QUEER WALES

Gender Studies in Wales
Astudiaethau Rhywedd yng Nghymru

Series Editors
Jane Aaron, University of South Wales
Brec'hed Piette, Bangor University
Sian Rhiannon Williams, Cardiff Metropolitan University

Series Advisory Board
Deirdre Beddoe, Emeritus Professor
Mihangel Morgan, Aberystwyth University
Teresa Rees, Cardiff University

The aim of this series is to fill a current gap in knowledge. As a number of historians, sociologists and literary critics have for some time been pointing out, there is a dearth of published research on the characteristics and effects of gender difference in Wales, both as it affected lives in the past and as it continues to shape present-day experience. Socially constructed concepts of masculine and feminine difference influence every aspect of individuals' lives; experiences in employment, in education, in culture and politics, as well as in personal relationships, are all shaped by them. Ethnic identities are also gendered; a country's history affects its concepts of gender difference so that what is seen as appropriately 'masculine' or 'feminine' varies within different cultures. What is needed in the Welsh context is more detailed research on the ways in which gender difference has operated and continues to operate within Welsh societies. Accordingly, this interdisciplinary and bilingual series of volumes on Gender Studies in Wales, authored by academics who are leaders in their particular fields of study, is designed to explore the diverse aspects of male and female identities in Wales, past and present. The series is bilingual, in the sense that some of its intended volumes will be in Welsh and some in English.

Also in series
Dawn Mannay, *Our Changing Land: Revisiting Gender, Class and Identity in Contemporary Wales*
Alice Entwistle, *Poetry, Geography, Gender: Women Rewriting Contemporary Wales*
Kirsti Bohata and Katie Gramich, *Rediscovering Margiad Evans: Marginality, Gender and Illness*
Angela V. John, *Our Mothers' Land: Chapters in Welsh Women's History, 1830–1939*

For all titles in the Gender Studies in Wales series please visit www.uwp.co.uk

QUEER WALES

The History, Culture and Politics
of Queer Life in Wales

Edited by

Huw Osborne

CARDIFF
UNIVERSITY OF WALES PRESS
2016

© The Contributors, 2016

Reprinted 2023

All rights reserved. No part of this book may be reproduced in any material form (including photocopying or storing it in any medium by electronic means and whether or not transiently or incidentally to some other use of this publication) without the written permission of the copyright owner except in accordance with the provisions of the Copyright, Designs and Patents Act. Applications for the copyright owner's written permission to reproduce any part of this publication should be addressed to the University of Wales Press, 10 Columbus Walk, Brigantine Place, Cardiff, CF10 4UP.

www.uwp.co.uk

British Library Cataloguing-in-Publication Data
A catalogue record for this book is available from the British Library.

ISBN (pb) 978-1-7831-6863-7
e-ISBN   978-1-7831-6864-4

The right of the Contributors to be identified as authors of their contributions has been asserted by them in accordance with 77, 78 and 79 of the Copyright, Designs and Patents Act 1988.

The University of Wales Press acknowledges the financial support of the Welsh Books Council.

Typeset by Mark Heslington Ltd, Scarborough, North Yorkshire
Printed by CPI Antony Rowe, Chippenham, Wiltshire

For Cory
In loving memory

Contents

Acknowledgements ix

List of Illustrations and Figures xi

Notes on Contributors xiii

Introduction 1
Huw Osborne

I. THE QUEER PAST BEFORE 1900

1. Queer Loss: Felicia Hemans, (Trans)nationalisms and the Welsh Bard 15
Daniel Hannah

2. 'Gender difference is nothing': Cranogwen and Victorian Wales 29
Jane Aaron

3. 'Please don't whip me *this* time': The Passions of George Powell of Nant-Eos 45
Harry Heuser

4. From Huw Arwystli to Siôn Eirian: Representative Examples of *Cadi*/Queer Life from Medieval to Twentieth-century Welsh Literature 65
Mihangel Morgan

II. PLACING QUEER WALES AFTER 1900

5. 'A queer kind of fancy': Women, Same-sex Desire and Nation in Welsh Literature 91
Kirsti Bohata

6. 'Not friends / But fellows in a union that ends': Associations of Welshness and Non-heteronormativity in Edward Thomas 115
Andrew Webb

7. Fairy-tale Drag and the Transgender Nation in Rhys Davies, Erica Wooff and Jan Morris 126
Huw Osborne

III. BUILDING QUEER WALES POST-DEVOLUTION

8   Lesbian Motherhood in the South Wales Valleys: A Narrative
Exploration   147
Alys Einion

9   Living in Fear: Homophobic Hate Crime in Wales   159
Matthew Williams and Jasmin Tregidga

10   Heb Addysg, Heb Ddawn (Without Education, Without Gift):
LGBTQ Youth in Educational Settings in Wales   177
John Sam Jones

IV. PERFORMING CONTEMPORARY QUEER WALES

11   Omnisexuality and the City: Exploring National and Sexual Identity
through BBC Wales's *Torchwood*   195
Rebecca Williams and Ruth McElroy

12 Queer/Welsh and Welsh/Queer: Performing Hybrid Wales   209
Stephen Greer

    Notes   224
    Select Bibliography   259
    Index   265

Acknowledgements

This project began several years ago, so there are many people who have contributed in small and major ways. I am indebted to colleagues who provided guidance and sensitive editorial advice on certain aspects of the book. Thanks to my colleagues in the Department of English at the Royal Military College of Canada, especially Drs Helen Luu, Laura Robinson and Chantel Lavoie. Katie Gramich was very supportive in the early stages, and directed me to many people who might be interested in contributing. I am especially grateful to Jane Aaron for her kind and consistent encouragement throughout these several years of the book's development. Jane nudged me back on track more than once and was always available with advice and guidance. There are many others (too many to list) at conferences and pubs (often both) who have shared ideas, sources and criticisms; thanks to everyone who so generously discussed this project with me. In fact, a great deal of this book emerged from panels at various conferences, especially the conferences of the North American Association for the Study of Welsh Culture and History and the conference of the Association for Welsh Writing in English, so I am grateful to all of my colleagues who participated in these panels and who gave such constructive feedback. Sarah Lewis at the University of Wales Press merits a very special thank you. Her support and guidance throughout this process have been invaluable. She has been remarkably patient with me through several delays, and her generous assistance was considerable at all stages, from proposal to publication. The research and travel required for this book was made possible in part through the financial support of the Royal Military College of Canada's Academic Research Program. Lastly, I must also thank the contributors to this collection from whom I have learned so much. I think one edits a collection of essays when one can't find the book one would like to read, and I am pleased to say that I have that book now, and I am honoured to be part of it.

List of Illustrations and Figures

Illustrations

1.	*Nant-Eos, today* (2012), by the author, photograph	46
2.	*Love Dreaming by the Sea* (1871), by Simeon Solomon, watercolour, School of Art Museum and Gallery, Aberystwyth University	50
3.	*Boy on a Dragonfly* [detail] (1866), by Johann Baptist Zwecker, watercolour with body colour, School of Art Museum and Gallery, Aberystwyth University	57
4.	*Satan Summoning His Legions* (1792), by Richard Westall, watercolour with washes and body colour, School of Art Museum and Gallery, Aberystwyth University	58
5.	*George Powell* (1860s), by unknown, photograph, School of Art Museum and Gallery, Aberystwyth University	62

Figures

1.	Sexual orientation by cohesion scale	162
2.	General fear of crime by sexual orientation	163
3.	Sexual orientation by general satisfaction	163
4.	HC a problem in level area by SO	164
5.	General fear of hate crime on the basis of sexual orientation	165
6.	Precautions scale by SO	165
7.	Impact of HC victimization worry by SO	166
8.	Who were you with at the time of the HC	167
9.	Where did the HC happen by PCG	168
10.	If you have been a victim of HC more than once, were any committed by the same perpetrator(s)?	169
11.	Perceptions of motivation for HC perpetration by SO HC victims	169
12.	HC perpetrator relationship by PCG	170
13.	Number of HC perpetrators by strand	171
14.	Gender of perpetrators by strand	171
15.	Age of HC perpetrators by strand	172
16.	Race of HC perpetrators by strand	172
17.	Satisfaction with contact with police by type of hate crime/incident reported	174

Notes on Contributors

Jane Aaron is Emeritus Professor at the University of South Wales. She is the author of *A Double Singleness: Gender and the Writings of Charles and Mary Lamb* (Oxford: Clarendon Press, 1991) and a Welsh-language book on nineteenth-century women's writing in Wales, *Pur fel y Dur: Y Gymraes yn Llên y Bedwaredd Ganrif ar Bymtheg* (Cardiff: University of Wales Press, 1998). She also co-edited the volumes *Out of the Margins: Women's Studies in the Nineties* (London: Falmer Press, 1991), *Our Sisters' Land: The Changing Identities of Women in Wales* (Cardiff: University of Wales Press, 1994), *Postcolonial Wales* (Cardiff: University of Wales Press, 2005), and edited a number of volumes for the Honno classics series, including an anthology of Welsh women's short stories, *A View across the Valley: Short Stories from Women in Wales 1850–1950* (Dinas Powys: Honno Press, 1999). Her latest books include *Nineteenth-century Women's Writing in Wales: Nation, Gender and Identity* (Cardiff: University of Wales Press, 2007), the first in the Gender Studies in Wales series, and *Gendering Border Studies* (Cardiff: University of Wales Press, 2010), co-edited with Henrice Altink and Chris Weedon.

Kirsti Bohata is Associate Professor and Director of CREW (the Centre for Research into the English Literature and Language of Wales) at Swansea University. She is the author of *Postcolonialism Revisited: Writing Wales in English* (Cardiff: University of Wales Press, 2004). Her most recent books are the co-edited volume of essays, *Rediscovering Margiad Evans: Marginality, Gender and Illness* (Cardiff: University of Wales Press, 2013) and a new edition of *Jill* by Amy Dillwyn (Dinas Powys: Honno Press, 2013). She is currently completing a monograph on same-sex desire and social disorder in the fiction of Amy Dillwyn and co-authoring an interdisciplinary book on Disability and Industrial Society, 1880–1948, arising from a five-year project funded by a Wellcome Trust Programme Award.

Alys Einion is Senior Lecturer in Midwifery at Swansea University. She has been a midwife since 1998 and has been researching lesbian parenting in Wales for many years. Her current research/writing interests are in women's life writing, lesbian parenting, midwifery and women's reproductive experiences, innovative approaches to teaching and learning, sustainability and ecology, spirituality and complementary therapies, feminism and narrative theory. Her other publications include the co-authored *Midwifery Essentials: Basics* (Edinburgh: Elsevier,

2012) and her biographical novel, *Inshallah*, which was published in the spring of 2014 (Dinas Powys: Honno Press).

Stephen Greer is Lecturer in the School of Culture and Creative Arts at University of Glasgow. His research focuses on the intersection of queer theory and contemporary performance, with particular interest in notions of identity and political community. He is the author of *Contemporary British Queer Performance* (Basingstoke and New York: Palgrave Macmillan, 2012) and is currently working on a book on the cultural politics of solo performance.

Daniel Hannah is Associate Professor at Lakehead University where he teaches and researches in the areas of American, Romantic and transatlantic literature. He has published on William Blake, Felicia Hemans, Herman Melville, Robert Louis Stevenson, Henry James, Joseph Conrad, Colm Toibin, David Lodge and Alan Hollinghurst. He is the author of *Henry James, Impressionism, and the Public* (Farnham and Burlington, VT: Ashgate, 2013). He is working on a monograph provisionally entitled *The Queer Atlantic: Masculinities, Mobilities, and Emergence of Anglo-American Modernism*.

Harry Heuser holds a PhD in English from the City University of New York. His research concerning the intersection of genres and disciplines culminated in his study *Immaterial Culture: Literature, Drama and the American Radio Play, 1929–1954* (Oxford: Peter Lang, 2013) and the exhibition *(Im)memorabilia: Ephemerality, Resonance and the Collector's Item* (School of Art Gallery and Museum, Aberystwyth University, 2015). With his husband, Robert Meyrick, he writes on Welsh and English art. Publications include the monographs *Gwilym Prichard: A Lifetime's Gazing* (Bristol: Sansom, 2012) and *Claudia Williams: An Intimate Acquaintance* (Bristol: Sansom, 2013), as well as a chapter for *Figure and Ground: Keith Vaughan Drawings, Prints and Photographs* (Bristol: Sansom, 2013). Also with Meyrick, he curated the exhibition *An Abiding Standard: The Prints of Stanley Anderson RA* at the Royal Academy of Arts in London and co-wrote the accompanying catalogue *raisonné* (Royal Academy, 2015). Heuser has previously written on George Powell for *New Welsh Reader* (2015) and, together with his undergraduate students at the School of Art, Aberystwyth University, curated *Queer Tastes: Works from the George Powell Bequest* (2015).

John Sam Jones has worked in education, as a chaplain in hospitals and prisons, and as a sexual health worker. He was the first co-chair of the LGB Forum Cymru, set up to advise the Welsh government of LGB issues in 2001. For six years, until 2010, he was the chair of the All-Wales Personal and Social Education (PSE) Working Group which met three times a year to discuss, debate and plan the recommendations for curriculum development and teachers training in all areas of PSE, including sex and relationships education. John studied creative writing at Chester. His fiction includes the short-story collections *Welsh Boys Too*

(Cardigan: Parthian, 2000), *Fishboys of Vernazza* (Cardigan: Parthian, 2003), and the novels *With Angels and Furies* (London: GMP, 2005) and *Crawling Through Thorns* (Cardigan: Parthian, 2008). *Welsh Boys Too* was an Honour Book winner in the North American Library Association Stonewall Book Awards.

Ruth McElroy is Reader in Media and Cultural Studies at the University of South Wales where she is Director of the Creative Industries Research Institute. Ruth's research and teaching interests lie in television studies, minority-language media, and media and culture in Wales. She is the co-editor (with Stephen Lacey) of *Life on Mars: From Manchester to New York* (Cardiff: University of Wales Press, 2012) and is completing an edited collection for Ashgate, *Contemporary British Crime Drama*. She has published in journals such as the *European Journal of Cultural Studies, Media History and Television* and *New Media*. With Caitriona Noonan she is currently writing *Mobile Fictions: Television Drama Production from Doctor Who to Game of Thrones* (Palgrave). Ruth is book reviews editor for the *European Journal of Cultural Studies* and is a corresponding editor for *Critical Studies in Television*. With Steve Blandford and Stephen Lacey, she is series editor of *Contemporary Landmark Television* (Cardiff: University of Wales Press).

Mihangel Morgan is a lecturer at Aberystwyth University. His main field of interest is twentieth- and twenty-first-century literature, although he has published an article on Ellis Wynne and is also a lecturer on the 'Llên 1640–1740' module. He has published two volumes in the Llên y Llenor series – *Jane Edwards* (Caernarfon: Gwasg Pantycelyn, 1997) and *Caradog Prichard* (Caernarfon: Gwasg Pantycelyn, 2000). His articles on John Gwilym Jones, Kate Roberts, Caradog Prichard and Waldo Williams have appeared in *Llên Cymru*, *Y Traethodydd* and *Ysgrifau Beirniadol*. He has also published studies on the visual arts, including a review on Catrin Howells's work, the work of the photographer Weegee and Welsh films. Mihangel Morgan's main interest is his literary work. To date, he has published three volumes of poetry, five volumes of short stories, seven novels, a novel for Welsh learners and a book of poetry for children.

Huw Osborne is Associate Professor in the Department of English at the Royal Military College of Canada. He is the author of *Rhys Davies* (Cardiff: University of Wales Press, 2009), and has contributed to such journals and books as *Almanac* (2009), *The International Journal of Welsh Studies* (2005) and *Military Culture and Education* (Farnham and Burlington, VT: Ashgate, 2010). He has recently completed an edited collection of essays titled *The Rise of the Modernist Bookshop: Books and the Commerce of Culture in the Twentieth Century* (Farnham and Burlington, VT: Ashgate, 2015).

Jasmin Tregidga is Research Associate in the School of Social Sciences at Cardiff University and Director of WestPoint Crime and Social Research Consultancy. Jasmin's research experience to date has focused predominantly on policing and violent victimization with a specific focus on domestic abuse and hate crime. She has worked on a number of research projects that have contributed to significant changes in the support afforded to victims of domestic and sexual violence. Between 2010 and 2013, Jasmin was the lead researcher on the All Wales Hate Crime Project which was the largest and most comprehensive academic study of hate crime conducted within the UK. The report, *Time for Justice*, was received by the Wales Minister for Communities at the project launch in the National Assembly for Wales and the findings formed the key source of evidence for the Welsh Government's Framework for Action on Tackling Hate Crime. Jasmin has published in the *British Journal of Criminology*, and she has co-authored several reports, including *Understanding Who Commits Hate Crimes and Why They Do It* (2013), *Time for Justice* (2013) and the *Final Evaluation Report on the Cardiff HomeSafe Project* (2010).

Andrew Webb is Senior Lecturer in the School of English Literature, Bangor University. He is the author of *Edward Thomas and World Literary Studies* (Cardiff: University of Wales Press, 2013). His research has also appeared in such books and periodicals as *Naked Exhibitionism: Gendered Performance and Public Exposure* (London: I.B. Tauris, 2013), *International Journal of Welsh Writing in English* (2013), *Textual Practice* (2012) and *The European Journal of American Culture* (2009).

Matthew Williams is Reader in Computational Criminology and Director of the Social Data Science Lab at Cardiff University. He has a long-standing interest in homophobic hate crime. In 2010, he led the Big Lottery-funded All Wales Hate Crime Project. This project built upon two previous studies into homophobic hate crimes in Wales (Stonewall Cymru Counted Out! Survey 2003 and Counted In! Survey 2007). More recently, he has studied the migration of hate crime and speech to the Internet. In 2013, he led the ESRC Google Data Analytics grant 'Hate Speech and Social Media: Understanding Users, Networks and Information Flows'. A major output from this project entitled 'Cyberhate on social media in the aftermath of Woolwich: a case study in computational criminology and big data' has been published in the *British Journal of Criminology* and was picked up in the international press and by the BBC.

Rebecca Williams is a lecturer in Communication, Cultural and Media Studies at the University of South Wales. Rebecca has produced articles on female fans of Doctor Who and David Tennant, participants in historical-reality television, representations of TV horror in *Torchwood*, fan responses to the demise of television shows, and (co-authored) transnational fans of the *Twilight* franchise. She is the author of *Post-object Fandom: Television, Identity and Self-narrative* (London and New York: Bloomsbury, 2015), and editor of *Torchwood Declassified: Investigating Mainstream Cult Television* (London and New York: I.B. Tauris, 2013) and *Endings, Transitions & Resurrections in Fandom* (University of Iowa Press, forthcoming).

Introduction

During the preparation of this book, the internationally successful film *Pride* (2014) was released, placing queer Wales on the world stage. This was a timely event for our project, and the film captures many of the themes and challenges explored in the chapters that follow. Most of this book's readers will be familiar with the film. It features the story of an unlikely partnership between the striking miners of a small Welsh town and a group of LGBT activists in London. I open this book with a brief discussion of *Pride* because I have mixed feelings about it, and these feelings are related to the difficulty of thinking about queer nations more generally. While I am drawn to the film's accommodating vision of a past and future of the nation that includes sexual diversity, I worry about sacrificing the particular narratives of loss, failure and trauma that this optimistic story of triumph cannot help but deflect. The queer nation resides somewhere between this hopeful need for a queer past and future and a more complicated search for belonging that requires the refusal of the terms on which this hope is offered.

I am pleased with the film's acknowledgement of the complex interplay of class, nation, sexuality and gender, and I like how it brings together two histories of oppression that one habitually thinks of as opposed. I appreciate the acknowledgement that while Welsh mining towns were in the closet, there were always people living queer lives, however repressed they may have been. I am also moved by the film's ending, which marks a powerful moment of public solidarity in the celebration of national, working-class and queer pride. And I enjoy the fact that this unusual story was no secret but largely unknown. Taken together, this film is a deeply affective argument for a Wales that has a queer history and that is already queer; we simply have to choose to see it. In some ways, *Pride* is Wales's coming-out narrative, the Welsh national equivalent to Hettie MacDonald's *Beautiful Thing* (1996), whose screenwriter, Jonathan Harvey, explained was written 'to have a hopeful, happy ending story about being gay and being working class and coming out'.[1] And it's important to have such stories that refuse the impossibility and death that too often characterize representations of non-heterosexual love.

In other ways, however, the film reinforces a division between 'Welsh' and 'queer' experiences. The film privileges metropolitan spaces in the formation of queer identities and denies any queer meaning to rural and non-metropolitan spaces. This upholds the myth that queer lives must almost always exist elsewhere, beyond Welsh borders – most likely in London. Where the film *does* acknowledge queer lives in Wales in Cliff's (Bill Nighy) coming-out scene, a lifetime of silence and struggle is dismissed in a comic line. I much prefer the treatment of Henry George (Islwyn Morris) in *Bydd yn Wrol* (Terry Dyddgen Jones, 1996) who shares a touching scene of implied outing with the younger Julian (Matthew Rhys). The metropolitan queerness of *Pride*, however, places the heroic narrative outside Wales and subsumes Wales into a larger transnational 'pride' that elides particular, national and local experiences. The coming-out story, for example, is generally a narrative of leaving the rural or peripheral environment to find oneself in the cities, which conceptually links rural life with the closet.[2] These peripheral sexualities, however, represent a further instance of the queer potential of Wales. As Richard Phillips and Diane Watt have argued, the non-urban and the rural are powerful interstitial spaces, 'for it is in such spaces that hegemonic sexualities may be least stable'.[3] Rural places and small towns, which are located at 'some material and metaphorical distance from both the regulation and the liberation of the center, in-between spaces on the margins of sexual geography[,] are simultaneously spaces of sexual "power and danger"'.[4] It is striking how many of the chapters collected here resist the metronormative narrative of *Pride*, whether it be the rural retirements and 'female friendship', or the homo-epistolary rural queer-space of Thomas and Frost, or *Torchwood* fans' celebration of a queer Cardiff, or Erica Wooff's return to Newport (to name only a few).

Pride also raises questions about the nature of queer histories, for history has often been in service of national narratives, and the act of 'recovering' a queer history is problematically bound to heteronormative stories of national origins, destiny and desire. Does *Pride* queer Welsh history, or does it merely – if dramatically – insert an LGBTQ footnote into a national and labour history that is largely unaffected? Or worse, does it sanitize 'queer history' by its association with more legitimate politics, relegating angry queer disaffection to dark streets of anonymous sex and death? Meanwhile, within Wales, Cliff is the one man who arguably needs alternative ways of knowing his home, and he is also the one who preserves and relates the stories of coal and castles that bind this working-class Welsh community, while the queer influence is more or less safely removed to London at the end of the film. In such terms, *Pride* raises the question of whether or not there can ever really be such a thing as a queer history. If one does try to tell this history, to what extent does any such triumphant narrative of queer rights replicate the political and national structures that have always silenced and policed queer sexualities? As some argue, just as the modern nation has required the de-legitimization of sexual difference, queerness necessitates the de-constitution of the nation's founding fictions. Lee Edelman, for instance, posits the queer as a negative force opposed not only to the coherence of the nation but to all 'progressive' politics that seek to incorporate sexual nonconformity into the nation. Properly conceived, Edelman argues, queerness 'can never define an identity; it can only ever disturb one'.[5] Therefore, the misguided political fight for a queer future *within* the nation will always fall into the forward-looking logic of politics in which all sides fight for the one side of the 'reproductive futurism' of the nation. From this perspective, the Queer Nation that arose in the wake of the AIDS epidemic of the 1990s – and which is seen in its nascent form in *Pride* – is a false promise, as are, latterly, homonormative rights-based politics – like gay marriage and gay adoption – that render queer people nationally meaningful only in terms of heteronormative citizenship.[6]

Pride, therefore, may contribute to a progressive history of gay liberation in nationalist terms, but is such a history desirable when it comes at the cost of forgetting trauma and suffering? When one creates a triumphalist narrative that claims 'queer figures from the past in a positive genealogy of gay identity, [one makes] good on their suffering, transforming their shame into pride after the fact'.[7] Heather Love argues that a queer approach to history must attend to the silence, failure and loss of the queer past while resisting a redemptive narrative of progress and contemporary social and political success that seals the past away in 'a superseded realm of ignorance, shame, and suffering'.[8] *Pride* is comic, colourful and cute, and it remasters a painful past, redeeming queerness in a properly oriented political guise of working-class solidarity. To be fair, the film does present the unsettling figure of Mark (Ben Schnetzer) haunting the road on the outskirts of Onllwyn in the months following his discovery that he has contracted HIV. His temporary removal from the action and narrative reminds us of the traumas that are difficult to make meaningful in this narrative of triumph, perhaps troubling its progress; however, this scene is short-lived and ultimately replaced by the progressive march of gay pride at the end of the film.

One might ask what an alternative to *Pride* might look like, and one answer is the treatment of trauma and passionate memory in Stevie Davies's novel *Impassioned Clay* (1999). Her queer historian protagonist searches, affectively and sensually, for a Welsh seventeenth-century figure of lesbian desire and transgender rebellion who is mutilated and silenced by history's power over queer bodies and voices. The narrator moves through her present desires while touching the trauma of the past. The result is not a confident recovery of the queer past, but a passionate and agonized feeling through obscurity and pain:

> I walked forwards facing perversely backwards, eyes straining for vision of the invisible, or cruising the endless terrain of text in the Bodleian. Antiquarian volumes became my passion. Their persons erupted from innards of books as the spines creaked open; and the dead spoke to me, with such vehement voices that when I looked up, my contemporaries seemed blurred and dull.[9]

Here we have a striking contrast to the queer historical project of *Pride*. The innards and creaked spines prefigure the trauma of her historical subject, sight is impossible, the project is 'endless', the desire unfulfilled, time's governing logic breaks down in the past and the present, and the progress of history's forward trajectory is deferred. This breaking, however, is also a breaking free from the bonds of that straight time and its foreclosure on queer desire.[10]

Whatever else it does, *Pride* compels us to think of the national, historical and contemporary place of the queer experience in Wales. Perhaps *Pride* is most valuable in highlighting the degree to which the idea of queering the nation is a fraught proposition that must be proposed despite the risks. There are many places within the nation's 'founding ambivalence' that expose and undo the heteronormativity of national belonging,[11] and a past that seems sealed away in straight time is also a past marked by difference, trauma, play, failure and loss, all of which revise and undo straight time, placing one in a queer relation to the nation. While people live within nations and often make the necessary error of identity coherence in the ritual practices of living, the nation conceived in the abstract is not the same as the particular and multiple nations that are experienced across the internal differences and external influences that make up communities. In her 1994 essay, 'Welsh Lesbian Feminist: A Contradiction in Terms?', Roni Crwydren writes from the problems and possibilities of queer Wales.[12] She begins in a familiar discourse of local and national desire: 'Wales is my home. I was born, and have spent most of my life, in one small area about which I feel deeply and passionately. I feel comfortable and at home in the woods, on its hills, moors and cliffs.'[13] However, Crwydren's lesbian identifications sit within matrices of national, linguistic and class-based inheritances that made a queer-Welsh belonging problematic and particular:

> Where did Wales and Welsh – people, culture, language – figure in all this: oppressors or oppressed? And where did I fit in with the picture? It was no problem for me to see the patriarchal nature of society around me, the sexism and heterosexism, and I wanted to live my life according to my new-found feminist beliefs and principles. I knew, however, that I came from a middle-class, English, and Anglicized Welsh background, from which I was not automatically freed by becoming a feminist.[14]

Her lesbian identity was never simply a sexual one, but one negotiated on the intersecting thresholds of nation, region, class, language, gender and sexuality.[15] These identifications, further, are simultaneous, sympathetic and conflicted:

> Was there a parallel between the oppression of lesbians and the oppression of the Welsh through language? To what extent is one weakened if such an integral part of one's life is devalued or not acknowledged? And what happens when you feel that two separate yet equally integral parts of yourself are simultaneously being oppressed – and when the oppressors of the one part include groups you identify with by virtue of the other?[16]

What happens? It's difficult to say, of course. These conflicts are really where Crwydren ends, and, as Stephen Greer explains in his chapter of the current volume, Dafydd James is still asking such questions almost twenty years later. Crwydren goes on to hope for integration, community and reconciliation, but only to hope and not necessarily to find. And perhaps the queer nation should be sought in such sympathetic incommensurabilities (rather than in their celebratory erasure in *Pride*). While it may not be possible to have something as neat and comforting as a queer nation and a queer history, one may, as Elizabeth Freeman puts it, be queer and find ways of living historically and nationally, and it is hoped that this collection will contribute to such a living.[17]

Identifying queer Wales is not an easy task, and I am certain (and certainly hope) that this collection of essays will not make this task any easier. It is hoped, rather, that this collection will address the challenges to understanding and reimagining the nation, that it will consider the places and times of many different experiences of queer Wales. It is hoped, in fact, that this collection will make it *less* easy to map and tell the time and place of the nation. In these terms, we might find a different kind of optimism, one that, in contrast to Edelman's formulation, reclaims the future. José Estaban Muñoz figures queerness as the desired and receding future towards which we may make optimistic use of a past and present that seem to lead only to the negation of non-heteronormative lives; that is, a queer future 'is always on the horizon', not an accomplished fact but a destabilizing ideal that assumes the potential for building communities.[18] Queerness, as Muñoz writes,

> is not here yet ... We have never been queer, yet queerness exists for us as an ideality that can be distilled from the past and used to imagine a future. The future is queerness's domain ... We must strive in the face of the here and now's totalizing rendering of reality, to think and feel a *then and there* ... Queerness is that thing that lets us feel that this world is not enough, that indeed something is missing.[19]

This multidisciplinary collection of essays straddles these paradoxical impulses: to render the Welsh nation queer and less knowable and to acknowledge that the nation is also a place and time in which people should be able (and proud) to live.

A queer Welsh past?

Several of the chapters in this book deal with the queer history of Wales. In the first section, we have literary, biographical, historical and art-historical approaches, some of which take a wide view across time and texts, while others focus on the lives and works of key figures. Whatever the scope, they all undo the sexual and gendered homogeneity of Welsh history and reveal a paradoxical phenomenon in that the Welsh national past is conceived in heteronormative terms yet inhabited by an equally defining queerness. The first chapter of the book presents the Wales of Felicia Hemans on the borders of nation and gender. Daniel Hannah's chapter addresses Hemans's uses of the Welsh bardic tradition in order to queer an English colonial imaginary, linking her poetry on Wales to her efforts to imagine national belongings that allow spaces for alternatives to normative matrimonial attachments. While English domination enshrines a female domesticity that limits the range of desire, Wales appears as a place of loss that empties and revises memorialized reproductive national myths. As Hannah explains, Hemans adopts an ambivalent bardic voice in which gender, desire and nation circulate and intersect, and her movement in and through national and gendered voices makes possible a queer Welsh (trans)nationalism that implicitly revises Wales's place as a site of British colonial desire.

Jane Aaron's chapter on Cranogwen (Sarah Jane Rees) is also concerned with a Welsh national identity formed in the gendered terms of English colonial influence, though Cranogwen occupied a very different national and linguistic position than did Hemans. Aaron reveals Cranogwen as a profoundly unconventional woman who confidently adopted many traditionally masculine roles and ultimately forged alternative homosocial networks of women. Her gender nonconformity and wide public acclaim in an age of largely unquestioned patriarchal ideology defies the idea of nineteenth-century Wales as a nation based in universally strict gender roles. Rising to prominence in the aftermath of the 1847 *Report of the Commission of Inquiry into the State of Education in Wales*, Cranogwen was received by her Welsh-language reading public as a symbol of feminine purity even as most of her published writing undermined the compulsory heterosexuality of her milieu and exposed the rituals and conventions that enforced it. In Aaron's analysis, Cranogwen emerges as an important figure of nineteenth-century gender-trouble.

Harry Heuser's chapter presents George Powell of Nant-Eos through Powell's eclectic collection of art, books and other materials, providing an alternative to a more conventional historicist frame that might domesticate Powell into the national narrative. There is, for instance, an enticing contrast between, on the one hand, the grand old family home of Nant-Eos or the national institutional solidity of the Aberystwyth University to which Powell bequeathed his collection, and, on the other hand, the disordered, irrational, nationally promiscuous and sexually perverse nature of the collection itself. Powell's collection is an incoherent record that defies any narrative that might straighten him out: it demands a queer embrace of diverse cultural materials and represents a kind of posthumous Victorian camp performance. In Heuser's treatment, Powell is a figure of excess that lived in queer opposition to the local, national and familial expectations of his milieu. In his general repudiation of his conventional role, he is, as Heuser suggests, a positive figure of queer failure who resists conventional forms of success in favour of a creative self-fashioning within and beyond his Welsh inheritance. In mind and body, Powell was a border-crosser whose associations and interests went far beyond local Welsh affiliations into national, cosmopolitan, sexual and aesthetic excesses while fashioning a pre-Wildean alternative queer existence.

Mihangel Morgan's discussion of Welsh literature challenges the presumed difficulty of expressing the queer experience in Welsh, arguing that the supposed impossibility of Welsh-language queerness capitulates to an imperial annexation by the English language. While acknowledging the heterosexist baggage of Welsh, Morgan claims that the history of the English language is no different, and Welsh may, in fact, provide more and better materials for articulating the queer experience in Wales. Following Richard Crowe, he describes what we may call the *cadi* tradition of Wales, and he turns to the less sexually determinate and less morally constrained literature of medieval Wales to build a vocabulary and ethos for queerness in Welsh. Morgan challenges presumptively heterosexual reading practices that desexualized and domesticated the sexual indeterminacy of medieval texts, texts that contain many examples of same-sex intimacy and desire. In placing these texts alongside more recent twentieth-century ones, he draws on Carolyn Dinshaw's affective approach to the past, applying a queer historical 'desire for bodies to touch across time'.[20] Against the pathologized, criminalized and foreign homosexual threat depicted in the Welsh present – the same homosexual threat that twentieth-century critics of medieval Welsh literature dismissed in their paranoid reading – Morgan traces the continued *cadi* strangeness of the Welsh medieval world in twentieth-century literature. In doing so, he presents a *cadi*/queer reclamation of eclectic Welsh-language traditions that do not conform to a monolithic heteronormative critical inheritance that would make the Welsh language into a foreign country for queer people in Wales.

All four of these chapters do more than simply uncover a hidden queer Welsh past. As discussed with *Pride*, there is always the temptation to build the heroic narrative of representative queers, to say 'Look, here we always were!', but, as discussed above, we must be wary lest our current political goals impose an unrealistic narrative of progressive queer liberation.[21] Also, one runs the risk of building a narrative of queer history that merely supplements the existing national narrative so that a disruptive figure like Powell becomes little more than a quirky character in the landscape of Welsh history, making for a colourful description in the tourist brochures.[22] This first part of the book does not uncover the hidden history of queer Wales; rather, it offers queer ways of knowing the nation and its history, society and culture. Many queer critics align national time with the 'time of reproduction'[23] and the 'chrononormative':[24] the inheritance across generations of wealth, goods, values and morals are family ties that connect 'to the historical past of the nation, and glance ahead to connect the family to the future of both familial and national stability'.[25] Queering the nation's history, therefore, must violate the 'notion that history is the discourse of answers', exposing it as 'a discourse whose commitment to determinate signification ... provides false closure, blocking access to the multiplicity of the past and the possibilities of different futures'.[26] Powell is a good example of these possibilities. The artefacts of his eclectic and nonlinear collection provide a way of looking at the national past through a queer refusal of historical determination. Morgan's affective connections across centuries do similar work. Further, all four chapters in this first section address and revise the nation's founding familial structures, whether it be Hemans's challenge to English colonial domesticity, Cranogwen's refusal of marriage and her building of an alternative homosocial community, Powell's queer resistance to the estate and his patriarchal inheritance, or the Welsh-language literary tradition's many playful indeterminacies within forms of marriage and courtship in texts from the Middle Ages to the present.

Queer borders

In the chapters in the second part of the book, the focus shifts to literature in the twentieth and twenty-first centuries. They are concerned with place, borders and belonging, and they, too, locate Wales at sites of queer national incoherence. Kirsti Bohata's chapter provides a transition from the previous section by situating her discussion in a lesbian 'tradition' that reaches back to the seventeenth century. This chapter provides the most complete survey of lesbian representation in Welsh literature to date, highlighting the intersection or inter-representation of lesbian and Welsh identities. Bohata's exhaustive chapter covers a wide range of figures and themes to demonstrate how tropes of Welshness are deployed in the depiction of transgressive female relationships. It addresses the rural retreats of Katherine Philips and the Ladies of Llangollen, and it explains the emergence of feminist consciousness alongside the struggle for Welsh national autonomy in the nineteenth century, most notably in Amy Dillwyn's fiction of genderqueer revolution. In much of the discussion, Wales is a representational space where ethnic and sexual differences coincide. It is, for instance, a gothic, haunted and witchy region in which lesbian desire is a monstrous threat, an apparitional absent/presence and a powerful alien otherness. In her treatment of important twentieth-century figures, Bohata addresses the work of Margiad Evans, Rhys Davies and Kate Roberts, among others, and, as she carries the analysis into the post-devolutionary context, Wales offers lesbian desire the possibilities of a national identity shaped in and through marginality. However, Bohata stresses that devolution also confronts that same desire with the heteronormative traditions that inhere within nation-building. Across this long 'tradition' of Welsh lesbian literary representation, Bohata argues, the figure of the lesbian is an especially indeterminate and unstable one that highlights Wales as a borderland, a place of unstable and contested national and sexual identities.

Like Bohata, Andrew Webb makes a compelling case for a Welshness that is always-already queer. His discussion of Edward Thomas's Welsh queerness troubles an Anglocentric 'normality' that has long subsumed Wales as its colonial other. This conflict registers in Thomas's writing as a dual repression of both his Welshness and his non-heteronormativity, and this struggle is most apparent in his collaborative male writing with Robert Frost. Drawing on notions of queer space, Webb presents Thomas's longing for, and oblique creation of, eroticized and nationalized spaces of male bonding that oppose the Anglocentric heteronormative repression of a doubly-divided identity.

My chapter on representations of transgender Wales in the work of Rhys Davies, Jan Morris and Erica Wooff discusses the ways in which the transgender experience further troubles the gendered borders of the nation. It draws on queer theories of time and performativity to identify what I refer to as a 'fairy-tale drag' in the representation of transgender and national experience. Read through Elizabeth Freeman's notion of 'temporal drag' and the ways in which drag is often outdated as well as cross-gendered, these uses of national and fantastic stories talk back to history and refashion the time and place of the nation for queer purposes. Rhys Davies has a long interest in transgender representation specifically in relation to nation and class, and often appeals to fantasy and the fantastic, as he does, for instance, in *The Painted King*. Jan Morris continues this trend in Welsh writing in her autobiography *Conundrum* and her national narrative *The Matter of Wales: Epic Views of a Small Country*, both of which infuse genres based in spatial and temporal coherence with appeals to fairy tale and myth that are inseparable from shaping of her Welsh transsexuality. Similarly, Erica Wooff's novel *Mud Puppy* deploys drag, fairy tale and fantastic displacement to fashion a Wales that accommodates alternative embodiments and eccentric desires.

Devolved Wales and the queer citizen

The first two sections bring us up to the present, where history and representation meet the social and political realities of post-devolution Wales and where recurring concerns about home and belonging are addressed through new disciplinary perspectives. The third section draws on the social sciences to address recent and contemporary experiences connected to law, politics, education, family and community. The section exhibits a common concern for lived social spaces and the need to shape visible and articulated queer identities within communities that passively or actively exclude non-heteronormative experience. While these chapters note that there is much more work to be done in order to make Wales a safe and healthy place for the full range of sexual lives, all are based in positive post-devolution changes to ideas of citizenship and national and local belonging. In the first chapter of this section, Alys Einion's analysis of lesbian mothers in the south Wales valleys returns to questions raised in previous chapters concerning place, home, family, domesticity and lesbian belonging. Based on interviews with lesbian mothers, she presents lesbian motherhood as a narrative identity adapted and validated for a particular time and place. Her chapter traces the conflicted position of queer parenthood that is excluded from heteronormative communities by virtue of queerness and from queer communities by virtue of its alignment with the homonormative family. The subjects of Einion's research negotiate this conflict through 'storied selves' that must be reworked and retold in the formation of a 'provisional unity' as both lesbian and mother. Through their emplacing narratives, Einion contends, 'valleys women can successfully negotiate the process of becoming that signifies their journeys as lesbians who are mothers, transgressing the boundaries of culture and creating new realities which acknowledge the strength of their history and culture whilst rejecting their limitations'. Einion's chapter is also compelling in its insistence that queer national identities are often local ones that must be negotiated outside the queer 'metronormative' spaces of major cities. While the valleys Einion describes may not destabilize hegemonic sexualities as described by Philips and Watt above, one might well say that the narratives in her chapter offer one of 'the hard earned protests of queer anti-urbanism', insisting that queer lives are built, albeit partially and conflictually, outside the transnational metropolitan 'queer' centres.[27]

Similar difficulties concerning the development of a non-heteronormative sense of self within Welsh communities are addressed in Matthew Williams and Jasmin Tregidga's chapter on homophobic hate crime in Wales. This chapter provides the only quantitative analysis in the collection, and it represents a sobering and urgent reminder at the heart of this book. The researchers surveyed and interviewed 535 LGBTQ people living in Wales, and their findings reveal that the respondents experience a disproportionately high level of hate crime, fear, violence and recurring victimization. Just as LGBTQ people are more likely to hide their sexualities within their communities, so too are they subject to victimization based on their visibility. These trends highlight the extent to which communal policing of gender and sexuality continues to restrict local experiences of belonging, despite the strides being made in the political and cultural life of Wales. Such restrictions inevitably affect, Williams and Tregidga stress, personal perceptions of 'self' and the presentation of identity in public settings. These quantitative results are matched and illustrated with the qualitative evidence of the interviews, which continue and broaden the experience of queer Wales voiced in Einion's chapter. The findings are bleak, but Williams and Tregidga note that the research of this chapter is part of the larger recognition of the problem and the need to address it. As part of the larger experience of queer Wales approached in this book, Williams and Tregidga's research contributes an important reminder of the concrete community-building that is still ongoing.

John Sam Jones writes from his experience as an educator of many years and as someone who participated in forming more inclusive educational policies in post-devolution Wales. Like Einion's, his chapter is based on the importance of personal narrative, and he merges his own story in education with the larger development of queer pedagogy in Wales. He argues that progress is made when education policies activate and make space for queer voices in school administration and curriculum development. Jones maps education in Wales from its pre-devolution commitment to family values and the vulnerability of the child to a post-devolution concern with the child as a citizen, which includes the child's right to sex and health education that accommodates sexual diversity. Jones presents today's Welsh classrooms as spaces where theory and practice meet and where inclusive queer communities can help revise the nature of Welsh citizenship.

All three of these chapters are concerned with the problems and possibilities of queer citizenship in Wales, particularly in terms of voice, self-formation, place and space. All three, further, necessarily take us outside the metropolitan centres to address the different experiences and needs of those whose sexualities do not conform to metronormative queerness. Like the chapters in previous sections, these urgent social analyses trouble the notion of 'home' and belonging in Welsh communities built on abiding heteronormative foundations.

Beyond time and place: a hybrid queer Wales

The final section draws the social, political and cultural interests of the book into a single focus with chapters dealing with creative industries and the place of these activities in the national, international, urban and cultural-institutional shaping of Wales. In these final chapters, the various elements of the book's diverse and extended examination of queer Wales looks most openly and positively to building a time and place for the queer future of Wales, a Wales that is more than ever a hybrid nation. Rebecca Williams and Ruth McElroy's chapter on *Torchwood* illustrates how much of the social and political work described in the third part of this book is carried on in Welsh media. Based partly in qualitative focus group research, the chapter is concerned with how Welsh sexualities are, as the authors write, 'made, lived and inhabited in place'. *Torchwood*'s Welsh setting coupled with its indeterminate sexual representation answers and complicates the need for national and sexual representation, positive portrayal and authenticity in the media. The show's alignment of the contemporary and 'real' Cardiff with the fantastic times and places of science fiction enable the expression and exploration of non-normative desire beyond the perceived limits of a given place and time. Williams and McElroy, therefore, further address queer temporalities. The second part of this chapter discusses an instance of queer memorialization of the *Torchwood* character, Ianto Jones. The memorial elaborates the book's general engagement with history, time and place in that it locates a particularly queer claim on Cardiff Bay, a powerful symbolic space of devolved national identity that appeals to a cosmopolitan hybridity and that promotes international contact through tourism and creative and cultural industries. *Torchwood* is an international media phenomenon predicated on the fantastic disruption of the straight space and time of the nation, making it a transformative vehicle of queer national belonging.

The closing chapter by Stephen Greer draws together the many themes of the book's engagement with queer Wales. The Wales that emerges in his discussion of Dafydd James's *Llwyth* and Ben Lewis and Dafydd James's *Village Social* is a hybrid, multiple and performative one produced and staged across local, national, international, linguistic and temporal borders. Greer does not present a fluid intersectional identity but a 'located hybridity' legible in the plays' production and reception within Wales and beyond Wales. In this movement outside Wales, the local becomes an intrinsically displaced and disoriented phenomenon that offers material for achieving queer futures. As Greer puts it,

> In this, the figure of the hybrid is never resolved as a new, coherent subject, but marks an ongoing project of hybridization – hybridity, if you will, as performativity. Set against the possibility of 'newness', then, is an apprehension of how bodies and their relations to space are materialised and made 'historical' through repetition, through gestures that make certain kinds of labour disappear as they become 'effortless'. On those terms, might we begin to understand belonging as a kind of methodology of place, a way of 'doing the local' to which we might become habituated? Which we pursue in the *hope* of habit, that it might become effortless rather than demanding our conscious labour? Or which we take up, queerly, in the hope of rewriting its terms to better include us?

Taken as a whole, this book presents queer approaches to the times and places of Wales, from the sexual indeterminacies of its early Welsh-language texts to the queer hybridity of nation-building and citizenship in devolved Wales. Wales is not inevitably tied to a heteronormative national history. On the contrary, it may be lived in the queer light of a past founded in ambivalences and reassessed to enable a queer vision of the future. As Stephen Greer says of *Llwyth*, 'Wales, the Welsh language and Welshness, then, are bound to sexuality and queerness ... in ways that are in turn optimistic and regressive, oriented on the future and demanding recognition of the past.'

Part 1
The Queer Past Before 1900

1

Queer Loss: Felicia Hemans, (Trans)nationalisms and the Welsh Bard

DANIEL HANNAH

Born in Liverpool, of Irish, Italian and German descent, Felicia Dorothea Hemans 'spent all but the first and last years of her life' in Wales.[1] Once read as an author engaged in 'chauvinistic, sentimental, and derivative' enshrining of decidedly *English*, Victorian ideologies,[2] recent approaches to Hemans's poetry have produced a realization of her work as, in Susan Wolfson's words, 'spectacularly unresolved'. Wolfson finds in Hemans's verse 'a poetry more apt to be strained by rhetorical effects and thematic configurations that tap into and voice a cultural unconscious of fragmented, contradictory awareness'.[3] Building on this suggestion, this chapter explores how an idea of Hemans and her work as queerly Welsh helps account for the awkward ambivalence that colours her seemingly eulogistic attentions to the 'Homes of England', to England's insistent ideological marrying of domesticity and national identity, in many of her best-known poems. Hemans's engagement with a Welsh bardic tradition in the early 1820s forms a crucial step in her works' emergent exploration of scenes that queerly and transnationally complicate the reproductive orientation of England's colonial imaginary.

Hemans's correspondence from her time in Wales documents her gradual, always uneasy acclimatization to her place in relationship to Welsh culture. For instance, an unpublished letter to Matthew Nicholson from her residence in Bronwhilfa on 23 June 1812 gives an early indication of both Hemans's attraction to Welsh history and her alienated distaste for contemporary Welsh culture:

> I certainly cannot recommend Wales for any thing but its air and scenery, & I believe that you will allow from experience that they deserve the highest eulogiums the poet or the painter can bestow; but I fear the spirits of its celebrated Bards, are entirely fled, for its present inhabitants seem to inherit nothing from their poetic Ancestors but their long pedigrees, & rooted dislike to the Saxon intruders. – I have seen so much of their illiberality, lately, (the effects of which, in ill-natured observations, have travelled, I understand, even to your part of the world,) that I feel no tie of *local* attachment would be strong enough to cause me any regret if I were to bid Wales farewell without any prospect of ever returning.[4]

Hemans, the 'Saxon intruder', remained in Wales, however, and ten years later she can be seen, in a letter from 19 December 1822, returning to her admiration of the Welsh scenery as a sign of her '*local* attachment': 'Although not born in Wales, my longtime residence here has sufficiently naturalized me to make your admiration of our mountain scenery highly gratifying.'[5] Nevertheless, her sense of naturalization remained always couched in liminal terms: in a later letter after a return from a trip to Liverpool, she describes herself as feeling 'as the Welsh countrypeople say in their griefs, "*very heavy*" just now. I had no idea I was growing by so many roots to this place, which – such is mortal inconsistency – I have wished to leave again and again.'[6] 'My whole life has lain within the wild circle of these wild Welsh hills', she declared in a letter from the same period, 'and I know nobody'.[7]

While, as Jane Aaron has noted, Hemans is best remembered for her 'constructive' English patriotism, her poetry also bears witness to her roaming identifications with peoples from varying locations and times, including Wales and the legacies of the Welsh bards.[8] Hemans's mobile approach to national belonging – an approach William D. Brewer has identified as embodying 'an ancient Welsh or British cosmopolitanism' – and her often queer play with gendered roles and forms of desire are, I wish to suggest, intimately tied.[9] While 'queer' might strike some as a surprising term for analysing what seems like an *oeuvre* predominantly concerned with romantic dramas and domestic exchanges between men and women, it is a particularly productive term for describing Hemans's 'undoing' of gender and desire in these transnational scenes (and her prescient representations of gender and desire as performatively formed through unstable acts).[10] Queer – as, in Elizabeth Freeman's terms, 'an ongoing breach of selfhood'[11] – concisely describes Hemans's returns to representations of desire as unseating and unsettling a gendered self. While this chapter will begin by mapping the queer interrelations specifically between desire and unsettling loss that mark out Hemans's general imagining of national belonging, my argument will move towards considering the resonance of that mapping for a reading of Hemans as a non-English, specifically, if contingently, Welsh writer. In Hemans's personal life, Wales offered something of a refuge from the loss of her marriage when her husband, Alfred, left her for Italy in 1818. In her poetry, her treatment of Wales and the Welsh bardic tradition need to be read in the context of her broader efforts to imagine national spaces in which alternative relations to normative matrimonial and domestic narratives might be forged. Wales, as an actual and imaginary space in her life and work, came to embody an experience of loss and desire that Hemans queerly positioned at the centre of (trans)national and domestic identities.

Contingent homes: domesticity, desire and loss in Hemans's poetry of the 1820s

In his veiled reading of the 'once so celebrated' poem, 'The Homes of England', Jerome McGann argues that while Hemans's 'bland[ness]' might seem to indicate 'sentimental attachment to' the poem's 'subjects', its style, 'so rich and so empty', its 'superficial superficiality' in fact suggests her commitment to the perpetual slippage of 'the images and forms that ideology requires for its sustenance', to its 'buildings of loss'.[12] Conscious of its own entry into a future of recitation, Hemans's poem, according to McGann, imagines both the nation and the text as sites of 'quotation', as a fulcrum for 'various inherited and signifying signs'.[13] While McGann acknowledges such a reading is 'not merely perverse but utterly resolute in its perversity', I want to argue that Hemans's project might be even more resolutely perverse than McGann's essay suggests.[14] 'The Homes of England' begins, in its eventual book publication, with an epigraph from the fourth canto of Walter Scott's *Marmion*, lines spoken by the youthful squire Fitz-Eustace: 'Where's the coward that would not dare / To fight for such a land?'[15] Fitz-Eustace's 'rapture' is, however, not, as one might expect from an epigraph to Hemans's poem, for the contested Northumbrian moor, the eventually English land of Flodden Field at the centre of the poem's battle; it is, rather, for the sight of Edinburgh and the gathering Scottish forces of James IV, viewed from atop Blackford Hill. Rather than opening out the poem's paean to English 'homes', the epigraph immediately evokes the colonial history by which the English have both viewed their homes as under threat and expanded their home in the isles of Great Britain. When, in the final stanza of the poem, the speaker of Hemans's poem calls for 'hearts of native proof' to be 'rear'd / To guard each hallowed wall' (35–6) of every 'hut and hall' (34), she produces an image of the English home, the domestic scene, as a site constituted by its own defence. Love of country and love of enclosure become the means by which England, in Hemans's poem, ensures a feminized domestic bliss – in which 'woman's voice flows forth in song, / Or childhood's tale is told' (13–14) – in its 'free, fair Homes' (33).

What 'The Homes of England' lays bare is Hemans's attentiveness to the home as the site of contingent imaginings of national belonging and contained domesticity. Throughout her career, Hemans's elegiac tone places pressure on the gendered norms of English national identity, even as it plays out a commitment to those norms. Indeed, in many of her well-known works, Hemans centres her refusal of both narrowly nationalist and domestic configurations around a 'queer art' of 'losing'.[16] In *Feeling Backward: Loss and the Politics of Queer History*, Heather Love seeks to re-direct critical attention to 'the association between homosexual love and loss – a link that, historically, has given queers special insight into love's failures and impossibilities (as well as, of course, wild hopes for its future)'.[17] Her work, here, on '[b]roken intimacies' seeks to build on Leo Bersani's and Lee Edelman's suggestions that queerness's critical value lies in its attentiveness to the losses that structure desire itself – Bersani, for instance, calls for a 'theory of love ... grounded in the very contradictions, impossibilities, and antagonisms brought to light by any serious genealogy of desire';[18] Edelman advocates an acceptance of queerness's 'figural status as resistance to the viability of the social while insisting on the inextricability of that resistance from every social structure'.[19] Loss – loss of the loved, loss of one's country, loss of one's home, loss of one's dead – is everywhere in Hemans's poetry and animates her poetry's explorations of the 'contradictions, impossibilities, and antagonisms' that structure desire. While it has become commonplace to ascribe this attentiveness to loss to the biographical facts of Hemans's father's and, later, her husband's abandonments of their families (her father relocated to Canada in 1810), such narratives have often sedimented an understanding of Hemans as a domestic writer, one whose status as housewife was unjustly hedged by irresponsible men and whose writing career served to mourn her loss of that status. But many of Hemans's poems queerly refuse such a trajectory, suggesting instead that loss and impossibility – an impossibility sometimes traced by the regulated impossibility of same-sex desire – work, from the start, to constitute desire; such a structure is always already in play, her poems suggest, before desire makes its home at the seat of the normative. Crucially, in ways that further complicate Hemans's domestic reputation, her conjoined imaginings of loss and desire mark out not only her structuring of romantic, marital and erotic relations but also infuse her treatment of national and transnational belonging and estrangement.

Hemans's entangled treatment of the erotic, the domestic and the (trans)national, cuts through many of her best-known works. In probably her best longer work, her two-part lyric narrative poem of 1825, *The Forest Sanctuary*, the story of the feminized Protestant Spanish narrator's flight from the Spanish Inquisition to America cannot be divorced from his stifled mourning after the execution of his 'heart's first friend' (I.xxii.198), Alvar, and the wedge this drives between himself and his wife, Leonor, who dies mid-Atlantic. The narrator's difficulties in mourning the loss of his intimate male friend become inextricably tied to the poem's insistence on exile as a loss of the quite-literal grounds for mourning – the figure that encapsulates this sentiment in the poem is that of the absent grave, tying Alvar's obliteration by fire to the graves of his ancestors in Spain and the gap represented by his wife's watery burial.[20] And estranged male intimacy and death at sea are, of course, also the key plot points of Hemans's most famous poem, 'Casabianca', which was first published in the *New Monthly Magazine* in August 1826 and later became Victorian England's most popular performance piece. The seeming simplicity of this poem's attentions to the ideally self-sacrificing patriotic subject plays out alongside a somewhat submerged querying of the forms by which patriotism becomes recognizable and reiterative. The poem famously centres on the 'boy ... on the burning deck' (1), whose absent grave (on account of his soon-to-be blasted body) figures forth the poem's reflection on its own strange ease in the presence of the boy's doomed commitment to his father (whose own unknown death off-stage is the absence that holds the boy in place). While it is a poem whose ostensible commitment to the boy's patriotic and patriarchal commitments gainsaid its anthologizing in recitation collections, it could just as well be remembered as a poem that performs the potentiality of such commitment to empty itself out as pure form (and in the process give itself up to recitations that seem to repeat the boy's own repetitions of commitment to himself and his absent father). That the poem perversely animates the fatal flames as a kind of ornamental compensation – the 'wreathing fires' (28) wrap 'the ship in splendour wild' (29) – might suggest, instead, that Hemans's poem revels in a feminized engulfment of masculinist nationalism, even as that fiery engulfment enshrines such attachment as heroic, if masochistic, heroism.

Where *The Forest Sanctuary* and 'Casabianca' explore male acts of abandonment and their queer effects on other males and on a masculine discourse of nationalist belonging, Hemans's most popular collection of poems, *Records of Woman*, first published in 1828, focuses on female acts of dedication, constancy and memorialization (even in the face of male abandonment or romantic estrangement), and ties these acts to a maternal concept of the nation. Yet, while the collection appears to espouse the importance of marriage and the nation and the willingness of women to sacrifice themselves for the sake of these institutions, the energy of the poems attaches not to the institutions themselves but to the sometimes-perverse acts by which such institutions are evoked and codified. By juxtaposing a wide range of memorial acts, the collection invites the reader to draw destabilizing analogies between the various 'records' of feminine remembrance. In a number of the poems, woman's fidelity and compassion or her maternal vision provide solace to abandoned men and women, with the womanly space of the home offering up refuge from a world of intra- and inter-national violence. This is the world traced by poems such as 'Gertrude, or Fidelity Till Death' (in which the title character comforts her husband as he is tortured to death), 'Costanza' (in which the eponymous heroine holds onto her 'crushed affection' and returns to provide a refuge for the dying soldier who abandoned her) and 'Madeline: a Domestic Tale' (in which a mother comforts her newly widowed daughter and brings her home from a faraway land). In 'The Switzer's Wife', such feminine compassion becomes the force that drives masculine nationalism, and in 'The American Forest Girl' (in which the girl intercedes in the execution of a fair English youth by a band of dark-souled Indians) compassion, as Tim Fulford has noted, positions the Victorian woman as a force for 'emotional work on the behalf of the new, evangelical, justification of empire as a civilizing mission'.[21] These poems, however, jar with various other poems that seem to call into question similar acts of feminine dedication. Gertrude's fidelity stands, in the collection, alongside Imelda's 'self-destructive sympathy'[22] as she sucks the wound of her poisoned lover after he is killed by her brother, or Properzia Rossi's homoerotic investment in the statue of Ariadne that she hopes will turn the head of her neglectful lover, or, in a later poem, Juana's passionate attendance to the body of her neglectful husband, Philip the Handsome, as she madly hopes to awaken a love she never experienced while he lived. In 'The Bride of the Greek Isles' (in which Eudora, the title character, self-immolates on a ship after being abducted by pirates on her wedding night) and 'Indian Woman's Death Song' (in which the woman sings as she rows herself and her children over a waterfall after having been abandoned by her husband for a white woman), sacrifice which might seem to signify fidelity to the principles of marriage also circulates, uncertainly, as a protest against the constraints marriage places on female agency.

'Those who are free throughout the world': bardic loss and mobility in Hemans's Welsh melodies

Much of Hemans's work of the 1820s, then, queerly resists the ways in which her own poems seem to reify normatively gendered accounts of national belonging. *The Forest Sanctuary* and 'Casabianca' were composed after Hemans's return to north Wales, where she would remain until relocating to Liverpool in 1827, a year before the publication of *Records of Woman*. So what connections might we draw between Hemans's queer (trans)nationalisms and her status as a Welsh writer and as a sometime writer of Wales? William D. Brewer locates in Hemans's work, in its persistent attempts to portray 'the emotions and experiences of people from various nations and historical epochs', a 'bardic ideology that has its foundation in ancient times and natural sites, subscribes to values endorsed by diverse cultures, and transcends national boundaries and ethnic allegiances'.[23] Brewer's reading of Hemans's 'international nationalism' proposes a fairly convincing explanation for her capacity to 'write both jingoistic poems praising England's military victories and sympathetic portrayals of England's enemies without perceiving a contradiction'.[24] Repositioning Hemans's more specific inscription of Wales as the site of Ancient Britain's birth and of Welsh bardic history as the embodiment of an aesthetics of loss can, however, allow for a more nuanced account of what she found when she turned from the fragments of contemporary imperial projects to the songs of Wales's past.

Hemans perceived her Welsh environment and its people as specifically marked, even exotic: in a letter to Mary Russell Mitford from 1827, Hemans encouraged the poet to visit her at St Asaph, promising she 'would find here new scenes, new people with many marked peculiarities (for the Welsh character is by no means yet merged in the English)'.[25] Yet if, as I am suggesting, Hemans's occupation of culturally liminal space – in north Wales, as a female poet, as a woman separated from her husband – shaped her quintessentially Romantic attachment to figures of loss and exile, her attention to the geographical space of Wales in her writing was, however, fairly slim. Her key exploration of Welshness takes place in her 1821 collection, *A Selection of Welsh Melodies*, the lyrics to which were set to arrangements of traditional airs by the prolific Welsh composer, John Parry. This volume, as Clare Simmons notes, needs to be read in the context of other Romantic liberal and antiquarian appropriations of folksong and folklore, of 'popular Medievalism', in such works as Thomas Moore's *Irish Melodies* (1807–34), Byron's *Hebrew Melodies* (1815) and Robert Burns's *Scots Musical Museum* (1787–1803).[26] Gary Kelly describes Hemans's appropriation of Welsh bardism as forming part of a broader effort, in Britain's 'Romantic liberal nationalism', to draw on 'remote and supposedly uncorrupted regions' as 'figures for the essential or "true" Britain, marginalised by the unreformed hegemonic order but a potential source of national, social, political, and cultural renewal, regeneration, reform, and reconciliation'.[27] But Hemans's bardism is, I would suggest, somewhat more complicated, for even as her original and transliterated Welsh airs evoke the possibility of Britain's renewal from the margins, they also inscribe her voice as part of an unclaimable loss at the site of national identity and mythology. Moreover, that loss (as with her other cosmopolitan works) figures as the space in which she problematizes her gendered identity as a female poet.

'The idea entertained of the bardic character', Hemans wrote in an 1823 letter to an unidentified recipient, 'appears to me particularly elevated and beautiful'. In particular, Hemans was drawn to the bard's mobility, to his ability to pass 'unmolested from one hostile country to another', and to the order's title, 'Those who are free throughout the world.'[28] Throughout *Welsh Melodies*, Hemans adopts a mobile, masculine bardic character that can only register its sense of possession, paradoxically, in terms of an emasculating loss. Her poems take both that mobility and that possessive loss as figures for their own movements between validation of and lament for her own necessarily limited attempts to possess the bardic voice. If loss became the queer figure by which Hemans simultaneously performed and deflated the values, or 'records,' of British domesticity in her later poems of feminine abandonment, in *Welsh Melodies* loss defines a national identity and the revivalism, or memorialism, that attaches to it – the analogies I will draw between these two narratives of loss in Hemans's career suggest oblique, not always clear, lines between the queer and Welsh strands of her writing. James Mulholland has recently argued for the formative role of the voice that Hemans adopts in these Welsh airs: 'her attempt to reinfuse wildness and vigor into Welsh poetic voices and to create viable publics around Welsh memories depended on the techniques of address that would eventually evolve into the dramatic monologue later in her career'.[29] Building on this, I want to argue such a forming of voice needs to be understood in the context of Hemans's mobile appreciation of an evanescent and contingent gendered national identity, embodied, at this stage, in the Welsh bard. *Welsh Melodies* traces the emergence of Hemans's structurally queer understanding of how ideologies of gender, desire and national belonging circulate and intersect.

In the third poem of the collection, 'The Green Isles of Ocean', Hemans uses a footnote to frame the melodies in terms of a mythography of loss, noting how the story of Gafran's voyage to discover the paradisiacal isles of the poem's title and his failure to return, along with 'the voyage of Merddin Emrys with his twelve bards, and the expedition of Madoc, were called the three losses by disappearance of the island of Britain'. This mythography proves crucial to Hemans's appropriation of the bardic voice – to act as a bard, in the collection, is to recall and regather a Welsh national voice characterized by its always-prior engagement in the act of recalling and regathering that which has disappeared. In the specific context of 'The Green Isles of Ocean' (which only death could bring searchers to), the quest for a lost land becomes, itself, a forfeiting of the grounds for narrating that loss (a forfeiting captured in that persistent Hemansian figure, the absent grave): 'To the winds of the ocean they left their wild story, / In the fields of their country they found not a grave' (9–10). In the succeeding poem, 'The Sea Song of Gafran', the 'wild story' of Gafran's voyage 'O'er seas unknown' (8) frames (as the opening and closing lines) the poem's more absorbing interest in the Welsh domestic hearths at which Gafran hopes to be recalled. Hemans returns to this mythography of loss with the poem 'Prince Madoc's Farewell' ('Madog's' in the original publication), a poem that, for her contemporary audience, would have immediately brought to mind Robert Southey's exploration of that same story in his epic poem *Madoc*. Initially aiming to cast a narrative of national transition from colonial Madoc to the rule over Incan Peru of Mango Capac, Southey's poem, as Lynda Pratt notes, with its distaste for tracing heterosexual romances, failed to locate a genealogy that would link the Welsh explorer to a new race of Welsh-Indians: *Madoc* became 'a foundation epic in which nothing lasting is founded and in which male friendship takes the place of the breeding of future citizens'.[30] Replicating Southey's queerly antifoundational colonial myth, Hemans's Madoc voices an ambivalent relationship to the song that becomes synonymous with Welsh land in *Welsh Airs*. While he calls for the 'free songs of the land / Where the harp's lofty soul of each wild wind is borne' (7–8) to '[b]e hush'd, be forgotten' (9) as a sign of his inability to 'return' (10), Madoc casts that same song ahead as the promise of the New World: 'No! no! let your echoes still float on the breeze, / And my heart shall be strong for the conquest of seas.' Recalling Southey's epic, genealogy again surfaces in Hemans's poem as a fraught figure for envisaging Welsh futurity:

> 'Tis not for the land of my sires to give birth
> Unto bosoms that shrink when their trial is nigh;
> Away! we will bear over ocean and earth
> A name and a spirit that never shall die.
> My course to the winds, to the stars, I resign
> But my soul's quenchless fire, O my country! is thine. (13–18)

Madoc's ''Tis not' signifies both the evidence of his own exile as the endurance of a Welsh name, spirit and soul, and a seemingly inevitable inscription of that name in the loss of a Welsh homeland. The suspension of the line ending through enjambment nods to the collection's consistent figuring of Wales as a land with no sire giving birth, as a land in which the bard's song of loss takes (to return to Pratt's reading of Southey) 'the place of the breeding of future citizens'.

As with her later inscription of woman's 'records' as a series of signs set in uncertain circulation, Hemans also frames the records of the Welsh bards – and her own effort to produce a bardic record – as unstable acts of memorialization. Shawna Lichtenwalner argues that Hemans's contextualizing quotations at the start of every poem in the collection and her 'extensive footnotes demonstrate a close familiarity with the work published by other contributors to the Welsh cultural revival, and an interest in representing Welsh history accurately'.[31] But Hemans's notes, which seek to recall and place lost Welsh cultural practices – and which usually invoke male scholarly voices in tension with the uncertain gendering of the poems' various speakers – sometimes stand in an unclear relation to the poems that enact those same practices. The tension between notes and poems ensures that the bardic records of Welshness in Hemans's collection continue a cycling of loss in their evasion of the masculine scholarly apparatus that Hemans invokes.[32]

The poem entitled 'The Mountain Fires' exemplifies this cyclical tension. Hemans's poem appears to draw on two personal experiences. The first she recorded in a letter discussing the beauty and bardic history of 'the valley of Llangollen' from 1822:

> I once passed through that scenery at night, when its sublimity was inexpressibly heightened by the fires which had been lighted to burn the gorse on the mountains. The broad masses of light and shadow which they occasioned gave it a character of almost savage grandeur, which made a powerful impression upon my mind.[33]

The second experience is rather more bizarre: in his memoir of Hemans, discussing the 'wildnesses' of her many unpublished occasional poems, Henry Chorley recalls how it was the 'livelier humour' she 'sometimes gave way ... to' in such verses that had once 'in a freak ... absolutely made her set one side of a furze-covered Welsh hill on fire, when abroad on a party of pleasure'.[34] Pulling these experiences together in the *Welsh Melodies*, 'The Mountain Fires' begins with a note that juxtaposes two modes for reading the fires, the first of which draws on an 1820 article on 'The Triads' from *The Cambro-Briton*:

> 'The custom retained in Wales of lighting fires (*Coelcerthf*) on November eve, is said to be a traditional memorial of the massacre of the British chiefs by Hengist, on Salisbury plain. The practice is, however, of older date, and had reference originally to the *Alban Elted*, or new-year.' – *Cambro-Briton*.
>
> When these fires are kindled on the mountains, and seen, through the darkness of a stormy night, casting a red and fitful glare over heath and rock, their effect is strikingly picturesque.

Rather than placing the poem, Hemans's note establishes three modes for reading the fires – as militaristic and anti-colonial memorial, as forgotten seasonal practice, as 'picturesque' scene. In this context, Hemans's poem, which in tension with the passive voice of the note takes up the imperative (and again perhaps freakish) 'Light the hills' (1, 5) as its opening refrain, bears an unclear relation to the failed Welsh resistance to Saxon imperialism that it may or may not record – if the flames, as the poem suggests, tell 'of Cambria's elder time' (16), it is unclear what they tell. The poem closes ventriloquistically with the 'voices' (21) of the 'noble dead' (20) sounding in the wind: 'Sons! though yours a brighter lot / When the mountain land rejoices, / Be her mighty unforgot!' (22–4). Yet even as the poem, thus, casts the fires as a grave-like remembrance of Wales's 'mighty' past (and its extinction at the site of the massacre), it refuses to specify the grounds of such a remembrance and, as such, forgets the very 'unforgot[ten]' voice that signs its final lines. As a 'picturesque' impression, the mountain fires become one more figure for the loss of a loss, one that locates that aesthetic of loss – and somewhat pyromaniacal desire to 'light' that fire in remembrance – in the unsigned, but seemingly autobiographical, voice of the headnote's second speaker.

Tensions – between poems and their apparatus, and between individual poems – also complicate the collection's ventriloquistic approach to the bardic voice. Take, for instance, the historically paired poems 'Chant of the Bards before Their Massacre by Edward I' and 'The Dying Bard's Prophecy'. The latter poem appears to rewrite Thomas Gray's fatalistic Pindaric ode, 'The Bard', warning the Saxon to 'think not *all* is won' (16) by laying out a prophecy of the Welsh song's re-emergence from the land: 'Though hush'd a while, that sounding flood / Shall roll in joy through ages yet to be' (27–8). The 'Chant of the Bards', however, pre-emptively frames this vision of futurity as purely figurative. Initially, the poem seems to proffer a vision of Welsh vocal freedom and resistance akin to that prophesied by the dying bard: 'So shall our spirits be free as our strains – / The children of song may not languish in chains' (3–4). But when this final phrase returns, with a difference, at the poem's conclusion, Hemans's incantatory style empties out the political promise of the first phrase to offer only a spiritual release – as the defeated Welsh spirits abandon their bodies, they must also leave behind empty chambers: 'Lonely and voiceless your halls must remain – / The children of song may not breathe in the chain!' (11–12). Hemans's footnote to 'Chant of the Bards' renders the resistance of the bardic song – which, of course, also synecdochically stands here for Hemans's own *Welsh Melodies* – only more equivocal by raising the possibility of her collective bardic voice occupying the space of historical fantasy: 'This sanguinary deed is not attested to by any historian of credit. And it deserves to be also noticed, that none of the bardic productions since the time of Edward make any allusion to such an event. – *Cambro-Briton*, vol. i, p. 195.' Just as the 'chant' of the poem both raises the prospect of a politically resistant voice even as it ascribes that voice to an apolitical spiritual realm, the footnote also performs a doubled role in positioning Hemans's Welsh ventriloquism in this and the succeeding poem – while the footnote casts doubt both on the occurrence of the massacre and the possibility of any bardic history of the event, it also lays out the imaginary gap which Hemans's 'bardic production' seeks to occupy. Like the neglected 'records of woman' that her later work will attempt to fill in, 'Chant of the Bards' figures as an attempt to remember an unrecorded history, but it also, in acknowledging its act of *re*memory, stages that attempt as a possible flight of fancy. Given that 'Chant of the Bards' references the most egregious story of Wales's colonization in the collection, it seems fitting that the Anglophilic Hemans ambivalently stages her 'record' of that event as something between a reimagining of something lost and a losing of something reimagined.

Hemans's performances are at their most ambiguous and queer in the best known poem of the collection, 'The Rock of Cader Idris', when the first-person narrator, who has physically taken the seat of the bard on the summit of Cader Idris for a night, awakes with a vision of uncertain significance. The poem can be read as a figure for Hemans's general reconstructive project (and for the Romantic period's more general enthusiasm for 'National Melody' as a genre)[35] – the effort of the modern-day poet to take up the voice of the bard by placing herself, ventriloquistically, in his seat (his 'cader'). Commenting on the poem's rather general treatment of nature and poetic inspiration, Tricia Lootens has read this poem as evidence of Hemans's universalist, non-specific and, as such, colonial use of the Welsh tradition: 'even as she celebrates the Welsh bards' national identity, Hemans colludes in the dispersion of that identity'.[36] William Brewer, by contrast, finds in the poem's 'extremely nonspecific account of the birth of a genius', Hemans's forging of 'spiritual and aesthetic', rather than 'ethnic', ties to the 'transcultural values' of 'Ancient Britain'.[37] Neither Lootens nor Brewer account sufficiently for the poem's actual refusal to gainsay the speaker's attainment of bardic genius. Where the majority of the poems in *Welsh Melodies* have circulated around questions of loss, 'The Rock of Cader Idris' offers up a contingent and queer vision of poetic achievement emerging from displaced and displacing desire. Laid out 'on that rock where the storms have their dwelling' (1), Hemans's unclearly gendered speaker gives herself or himself up to the 'swelling' (3), 'fitfully streaming' (5), 'moan[ing]' (6) voice of '[t]hings glorious, unearthly' (11). '[A]lmost faint[ing] with rapture and awe' (12) yet 'triumphantly liv[ing]' (26) through the experience, the speaker's encounter with the mountain's phallically sublime 'dread ... grandeur' (8) positions his or her ventriloquistic attainment of 'a voice, and a power' (28) the morning after as an erotic, even reproductive, exchange of uncertain import.

'The Rock of Cader Idris' was later published in *The New Monthly Magazine* in 1834 and the differences between the supplementary material accompanying the two versions of the poem complicate the poem's apparent celebration of genius's birth. The original book version concludes with an endnote explaining that according to 'an old tradition of the Welsh bards' it is believed 'that whoever should pass a night in that hollow, would be found in the morning either dead, in a frenzy, or endowed with the highest poetical inspiration'; however, the magazine version rewrites this material in a headnote to suggest that according to 'popular Welsh tradition ... whoever should pass a night in that seat, would be found in the morning either dead, raving mad, or endowed with supernatural genius'. The rewrite suggests Hemans returned to her source material, Edward Davies's *Celtic Researches, on the Origins, Tradition, and Language of the Ancient Britons* (strangely, Hemans misspells his name as Davis in *Welsh Melodies*, and then, in the later magazine version, omits any reference to him altogether). The original unacknowledged quotation reads as: 'On the very summit, we are told there is an excavation in the solid rock, resembling a couch, and it is pretended that, whoever should rest a night in that seat, will be found in the morning, either dead, raving mad, or endued with supernatural genius.'[38] Hemans's rewrite suggests a desire to close off ambiguities raised by the earlier version's hazy distinction between 'frenzy' and 'high ... inspiration'. But if Hemans's rewrite suggests a desire to tame the suggestiveness of her earlier collection's conclusion, they also inadvertently direct us to reconsider the oddity of that closing gesture. Returning to yet eliding the presence of a masculine scholarly apparatus, Hemans's ambivalent refashioning of the epigraph points to the poem's own uncertain negotiation of the relationship between a visionary loss of self and a masculinized birthing of the self's poetic voice.

Hemans's poem ties the uncertainty of the speaker's reproductive attainments to the uncertainty of the process by which the speaker emerges from his or her vision. When the speaker awakes 'to inherit / A flame all immortal, a voice, and a power' (27–8), it leaves the poem unclearly positioned in relation to the eroticized phantoms of Wales's dead, 'the mighty of ages departed' (21) that the speaker has encountered. The speaker survives the night, we are told, because 'my spirit / Was strong, and triumphantly lived through that hour' (25–6). So should the speaker's subsequent attainment of voice be read as an effect of these phantoms on her sensibility ('I *felt* their deep presence – but knew not their forms' (20)), or a sign of his or her independent triumph over their 'cold radiance' (23)? While, midway through the poem, the speaker reflects on an internal battling 'of madness and death' (16), it is unclear to what extent that battle has been resolved by the speaker's awakening at the poem's end.

Hemans's ambivalent taking up of the bardic voice in 'The Rock of Cader Idris' (which was often published as the closing poem in the collection) ought to be reassessed in the context of her approach to the source material that she oddly returns to yet buries in the magazine rewrite. In the opening dedication of *Celtic Researches*, Edward Davies depicts himself as a mediating figure, a necessary supplement to druidic culture, which could not, by virtue of its defining characteristics, be trusted to document itself: 'Simplicity of manners, and superstitious credulity, which constituted the most prominent features of characters in the votaries of that religion, obstructed the solution of its riddles, and consigned its legendary tales to their fate, as oracular mysteries too deep to be fathomed.'[39] The passage describing Cader Idris in Davies's book comes in the middle of a section in which Davies, himself, positions his work in an ambivalent relationship to the druidism, or bardism, that he seeks to document and analyse.[40] Just a page prior to the account of Cader Idris, Davies describes how the peaceful druids' only instrument of power, 'the rod of *excommunication*', left them powerless 'in the eyes of strangers' and rendered the unarmed *Celtae* ill-prepared for invasion. 'As our nature is constituted', Davies declares, the institution of druidism 'seems neither to have been calculated for the liberty of the individual, or the independence of the nation: and I regard its prevalence, as one main cause of the general subjugation of the *Celtae*'.[41] The mythology of Cader Idris circulates, then, in Davies's imperialist work as a sign of druidism's overinvestment in the authority of passively prophetic vision. It takes its place in Davies's tracing of a teleological arc of doom for Wales's aboriginal inhabitants that closely echoes Britain's more contemporary narratives of imperial destiny, one that condemns the peaceful bards both to necessary rewriting by scholars like Davies and to inevitable colonization by the better-armed Romans.

Hemans's curiously poised rewriting of her source material in *Welsh Melodies* suggests, then, an ambivalent response to the teleologies she draws on. By rendering ambiguous the speaker's erotic achievement on awaking, by tracing an uncertain distinction between 'frenzy' and 'inspiration' in the speaker's concluding rhapsody, Hemans frames what would seem to be a scene of attainment as one more potential cycle in her Welsh songs of loss. At the same time, Hemans, somewhat perversely, suggests that this wavering vision of a speaker who has either attained or lost the phallic voice of Wales might serve as a more fitting descendant of the bards whose losses, whose absences, writers like Davies would seek to fill in. And this contingent imagining of poetic and erotic achievement comes, in the poem, as an effect of the text's insistently queer refusal to place desire. While the poem's note establishes the speaker's passing of 'a night in that seat' as the fulfilment of a Welsh 'tradition', the poem itself refuses to account for the motivations behind the speaker's presence on the mountain. Anaphorically, the opening two stanzas place the speaker without situating the desire that has led her or him to this place: 'I lay on that rock' (1); 'I lay there in silence' (9). The final two stanzas balance this uncertain placement with anaphoric accounts of the speaker's subsequent, no-less ambiguous, vision: 'I saw them' (17); 'I saw what man looks on, and dies' (25). On the surface, Hemans's poem traces how a quintessentially Romantic encounter with an ineffable sublime – an experience that 'Man's tongue hath no language to speak' (10) – brings the speaker a 'sense' (32) that allows her/him to perceive a 'new glory' in 'all nature' (31). Its play, however, with the ambiguity of its endnote/headnote frames the speaker's sublime resurrection ('as from the grave, I awoke' (27)) as emerging from an uncertain attraction to and erotic encounter with a site of Welsh bardic loss. The speaker's visionary encounter suggests that it is the enduring presence of the 'departed' (21), 'the dread beings around us that hover, / Though veiled by the mists of mortality's breath' (13–14), that 'gives soul to' nature's 'beauty' (32) – a Romantic realization of the self's visionary capabilities comes, here, with a recognition of loss's shaping of the landscape. Yet the poem has 'no language to speak' the desires that may or may not bring it into communion with 'the dead' (22) of Wales's lost past.

If loss became the queer figure by which Hemans both performed and deflated the 'records' of British domesticity in her later poems of feminine abandonment, in *Welsh Melodies* loss defines a national identity and the charged memorialism that attaches to it – in 'The Rock of Cader Idris', the collection strikes an uncertain note with the unclearly gendered, would-be bardic speaker poised between a reproductive coming into voice and a rapturous loss of the self. As with the inconsistent tone and politics of *Records of Woman*, *Welsh Melodies* offers up acts of ventriloquistic bardism that at times reinforce the reifying moves of her masculine scholarly notes and, at other times, refuse the very project of documenting Celtic aboriginality. Complicating the relationship between Hemans's poetic voice and the masculine bardism and Celtomania it rehearses, Hemans's mythology, and demythologization, of loss in *Welsh Melodies* anticipates the losses that structure her later perverse, aesthetic attentions to 'The Homes of England' and the unhoming of various cultural others. A reading of *Welsh Melodies* suggests that the queer (trans)nationalisms that map Hemans's poems of the 1820s emerged from an aesthetic honed by her immersion in an imaginary of loss that inscribed Wales as both resistant to and the seat of British colonial desires. 'The Rock of Cader Idris' ultimately situates Hemans's ventriloquistic efforts to occupy the seat of the Welsh bards as a disorienting, erotic event – the poem traces Hemans's (trans)national bardism, 'free throughout the world', to desires that refuse any easy disentangling from experiences of loss.

2

'Gender difference is nothing': Cranogwen and Victorian Wales

JANE AARON

I

In February 1887 a craze for 'bobbing' was troubling a correspondent to the 'Questions and Answers' column of the Welsh-language women's magazine *Y Frythones* (The Female Briton). She wrote to its editor asking: 'What do you say about women cutting their hair like boys? In some shops sometimes, it's difficult to know whether the person serving is a boy or a girl' (*Beth a ddywedwch am fod merched yn tori eu gwallt fel bechgyn? Mewn ambell siop weithiau, bydd yn anhawdd adnabod pa un ai bachgen ai merch a fydd y rhywun ger bron*). Given the dress code of commercial enterprises in Wales in the 1880s, it is unlikely that 'M.T.', as the correspondent signs herself, was in any real confusion as to the gender of the server; however, the editor of *Y Frythones* takes her question in all seriousness, replying, 'First of all, then, ask that person which he or she will be, a boy or a girl? Then proceed with your business' (*Yn gyntaf peth gan hyny, gofynwch i'r person pa un fydd, ai bachgen ai merch? Yna ewch yn mlaen a'ch neges*). Interestingly, the editor, Sarah Jane Rees (1839–1916), generally known by her bardic pseudonym Cranogwen, does not suggest that her correspondent when questioning the server should use the present tense ('which he or she is' – *pa un ydyw*), which would imply a query after his or her biological sex, but rather the present future ('which he or she will be' – *pa un fydd*), suggesting the possibility of gender self-identification on the part of the server. And Cranogwen concludes her response to this particular instance of gender trouble by warmly encouraging her readers not to demur at such diversities from the expected norms but to welcome them as part of life's rich variety: 'Some in this way and some in that is the order and excellence of the creation' she declares (*Rhai yn y modd hyn a rhai yn y modd arall yw trefn ac ardderchawgrwydd y greadigaeth*).[1]

'M.T.', if she was a regular reader of *Y Frythones*, should in fact have known better than to expect of its editor any critique of unconventional gender performativity. By 1887, Cranogwen had already made her refusal to accept conformist notions of gender roles quite clear, particularly in her role as 'agony aunt' in the 'Questions and Answer' column. In September 1881, another correspondent had asked her, 'Is it through marrying or through not doing so that a woman best meets the purpose of her existence?' (*Pa un wrth briodi ai wrth beidio yr etyb merch ddyben ei bodolaeth yn oreu*?) In responding, Cranogwen refuses the invitation to provide any generalization of women's role:

> *Anwyl chwaer, pwy yw y ferch yr ymholwch o berthynas iddi, a pha beth, dybywch, ydyw dyben ei bodolaeth? Os y gellwch roddi i ni yr hysbysrwydd hwn, ni a'ch atebwn ar unwaith. Y mae merch fan yma ar ein pwys yn cyfrif, meddai, ei bod hi yn ateb dyben ei bodolaeth yn dda iawn trwy beidio, ond nid hi yw pawb; y mae y fath wahaniaeth rhyngom a'n gilydd, wyddoch.*²

> Dear sister, who is the woman of whom you ask, and what, by your reckoning, is the purpose of her existence? If you can give us this information, we will give you an immediate answer. There is a woman here at our side who, she says, meets the purpose of her existence very well by not marrying, but she is not everyone; there is so great a difference between us and one another, you know.

The woman to whose position 'here at our side' Cranogwen draws her readers' attention was probably Jane Thomas, with whom the *Frythones* editor lived for the last twenty-three years of her life. While her parents were alive, Cranogwen's home was with them, but during the 1880s Jane moved into the house next door, and after her widowed father's death in 1893 Cranogwen joined her.³ Heterosexual relationships had not featured as part of 'the purpose of her existence', any more than Jane's; from the perspective of her lived experience, then, Cranogwen was unlikely to subscribe to any conventional generalizing view of womanhood.

In her role as 'agony aunt', she tries to impress upon her readers the importance of concerning themselves not with traditional gender definitions or the nonconformities of others, but rather with the discovery of their own individual potential and ways to its fulfilment. Responding to a further query in December 1881 on the nature of women's proper sphere, the 'Ed.' (*yr Ol.*) as Cranogwen liked to sign herself, writes, 'Everyone's sphere and work is obvious enough, male or female ... in the light of that which he or she *is*, and *can do*' (*Y mae lle a gwaith pob un, gwryw ai benyw, yn ddigon amlwg ... yn ngoleuni yr hyn ydyw efe neu hi, a'r hyn a all*). 'Our advice always to everyone,' she adds, 'is and will be, if you feel certain you can do something well ... offer to do it; if you are prevented, no doubt you will feel ... within you guidance as to how to act.' (*Ein cynghor ni bob amser i bob un, ydyw ac a fydd, os y teimlwch yn sicr y medrwch wneyd rhywbeth yn dda ... cynygiwch ei wneyd; os y gwaherddir chwi, ond odid na theimlwch ynoch ... gyfarwyddyd pa fodd i weithredu.*)⁴ Though familial and societal influences may attempt to mould the individual in accordance with conventional gender patterns, such constructions should be resisted if they do not accord with the inner sense of authentic identity. Cranogwen in effect replaces one form of essentialism with another: biological definitions of the woman's role as primarily reproductive are spurned in favour of a committed belief in individual selfhood, knowledge of which is arrived at through intuition. Unique to each individual, and created by his or her Maker, this is the core identity which may or may not accord with conventional gender ideology. This was the template by which Cranogwen herself had lived, but her readers had difficulty accepting it, or so at least their numerous questions on the same issue would suggest. In 1883, another correspondent who called herself, pointedly, 'Deborah' asked 'Do the scriptural examples of public women in war, song, and prayer, provide a warrant for others, in these days, to be the same?' (*A yw yr enghreifftiau ysgrythyrol o fenywaid cyhoeddus mewn rhyfel, a chân, a gweddi, megys yn gwarantu ereill, yn y dyddiau hyn, i fod yr un peth?*) The Ed. replies, with some impatience by now, 'There is no need of a warrant for that, apart from *being* that which would make them the same ... It is a pretence in everybody, men and women alike, to try to be what they are not; and it is a loss for anybody not to be what they are.' (*Nid oes eisiau gwarant i hyny, heblaw bod y peth a'u gwna yr un fath ... Ymhongarwch yn mhawb, meibion a merched yn ogystal a'u gilydd, ydyw ceisio bod yr hyn nad ydynt; a cholled ydyw i un beidio bod yr hyn ydyw.*)[5]

Her advice was nothing if not consistent: no essential self can be imposed from without; the essence is within the individual, the life task is to find it and be true to it, whatever the obstacles. But she was still answering similar questions in the same manner in 1888, when two female correspondents from Dolgellau raised a query as to the suitability of women becoming preachers. 'Everyone,' replied the Ed., 'should preach the Gospel who feels a desire to do so, and can do so, and can get people to listen' (*Dylai pawb bregethu yr Efengyl y sydd yn teimlo awydd i wneyd, ac yn medru gwneyd, ac yn cael pobl i wrando*). The biological sex of the preacher is immaterial to the case: it is her or his desires and talents that count, God-given talents according to Cranogwen, which no social fabrication has the right to frustrate. 'Gender difference is nothing in the world' she concludes authoritatively (*Nid yw gwahaniaeth rhyw yn ddim yn y byd*). Literally, this last pronouncement translates as 'Difference of sex is nothing in the world'; the concept of gender (*rhywedd*) did not exist in nineteenth-century Welsh, but given the context of Cranogwen's argument here, she is clearly speaking of what would today be called gender difference rather than sexual difference. The fact that there were as yet no words for what she was trying to communicate to her readers indicates the progressiveness of her ideas, and the difficulties of her readers in following them. But she softens her tone to these two would-be female preachers from Dolgellau, as if in sympathy with them for the struggles which lie ahead, saying, 'you are brave girls, we believe; take care then to form a correct and mature opinion about everything ... Among pioneers, some succeed, and some run to destruction' (*Yr ydych yn enethod gwrol, ni geliwn; cymerwch ofal gan hyny i ffurfio barn gywir ac aeddfed ar bobpeth ... O blith pioneers, y mae rhai yn llwyddo, a rhai yn rhedeg i ddinystr*).[6] For all the firmness of her pronouncements to the effect that 'gender difference is nothing', she did not assume it would be easy to succeed as a woman in nineteenth-century Wales. The Dolgellau correspondents would be pioneers on unchartered seas, and would need not only courage but all the right-thinking maturity they could muster to hold to their course.

But at least one outrider had gone before them, viz., Cranogwen herself who by 1888 had been for some twenty years preaching up and down the length of

Wales, and to Welsh communities in the United States as well. And preaching was by no means the first traditionally masculine occupation to which she had turned her hand. From fifteen to seventeen she worked as a sailor, manning her father's small trading vessel along the shores of Cardigan Bay and down to the Bristol Channel ports. From 1860 to 1866, armed with a mariner's Master's Certificate from a London Nautical School, she taught navigation amongst other subjects, preparing young seamen to take their marketing board certificates. In 1865, she shot to fame in Wales when she competed – anonymously, of course, according to the tradition – in a National Eisteddfod poetry competition. When the prize poet's name was announced, and it was revealed that a woman had triumphed over the two leading (male) poets of her day, Islwyn and Ceiriog, Cranogwen was suddenly in the limelight. And yet, apart from the fact that she was never listed as an accepted lay preacher in the diary of her sect, the Calvinist Methodists, and was often not permitted to ascend to the pulpit of the chapels she visited but had to preach from the *sedd fawr* (deacons' pew), she did not suffer the usual ostracized victimization of the born-too-soon pioneer; on the contrary, she was generally venerated during her lifetime, by both sexes. Her first biographer, the Reverend D. G. Jones, recalls the impression she made when visiting on her preaching and lecturing tours the industrial villages of the Rhondda valley in his childhood in the 1870s. 'She was looked upon,' he remembers, 'as a great wonder. The village poets were gratified to have the honour of seeing her walk down the street; truly, they thought of her as a supernatural being.' (*Edrychid arni fel ... rhyfeddod mawr. Yr oedd yn dda gan feirdd pentref gael y fraint o'i gweled yn cerdded yr heol; yn wir meddylient amdani fel rhywbeth goruwchnaturiol.*)[7] As for her female admirers, Catherine Jane Prichard, known by her pseudonym, Buddug, who worked with Cranogwen in the temperance movement, spoke for many when she wrote:

> *Rwyf bron a'th addoli, anfarwol Granogwen,*
>   *Rwyt wedi fy synnu, a'm swyno yn lan ...*
> *Dy ryfedd hyawdledd a'th ddwys dduwiol-frydedd,*
>   *A'th ddoniau gwahanol enillodd fy serch:*
> *Pwy bellach faidd wadu nas gall arucheledd*
> *A mawredd meddyliol babelli mewn merch?*[8]

> I nearly worship you, immortal Cranogwen,
>   you have amazed and charmed me utterly ...
> Your strange eloquence and profound piety
>   and your different talents have won my love:
> who further dares deny that sublimity
> and greatness of mind can reside in woman?

Cranogwen's unusual career gives rise to at least two questions, both of significance in relation to the nature and history of gender relations in nineteenth-century Wales. First, what gave a seaman's daughter from Llangrannog, whose father's trade barely raised the prosperity of the family above that of their farm labourer neighbours, the confidence and drive to burst with such gusto through a succession of gender glass ceilings? Secondly, why, during an age in which the patriarchal ideology of the proper sphere still confined the majority of women to domesticity and recommended the adoption of the passive feminine role, was her success greeted with such acclaim? None of her admirers went as far as to suggest that there was anything ladylike or feminine about Cranogwen; on the contrary, they tend to prize what are presented as her masculine attributes, with many references to her strong rough voice, 'like a man's', and her authoritative presence, which apparently tended to dominate all meetings she attended, whether or not she was officially in the chair.[9] 'The chosen child of nature, / Honest, rough, strong was she ... She was born to lead an army,' wrote the poet Nantlais, in her praise (*Etholedig blentyn natur, / Gonest, garw, cryf oedd hi ... Ganwyd hi i arwain byddin*).[10] And she made no bones about the difference between her life and that expected of women but celebrated it, writing openly of the fact that her strongest affections were for women. Yet she was held in high esteem by her compatriots, women and men alike: the character of a culture which, against all expectation, made her its heroine needs further explication. The next two sections of this chapter examine these questions, before turning in the last section to examine more closely Cranogwen's relations with women.

II

Sarah Jane Rees was born in 1839, the third child of John and Frances Rees of Dolgoy-fach, a small thatched cottage two miles inland from the fishing village of Llangrannog, from which she later took her bardic name, Cranogwen. John Rees owned a sketch, a small sailing vessel on which he carried local cargo to and fro from the Welsh ports, rarely venturing further afield than Bristol. In a series of autobiographical pieces – initially entitled 'Cranogwen' and subsequently 'Hunan-goffa' (Autobiography) – published in *Y Frythones*, Cranogwen, writing of herself in the third person, focuses on her early infancy and childhood. Her birth she claims was much welcomed not in spite of but because of her gender: 'A *daughter* had been given', she writes; 'she was the first *girl* in the little family, and ... it appears she was much awaited for' (*Yr oedd yr hyn y cyfeirir ato yn dipyn o amgylchiad yn y ty a'r teulu bychan dan sylw; cawsid merch ... Hi oedd y ferch gyntaf yn y teulu bychan, ac ... mae'n ymddangos y dysgwylid am dani.*)[11] It was the family's female members who gave so warm a welcome to this new arrival; her father's mother, who lived with them, 'a little woman, full of quicksilver, ... full of energy in her ways, very unyielding' (*dynes fechan, llawn arian byw ... llawn yni yn ei ffordd, di-ildio iawn*), declared that her new grandchild, who had been given her name, 'resembled her and that something might come of her better than being *wholly* useless' (*yn meddwl ei bod yn debyg iddi, ac y daethai rhywbeth ohoni yn well na bod yn hollol ddiddefnydd*).[12] The grandmother's low standard of expectation was possibly influenced by her disappointment in her son, Cranogwen's father, who according to her biographers was prone to alcoholism, but his absence at sea for much of her childhood left the family secure from any potential disturbance from that quarter.¹³ Frances Rees appears to have shared her mother-in-law's great expectations for the new daughter; later in 1870 when she published her first and, in the event, only poetry collection, Cranogwen dedicated it to her mother explaining that though she knew her work was not yet ripe for publication, she hesitated to delay further for fear that Frances Rees might not live to taste the anticipated fruit of her daughter's promise:

> *A rhag i tithau orfod rhoddi cam*
> *I arall fyd, – i'r dieithr fyd a ddaw, –*
> *Cyn derbyn unwaith, i dy anwyl law,*
> *A gweled, o ffrwyth y gangen hon*
> *A dyfodd yn dy gysgod, ar dy fron,*
> *A phrofi ei flas, – mi benderfynais i*
> *Ei dynu: – wele ef, fy mam, i ti.*

> And rather than you should have to step
> into another world – the strange world to come –
> without once receiving, in your dear hand,
> and seeing, the fruit of this branch
> which grew in your shadow, on your breast,
> and tasting its savour, – I decided
> to pluck it: – here it is, my mother, for you.¹⁴

The dedication binds mother and daughter very closely together as the one tree from which the poetic fruit grew, harvested before its time so that the mother should not face death empty-handed. According to patriarchal conventions, it was the birth of sons rather than daughters that fulfilled a woman's existence but in Cranogwen's family romance, in contradistinction to prevailing norms, the daughter is the mother's fulfilment. All the stronger, then, would have been her discomfiture when she emerged from this supportive female cocoon into the world at large to discover that, as she says, 'outside the family, whatever, she was nothing' (*y tu allan i'r teulu, pa fodd bynag, nid oedd yn ddim*).¹⁵

However, the immediate neighbourhood in Llangrannog into which she issued seems initially to have protected her from the full realization of female insignificance, inhabited as it was, in Cranogwen's recollections at any rate, by a number of strikingly strong-minded women. Of course, a predominantly fishing and sailing community must often have been in fact female-dominated, with the males absent at sea for long stretches of time. Nevertheless, even when men are present in Cranogwen's remembered Llangrannog, they are much overshadowed by their women. Of one married pair in the small community she records that the wife 'had the gift to speak and rule, his gift was more towards obedience', and adds, characteristically, 'What can be better than that each should do according to his gifts – doing that which they do best?' (*ganddi hi oedd y ddawn i siarad a llywodraethu, ei ddawn yntau yn fwy tuag at ufuddhau. Beth all fod yn well nag i bawb wneyd yn ol eu doniau – gwneyd yr hyn a allont oreu?*)¹⁶ In the case of another neighbouring couple the husband was an 'innocent' (*gŵr diniwed*) while his wife had a 'strong common sense and many opinions' (*synwyr cyffredin cryf, a llawer o farn*). It was 'Mrs C.-' rather than her husband who was accounted 'a person of significance' (*dynes a gyfrifid yn 'rhywun'*) in the small community, in which another of the female cottagers is described as Mrs C.-'s 'beloved' (*ei chares*), though what precisely Cranogwen intended to imply by such a term is unclear.[17]

The neighbour whom she remembered with the most ardent affection, however, bordering on veneration, was none of these but a solitary pauper, Esther Judith, to whom she devotes not only key passages in her autobiographical articles but also a separate extended series of seven articles published from 1880 to 1881 in *Y Frythones*. Esther Judith is praised primarily for her 'intellectual strength' (*cryfder deall*)[18] and her impassioned expression of it; according to Cranogwen, 'had the circumstances, *many* of them, been different, and she exactly as she was, she would have made an incomparable orator ... she would have set the world on fire with the power of eloquence, enthusiasm of spirit, and zeal for the truth' (*pe y buasai yr amgylchiadau yn wahanol, lawer o honynt, a hi yn hollol yr un, gwnaethai areithiwr o'r bron digymar ... rhoddasai y byd ar dân gan nerth huawdledd, brwdfrydedd ysbryd, a sel dros y gwirionedd*).[19] Repeatedly, Cranogwen stresses the wastage of human potential and the unnaturalness of forcing such an individual as Esther into the conventional female role: 'whoever was called to "keep house" ... Esther was *not*; she possessed little more aptitude and ability for that than did John the Baptist' (*Gan nad pwy a alwyd i 'gadw tŷ' ... ni alwyd Esther; ni feddai fawr fwy o gymhwyster a gallu i hynny nag a feddai Ioan Fedyddiwr*).

For all her poverty, had Esther Judith been male she might well have been afforded the opportunity to train for the ministry; within her chapel community, her intelligence would not have gone unnoticed, and could well have won her a community-funded place at a theological college. Cranogwen's portrayal of Esther Judith emphasizes the manner in which women's potential was underdeveloped, much to their culture's loss, and to their personal frustration. The series 'Esther Judith' is a lament for the lost women preachers and writers of Wales.

Anger in response to the gender system's injustice and its wastage of human potential continued to characterize many of Cranogwen's later essays. In 1887, while commenting on developments in Welsh women's education, she takes issue with Elizabeth Phillips Hughes, headmistress of the Cambridge Training College for Women Teachers, who had apparently argued for advances in this sphere on the grounds of 'suitability' (*cymhwysder*) (that is, girls should be educated so as to make them suitable partners for educated men and suitable mothers of their children). The *Frythones*'s editor insists instead on 'justice' (*cyfiawnder*) and 'woman's rights' as the more appropriate rallying call, claiming that woman 'has an old right, as old as man's, to all the privileges within reach' (*mae ... ganddi hawl hen, gan hyned a dyn, i'r holl ragorfreintiau a fewn cyrhaedd*).[20] No doubt her sense of the injusice she had witnessed in childhood also fuelled much of her early drive towards fulfilling her own potential. Apparently, her parents had not envisaged sending their daughter to school after her brothers, who attended a small local school held in a farmhouse barn in nearby Pontgarreg. But Sarah Jane

Rees according to her own account was a tomboy (*rhoces*) who copied her older brothers in all they did, and in so doing learnt to write at a precociously early age; so impressed were John and Frances Rees by their daughter's evident ability to learn that they let her join her brothers.[21] After a few years of schooling in the farmhouse barn, she was apprenticed to a local milliner; this attempt by the parents to encourage their daughter down a conventional feminine route proved, however, a complete failure, and eventually, at fifteen, she succeeded in persuading them to let her go to sea with her father instead.

During the next two years, she and her father worked daily side by side, often under dangerous conditions. According to her biographer, on one particular occasion, during a heavy thunderstorm, the father gave orders to turn inland to seek harbour, but the daughter disagreed, arguing instead that to head further out to sea would be the safer option. 'A storm rose between the two of them', says the Reverend Jones; 'at last she stamped her foot with force on the deck; she challenged the authority and experience of her father, and forced him to bend to her judgement' (*Aeth yn storm rhwng y ddau, o'r diwedd trawodd hi ei throed gyda grym ar y dec; heriodd awdurdod a phrofiad ei thad, a gorfododd ef i blygu i'w barn*).[22] If Cranogwen had early won over her mother simply by being born a long-awaited daughter, it would appear that during those two years at sea, she also won ascendancy over her father. At any rate, by the time she was seventeen, no other obstacle was put forward by her family against her desire for further education. As her two older brothers were by now earning and could contribute to the family income, money was found for her to attend private schools at New Quay, Cardigan and London, from where she returned at twenty-one to preside as teacher over the school in Pontgarreg, with her Master's Certificate in navigation. At every stage in her early career, she had succeeded by refusing to accept the limited role afforded to the women of her epoch and social class: she was not obedient and not docile; she insisted on acquiring an education, and she insisted on stepping outside the domestic sphere and doing a man's work rather than a woman's.

In 1865, however, the route ahead was made substantially easier for her by her National Eisteddfod success. The title provided by the adjudicators for that year's prize poem was 'Y Fodrwy Briodasol' ('The Wedding Ring'); strikingly, Cranogwen's winning entry, though it treats the question of marriage from many differing perspectives, at no point features a bridegroom. Divided into four 'portrayals', the poem depicts four working-class wives, each contemplating her ring in solitude and reflecting on her marriage. The first voices the doubts and fears of a young woman on her bridal day, realizing that for many the ring has only brought sorrow and disappointment; the second, by far the most impassioned and memorable portrayal, is spoken by a drunkard's wife who knows her spouse will soon return from the tavern to abuse her infant and herself, while the third is a sailor's wife, surrounded by her happy brood of children with the husband safely absent at sea; and the last features a woman on her death-bed of straw, bidding farewell to her ring from which she turns to a better world. The second 'portrait' in particular reads like a 1970s feminist polemic. Roundly cursing the ring which chains her and her infant to violent disorder, the drunkard's wife tells it:

> *Breuddwydiais, – credais dy fod di*
> *Fel carreg yr athronydd,*
> *Yn meddu'r hynod rin i droi*
> *Y cwbl yn aur o ddefnydd.*
>
> *'Ond O! y siomedigaeth flin*
>
> *Nid allaf siarad allan byth*
> *Fy ing! – mae yn anrhaethol!*
> *A dyma ffrwyth dy weniaeth di,*
> *Fy 'modrwy briodasol'.*
>
> *Gwyn fyd na allwn sangu'n ol*
> *Ar lannerch deg gwyryfdod;*
> *Dialedd melus fyddai i ffwrdd*
> *Dy daflu mewn dibrisdod.*[23]
>
> I dreamt – I thought you were
> the stone of the philosopher,
> possessing the rare virtue to turn
> the whole to gold material.
> But O! the bitter disappointment
>
> I cannot ever speak of it,
> my anguish! – it's unutterable!
> And this is the fruit of your flattery,
> my 'wedding ring'.
>
> Blessed would I be could I step back
> to virginity's fair glade;
> it would be sweet revenge
> to throw you away as contemptible.

But do so she cannot, and she has little to hope for except her own death or that of her groom. This was the poem which so delighted its audience that Cranogwen became a celebrity on the strength of it. Arguably, however, she owed the success of this poem and her subsequent popularity to a significant extent to a central traumatic event in the history of nineteenth-century Wales, as the next section explains.

III

Cranogwen rose to fame during the aftermath of the 1847 *Report of the Commission of Inquiry into the State of Education in Wales*. Initially commissioned to investigate why the Welsh population was by and large so resistant to acquiring English at a time when vast tracts of the rest of the globe were rapidly becoming anglicized, the *Report* went way beyond its brief and listed in detail the failings of the Welsh, ascribing each lapse from grace to their lack of the civilizing English tongue. Jelinger C. Symons, one of the commissioners who prepared the *Report*, gave it as his considered opinion that though 'the Welsh are peculiarly exempt from the guilt of great crimes', there are 'few countries where the standard of minor morals is lower'.[24] 'Petty thefts, lying, cozening, every species of chicanery, drunkenness (where the means exist), and idleness' were characteristic failings of the Welsh, a race incapable of greatness even in crime, except for one large-scale vice: many of the witnesses to the *Report* informed its commissioners that 'want of chastity is the giant sin of Wales'.[25] According to the 1851 religious census, 75 per cent of the Welsh population were Nonconformist, the majority attending Welsh-language chapels,[26] and the clergymen of the emptying Church of England in Wales who bore witness to the *Report*'s commissioners frequently blamed the Nonconformist sects in particular for Welsh failings, as if they sought to shame their parishioners back into the Anglican fold. The Reverend John Price, rector of Bleddfa and a magistrate, told Symons that

> the chief causes of this disregard to modesty and chastity may be referred ... to the bad habit of holding meetings at dissenting chapels or farmhouses after night, where the youth of both sexes attend from a distance for the purpose of walking home together. As a magistrate, I can safely report that in the investigation of numerous cases of bastardy I have found most of them to be referred to the opportunities of meeting above mentioned.[27]

The English press further sensationalized the *Report*'s findings, the *Morning Chronicle* claiming that 'Wales is fast settling down into the most savage barbarism', while the *Examiner* reported of the Welsh that 'their habits are those of animals and will not bear description'.[28] The Welsh-language mouthpiece of the Church of England, *Yr Haul* (The Sun), also proclaimed that, 'morality is so low amongst the Welsh Dissenters that it would make many pagan nations blush were they in the same condition' (*mae moesoldeb mor isel yn mhlith yr Ymneilltuwyr Cymreig ag a wnelai i amryw genhedloedd paganaidd wrido pe byddent yn yr un cyflwr*).[29]

For members of the outraged Welsh Nonconformist sects, it became a matter of the first importance to restore virtue to the tarnished image of the nation, particularly its Nonconformist women. In accordance with the double standard of Victorian sexual morality, the *Report* had implied that the primary cause of the Welsh nation's barbaric libidinousness was a lack of moral rigour amongst its womenfolk rather than its men. In fact, according to the *Report*, 'want of chastity in women ... is sufficient to account for all other immoralities, for each generation will derive its moral tone in a great degree from the influences imparted by the mothers who reared them'.[30] Suddenly, the attention of Nonconformist Welsh-speaking Wales was focused on the heterosexual behaviour of its women, as the chapel leaders sought to find clear proof of their virtue and so expose the *Report*'s findings as perfidious libel.

When Cranogwen shot into the limelight almost two decades later at the 1865 eisteddfod, it was as if in answer to a still stricken nation's prayer. The choice of 'the wedding ring' as the topic of the prize poem in itself indicates the culture's continuing obsession with the 1847 *Report*. With Cranogwen's winning entry, Welsh-speaking Wales acquired excellent first-hand evidence for its cause: a Welsh-language poem by a woman whose roots were firmly in the Dissenting lower class, who took a stand against alcoholism, also a particularly Welsh weakness, according to the *Report*, but more significantly presented the Welsh woman as one who preferred 'fair virginity' not only to extra-marital dalliance but to any association with errant males, was a treasure indeed. When she went on to edit *Y Frythones*, her contributions, particularly to the 'Questions and Answers' column, provided on many occasions further precious evidence of Welsh Nonconformist women's propriety.

Take, for example, her comments on the practice of 'courting on beds' which, according to the 1847 *Report*, was widespread in Wales. Courting on beds, or 'bundling', referred to the custom of acknowledged lovers getting to know one another better while lying, supposedly fully clothed, on the woman's bed, with the woman 'bundled' into a pillow-case or sack for extra precaution. For lack of any other private space during the winter months, the practice had been common in other parts of rural Europe too before the mid-nineteenth century,[31] but the Victorian morality of middle-class England, with its stress upon the sanctity of the marriage bed, was by now demanding a change in sexual mores. Only in one place in *Y Frythones* is there any reference to 'courting on beds'. In 1885, Gwladus Ruffydd of Penrhos wrote to its 'Question and Answer' column to enquire 'Why does the *Frythones* not speak against night associations?', that is, courting on beds ('*Paham na ddywed y Frythones yn erbyn cyfeillachu y nos?*'). Cranogwen replies, 'Because she does not assume that any of her readers practice it ... Is there much of that to which you refer still carrying on? We are so ignorant in these matters' ('*Am nad yw yn tybied fod un o'i darllenwyr yn arfer hyny ... A oes llawer o'r hyn y cyfeiriwch ato eto yn parhau? Yr y'm mor anwybodus yn y materion hyn*').[32] Historical studies of the lovemaking habits of the Welsh have shown that these 'night associations' did in fact continue into the twentieth century: only slowly between 1920 and 1930 did the practice of 'courting on beds' die out in rural Wales, according to Catrin Stevens.[33] But Cranogwen's response was exactly what the Welsh Nonconformist leaders of her day needed to hear: here was a woman reared amongst Welsh rural labourers who could state with transparent honesty that she and, she believed, her host of female readers knew nothing whatsoever about 'courting on beds', thus contradicting all malicious reports as to its continuing ubiquity in Wales.

Much of the characteristic humour of Cranogwen's 'agony aunt' column stems from the fact that this would-be adviser is self-confessedly unfamiliar, and often impatient, with the anxieties preoccupying many of her heterosexual readers. In April 1880, for example 'Claudia' from Aberporth asks 'What age do you think is the safest for women in general to enter into the state of matrimony?' (*Pa oedran tybed, yw y dyogelaf i ferched yn gyffredin fyned i'r ystad briodasol ynddo?*), to which the Ed. replies, 'Such a question is not appropriately addressed to us, but we'll take the freedom to reply that the safest thing for those who can't decide this question for themselves is not to enter that state at all' *(Nid atom ni, bid sicr, y cyfeirid y gofyniad hwn; ond cymerwn ein rhyddid i ateb mai y dyogelaf i'r rhai y byddont yn methu penderfynu y cwestiwn ar eu rhan eu hunain, yw peidio myned o gwbl)*.³⁴ Four months later, 'R.A.' from Cwmceri wants to know 'Are there not many more girls in the world than boys? How then is it possible for them all to be given in marriage?' (*'Ai nid oes llawer mwy o ferched yn y byd nag o feibion? Sut gan hyny y mae yn bosibl iddynt oll gael eu rhoddi mewn priodas?'*), and the 'Ed.' responds 'No, the number is pretty equal. Not "all" of them choose marriage presumably ... Be comforted, sisters, and try to find something to do. A little *singing* could be a happy admixture' (*'Nac oes; y mae y rhif yn bur gyfartal. Nid ydynt "oll" yn dewis hyny dybygid ... Byddwch gysurus chwiorydd, a cheisiwch rywbeth i'w wneyd. Gallai ychydig o ganu fod yn gymysgedd hapus'*).³⁵

On another occasion, in April 1882, an anonymous correspondent, reacting it would appear against the unexpected establishment of a new choir in his or her neighbourhood, asks her, 'is it not very objectionable and purposeless that an old lad [i.e. a bachelor] should dedicate two nights a week to try to teach completely talentless old lads and old maids to compete as singers?' (*onid yw yn wrthun a diamcan iawn fod hen lanc yn ymroddi ddwy noson yn yr wythnos i geisio dysgu hen lanciau a hen ferched, hollol ddidalent, i ymgystadlu mewn canu?*). With delighted surprise, the Ed. replies,

> *hen lanc yn dysgu hen lanciau a hen ferched i ganu ar gyfer cystadleuaeth! ... [Y]n mha le y mae yr urdd mor gryf a chyffredin fel y gellir gwneyd côr canu o honi, a hi yn unig! Byddai yn olygfa y teimlem yn werth myned yn bur bell i'w thystio ... Ond dyna, fe all nythaid fel yna fod rhywle, mewn rhyw gongl ddyddan, ddiniwed o'r byd.*³⁶

> an old lad teaching old lads and old maids to sing for a competition! ... [I]n what place is the order so strong and numerous that a choir of singers may be made of it, and it only! It would be a scene we would feel it worthwhile to travel pretty far to witness ... But there, some such nest could exist somewhere, in some interesting, innocent corner of the world.

Gleefully, she welcomes the prospect of the existence of such an 'interesting, innocent corner of the world', far removed from the constrictions of compulsory heterosexuality, where a different 'order' sings and flourishes.

It could be argued, however, that between the publication of the education *Report* in 1847 and the dissemination of the sexologists' findings on 'sexual inversion' towards the close of the century, Welsh Wales was itself such an 'innocent corner', for 'old maids' at any rate, if not 'old lads'. Only with the publication of studies like Havelock Ellis's *Sexual Inversion* in 1897 were suspicions first raised about the nature of 'romantic friendship' between women.³⁷ As in the case of the Ladies of Llangollen, before then such relationships were accepted and, indeed, admired as proof of the fact that women could love faithfully on a level above the physical.³⁸ By rejecting men, and maintaining an entirely pristine image in the heterosexual context, a woman like Cranogwen appealed to audiences who saw in her proof of the iniquity of the *Report*.

'Gender difference is nothing'

IV

A year after her eisteddfod win in 1866, she was able to give up school-teaching, and she spent the rest of her days as both a woman of letters, editing *Y Frythones* from 1879 to 1891, and a campaigner, founding the South Wales Women's Temperance Union in 1901. From this time on also, she moved largely in the company of women, many of whom she had herself encouraged out from their homes into more public spheres as writers, lecturers and campaigners. To have about her a supportive community of women appears to have been throughout her life an emotional necessity for Cranogwen. Women were her all in all, in a manner which no doubt made her all the more effective as the inspirer and leader of a new wave of women writers. Maybe she was not as a result knowledgeable in every aspect of her readers' relationship problems, but not one of them could doubt the wholeheartedness of her concern and dedication to their progress as women.

In her poetry collection, *Caniadau Cranogwen* (1870), she published a poem, '*Fy Ffrynd*' ('My Friend'), in which she attempted to explain the nature of her feelings for women or, rather, in this case for one woman in particular. Although she is careful in the opening stanzas to categorize the attraction as a romantic friendship rather than a love affair, as the poem proceeds, its tone becomes unambiguously passionate:

> *Ah! anwyl chwaer, 'r wyt ti i mi,*
> *Fel lloer i'r lli, yn gyson;*
> *Dy ddilyn heb orphwyso wna*
> *Serchiadau pura'm calon*
>
> *I seren dêg dy wyneb di*
> *Ni welaf* fi *un gymhar ...*
> *Mae miloedd eraill, sêr o fri,*
> *Yn gloewi y ffurfafen;*
> *Edmygaf hwy, ond* caraf *di,*
> *Fy Ngwener gu, fy 'Ogwen'.*[39]
>
> Ah! dear sister, you are to me
> as the moon to the sea, constantly;
> following you restlessly are
> my heart's purest affections
>
> To the fair star of your face
> *I* see no equal ...
> A thousand other stars of distinction
> brighten the firmament;
> I admire them, but I *love* you,
> my beloved Venus, my 'Ogwen'.

Here, particularly with the reference to 'Ogwen', the female love-object in a popular romantic ballad of the period, Cranogwen places herself unequivocally, and without any apparent embarrassment or self-consciousness, in the male lover's role.

To whom was 'Fy Ffrynd' addressed? Her biographer, the Reverend D. G. Jones, who only got to know Cranogwen personally during the last years of her life, when she was living with Jane Thomas, mentions only Jane as her constant companion and support. But in 1886 in a two-part essay in *Y Frythones*, Cranogwen remembers with profound grief another woman who twelve years previously had died in her arms. Writing of herself in the first person plural, as was her practice in *Y Frythones*, she can barely credit the fact that 'bound to her as we were in many ways, and professing while she was still with us, an unusual attachment to her and admiration of her' (*a ni yn rhwym iddi mewn llawer o ffyrdd, ac yn proffesu, tra yr oedd eto gyda ni, ymlyniad anarferol wrthi ac edmygedd o honi*), it is only now that she is 'starting to plant a flower' (*cychwyn i blanu blodeuyn*) of public commemoration on her grave. It is unlikely, she says, that the object of her attachment would have remained silent for so long had the case been reversed and it had been Cranogwen who needed memorializing (*Nid yw yn debyg y gwnaethai hi felly â'n heiddo ni, pe felly y buasai yr achos*). But her apparent neglect was not due to lack of feeling, Cranogwen protests, but too much feeling: 'the true explanation is, it is difficult work to treat the remembrance of our beloveds – *very difficult*' (*yr esboniad cywir yw, gwaith anhawdd yw trin coffadwriaeth ein hanwyliaid – anhawdd iawn*).[40]

The woman so much missed she names as Fanny Rees (1853–1874), a miller's daughter from Troedyraur in Cardiganshire, a hamlet just inland from Llangrannog. Fanny, like Cranogwen, was an autodidact who had published in the Welsh-language periodicals of her day under the pseudonym Phania, and who had, also like Cranogwen, persuaded her parents in 1873 to release her from her labours at the mill to undertake further education in London. There she contracted tuberculosis and returned to Wales to die, but not to her parents' home. 'This was under the roof of the writer of these lines,' says Cranogwen of Fanny's death, 'and from then to this day she has considered that a special favour to her from the one to whom "the death of his saints is precious in his eyes"' (*Bu hyn o dan gronglwyd ysgrifennydd y llinellau hyn, ac er hyny hyd yn awr, y mae wedi ei hystyried yn ffafr arbennig iddi oddiwrth y neb y mae 'marwolaeth ei saint yn werthfawr yn ei olwg'*).[41] To choose a friend's house in which to die, as opposed to one's nearby family home, and to know that one's dying presence there would be considered a profound gift, does suggest a requited affection stronger than friendship. Furthermore, when Cranogwen speaks of herself as having formerly publicly 'professed while she was still with us' her 'unusual attachment' to Fanny she may well have been referring to the poem 'Fy Ffrynd'. Fanny, Cranogwen knew, 'loved her friends *intensely*. In her it was completely true that "Love is strong like death"' (*[e]i chyfeillion a garai yn angerddol. Ynddi hi yr oedd yn hollol wir, 'Cariad sydd gryf fel angeu'*), and the same degree of particularly passionate feeling, on the part of the beloved as well as the lover, is suggested in 'Fy Ffrynd'. Addressing the 'friend', the poet tells her that 'I do not know whether any language ... can express, even *in part*, how dear you are to my heart; but you know all my heart' (*Ni wn y medr unrhyw iaith ... eglurhau, mewn rhan, / Mor gu wyt gan fy nghalon; Ond gwyddost ti fy nghalon oll*).[42] At any rate, whether or not this relationship, and the later relationship with Jane Thomas, was emotional alone, or also sexual, it is clear that to Cranogwen there was no idea of sin or shame attached to such a tie. Fanny, like Cranogwen herself, was to the end a profound Christian, for whom, as she writes in the extracts from her diaries quoted in *Y Frythones*, human love was precious to the extent that it 'beamed from the warmth in the Divine breast' (*yn belydru o'r gwres yn y fynwes Ddwyfol*).[43]

Much of Cranogwen's energies from the mid-1870s to her own death were exerted in encouraging other Welsh women to develop their writing and speaking talents, and extend their education, in the same way as she had no doubt encouraged Phania. *Y Frythones* ran literary contests, open to both sexes, but its editor confessed that encouraging female talent was her main aim. Initially, she had to reprimand her female readers for their tardiness in submitting material. In 1879 after receiving entries for a young people's competition, she writes 'Come on, girls, where are you? Most of the writers are boys, and you know that it was to *you* chiefly that we looked' ('*Deuwch, ferched, yn mha le yr ydych? Bechgyn yw y rhan amlaf o'r ysgrifwyr, a gwyddoch mai arnoch chwi yn benaf yr oedd ein golwg*').[44] Welsh women responded to her call, knowing their work would be welcomed by Cranogwen and given a sympathetic reading, if only by virtue of their sex. Through openly and enthusiastically favouring female talent in this way, Cranogwen succeeded in producing for ten years, between January 1879 and February 1889, a substantial monthly journal (some thirty pages of small double column print every month) with nearly as little work by men in it as there was of women's writing in Ieuan Gwynedd's *Gymraes*. The essayist Ellen Hughes of Llanengan (1862–1927), the poet and later editor of the second *Gymraes*, Ceridwen Peris (Alice Gray Jones, 1852–1943), the novelist Mary Oliver Jones (1858–1893), all published their first writings in *Y Frythones* and went on to become household names before the end of the century. In 1900, Cranogwen, as she looked back on Ellen Hughes's successful career, could take pride in her early discovery: 'I felt like one who had gained much booty when, years ago … Ellen Hughes came into view,' she wrote in the second *Gymraes*, adding,

> *Ni wyddwn, waeth i mi gyfaddef, fod yr ohebyddes ddyddorol o Lanengan i dyfu cyn y byddai hir o amser, i fod yn un o wroniaid meddyliol ei hoes, a hyny, pe y byddai bwys i'w ddweyd, heb gyfrif rhyw.*[45]

> I did not know, I might as well confess, that the interesting correspondent from Llanengan was to develop before very much time had passed to become one of the intellectual heroes of her age, and that, if it is of any significance to say so, without counting gender.

By 1900, there was less need to place emphasis on gender: Welsh women had proven their literary ability. Cranogwen had succeeded in creating a network of Welsh-language women writers who knew one another, wrote about and for one another, and received inspiration and encouragement from one another, and particularly from 'the Ed.'

In 1886, Cranogwen wrote of the question of women's enfranchisement,

gwyddom nad yw ond cwestiwn o amser iddo ddyfod yn ffaith ... I rai, deallwn yr ymddengys megys yn wyro oddiar y ffordd uniawn i dir afleidneisrwydd, a rhywbeth gwrth-wyneb i'r hyn sydd bur fenywaidd a dyrchafedig, ond yn mhen can' mlynedd, diau genym yr edrychir yn ol ar y syniadau hyn gyda thosturi, gan ryfeddu mor blentynaidd yr edrychid ar ddiwygiad cyn ei ddyfod. Cam ydyw yn ddiau, a fydd, wedi ei gymeryd, yn dwyn y ddynoliaeth fenywaidd yn nes yn mlaen ar raddfa eu dyrchafiad cyfreithlawn.[46]

we know it is only a question of time before it becomes a fact ... To some, we understand, it seems like a turning away from the straight path to indelicate terrain, and something opposite to pure and exalted femininity, but no doubt people will look back at such ideas with pity in a hundred years' time, marvelling at how childishly reform was viewed before its coming. It is a step which, once taken, will lead womankind closer to its legitimate elevation.

What is most striking about Cranogwen's career is the progressive nature of her ideas and the boldness with which she lived them and made them real. It was not until 1990 that Judith Butler in effect launched the school of queer theory with her arguments that 'gender identity ... is a regulatory fiction', a '*stylized repetition of acts*', rather than 'a true or abiding masculinity or femininity'.[47] Yet the editor of *Y Frythones* in the 1880s, in answering question after question from her correspondents as to women's appropriate work and sphere, preached virtually the same message. Notions of 'pure and exalted femininity', or by implication masculinity, are 'childish', regressive fictions in her view too. By exposing their unreality through working, speaking, writing and loving in conscious opposition to the gender constrictions of her day, she helped her contemporaries to achieve their potential. As she said and repeatedly proved by example, 'gender difference is nothing in the world'.

3
'Please don't whip me this *time':*
The Passions of George Powell of Nant-Eos

HARRY HEUSER

Introduction

A few miles inland from the Welsh seaside town of Aberystwyth lies the country estate of Nant-Eos (see illustration 1). Bearing a name that is Welsh for 'nightingale brook', the secluded spot has long been steeped in romance. Among the most fanciful legends surrounding the place is that, in the shape of a wooden chalice known as the Nanteos Cup, it held the Holy Grail, the sight of which was to have inspired Wagner to compose *Parzival*.[1] Rather less inclined to be rhapsodic about the Georgian pile, now a luxury country house hotel and restaurant, was George Ernest John Powell (1842–82), to whom the 'splendid old place' was '*home*' in all but a 'sentimental sense'.[2] Powell has been called the 'most extraordinary figure' in the history of Nant-Eos – and over the past 150 years or so he has been called much else besides: 'eccentric', 'rather sinister' and, the anachronism of the tag notwithstanding, 'homosexual'.[3]

Resisting classification yet goading us in our attempts at labelling, Powell asserts himself as a straddler of worlds that, traditionally, have been seen as poles apart. Crossing boundaries – be it literally, by living in London and Normandy, or figuratively, by translating Icelandic legends rather than Welsh mythology – the English-born 'Welshman' has long been a doubly marginalized figure, both queer and queerly Walian.[4] The fact that much of what is known of him is not verifiably factual but instead the stuff of hearsay has further contributed to making Powell an academic nonentity. Of all this, the man in question was keenly aware. Indeed, he seems to have anticipated – and to some extent engineered – our reception of him. He left behind a number of self-conscious clues about his inner world and, through his conspicuous bequest to what is now Aberystwyth University, he made a lasting public display of his short private life.

1 *Nant-Eos, today* (2012), by the author, photograph.

'Corruption, Incorruption, both': influence and the queer talent

'Not an altogether appealing figure', remarked Cecil Y. Lang, who, like most scholars, encountered Powell as a correspondent and close friend of Algernon Charles Swinburne. Lang's 1959–62 edition of Swinburne's letters – over one hundred of which are addressed to Powell – did much to open our eyes to Swinburne's world; at the same time, it cast his confidant as a tenebrous character of questionable morals and dubious merit. Lang summarily dismissed the 'well-to-do Welshman' as having been 'by no means the best possible influence on Swinburne during the sixties and seventies'.[5] Whatever the 'best' or worst influence may be, Powell's potentially significant part in shaping the work and *Weltanschauung* of a major British poet warrants speculation. The phrase 'well-to-do Welshman' deserves questioning, too, as it implies a privileged existence and a sense of national identity that Powell had neither quite the means nor the mentality to enjoy. In fact, Powell spent little time at Nant-Eos, even when he, an only son, inherited the estate upon his father's death in 1878. And although he is sometimes assumed to have been a 'well-to-do Welsh landowner', it was not his father's land but his mother's comparatively modest legacy that allowed Powell to indulge his passion for art and music.[6] It also enabled him to travel abroad, to Europe, Russia, North Africa and Iceland, to live in France and maintain rooms on Mornington Crescent in what is now the London borough of Camden. Still, it was Nant-Eos, its formidable presence and ineluctable past, that shaped his pre-Wildean queer existence, the private sphere and public image that Powell, in the absence of scientific parlance or social precedents, struggled to define for himself. Just who was this ignominious sidekick that, to most scholars of Victorian culture, exists mainly as a footnote to writings on Swinburne, as a companion to whom he is argued to be 'best remembered'?[7]

Approaching him by letter, Powell sought Swinburne's friendship because the poet was far removed from the locals and relatives that Powell associated with Welshness. Elizabeth Berridge, whose grandmother was a distant cousin of Powell's who remembered the youth as '[u]ndutiful and extravagant', commented that it

> must have been a marvellous release for George, to walk and talk with a man who had already made his mark in that larger world he longed to enter. For no one on his father's estate, no one in the county, cut off as it was by bad roads and mountains, spoke his language. He was starved of affection and that essential interchange of ideas and emotions denied him in the blunt society of his Welsh neighbours.[8]

Similarly blunt, Lang's assessment of Powell's influence on Swinburne echoes the sentiment of one of Swinburne's contemporaries, the critic William Michael Rossetti (brother to Dante Gabriel and Christina), who observed that Powell's 'acquaintance has ... been a very disastrous thing for Swinburne, confirming him in the drinking-habits he was already too prone to'.[9] Together with Swinburne, who was five years his senior, Powell reportedly 'haunt[ed] a certain low-class inn at Aberystwyth' and 'caroused', as Berridge puts it, where 'no Powell or the guest of a Powell would ever show his face'.[10]

Lang went so far as to claim that Powell 'accumulated a reputation of which the odor linger[ed]' in the 'small community' some 'seventy-five years after his death'.[11] To what extent the locals were scandalized by – or even aware of – Powell's private life is not sufficiently documented. In one contemporary guide to Aberystwyth, Powell was singled out as 'an elegant literary and musical scholar';[12] besides, the community, as Powell was eager to divulge to Swinburne, could hardly lay claim to being a model of decorum: 'We have just had in Aberystwith (account suppressed in the newspapers, of course – British virtue!) a most extraordinary case of incestuous rape, which I will reserve for your entertainment when we meet.'[13]

Most of the rumours that circulated about Powell originated in France, where Powell entertained guests at the Chaumière de Dolmancé, his small cottage in Étretat on the Normandy coast. By all accounts – Guy de Maupassant's dark, romantically embellished 'L'Anglais d'Étretat' foremost among them – the cottage lived up to what Edmund Gosse declared to be a 'preposterous' name.[14] It was a reference to *La philosophie dans le boudoir* by the Marquis de Sade, whose works Powell and Swinburne admired and quoted in their correspondence. Swinburne later denounced reports of the excesses at Étretat as 'absurdly impertinent inventions'.[15] Whatever the correspondents may have experienced in the flesh, Swinburne's letters to Powell communicate a philosophy of their own, a proto-Wildean dialogue in which their felt otherness could be articulated and exalted. As Terry L. Meyers suggests, Swinburne's exchanges 'help vivify' aspects of the poet's world that are 'at once aesthetic and, in some of their intimations, other than aesthetic'.[16]

While still at work on his novel *Lesbia Brandon*, in which flogging features prominently, Swinburne thanked Powell for a 'gift' he deemed 'trebly valuable for interest and external belongings and as the seal of friendship' – a photograph of the birch that was used for the disciplining of schoolboys. Former Etonians both, Powell and Swinburne had first-hand knowledge of corporal punishment that, in adulthood, would become the stuff of longing, of eroticism mingled with nostalgia. The birch, fresh application of which Powell and Swinburne may have experienced at Verbena Lodge, a brothel in the London suburb of St John's Wood, was an instrument of chastisement invested with liberating potential, a receptiveness to as yet indeterminate impressions and sensations.[17] 'I long to thank you in person', Swinburne wrote, 'and to enjoy the sight and touch of the birch that has been used. I don't think that I ever more dreaded the entrance of the swishing room than I now desire a sight of it. To assist unseen at the holy ceremony ... I would give *any* of my poems.'[18]

All along, the closeness of their bond was being compromised by Powell, whose yearning for intimacy was tempered by the compulsion of making a record of his associations. Writing on the subject of 'privacy' to Dante Gabriel Rossetti, Swinburne declared that 'if we are to be shackled in our inmost intercourse with our closest friends by the fear of future vermin, we may as well resign all liberty, and all thought of elbow-room for fun or confidence of any kind, at once'. And yet, he added: 'I told Powell that his fashion of binding my epistles to him in small volumes with leather covers might be compromising – and he promised to take every care to prevent their falling into Philistine hands.'[19] Consequently, Powell made his secret sharer a 'good deal more guarded and decorous than might otherwise have been the case'.[20] For biographers of Swinburne, Lang suggests, Powell is a decided liability: an obscure source that not only corrupts the subject but hinders it from speaking freely.

For anyone approaching him as a subject as well as a source, Powell poses greater challenges still. Although he corresponded widely – with Henry Wadsworth Longfellow, Simeon and Rebecca Solomon, Felix Mendelssohn and Cosima Wagner – few of Powell's own letters are known to be extant; nor did he leave behind any diaries or reminiscences through which we might gain access to his thoughts and experiences. As a frequent addressee of Swinburne and a named character in 'L'Anglais d'Étretat', Powell could not entirely escape notice. To be sure, few who heard of the mysterious, monkey flesh-eating 'M. Powel' by way of Maupassant's autobiographical sketch guessed the identity of the host; one early twentieth-century German scholar, for instance, presumed the reference to be to historian Frederick York Powell.[21] A biography of George Powell 'should certainly be written', an intrigued critic parenthetically remarked in his review of Lang's *Swinburne Letters*;[22] yet although he featured in subsequent fictionalizations of Swinburne's life, George Powell has never been the main subject of a major critical study.[23] That Powell was concerned about his legacy becomes manifest in the books and artefacts he bequeathed to Aberystwyth

University. Making our possessions public is a way of coming out, as it invites others to enquire into our past and appraise our worth. Quite literally, it means saying 'I matter'. Considering that Powell's eclectic collection seems to draw so little on identifiably Welsh culture, his bequest asserts a queer identity by declaring the man to have mattered differently.

As former Aberystwyth University librarian Richard Brinkley pointed out, Powell can be most fully considered not only by 'looking at his friends' but also by examining 'his literary works and his collections of books and works of art'.[24] Unlike his associations, Powell's 'literary works' have received little attention, least of all from cultural historians of Wales who have dismissed his writings as inferior or irrelevant. Even those who did venture a closer look felt obliged to concede that the 'young and rich dilettante ... might not seem worth such attention'.[25] As a subject, Powell has fallen short precisely because he is singular rather than exemplary; and it is for this reason that only a queer reading can make sense of and do justice to his life by arguing its worth – its significance, its merit and its allure – to lie in what strikes specialists as inartistic failure or outright lack: the distinct, binaries-resistant quality of being neither here nor there. Termed a 'misfit in the squirearchical society' of Wales, Powell is a queer subject in more than one sense.[26] He did not conform to the nineteenth-century image of a country squire; nor does he match ours. He does not rank among eminent Victorians and does not gain in our appreciation by being compared to them. As a 'man of letters', he has justly been rated 'minor'.[27] Apart from *Legends of Iceland* (1864–6), two volumes of translation on which he collaborated with Norse scholar Eiríkr Magnússon, Powell left only a small number of juvenile poems and sketches. As documents of nineteenth-century Welsh culture, Powell's writings have been deemed wanting. Indeed, the mere mention of Powell in the context of Anglo-Welsh poetry has been greeted with hostility.

One such attempt was made in 1970, when the poet and literary scholar Raymond Garlick named Powell alongside George Herbert, John Dyer and Dylan Thomas. To Garlick, 'Anglo-Welsh' was a 'convenient shorthand' for 'writing in the English language by Welshmen' and therefore implied 'no reflection upon the Welshness of the writer in question'.[28] To this, critic David Lewis Jones responded that an 'Anglo-Welsh tradition' of poetry that 'must include figures like Powell seems to be worthless'. According to Jones, it is 'impossible to detect any meaningful Anglo-Welsh traits' in Powell, 'other than that he was Welsh (albeit a member of the anglicised gentry) and wrote in English'.[29] To some chroniclers of the far from homogenous culture of Wales, this constitutes a betrayal of his heritage. He 'spent a fortune promoting the customs and heritage of Iceland', argues one social historian, 'but for the culture and history of the land that gave him his wealth, his heart was just as ice'.[30]

In fact, Powell expended considerable effort to ensure that the collection of books and artefacts he amassed during his short lifetime would come to Aberystwyth. He supported a number of local causes, served as president of the Aberystwyth Literary Institute and Working Men's Reading Room, and contributed £200 towards the rebuilding of the ancient Church of St Padarn

– where members of the Powell family are buried – thus matching the highest sum, which was donated by his father.[31] As pianist, Powell participated in several concerts at Aberystwyth's Assembly Rooms and 'kindly consented' to preside over the 'Penny Readings and Musical Entertainment' in the town's Temperance Hall.[32] Not that such occasions were celebrations of Welsh culture for Powell, who performed the works of German Romanticism like Schumann's 'Einsame Blume' or 'Liebeslied' by Adolf von Henselt. That is, whatever 'influence' Powell exerted, particularly on 'Welsh musical life', came from without rather than within Wales.[33] In later years, when he held the office of High Sheriff of Cardiganshire, Powell looked upon this representational role as if it were some kind of masquerade, a 'get-up' and 'turn-out' in 'splendid' costume, apparently of his own choosing.[34] 'A pretty High Sheriff, ma foi!',

2 *Love Dreaming by the Sea* (1871), by Simeon Solomon, watercolour, School of Art Museum and Gallery, Aberystwyth University.

Powell told Swinburne: 'Picture me to your mind's eye, next July, in the garb of a flunkey, with the addition of a cocked hat and sword, kootooing to the Judge and *sitting on the bench*! ... My undersheriff does all the *work* luckily (except this) and I *pay*.'[35]

Judged on nationalist terms, Powell, as poet, may have fared better if he had, as 'originally intended', concluded work on 'Eleonora', a 'romance of Aberystwith Castle'. He had 'carried it to some length' but became so 'disgusted with' it that he 'abandoned it' as 'miserably weak and far too melo-dramatic'.[36] This statement, made on the pages of a second volume of poetry that Powell, still in his late teens, published privately in 1861, may have been meant as an apology for – or at least an explanation of – the derivative and apparently generic quality of his writing. Powell himself acknowledged a debt to Longfellow, to whom some of his poems were dedicated. Shared exclusively with acquaintances, friends and relations, Powell's verse is nonetheless personal, directed towards those who might be able to glean the tenor of his coded language. For instance, in a poem dedicated to his close friend, the future Reverend Claude Fox Chawner, Powell creates the conceit of an idealized friendship in a series of similes in which boon companions are likened to sources of light and life, to 'steadfast' beacons, 'mirrors clear' and 'showers of rain' that draw out 'harvests / From the once so sterile dearth'.[37] According to Berridge, Chawner had become the 'object of George's passionate attention'.[38] His name appears in a number of letters addressed to Powell, including Swinburne's, mostly with reference to his poor health. Chawner, who died of consumption when he and Powell were in their mid-twenties, may well be the 'very dearest and best one' whose recovery Powell memorializes in 'The Wreaths':

> You are wasted and very white, dear;
> But you are once more ours again;
> You drooped, as the blushed anemone
> For cool, west rain.[39]

Whether or not it would be 'generous to describe Powell even as a poetaster', as one commentator has it, his poetry should not be discounted on the basis of lacking in identifiably Welsh themes, cultural references and regional inflections.[40] Choosing for himself the un-Christian pseudonym Miölnir, the hammer of Thor, Powell was ready to weaponize his Oxonian education and smash what he perceived to be the stultifying conditions of his home, which he – whether anxious not to go unrecognized or eager to name what he was up against – identified as 'Nant-Eos'. Ultimately, what 'Miölnir' hammered out for Powell was an alternative, queer existence that was not quite a breaking away from the past.

Powell's desire to be other was rooted in his family history, particularly in his relationship with his father. After all, Powell's absence from Nant-Eos in adulthood was not entirely by choice. By his own accounts, he was at one point 'formally forbidden the place' and had 'not the faintest inclination to set foot in it henceforth and for ever'. In a letter to Magnússon, Powell refers to his father as a 'stuffed dummy', who, standing for the county, was 'about as useful in the House of Commons as a straw effigy of Guy Fawkes would be in the same place'.[41] Writing from his cottage at Étretat, Powell told Swinburne of news that 'a certain Col. P.' was 'twice as fat as before, heavy even to stupidity, always absent in mind, and just gone to Nice. Whether the fact of his shadow growing in breadth is any proof that it is diminishing in length, I cannot say, but there is perchance room for hope.'[42]

An Eton-schooled Oxford dropout, George Powell appears to have found it impossible, and indeed insufferable, to live up to expectations, especially by assuming the part of a country squire, a life to which he as heir to Nant-Eos seemed destined. It was less a rejection of his forefathers than it was a direct response to his father, whose bloated shape was an embodiment of self-indulgent entitlement. According to one apocryphal account of the father-son relationship, Powell made a mockery of conformity by obeying to the letter his pater's command that he go hunting, only to return home having shot one of the colonel's own bullocks.[43] What was more objectionable to Powell than cruelty was hypocrisy, and his father was the proud bearer of double standards. In 1853, when George was eleven years old, the colonel had accused his wife Rosa of an undue attachment for a family friend in whose company Rosa may have found some comfort while the squire went hunting or was 'engaged in other pursuits'.[44] In a letter to his father-in-law, Colonel Powell vowed 'as a father, a man of honour and a gentleman', never to see his wife again, nor let his wife raise their two children, George and his younger sister Harriet.[45] Meanwhile, it was the colonel who had an affair, with the children's governess, Sarah Lord, together with whom he plotted to discredit his wife by accusing her of infidelity.[46] Rosa Powell suspected that her husband was abusing the influence he enjoyed as a squire in order to 'try and collect evidence' against her alleged lover. This 'mission must have utterly failed', she declared, 'unless *bribes* for falsehood have been offered and accepted. The *Welsh* are I know somewhat notorious for accepting *bribes*.'[47]

The legal documents and letters exchanged between 1853 and 1856 during the negotiations leading up to a Deed of Separation provide a glimpse at Powell's troubled childhood and youth. They help to explain not only his affection for his mother and his animosity towards his father, whom he nevertheless in some ways resembled, but also his attitude towards what he assumed to be Welsh traits. His response, in turn, sheds light on his sense of otherness, his need to escape the conditions he experienced as stifling and the conventions he came to distrust. The colonel had long neglected his wife and children, leaving them 'alone and unsupported for periods of six to eleven months together' while 'amusing himself in Ireland' and allegedly indulging in 'promiscuous amours' as a result of which he was said to have 'contracted the most foul and disgraceful of diseases'.[48] Whatever the foundation of these claims, Powell and his sister were exposed to such accounts, as the tales their governess told them were not all of the nursery rhyme variety. She 'talked the whole matter over *before my children*', Powell's mother complained, adding how 'needless, how cruel' it was to 'speak to the children *at all* on the subject. How easy to their young minds to form some excuse for [their mother's] absence from them, and how inconsistent must their father's conduct appear.' Her son, she assumed, was at least 'old enough and clever enough to fully comprehend this'.[49]

Eventually, Colonel Powell withdrew his accusations even as he continued to pursue the separation. He called it 'very wrong and foolish of Rosa to allow the people in this county to talk at all' about the matter. No doubt he was concerned about gossip amongst the county set, especially at a time when he was expected by 'some of the gentry' to stand for Parliament. 'You know what they are here', the colonel complained to his father-in-law, 'and the only people against me *are my relations* down here'.[50] After the separation, Powell's father granted his wife just £300 a year, and that only on condition that she admit her guilt. He reasoned that she had, 'through her conduct, forfeited the ability to indulge in all the gaiety and luxury which she might have expected had she lived to become the wife of a gentleman of £8,000 a year'.[51] Nor would he permit his children to stay with their mother, who declared, 'I must abide as best I may to the unjust law which gives a father such tyrannical power over them.'[52] By May 1856, the colonel had forbidden his wife to visit either of her children at their schools and, a few weeks later, demanded that she stop corresponding directly with them.[53] George had by then left Blackheath Proprietary School and was enrolled at Eton, where letters from his mother were intercepted at the colonel's request.[54]

For all his scheming, Colonel Powell was without guile when it came to indulging his pleasures. According to his outraged father-in-law, Powell's father 'often brought his wife' books of the 'most vile, gross, low and disgusting obscenity', among them 'one of the most immoral ever printed' – the, to him, unmentionable *Memoirs of a Woman of Pleasure*, commonly known as *Fanny Hill*.[55] After his wife refused to read it, the colonel told her that he would offer it to the man he alleged to be her lover.[56] Another claim made by Rosa Powell's father was that, in the smoking room at their house on the seafront at Aberystwyth, there hung the 'most indecent pictures' and that the colonel had a 'collection of prints of the most obscene and coarse description'; 'open to the whole house', the prints were 'remarked upon' by the couple's young daughter.[57] Master Powell, too, took note; but such was the '*evil* influence' these prints had 'over the mind of the child' that he reportedly 'pointed them out as *very* pretty'.[58] As an adult, the colonel's impressionable offspring would himself become a collector of art and artefacts expressive of his own passions and desires. As an adolescent, though, Powell had no such outlet. He turned to writing instead. And what he explored in some of his verse was not only the corruption of mind and body but also the fascination this presumably '*evil* influence' held for him.

Morbid and brooding, Powell's juvenile poetry is to some extent a response to the decline of Nant-Eos and the deterioration of family relations. What is more, during the late 1850s and early 1860s, the Powell family was fast losing its branches. George's sister Harriet died from tuberculosis in 1857. By 1858, his father was partially paralysed and remained confined to a wheelchair following an unspecified illness. In May 1860, his mother, Rosa Powell, who declared that her children had 'for years been all that bound [her] to life in [her] most miserable marriage', died 'from the breaking of a blood vessel'.[59] Later that year, her adolescent son issued his first, self-published volume of poetry:

> That sad odour of the dead leaves;
> Always bringing back before me
> Memories of pain and sorrow,
> Memories I love avoiding.
> Always that sad odour gives me
> Deep, vague fearings of the future.[60]

The 'fearings' alluded to in 'Autumn Wind' continued to haunt Powell, and any sense of personal triumph was blighted by anxieties about his heredity and a legacy of his own. As Herbert M. Vaughan comments, there is an 'element of mystery and sadness' that 'suffuses nearly all his verse'.[61] Meanwhile, the same poem that claims the past to be inescapable also speaks of the love of eluding it, of being 'Half entranced by melancholy, / Half again entranced by pleasure' – the perverse pleasure of the guilt arising from a desire to forget in the very act of remembrance.

Born half a century before gothic literature 'reached its apex', as George E. Haggerty puts it, at a time 'when gender and sexuality were beginning to be codified for modern culture', Powell, whose adult library contained works by Poe and Baudelaire, felt compelled to couch his experience of queerness in terms that now strike us as decadent and dark romantic.[62] According to Ellis Hanson, the 'Gothic often reproduces the conventional paranoid structure of homophobia and other moral panics over sex, and yet it can also be a raucous site of sexual transgression and excess that undermines its own narrative efforts at erotic containment.'[63] In Powell's 'Vale', for instance, the poet's 'mystic' lyre is rendered mute by the creeping, 'parasitic leaves' of 'carnal love', his 'robe of stainless poesy' lost among the 'flame-leafed flowers of man's desire'.[64] In 'What Spirit?', likewise, Powell writes of the 'faint dungeon of Despair', a 'heart forsaken' in a 'tower of Hopeless Love', while a pulsating energy makes itself felt below: the 'ocean's hidden thunders' that '[e]bb and flow' in the 'creaming bosom of the deep, / With murmur and with moan.'[65]

'A Fever Vision' comes closest to the formulation of a queer identity: 'A double spirit seem'd to be / Given to me within myself.' Lying, limbs 'aching', in a 'wakeful dreamy state' '[b]eyond the very thoughts of men', the speaker undergoes, witnesses and rehearses a violent, transformative experience – a *petite mort* of epic proportions:

> Though death was pass'd, and dead I lay,
> Yet lived in very death; my soul
> Free, yet restrain'd in liberty,
> A forced partner was compell'd
> To watch my mortal change, and see
> Corruption at its horrid work.
> So, mentally I saw it steal,
> E'en saw it in its sable pall,

> Creeping upon my ashy corpse,
> Change with its awful tints my skin,
> And waste by slow degrees my flesh ...
> Through all this time my spirit pray'd,
> Humble, before th' Omnipotent,
> For access to the great White Throne.
> But no! that vast opposing mass
> Kept back my prayers and yearning soul,
> Inexorable in its strength.
> At last, a bleachèd skeleton,
> Clothed in a robe of scarlet weeds,
> Flaunting as if in mockery
> Of death, for ages I remain'd
> Alone in ghastly solitude;
> A soul and body separate
> Yet one. A life in graveless death;
> Corruption, Incorruption, both
> So opposite, together bound.[66]

The anxieties of influence,of heredity and hybridity, expressed in such images would gradually, though never quite entirely, make way for an embrace of multiplicity, as Powell shifted his attention from creating a poet-persona to the fashioning of a dilettante self.

'onions, a lemon, and a young lady': towards a queer legacy

Years before he set out building his collection and entered into a drawn-out process of gifting it to Aberystwyth, Powell slyly commented on the state of culture in the Welsh town. In 'An Eye-witness at a Bazaar', one of the sketches in his privately printed volume *'Quod-Libet'* (1860) – for the publication of which he identified himself as G. E. J. P, Nant-Eos – Powell offers an imaginary impression of life in the 'interesting old town of Abersnitchwitch'. Looking at a stall ostensibly 'devoted to the fine arts', his narrator marvels:

> Here were suspended specimens of all styles, secular and sacred, grave and funny ... [The owner] seized upon me, and offered me, in succession, drawings of a red cow, a landscape, fruit, another cow, a boat, a bull, a bundle of fishing baskets, a rope of onions, a lemon, and a young lady. At last, she contrived to force three drawings upon me, for which she benevolently charged two pounds.[67]

Setting himself apart from the indiscriminate collector, Powell presents his first-person narrator as a connoisseur who, though unable to withstand the onslaught of fabled greatness thrust upon him, can nonetheless tell tat from the real thing:

> The next drawing represented 'The Cavalier'. This person stood in a melo-dramatic attitude, and was attired in a slightly anachronistic costume, having the upper portions of his frame clothed in that of a member of the court of Charles, while his lower extremities presented a combination of the modern gamekeeper, and the ancient Greek warrior: at any rate he looked horribly fierce, which was all that was required.

The remaining drawing was called 'A Study', which it certainly was, being an elaborate, but rather confused arrangement of articles of every kind and description. In one corner of this work, a statue of Phoebus could be seen, backed up by a willow pattern plate, full of stewed pears; while, a little further on, was a most interesting group consisting of a hair brush, a blacking bottle, a jerkin and a bust of Milton ... What a gigantic mind must *that* have been, that conceived the artistic arrangement of dolls and sachets, scent bottles and embroidered braces, juvenile pistols, and adult nail scissors. Oh, how grand it was!

It is art historical and literary discernment that makes it possible to appreciate – recognize and relish – this genre, period and class-defying jumble sale of Western culture, high and low. At last, the narrator tears himself away, only to be 'loaded with articles of every description, all more or less useless'.[68] The 'Eye-witness' has become party to and perpetuator of a cultural mash-up in an experience of delight in disorder rather than its dismissal, a perversion of high culture made possible by higher education.

The collection that Powell subsequently amassed was similarly undisciplined: representative of his passion, it was otherwise all over the place. In his own estimation, it was all he possessed of 'bigotry and virtue', whichever the judgement of those living in his 'dear but benighted town'[69] for whose enlightenment or mystification he determined to bequeath what was estimated to be 150 oil paintings, prints and drawings, over 2,500 books and manuscripts, as well as curiosities ranging from a pair of Canadian snowshoes to a fragment of Robert Schumann's coffin in a silver enamelled rock crystal casket. In the 1883 edition of the *University College of Wales Calendar Advertiser*, the university declared itself 'deeply indebted for so many valuable donations', listed among which were 'nineteen very curious and rare Japanese nitskeys [netsuke] or waistband fasteners', 'seven small bronzes from the temple of Juno at Argos', as well as autographed letters by Schumann, Weber, Cherubini, Hummel and 'other celebrities'.[70] His inclusive, culturally diverse collection provides us with telling insights into Powell's queer worldview.[71] It is through his idiosyncratic hoarding and wholesale giving away of disparate objects that Powell sought to construct his image and communicate his desires. A lock of Swinburne's hair and a cast of Mendelssohn's hand had, as curator Neil Holland points out, 'strong significance' as 'souvenirs of friends' and 'relics of heroes'.[72] Among the portraits in chalk that he commissioned from his friend Wilhelm Kümpel were likenesses of men Powell knew personally or admired from afar. They range from his manservant Edwin Callaway to *Märchenkönig* Ludwig II of Bavaria; they include his beloved Chawner but also Schumann, Longfellow and Wagner, with whom Powell claimed to have dined at Bayreuth in 1876.[73]

According to Holland, 'homoeroticism' was 'one of the prime organising principles' of Powell's art collection.[74] His bequest included a study in red chalk of a pipe organ pumper for *The Love Song* by Burne-Jones, a painting now in the Metropolitan Museum of Art in New York; Solomon's androgynous *Roman Youth* and *Love Dreaming by the Sea* (see illustration 2), the latter executed expressly for Powell; *Young Bacchus* teasing a leopard by Kümpel; and a naked boy astride a phallic dragonfly by German-born illustrator Johann Baptist Zwecker, who also illustrated Powell and Magnússon's *Legends of Iceland* (see illustration 3). Rather than any particular physique, what appears to have attracted Powell as a collector were narratives of corruption or transgression, as exemplified by Richard Westall's dramatic watercolour paintings *The Birth of Sin* and *Satan Summoning His Legions* (see illustration 4) or by Étienne-Barthélémy Garnier's pencil drawing *Ajax the Great*, which shows the gods-defying warrior wearing only a helmet, a scabbard dangling between his legs. Meanwhile, a fascination with bodily decay is apparent in Powell's collection of forensic studies by Jacques-Hippolyte van der Burch, watercolour paintings designed to document the transformation of human cadavers under various conditions. A selection of his pictures would have been displayed alongside European bronzes of male nudes, some thirty of which Powell purchased on his travels on the continent. Powell generally acquired objects that were small enough for display in his rooms in Mornington Crescent; among them reduced copies of Giambologna's bronze *Mercury*, Michelangelo's *Dying Slave*, the Pompeian *Dancing Faun* in Carrara marble and a porcelain figure group of *Castor and Pollux*.

3 *Boy on a Dragonfly* [detail] (1866), by Johann Baptist Zwecker, watercolour with body colour, School of Art Museum and Gallery, Aberystwyth University.

In addition to shedding light on a not quite eminent but eminently queer Welsh Victorian, Powell's eclectic bequest to his countrymen and women also encourages us to ponder the politics behind the construction of national character and the marginalization of those presumably not fit for that purpose. As a teenager, Powell vowed that being one of a kind was less desirable than reaching out for kindred spirits and exploring elective affinities. 'I have decidedly come to the conclusion, not without much thought, that any hopes I may have entertained of being original in the slightest degree, are without foundation, and perfectly groundless', he declared in his preface to *'Quod-Libet'*. Adding, as in all of his published writings, the name of his father's estate to the moniker he chose for himself, the individual talent owns to a sense of tradition. The numerous dedications to friends and relatives and the acknowledged debt to fellow writers suggest that it was not originality to which Powell aspired but communion.

Anticipating his readers' judgement, he added the sly and disarming plea: 'Oh, spare me the scorpion-lashes of your elevated wit. I plead guilty, and commending

4 *Satan Summoning His Legions* (1792), by Richard Westall, watercolour with washes and body colour, School of Art Museum and Gallery, Aberystwyth University.

myself to your mercy, I say, like a whimpering school-boy, "Please don't whip me *this* time, I did my best."'[75] Like his volumes of poetry, *'Quod-Libet'* ends self-consciously: 'Reader, – You have, probably, remarked the diversity of styles, both of narrative and of writing: it is intentional, and the reason is, of course, obvious.'[76] What becomes 'obvious' is that Powell adopted a series of guises in order to arrive at a persona that was not quite masking the learned, yearning young man who, striving to distance himself from his father, reimagined himself as aesthete, antiquarian, collector and benefactor.

Anxious to present himself as informed, inclusive and broadminded, Powell made a meticulous record of the widening knowledge and diversification of culture in contemporary journalism. From 1875 onwards, he compiled his own miscellanies of writings he came across in periodicals such as the *Fortnightly*, the *Contemporary Review* and *Gentleman's Magazine*, articles from which he extracted liberally and bound in nearly one hundred volumes bearing the embossed title *Essays, Poems and Reviews*. Many of these writings reflect the debates of the day, be it on evolution or socialism, atheism or vivisection. There are tantalizing traces of Powell's predilections in articles like 'Flogging in the Army' or fictions such as Sacher Masoch's erotic story 'Mondnacht' (in a French translation). In the handwritten tables of content, each of which bears his signature, Powell cross-referenced the articles, pointing out a continued discussion or articles on related topics. Cataloguing his readings, he was both librarian and autobiographer. Even in 'Gleanings', his scrapbook of newspaper clippings and mementoes, Powell took pains to point out to us what to him required no explanation. Marking with an 'x' some lines from Swinburne's poem 'Ex Voto', which draws upon the poet's near drowning in Normandy without stating the location, Powell added 'Étretat' in the margins and, in a handwritten note, offered his account of the event.[77]

Though it was obviously made for posterity, Powell's leather-bound collections of journal articles is highly individualistic: an article on 'Fermentation, and Its Bearings on the Phenomena of Disease' appears alongside Pater's 'Study of Dionysus' and John Addington Symonds's 'Sophocles', all of which were published in the *Fortnightly*; so do a number of articles by St John Tyrwhitt, who had attacked Pater and Symonds on the issue of 'Greek Love'. Meanwhile, the article at the centre of the controversy, Tyrwhitt's 'Greek Spirit in Modern Literature', published in the *Contemporary Review*, is not included and was perhaps deliberately omitted for being beneath contempt. Since Powell left no commentaries, we can only guess at his attitude towards the thoughts expressed or the writers who expressed them. What did Powell make of the texts whose authors we now read as being part of an emerging queer canon: Vernon Lee, Roden Noel, Whitman, Pater, Symonds and his lover Frederic William Henry Myers? Did Powell see himself in Tennyson's lifelong friend James Spedding, who, as Richard Dellamora suggests, 'may deliberately have translated into scholarship the affective and sexual preferences that his society otherwise denied licit expression'?[78] As Dellamora argues in the case of Powell's male contemporaries, Swinburne among them, their writings indicate 'ways in which men seek to express desire for other men, even when such desires are rarely or never consummated in the flesh'.[79] Such yearnings and leanings may be readable as well in the published writings these men collected and shared. Clearly, Powell sought to keep up in print with writers he knew personally: old friends, acquaintances and fellow Oxonians; but he also appears to reach out to us. What, we can only wonder, were his feelings upon reading Swinburne's article 'Simeon Solomon', published in the July 1871 issue of the Oxonian journal *Dark Blue*, which, by referring to Solomon as 'perverse', contributed to the unmaking of the painter as a *persona non grata*?[80]

Powell rarely made notes in the margins or underlined passages to indicate his responses to the books in his library. There is no proof that he read the books he owned. The collection nonetheless calls for conjecture as to his reasons for choosing specific volumes and for making them part of his bequest. Some of these volumes seem to speak to us not simply of the period in which they were written and received but of their owner's desires and anxieties, and it is tempting to read them as expressions or extensions of his queer identity. Next to the many titles that would have been found in the library of any Victorian gentleman – the writings of Thomas Carlyle, for instance – there are others, including the works of George Sand, as well as lesser or at any rate lesser-known works that bespeak Powell's sense of marginalization and his attempt to communicate, through his bequest, the truths he may not have been able to articulate otherwise.

The collection of articles and books now at Aberystwyth University, exclusive of those volumes he gifted to the town library, suggests that Powell had an interest in demonology and witchcraft, in diseases, suicide, as well as in alternative definitions of matrimony (*Marriage of Near Kin*, 'Consanguinity in Marriage' and 'Marriages between First Cousins in England and their Effects'), which were of particular interest to him, no doubt, because his grandmothers were sisters and his parents first cousins. Powell also collected books on mental illness, among them *On the Writing of the Insane* (1870) and *My Experiences in a Lunatic Asylum* (1879). The former proposed a 'series of pictures of insane minds, painted by themselves', albeit without providing any definition of the term: 'The line must be drawn somewhere between the sane and the insane for purposes of public convenience.' Powell may have identified with the portrait of a 'young man who had been respectably brought up, and had some little property' but who was, in 'consequence of some extravagancies of conduct', placed in an asylum.[81]

My Experiences in a Lunatic Asylum, ostensibly penned 'by a Sane Patient', opens with remarks that Powell may well have read in light of the developing pathologizing and criminalization of desire and of the threat posed by authorities in the fields of science and law who endeavoured to classify and contain the unspoken:

> There are odd corners in the brains of most of us, filled with queer fancies which are as well kept out of sight; eccentricities, I suppose they may be called. The man who is so 'concentric' as to be innocent of peculiarities is a companion of a dull sort. But Heaven help us all when such things may be called, and treated as, madness. For, if all of us were used according to our deserts in that way, who should escape the modern substitutes for whipping?[82]

Owing to his expression of such 'queer fancies', Powell's far from 'concentric' friend Simeon Solomon faced social and financial ruin. Swinburne's response to Solomon's apparent need for openness echoed the flippant statement – presumably quoted from George Sala's 'columns of gossip' – that precedes the above passage: 'What a fool he must be! For years I have been as mad as he, only I took care never to say so.'[83] This is just how Swinburne reacted to Solomon's refusal to make a secret of his desire, a wilful act of exposure by someone who, in Swinburne's estimation, had 'deliberately chosen to do what makes a man and all who associate with him infamous in the eyes of the world'.[84]

Writing to his watchful friend, the poet-critic Theodore Watts (later Watts-Dunton), Swinburne made it known that he had advised Powell to distance himself from one so out to disgrace himself and make ignominious the desire that as yet had no single, universally understood label attached to it:

> I do think a man is bound to consider the consequence to all his friends and to every one who cares for him in the world of allowing his name to be mixed up with that of a – let us say, a Platonist; the term is at once accurate as a definition and unobjectionable as an euphemism.[85]

In an anonymous 1874 article on Ralph Waldo Emerson, purportedly an interview with the American poet, Swinburne himself was referred to as 'a perfect leper and a mere sodomite'; wary of such branding, Swinburne wrote a notoriously foul-mouthed reply to Emerson, a copy of which Powell 'indiscreetly' forwarded to the *New York Daily Tribune*.[86]

Another volume in Powell's library was an 1869 edition of Wilson and Caulfield's *Book of Wonderful Characters*, which promised readers the biographies of 'men who have essentially differed from the rest of the human race', whether by having 'some peculiar congenital defect' or an 'eccentricity of character' that 'inevitably impels them to overleap and trespass from the boundaries of the beaten highway of conventional life'. In it, Powell would have encountered the transvestite Chevalier D'Eon, based on whose famous case Havelock Ellis later coined the term 'eonism'. Though 'far from being prudish', as Wilson and Caulfield put it, D'Eon maintained the 'most inviolable secrecy on the subject of his sex, to the day of his death'.[87] As a teenager, Powell had created a cross-dressing character in 'The Femme de Chambre', one of the stories collected in *'Quod-Libet'*. It is a mystery involving a thieving lady's maid with 'curious blue marks' around her upper lip and chin – signs that, 'to one more attentive' than her ladyship, suggested that the maid's 'face had felt the razor'. There are shades of Powell in the figure of the equally unsuspecting Lord Roseley, who, like Powell, 'had been educated first at Eton, and then at Oxford', instruction apparently insufficient for the identification of a cross-dressing convict escaped from Botany Bay.[88]

That Powell related cross-dressing to crime, treachery and its detection invites speculation both as to his attitude towards gender ambiguity and his experience of sexual pleasure. However, historian H. G. Cocks cautions not to approach Victorian cross-dressing – specifically celebrated cases such as Boulton and Park

– with a twentieth-century understanding of transvestitism or drag.⁸⁹ As recorded in his scrapbook, Powell himself found occasion to cross-dress publicly when, in January 1866, he appeared in amateur dramatic performances of two one-act comedies: *A Terrible Secret* (1861) by Joseph Stirling Coyne, in which he played Mrs Henpecker, a woman suspicious of her husband's dealings with another man, and *Delicate Ground* (1800) by Charles Dance, in which Powell was seen as Pauline, a woman who has to choose between two men: her husband and her lover. Significantly, the plays were performed at the Corn Exchange in Tenbury, England, the hometown of one of Powell's 'True Friends', the aforementioned Claude Fox Chawner.⁹⁰ Whatever the pleasures he may have derived from it,

5 *George Powell* (1860s), by unknown, photograph, School of Art Museum and Gallery, Aberystwyth University.

Powell clearly enjoyed dressing up and down, an appropriation of styles and traditions to which his albums of personal photographs attest (see illustration 5). As his experience as High Sheriff drives home, Powell was a cross-cultural dresser-upper at heart.

The 'true' nature of Powell's relationships with men and his understanding of gender may ultimately be nothing more – nor anything less – than the truth of our own desires. Yet whatever our construct of Powell, his experience calls to mind the lives that were lived beyond conventions, lives that defied fixed categories of gender and sexuality. In May 1881, 'unattended by any approach to display', George Powell was legally married. His bride, Dinah Harries, was a housekeeper from Goodwick, a small fishing village near Fishguard in Pembrokeshire. Though the ceremony was performed at St Matthews' Church, Camden, 'all persons formally associated' with it were 'natives of Wales', suggesting that Powell did not feel a need to keep secret what, in the eyes of the public, was certainly no match befitting a High Sheriff.[91] According to one account, Powell had met Harries while '[s]eeking a bed one boisterous winter's night in Goodwick'; he had been 'turned away from many a doorstep until he was admitted into the cottage of a seaman'. Powell 'woo'd and won' his daughter, who was apparently 'quite ignorant of her husband's social position'. Just how long had Powell known his future bride, considering that he, years prior to their first meeting, had owned a cottage in Goodwick, from which several of his letters to Swinburne were sent? Had Powell, approaching middle age, intended to secure his legacy by producing an heir? Some seventeen months later, Powell died 'without issue'; his widow emigrated to America, where she remarried.[92]

Having distanced himself somewhat from the companion of his youth, a 'startled' Swinburne expressed himself 'much grieved' by the 'news of poor George Powell's death'. In a letter to Watts, dated 8 November 1882, Swinburne wrote:

> I can hardly realise the idea that I shall never see him again with whom I have spent so many days and weeks together and exchanged so many signs of friendship in past years ... The poor fellow was one of the most obliging and kind-hearted of men, and wonderfully bright-spirited under severe trial and trouble. I shall always have a very tender and regretful remembrance of him.[93]

Publicly, Swinburne bade farewell to his 'Dead Friend' in a performance that honoured the lost bond and kept secret the identity of a 'Friend of hopes foregone' whose name would have signified little to most:

> Known and loved of few,
> But of these, though small their fold,
> Loved how well were you![94]

Loved, perhaps passionately, but also imposed upon and exploited for his compassion. 'Powell has been at great pains to do your behests', Solomon once reminded Swinburne; 'he is very unselfish and only happy when he is doing some service for others'.[95] There is evidence, too, that this yearning for companionship made Powell vulnerable to abuse and betrayal. In 1871, Powell, who was described in the press as 'a gentleman not in business', appeared in court following the arrest of his 17-year-old former houseboy.[96] Having forged Powell's signature on several cheques, the youth had spent the money at his tailor's and, together with a male companion, lived it up in Gay Paree.[97]

'A nobler or more generous heart than his seldom beats in the bosom of man', Eiríkr Magnússon declared some two decades after Powell's death. Responding to the historian George Eyre Evans, Magnússon explained what he saw as the duality of Powell's life – the potential for 'good' and the otherness that, in post-Wildean reflection, had come to be outlawed and pathologized:

> His gifts of mind were great and beautiful. His musical talent was extraordinary. His poetical talent if it only had been assiduously cultivated would certainly have ranked high among his contemporaries. His love of art was wonderfully intense and his taste very sound at least in his earlier years. Like other mortals he had his weaknesses, but he had really an immense store of good in him for a counterbalance.[98]

A dabbler who strove to matter, a misfit who dwelled on his legacy, Powell struggled to strike such a balance. Articulating what Judith Halberstam in *The Queer Art of Failure* posits as 'an alternative vision of life, love, and labor', Powell nonetheless aimed for validation and inclusion.[99] 'Let us not live in sloth, nor walk in the deceitful ways of pleasure; neither let us remain idle, and put off salvation till the morrow', a teenaged Powell sermonized in 'A Psalm of the New Year', a poem dedicated to his 'Dear Father'.[100] On the face of it a remorseful son's promise to mend his ways, the 'Psalm' is a vow to reject the squire's life of entitlement. It may also have served as a warning to himself not to squander the means for cultural enrichment that his station could provide for himself and, through his efforts, for others. Unlike the proud but ruinous colonel, George Powell sought 'salvation' – rebirth and afterlife – in art, literature and music, and in the bonds that dilettante pursuit of culture, history and the sciences can promote. It was the pursuit of a little learning and a quest for some other truth and beauty that was not meant to perish with its heirless possessor but that, through Powell's idiosyncratic collection of books and artefacts, was intended to take its place in the repositories of Welsh culture and assert, obliquely, a queer influence on the academia of Wales.

4
From Huw Arwystli to Siôn Eirian: Representative Examples of Cadi/Queer *Life from Medieval to Twentieth-century Welsh Literature*

MIHANGEL MORGAN

Introduction

In a recent edition of the Welsh literary magazine *Taliesin* which was devoted to the subject of gender, Angharad Elen writes in her editorial about the fifty-eight different terms for defining gender available to users of Facebook, and then she goes on to lament:

> *58, meddyliwch! A'r rhan fwyaf ohonyn nhw yn anghyfieithiadwy i'r Gymraeg – ar hyn o bryd beth bynnag. Fel y sonia Dafydd James yn ei erthygl, does gennym ni ddim gair Cymraeg boddhaol am 'gay' hyd yn oed, heb sôn am eiriau am bron i drigain o ddiffiniadau gwahanol. Beth mae'r diffyg yn yr eirfa yn ei ddweud amdanom ni fel Cymry, tybed?*[1]

> 58, think of it! And most of them untranslateable into Welsh – for the moment at least. As Dafydd James mentions in his article, we don't even have a satisfactory word for 'gay' in Welsh, not to mention the words for almost sixty different definitions. What does this deficiency in the vocabulary say about us as Welsh people, I wonder?[2]

Well, it says a lot about the lack of status of our language and our culture, but it also does an injustice to the complexity of Welsh literature and of the Welsh language. Dafydd James makes a similar point in his article – referred to by Angharad Elen – 'Y Queer yn Erbyn y Byd' ('The Queer Against the World'),[3] citing his own play *Llwyth* (Tribe):

> GAVIN: *Ond beth am y gair 'gay' yn Cymraeg [sic] ... gwrw-thingy?*

> DADA: *... gydiwr. Gwrywgydiwr.*

> GAVIN: *Ie, that's it. Gwrywgydiwr! Man-gripper. What's that about? Makes me sound like a JCB.*

> DADA: *Beth am hoyw?*

> GAVIN: *That's equally shit.*

DADA: *Pam?*

GAVIN: *Mae'n soundo'n gay.*[4]

I hardly need to translate, but:

GAVIN: But what about the word for 'gay' in Welsh ... *gwrw*-thingy?

DADA: ... *gydiwr. Gwrywgydiwr.*

GAVIN: Yes, that's it. *Gwrywgydiwr*! Man-gripper. What's that about? Makes me sound like a JCB.

DADA: What about '*hoyw*'?

GAVIN: That's equally shit.

DADA: Why?

GAVIN: It sounds gay.

Of course there is a comic vein to this scene, and Gavin is clearly struggling with his Welsh; however, the misunderstanding of the Welsh word *gwrywgydiwr* is a sad reflection of how out of touch many Welsh speakers are with their own language. Gavin is not alone in misinterpreting the elements of the word as 'man-gripper' or 'man-grabber'. It's as if someone were to look in *Y Geiriadur Mawr* (The Big Dictionary, 1958) and translate *prifysgol* as 'main ladder', by going through the secondary meanings, rather than finding the correct meaning and understanding of *prifysgol*, which is 'university'. Even if one were to do so, it would be wrong to translate *gwrywgydiwr* as 'man-gripper'. *Gwryw* means 'male'; the second part comes from *cydio* and means 'to copulate', and this is a very old word and very old meaning. *Cydiwr* in the sexual sense of 'copulator' goes back to 1450. *Gwrywgydiwr*, or at least its plural, goes back to 1547, when William Salesbury used it in his translation of the Bible into Welsh, albeit in a somewhat negative context. Among those who are unrighteous and cannot therefore inherit the kingdom of God are listed:

Na godinebwyr, nac eilun-addolwyr, na thorwyr priodas, na masweddwyr na gwryw-gydwyr.

I Corinthiaid vi.9

Now if we look in the corresponding verse in the English King James version, we find no single word in the place of '*gwryw-gydwyr*' but the much more cumbersome 'men that abuse themselves with mankind'. Welsh, it would seem, has a long and useful vocabulary, one that is and should be more adaptable than English.

There were in fact many other words in Welsh, although usually with negative associatons, that refered to same-sex acts and to those that practised them. While *bwgerydd* ('bugger') dates back to 1567 in Welsh, there is also the verb *tinhwygo*, which refers to anal sex recorded in 1400 and which would give the noun *tinhwygwr*. And what about the word *hoyw*? In rejecting this word because it 'sounds gay', the character Gavin signals the difficulties of finding an accomodating queer place in any language and inadvertently makes *hoyw* an even more attractive option. Just as the English word 'gay' was often used in bawdy contexts and held sexual connotations long before it was appropriated in its modern sense in the late 1960s and early 1970s, so was the word *hoyw* often used along with sexual meanings. A very apposite example can be found in Huw Arwystli's poem about the boy in girl's clothes discussed below. There we have '*gwidw hoyw*', which Dafydd Johnston translates as 'lusty widow'.[5] This is not a rare instance of the use of the word in a sexually suggestive context. Of course, I am not saying that the word/s meant then what they do now, but perhaps we need to remind ourselves that when the word 'gay' was first taken up it was not instantly embraced; many people within the movement for homosexual equality disapproved of it. Both 'gay' and *hoyw* have a long history of sexual innuendo, and the Welsh language should not always be thought of as having to catch up with English. And what about those fifty-eight 'untranslatable' definitions? How old are they, I wonder? And how untranslatable? We find that *gwryw-fenywaidd* ('bisexual', 'hermaphrodite') dates back to 1866, *deuryw* ('bisexual') to 1604, *cyfunrhywiol* (which has become a synonym for *gwrywgydiol*, 'homosexual') was first used in 1785. I could go on. The language has the resources. The users of the language need to avail themselves of them and stop seeing English as a sort of default language of the world.[6]

Further, when it comes to the word 'queer', Dafydd James feels confounded by the Welsh language. He cannot find a suitable word in the language to convey 'queer', specifically in the sense in which it is used in the term 'queer theory':

> *Fe fuaswn i wrth fy modd yn cael dweud wrth bobol [sic] fy mod i wedi fy ngwneud yn ddoctor trwy sgwennu [sic] traethawd am 'Berfformio a Damcaniaethau Cadiffanllyd', ond rywsut, dwi'n teimlo nad yw hynny yn gweddu.*[7]
>
> I would be happy if I could say to people that I was made a doctor through writing a thesis on 'Performing and *Cadi-ffan* Theory', but somehow, I don't think that's appropriate.

Actually *cadi* has a very interesting history and should not be dismissed so readily. It comes from the personal name Catrin, so it's a bit like the words Molly or Nancy in English and the *Geiriadur Prifysgol Cymru* (The University of Wales Dictionary) definition says: 'Hen ferch o ddyn neu fachgen, busnesgi, ymyrrwr; un o'r dawnswyr haf gynt wedi gwisgo fel merch: effeminate man or boy, sissy, busybody, meddler: May dancer dressed as a girl.' This usage dates back to 1600–30. Once again, this pre-dates the use of 'queer' to mean homosexual, which goes back to only about the 1890s. Certainly, *cadi* has a past of stigma, but 'queer' has baggage of its own and should not be universally imposed upon and applied within diverse linguistic cultures. When Queer Nation was formed in the 1990s, its founders did not confer with people of the world, and they did not ask people in the Rhondda valley if they approved of it. The word 'queer' in south Wales is still an insult and hurtful; hardly anyone there knows that it has been 'reappropriated' by academics, and the same can be said of *cadi, cadi-ffan* in north Wales. The decision to use the term 'queer theory' was not arrived at by some kind of international democratic consensus; rather, it has been imposed on us through a form of imperialist, American, linguistic annexation. So, to return to the word *cadi, cadi-ffan*, and bearing in mind its history as part of our hidden national narrative, why shouldn't we talk of *damcaniaethau cadi, 'cadi* theory'? I think it is time for us to reappropriate *cadi* or *cadi-ffan* in Welsh. Sometimes a word or term used in a new way just takes a little time to become accepted and familiar; they 'sound gay' at first, as did 'gay' in fact, and *hoyw* and, indeed, 'queer', until they don't.

A start has already been made in the reappropriation of *cadi* in an excellent and forward-thinking article by Richard Crowe:

> *Ond beth yw'r traddodiad hoyw? Yn sicr, nid yw'n fonolith. Swp o draddodiadau ydyw sy'n amrywio o oes i oes ac o le i le ac eto sy'n dangos unoliaeth syfrdanol ar adegau. Fe ddeallai hoywon Venezia'r bymthegfed ganrif arfer breninesau Aberystwyth yr ugeinfed ganrif o ofera mewn caffe ar brynhawn Sadwrn i'r dim. A dwi'n siŵr y byddai'r Cadi Haf yn ei wisg hanner dyn a hanner menyw wedi cael croeso gan berdaches yr Americaniaid Cynhenid. Wrth wraidd y traddodiad hoyw y mae camp – yr ymwybod o gelfyddydolrwydd (artiffisialrwydd) dosbarthiadau wedi ei dymheru â dogn gref o afiaith. Ysbryd y Mabinogi – campau ieuenctid – os liciwch chi. Mae'r egwyddor a eilw Twm Morys yn sgwarnogrwydd yn perthyn yn agos. Mae hoywder yn herio'r gyfundrefn ryweddol sy'n mynnu mai dwy rywedd sydd – gwryw a benyw – sy'n cydfynd yn union â rhyw biolegol – gwryw a benyw – yr unigolyn.*[8]

But what is the gay tradition? Certainly it is not monolithic. It's a bundle of traditions that vary from age to age and from place to place and which yet reveal an amazing uniformity at times. The gays of fifteenth-century Venezia would perfectly understand the tendency of queens in Aberystwyth in the twentieth century to waste time in a cafe on a Saturday afternoon. And I feel sure that the Cadi Haf in his half-man half-woman outfit would have been welcomed by the *berdaches* of the Native Americans. At the root of the gay tradition is camp/an achievement[9] – the awareness of the artificiality of definitions tempered with a good dollop of humour. The spirit of the Mabinogi – the games of youth/the campyness of youth[10] – if you like. The concept that Twm Morys calls *harelikeness* is very closely related.[11] Gayness challenges the system of sexual orientation that insists that there are two genders – masculine and feminine – which complies exactly with the biological order – masculine and feminine – of the individual.

Crowe presents a different way of approaching the question of articulating queerness in Welsh, now and in the past. He writes of a tradition, but not a singular or monolithic one; it is an eclectic one within which Wales may stake a *cadi*/queer claim. To abandon Welsh as a backward language that has not kept pace with the needs of sexual identity would amount to little more than a capitulation to a linguistic imperialism that offers an impossible choice: be queer or be Welsh, but never both. Crowe tells us to look to the variety, diversity and uniformity across traditions, times, places and languages for a playful achievement of Cymru *cadi*. He refers to the Mabinogi to begin locating this mercurial *cadi* Welsh tradition, and well we might, for here we find the tale of *Math fab Mathonwy*, the Fourth Branch (*c*.1200), a tale that magically undoes bodies and their prescribed relations and desires. In this tale, as punishment for Gilfaethwy's having raped his foot-holder, Goewin ferch Bebin, Math turns his nephews, Gilfaethwy fab Dôn and Gwydion fab Dôn, first into a hind and a stag who then mate and produce a young deer. The next year, he turns the one that was a hind into a boar and the one that was a stag into a sow who then between them produce a piglet. The following year, he turns the one that had been the boar into a wolf bitch and the one that had been a sow into a wolf dog; they mate and produce a cub. The offspring of all three matings are then turned into human boys by Math. In this, the 'queerest' of all stories, the boundaries of gender, family and even species are broken down as the brothers criss-cross from male to female and back again. Here we have incest, homosexuality, transgender and temporary heterosexual fertility, with both brothers experiencing being female and giving birth. Surely this must be one of the fullest expressions of the whole range of 'queerness' in any literature. Although Math uses his magical powers to humiliate Gwydion and Gilfaethwy, the episode seems to suggest the amorphous potential of the bodies, genders and sexualities.

There is, therefore, a double challenge in this chapter. First, we must turn unapologetically to the Welsh language, with all of its heterosexist baggage, in order to give it the same chance that English had to fashion a *cadi*/queer experience with local linguistic resources. Secondly, we must turn to the Welsh past to shape a meaningful *cadi* Welsh present, and we must do so by recognizing the hare-like (*sgwarnoglyd*) indeterminacies of the past, those sites of narrative and lyric possibilities that constitute the resources for building community in the present. Along these lines, Crowe's argument is similar to Carolyn Dinshaw's affective approach to the queer materials of the past as she applies a 'queer historical touch' in 'a desire for bodies to touch across time', exposing 'indeterminacies, contradictions, and slippages' within the presumptively 'determinate oppositional structures' of the past.[12] For Dinshaw, 'queer histories – affective relations across time – recognise the historical past as a vibrant and heterogeneous source of self-fashioning as well as community-building'.[13] Following Dinshaw (who draws on Foucault), therefore, the rest of this chapter examines representative examples of *cadi* life in medieval and twentieth-century Welsh literature, bringing into contact the long past and the near present in a camp achievement of Welsh queerness.[14] The medieval context is far from our more recent twentieth-century one, most usefully in that it did not imagine sexuality as a '"fictitious unity" of normative heterosexuality', and, through this revisiting of the *cadi*/queer Welsh past, we may 'understand the kind of liberatory potential that is offered by a realm of acts without essential identities',[15] and not feel obliged to think of Wales, Welsh and the Welsh past in solely alienating and heterosexist terms. And this may help, in the long run, as we revisit the more recent past, and 'with these new pieces of history ... make new relations, new identifications, new communities with past figures who elude resemblance to us but with whom we can be connected partially by virtue of shared marginality, queer positionality'.[16] As we read these texts, therefore, we will resist the presumptively heterosexual reading practices of the twentieth century in order to illustrate the ways in which queerness emerges within the many gender-indeterminate texts that appear alongside more explicitly queer ones. Indeed, the half-told stories of queer desire within Welsh literature should not be read as the absence of proof of queer life but as the presence of a sexual ambiguity and freedom that defies heteronormative definition. And we will find, in fact, that Welsh is a very queer language after all.

Medieval cadi Wales: a boy in a frock

The story of Amlyn and Amig (Amis and Amiloun in English) is a prime example of this long tradition of hare-like *cadi* strangeness in the presumptively straight tradition of Welsh language literature. It seems that this Welsh tale *Kedymdeithyas Amlyn ac Amic* (The Friendship of Amlyn and Amig) dates from around the early fourteenth century, and clearly it was well known as it is referred to by Dafydd ap Gwilym (*fl.* 1334–80) and by the poet Iolo Goch (*c.*1320–*c.*1398).[17] In all the renditions and in various languages, one element of this well-known story of friendship stays constant: the heroes share a deep intimacy and pledge to be faithful to one another until death, and are ostensibly joined by institutions of faith, family and blood. Early versions are thought to be pagan and the two friends drink blood to seal their bond, but later European retellings of the story bring in Christian elements, so in *Kedymdeithyas Amlyn ac Amic* the oath is sworn in the monastery of St Germain over the sacred relics there: 'that one would not fail the other in love nor in advice nor in help while they lived in accordance with the justice of the law of God in everything that belonged in a true friendship' (*'na phallei neb ohonunt y'w gilyd, nac o garyat nac o gynghor, nac o ganhorthwy tra vei vyw, herwyd kyfyawnder kyfreith Duw o bop peth a berthynei ar gedymdeithyas gywir'*).[18] The two friends are born at the same time and when they are brought together they are like identical twins: no one can tell them apart. They are baptized by the pope in Rome. As children, they could not be separated: 'neither of them would eat or drink or sleep without the other' (*'na mynnei yr vn onadunt na bwyt nac yvet na chysgu heb y gilyd'*).[19] After their baptisms, their fathers take them their separate ways. They grow up and go through many trials apart and then begin their search for one another. Eventually, they are reunited and that's when they pledge their oath in the monastery. Rather like Pwyll and Arawn in the First Branch of the Mabinogi, the two change places with one another. Amig takes Amlyn's place in a duel, while Amlyn stands in for Amig at Amig's home, and here again like Pwyll, although he sleeps in the same bed as Amig's wife, he places a sword between them so that they never touch. Through the surrogate erotic space of the marriage bed, they prove their complete faith in one another.

The most important episode in the tale comes after God strikes Amig with leprosy, and Amig turns to his friend Amlyn who takes him in, following which the two men affect a kind of procreative and lineal marriage through the death and rebirth of children. One night, when they are sleeping in the same bed (*'yn kysgu yn yr vn gwely'*),[20] Amlyn's wife having gone to church, God sends the archangel Raphael to tell Amig that in order to cure his leprosy Amlyn has to kill his two little sons and wash his friend in their blood. Amlyn is, not unreasonably, difficult to persuade, but in the end Amlyn complies. He kills his children, washes Amic from head to toe in their blood, and the cure is achieved. Marvellously, the little boys are soon restored to life. These children might be seen as the newly reborn offspring of Amlyn and Amig's union. Finally, Amlyn and Amig die side by side on the battlefield defending Christianity. They are laid to rest in separate churches, but overnight God miraculously transports the body of Amlyn and puts it in with that of Amig in the same grave in a marriage that is more sacred and enduring than their institutionally proper marriages. This is not a native Welsh story, but it is one that found expression in Welsh, that celebrates true love between two men and that queerly unsettles the heterosexual tradition.[21] Despite the possibilities of this tale, the tendency is to read it within the conventional tradition of chaste comradely love.[22] In her excellent scholarly edition of *Kedymdeithyas Amlyn ac Amic*, neither in her introduction nor in her notes does Patricia Williams allude to the possibility of same-sex love as being part of the tale (in her presumptively heterosexual reading practice, it probably never even crossed her mind). And the question does not seem to have been raised in any of the discussions of the various other European versions of the story; however, the tale may be read as an expression of the *cadi*/queer desire that disarticulates and undermines heterosexual institutional love. This story of intense male-bonding implicitly revises family, marriage, bloodline and tradition through a destabilizing yet abiding queer/*cadi* desire.[23]

Similar queer bonds and marriages between men appear elsewhere in medieval Welsh poetry. Peter Busse, in his admirable article 'The Poet as Spouse of his Patron. Homoerotic Love in Medieval Welsh and Irish Poetry?', points to examples from the poet Taliesin (*fl.* end sixth century). He also discusses Aneirin (*fl.* second half of the sixth century) and goes on to show later poets 'expressing their deep affection and love for their patron'.[24] He finds further instances in the work of Cynddelw (*fl.* 1155–95), Dafydd ap Gwilym, possibly the most important of all Welsh poets, and Guto'r Glyn (*fl.* 1440–93). Though not wishing to cover exactly the same ground as Peter Busse's study, it is worth looking at lines he quotes from Dafydd ap Gwilym's *cywydd*[25] for his patron Ifor Hael:

> *Dywed, o'm gwlad ni'm gadwyd,*
> *Duw a'i gŵyr, dieuog wyd,*
> *Fy mod ers talm, salm Selyf,*
> *Yn caru dyn uwch Caerdyf.*
> *Nid salw na cham fy namwain,*
> *Nid serch ar finrhasgl ferch fain.*
> *Mawrserch Ifor a'm goryw,*
> *Mwy no serch ar ordderch yw.*
> *Serch Ifor a glodforais,*
> *Nid fal serch anwydful Sais,*
> *Ac nid af, berffeithiaf bôr,*
> *Os eirch ef, o serch Ifor,*
> *Nac undydd i drefydd drwg,*
> *Nac unnos o Forgannwg.*[26]

> Say, from my country I have not been allowed
> – You bear no guilt [for it], God knows –

>[but that] I have now been a while[27]
>Courting a being near Cardiff [here].
>No fortune ugly or perverse is mine,
>No love for slender, smooth-lipped (?) girl,
>But I am overwhelmed with love for Ifor,
>More than the love of any girl it is.
>I have celebrated Ifor's love
>Which is not like the love of stupid Saxon churl;
>Nor will I go, most perfect lord,
>For Ifor's love, if he should ask –
>One single day to wicked towns,
>Or pass one night [away] from Morgannwg.[28]

What is striking here is the repetition of the word *serch* (love), six times within fourteen lines. It is not a girl he loves, he stresses, but a man, and it is overwhelming. Peter Busse is measured when he says, 'The keywords in these poems are *serch* "love" and *caru* "to love" and they do mainly express friendship and not love, or to put it more precisely, we should use the terms *agape* and *eros*.'[29] I am not sure of the distinction here between *serch* and *caru/cariad*. In Welsh, *serch* usually means 'love', *eros*. Apart from that, the repetition of the word *serch* is so emphatic that it borders on the importunate. I would like to come back to this point after examining another poet that Peter Busse discusses, namely Guto'r Glyn and, in particular, his 'Moliant i Ieuan Fychan o Foeliwrch' (Praise for Ieuan Fychan of Moeliwrch):

>*Rhoed priodas, urddas oedd,*
>*Rhwym Un Duw, rhôm ein deuoedd.*
>*Annhebig, heb gyngigen,*
>*I briodas gwas a gwen,*
>*Nis gwnaeth, digaeth ostegion,*
>*Brawd Sais y briodas hon;*
>*Duw Tad wedi deuoedd dydd*
>*A'th brïodes â'th brydydd ...*
>*Ni ad Duw, annwyd diwael,*
>*Ysgar rhôm, ysgwïer hael;*
>*Ni thyr rhwym a wnaeth Iôr hir ...*
>*Nawdd Dduw Tad ni ddatodir ...*
>*Y mae deupen carennydd*
>*Y rhôm, nid â byth yn rhydd ...*

>A marriage was made between the both of us,
>It was dignity, the One God's bond.
>Dissimilar to a young man and woman's marriage,
>Without jealousy,
>This marriage wasn't made by an English brother,
>Free banns;
>God the father after two trysts
>Married you with your poet ...
>God won't allow a separation between us

> Excellent disposition, generous esquire:
> A bond made by eternal God won't break
> God the Father's patronage cannot be undone ...
> The two ends of love
> Are between us, it will never be undone ...[30]

The notes that accompany this poem state, 'What is highly relevant to this poem is that expressing love for a patron was certainly a topos in Welsh poetry from an early date.'[31] But what is remarkable about this topos, which we saw at work earlier in the quotation from the poem by Dafydd ap Gwilym, is that the culture of that time found nothing questionable or peculiar (queer?) in this sort of language and imagery. It seems to have been not only perfectly acceptable but positively commendable for a poet to talk about his patron as his beloved and even as his spouse. There seems to be no fear here of accusations of sin or lack of virtue. As with Amlyn and Amig, the loving bond between poet and patron even stands under God's blessing: '*Nawdd Dduw Tad ni ddatodir*' (God the Father's patronage cannot be undone). These poems are only acceptable to modern-day critics and scholars as long as they are read as being purely formulaic: a topos or a literary conceit. Even as a conceit, however, these poems depend upon a queer address that some argue is always at the heart of the love lyric. As Carla Freccero has argued, the 'I' and 'thou' of the love lyric from Petrarch to Melissa Etheridge is notoriously unstable and shifts ambivalently across genders.[32] These homoerotic lyrics cannot simply be dismissed as conceits, for they express an inherent queer desire/identification (as Freccero puts it, Petrarch does not love Laura but loves himself in drag). The lines of love and power between men in these poems render this dynamic more explicit, and we see again that abiding destabilizing force in a love that can 'never be undone' at the very moment it undoes the matrimonial pronouncements of heterosexual union.

A direct challenge to the heterosexual love lyric of the male poets and the institutions that this love upholds may be found in women's poetry of the period, especially in the work of the poet Gwerful Mechain (*fl.* 1462–1500). In her 'I Wragedd Eiddigeddus' (To Jealous Wives), she stands up to the male poets who sing endlessly about 'Y Gŵr Eiddig' (The Jealous Husband), but there is more subtlety in her 'Cywydd y Cedor' (The Female Genitals). To begin, she parodies the male poets' love songs:

> *moli gwallt, cwnsallt ceinserch,*
> *a phob cyfryw sy fyw o ferch*
> *ac obry moli heb wg*
> *yr aeliau uwchlaw'r olwg:*
> *moli hefyd, hyfryd dwf,*
> *foelder dwyfron feddaldwf*
> *a breichiau gwen len loywlun*
> *dylai barch, a dwylaw bun.*

> praising the hair, gown of fine love,
> and every such living girl,
> and lower down praising merrily

> the brows above the eyes;
> praising also, lovely shape,
> the smoothness of the soft breasts,
> and the beauty's arms, bright drape,
> she deserved honour, the girl's hands.³³

In these lines, she names and claims the conventional male gaze of the *blason* before turning it to her own desire. This is her own voice: she's speaking for herself. And she goes on to speak in a way and of things no male poet had ever spoken – this is the whole point of her poem:

> *a'r plas lle'r enillir plant,*
> *a'r cedor clyd, rhagor claer,*
> *tynerdew, cylch twn eurdaer,*
> *lle carwn i, cywrain iach,*
> *y cedor dan y cadach.*
> *Corff wyd diball ei allu,*
> *cwrt difreg o'r bloneg blu.*
> *Llyma 'ynghred, teg cedawr,*
> *Cylch gweflau ymylau mawr,*
> *Pant yw hwy na llwy na llaw*
> ...
> *gadewch heb ffael er cael ced*
> *gerddau cedor i gerdded.*
> *Sawden awdl, sidan ydiw,*
> *sêm fach, len ar gont wen wiw,*
> *lleiniau mewn man ymannerch,*
> *y llwyn sur, llawn yw o serch*
> *fforest falch iawn, ddawn ddifreg ...*

> and the place where children are conceived,
> And the warm quim, clear excellence,
> Tender and fat, bright fervent broken circle,
> Where I loved, in perfect health,
> The quim below the smock.
> You are a body of boundless strength,
> a faultless court of fat's plumage.
> I declare, the quim is fair,
> circle of broad-edged lips,
> it is a valley longer than a spoon or a hand
> ...
> let songs to the quim circulate
> without fail to gain reward.
> Sultan of an ode, it is silk,
> little seam, curtain on a fine bright cunt,
> flaps in a place of greeting,
> the sour grove, it is full of love,
> very proud forest, faultless gift ...³⁴

Gwerful Mechain's *cywydd*, in spite of the rather colourful vocabulary, is tender and sensual. The imagery is intimate, detailed, even visceral. Although she talks of sex with men in the poem, she implies that it is a duty. We sense that her real feelings are for other women. She is ostensibly addressing male poets, but she sings from the female body to the female body. In moving from conventions of male poetry to a new country of desire, she queerly claims the territory of language and poetry for herself. She connects with other women, empathizes through herself with them.

Gwerful Mechain's poem does not stand alone as an expression of love between women in Welsh literature. A number of poems from the Middle Ages written by or for women and addressed to other women use the convention of the *llatai* or love-messenger. A striking example is 'Cywydd i yrru gleisiad yn llatai oddi wrth ferch at ferch arall' (A *cywydd* to send a young salmon as a *llatai* from one girl/woman to another girl/woman).[35] There are some quite beautiful touches in this poem. It begins, as is usual in this kind of poem, with a detailed evocation of the chosen *llatai* using the technique of *dyfalu*, multiplying metaphors and colourful descriptions of the object: '*Mellten dwfr, nid mall tan don, / Mal draig yn moldior 'r eigion.*'[36] (Lightning water, not evil beneath the wave/Like a dragon moulding the deep.) Then the poem says that the salmon is noted for having within it '*natur merch: / A dyn ...*' (The nature of woman: / And man ...) The use of *dyfalu* and the transgender salmon suggest the same shape-shifting indeterminacy of *Math fab Mathonwy*. Further on, there is a lovely observation of 'natural history' when the poem describes the salmon in specifically feminine imagery going to the furthest parts of the sea '*â 'th wyau mân*' (with your tiny eggs). Then, continuing to follow the convention of a *llatai* poem, the poet hopes the fish will not come to harm and urges it to seek the love object with care and to avoid danger and enemies on its journey. The allusion to '*Môn, ag enw mam ynys*' (Anglesey, named mother island) again seems to emphasize the feminine background and imagery that runs through the poem. '*Dos i drin fy nghyfrinach*' (Go and deal with my secret), says the poet, introducing a sense that here is a love that is not entirely out in the open, but rather hidden. Then Siân is named: she is married now; she used to be Siân Owain, and now she is Siân Griffith. '*Bu rydd*' (she used to be free); '*Bun a roed dan ben yr iau*' (a maiden put under the yoke). The sense of regret at her marrying is enormous. She's enslaved, and it's as if a bond has been broken: '*Torrodd â Marged Harri*' (she broke from Marged Harri). The marriage was not an *athrod*, the breaking of a legal bond, but before the marriage, Marged says of Siân '*A chur maith, fel chwaer i mi*' (with a painful longing, like a sister to me). The image of sisterhood is repeated and expanded for several lines until, she says, she took another companion, a man, a husband. The poem moves from shape-shifting freedom found in feminine love to the restrictions of the heterosexual marriage contract to which women were bound, but the *cadi*/queer desire of mobile bodies meeting in this Welsh-language poetic tradition is not reducible to that binding.

The troubling of gender in these patronage poems and *llatai* finds most explicit expression in a mysterious piece from this period by Huw Arwystli (*fl.* 1542–78), and here more than anywhere we detect the *cadi*/queer potential of a Welsh past outside the normalizing heterosexual fictions of the present. Arwystli describes a boy dressed as a girl, a thing he finds both perplexing and alluring, and the speaker seems drawn to the pretty girl but terrified by the complicating fact that 'she' is a 'he'. He expresses his conflicted, ambivalent feelings in the opening couplet:

> *Y ferch fwynddadl, lygatlws,*
> *a hed a dwygaill a hws ...*
>
> The soft-spoken girl with pretty eyes,
> With a hat and two balls and a mantle ...[37]

At no point does the poet use the masculine personal pronoun; the mutations and adjectives in the Welsh always agree. Several times, he remarks on her striking beauty: she is '*[l]ygatlws*' (beautiful eyed), '*[g]loywlun lwyd*' (fair of form, pale), '*[t]eg iawn*' (very pretty). Yet he cannot refrain from considering 'her' sexual apparatus: 'she' has '*[t]ri morddwyd*' (three thighs), 'she' has '*unllath o fonllost*' (a yard-long cock), 'she' has '*brwysg dewgyn braisg a dwygaill*' (a hefty fat chisel and two balls). Nevertheless, the poet insists she prefers the opposite sex:

> *Gwell gan dda'i llun, fun feinwar,*
> *neges â'i chares no'i char.*
> *gwell genti serch merch no mab.*
> *Mwy'n ddigwmpar y carai*
> *Ei nith, o'r hanner, no'i nai.*
>
> The slender shapely maid prefers
> Intimacy with her girlfriend than her boyfriend
> she'd rather have the love of a girl than a boy.
> Incomparably more would she love
> her niece, by half, than her nephew.[38]

Very pointedly he declares:

> *Ni bu uchod yn bechwr*
> *erioed rhwng ei deudroed ŵr.*
>
> No sinful man was ever up
> between her two feet.[39]

However, a few lines further on, he seems to quote a '*gordderchwr*' (adulterer, fornicator):

> '*Rhan fry'n ferch*', *medd gordderchwr,*
> *rhan ôl, er hynny, 'n ŵr.*
>
> 'The upper part is a girl' says a suitor,
> The remaining part, nevertheless, is a man.[40]

One wonders how this person knew that.

This troubling figure of transgender desire is filled with queer potential, but if we turn to the editor's comments on this poem we should by now be unsurprised by the heterosexual realignment of this unruly body: 'Although the boy is referred to as a girl, it is important to realise that he is not homosexual, since the whole point of the poem is that he has male desires despite his clothing. He was perhaps an actor in a play or pageant.'⁴¹ This pushes aside any hope of claiming that this poem comes outside the orthodox, conventional, straight frame, but in fact, neither the reader, the editor nor the speaker know anything definitive about the boy. The boy does not get a chance to speak through the poem, and the only way the poet can make sense of the unusual situation that confronts him is by admitting that he is attracted to the 'girl', thus exonerating him/her from 'sin', and, in doing this, he deflects his own sexual excitement caused by thoughts of the boy's genitalia and being '*uchod rhwng ei deudroed*' (up between her two feet). The allure is there, but it is a threat; it is not permitted. What we have in this poem is Huw Arwystli's confusion, and a confusion of the codes and categories that render gender legible. This is a fascinating, enchanting poem, a rare, precious text, giving as it does a glimpse into the complexity and richness of sexuality and indeed attitudes to sexuality in the Middle Ages. Who was the mysterious, queer boy? There is a story here that refuses to be straightened out by any normalizing hypothesis.

In the Mabinogi, in the tale of Amlyn and Amig, in patronage poems, in lesbian *llatai* and in unsettling transgender embodiment, a *cadi*/queer desire has been articulated in Welsh and in indifference to the normalizing constraints of a twentieth-century critical reception. The editors and scholars who reframe these *cadi*/queer texts within safely heterosexual terms do so in a twentieth-century reactionary fear of a homosexual identity that did not in fact apply to the Middle Ages, and when we refuse to read these texts outside this homophobic frame, we may access their destabilizing potential as resources for *cadi*/queer Welshness. As we move now to the twentieth century when sexuality was constrained by homophobic discourses, we will miss the playful and troubling transgender figure in Huw Arwystli's poem; however, she is still legible, and the rest of this chapter will work to recover her confusing presence from the generally negative representations of sexual difference.

The twentieth century: Gwenallt's hedgehog

Negative representations of homosexuality recur in much twentieth-century Welsh-language literature. We must now contend with the likes of Saunders Lewis, whose chauvinism relegated homosexuality to a realm of foreign deviant criminality. For example, in his political drama, *Cymru Fydd* (Wales to Come, 1967), Dewi, the son of a minister, has escaped from prison where he has been held for petty crimes. He returns to his home and explains why he has escaped in terms that pervert faith and family:

> DEWI: *Bocsiwr deg ar hugain oed o Stepney ydy fy mhartner i. Rydan ni wedi'n cloi gyda'n gilydd mewn cell fach gul ac uchel o chwech bob pnawn hyd at chwech bob bore, deuddeg awr gyda'n gilydd, fel Adda ac Efa ym Mharadwys. Yr hyn mae'r Saeson yn ei alw'n marriage of convenience ... Sodom a Gomorra ydy carchar, a'r muriau a'r drysau clo i ofalu nad oes na dewis na gwrthod ... Mae 'na bethau na fedra i mo'u hadrodd yn digwydd ym mharêd y lle chwech bob bore.*⁴²

DEWI: A thirty-year-old boxer from Stepney is my partner. We are locked in a small narrow, tall cell from six in the afternoon until six in the morning, twelve hours together, like Adam and Eve in Paradise. What the English call a marriage of convenience ... Prison is Sodom and Gomorrah, and the walls and the locked doors make sure that there's neither choice or refusal ... There are things I can't talk about which happen in the toilet parade every morning.

This perverted English 'marriage' in an English prison suggests that his Welsh home provides a more pure escape, and it's worth reminding ourselves that Lewis spent nine months in Wormwood Scrubs in 1936 for his part in a nationalist political protest. Another erstwhile prisoner (for conscientious objection), D. James Jones, known as Gwenallt (1899–1968), made similar use of his negative experiences of homosexuality in his prison-based novel *Plasau'r Brenin* (The King's Palaces, 1934), but an even more unfavourable view can be found in his poem 'Y Draenog' (The Hedgehog). It starts with the poet taking a walk towards Nanteos (a mansion near Aberystwyth).[43] Predictably, he finds a subject for his muse. He uses the hedgehog as a symbol of everything that is primitive, savage and revolting. In one verse he says,

> *Ynddo ef y mae cyltau cyntefig y Congo,*
> *Demoniaid rhwydd y gwylltiroedd tan,*
> *Miwsig yr eilunod ym Malaia a Tahiti,*
> *Duwiau a duwiesau silindrig Iapan.*[44]

> In him are the cults of the Congo,
> The swift demons of the brown plains,
> The music of the idols in Malaya and Tahiti,
> The cylindrical gods and goddesses of Japan.

This says more about Gwenallt, a man teeming with all kinds of prejudices, than it does about a hedgehog. But it is the verse that precedes this which is of interest to us. He says:

> *Yn y tywyllwch crwn y llam y llyffaint*
> *Ac y cân y brogaid a phryfed fel cloch,*
> *A'r greddfau hen yn llifo fel dyfroedd*
> *Dwyfol, gwryw-gydiol a choch.*[45]

> In the rounded darkness the toads jump
> And the frogs sing and insects ring,
> And the old instincts flow like
> Divine rivers, homo-sexual and red.

Why must the poor hedgehog be '*gwryw-gydiol a choch*' ('homo-sexual and red')? Apparently, only in these terms could Gwenallt fully express the horror and revulsion he felt for all things primitive: the words are merely threads in the fabric of his nausea. In the last couplet he says: 'He it was that filled in the emptiness where the Trinity used to be, / Oh! Immortal ball. Oh! Godliness of thorns' ('*Efe a lanwodd y gwacter lle bu'r Drindod, / O! Belen anfarwol. O! Dduwdod y drain*').[46] The hedgehog has come to stand for all that is ungodly, specifically unchristian, and that includes homosexuality and, for some reason, redness. As with Saunders Lewis, Gwenallt defends the boundaries of the proper and pure as he strolls by the old Welsh manor house.

A similar monstrous threat to the 'natural' heterosexual order is found in *Ffenestri Tua'r Gwyll* (Windows Towards Twilight, 1955) by Islwyn Ffowc Elis (1924–2004). In this novel, it is immediately clear that the character is meant to be a homosexual from his name – Cecil. This was the name given to many effeminate men in books, films and plays in the 1940s and 1950s. Never above judging his own characters, this is how Islwyn Ffowc Elis introduces Cecil through the eyes of Ceridwen, the focus of the story:

> *Syllodd Ceridwen drwy'r drws a gweld Cecil yn dod i mewn. Er eu bod yn hen ffrindiau bellach, yr oedd gweld Cecil yn gyrru ias fach anghynnes drwyddi bob tro, fel petai'n cyffwrdd â llyffant. Yr oedd ei wyneb a'i lais a'i osgo mor fenywaidd, yr oedd hi'n siŵr fod ei Grëwr wedi gwneud camgymeriad ynglŷn â'i ryw.*[47]

> Ceridwen looked through the door to see Cecil coming in. Although they were old friends by now, she felt an unpleasant little chill go through her every time she saw him, as if she had touched a toad. His face and his voice and his manner were so womanly, she was sure that his Creator had made a mistake with his sex.

A friend is suspicious of the time Cecil spends at the home of Ceridwen, a respectable widow, and this gives the author another opportunity to make Cecil's nature clear:

> '*Wyt ti'n siŵr nad ydach chi ddim* mwy *na ffrindiau?*'
> '*Nac yden. 'Does gan Cecil ddim i'w ddweud wrth ferched.*'
> '*Mae o'n ddyn annaturiol 'ta.*'
> '*Ydi, mae o.*'[48]

> 'Are you sure that you are not *more* than friends?'
> 'We aren't. Cecil has no interest in women.'
> 'So he's an unnatural man then.'
> 'Yes, he is.'

Cecil is one of the Creator's mistakes, and he's unnatural. For this he is despised: he brings to mind the touch of a toad, so revolting is his presence, almost as revolting as Gwenallt's hedgehog. And there is much more along these lines. When a poet, Alfan Ellis, comes to stay with Ceridwen both she and Cecil are attracted to him. There is a horrible scene (chapter 30 in the novel) when Cecil tries to force himself into Alfan's bedroom. The noise of Alfan's refusal wakes Ceridwen who insists that Cecil return to his own room. After the incident Ceridwen considers what she has just witnessed:

> *Cofiodd amdani hi a Jane Penclawdd, pan oeddynt yn gwneud y Rhufeiniaid yn yr Ysgol Sul erstalwm, yn gofyn i John Jones yr athro beth oedd Paul yn ei feddwl wrth sôn am y 'gwŷr ynghyd â gwŷr yn gwneuthur bryntni', a John Jones yn mynd yn goch yn ei wyneb ac yn dweud na wydde fo ddim. Yr oedd Paul yn gwneud pechod ohono, ac yr oedd seicoleg fodern yn gwneud afiechyd ohono, ac ni allai'r ddau fod yn iawn. Ni wyddai hi; ni allai wybod; ond dechreuodd feddwl iddi fod yn greulon wrth Cecil lawer tro wrth wneud gwawd o'i wendid. Yr oedd yn ddigon tebyg ei fod yn groes y byddai'n rhaid iddo'i chario ar hyd ei oes, fel yr oedd yn rhaid i ambell un gario dau lygad dall neu grwb ar ei gefn.*[49]

> She recalled when she and Jane Penclawdd were doing Romans in Sunday school long ago, asking John Jones the teacher what did Paul mean when he spoke of 'men with men working that which is unseemly',[50] and John Jones turning red in the face and saying he knew nothing. Paul made it a sin, and modern psychology made it an illness, but they couldn't both be right. She didn't know, she couldn't know, but she began to feel that she had been cruel towards Cecil on several occasions in mocking his weakness. It was probably a cross he would have to bear all his life, just as some have to bear two blind eyes or a hump on their back.

It is almost embarrassing to draw attention to texts like this. Of course, it could be argued in his defence that Islwyn Ffowc Elis is simply conveying the thoughts of his homophobic female character, but Ceridwen is presented as a sophisticated, educated woman, a musician who surrounds herself with writers and artists. So Islwyn Ffowc Elis had a perfect opportunity here to explore a more nuanced view of homosexuality. Sadly we sense no encroaching enlightenment. Instead, the chance to think about the matter is sidestepped and the 'It Is Written' approach is embraced. Homosexuality is equated to blindness or a spinal deformity.

In texts like the ones above, we see how far we have come from the spirit of the Mabinogion to which Richard Crowe appeals, but we needn't resign ourselves to such embarrassing and negative portrayals. Despite the generally homophobic stance of Saunders Lewis, Gwenallt and Islwyn Ffowc Elis, the *cadi* hare-likeness persists throughout the twentieth century, and there is always a queer presence within these heteronormative contexts as long as we accept the invitation to read them there within the heteronormative fictions that surround them. John Gwilym Jones, for example, provides an alternative to these restrictive Welsh perspectives in his last play, *Yr Adduned* (The Promise, 1979). In one very funny scene between Ifan, a schoolteacher, and his condescending headmaster, John Gwilym Jones sneaks in a clear reference to homosexuality. Ostensibly, Ifan has been brought before the headmaster because one of the parents has complained that he is promoting Welsh nationalism in his Welsh literature class. Ifan argues that in order to teach the work of writers like Saunders Lewis, Gwenallt and Waldo Williams, he cannot avoid the subject, as they were nationalists. Then, using a sort of Trojan horse, he compares this to his fellow teacher who in teaching English has to say, among other examples, 'there is enough evidence in Tennyson's *In Memoriam* to accept that he was in love with Arthur Hallam' (*'fod digon o brofion yn* In Memoriam *Tennyson i dderbyn ei fod mewn cariad ag Arthur Hallam'*), and the French teacher who has to say 'that Rimbaud and Verlaine lived together. How can the lifestyles of Gide and Cocteau and Genet be ignored? (*'bod Rimbaud a Verlaine wedi byw efo 'i gilydd. Sut medrir anwybyddu bucheddau Gide a Cocteau a Genet?'*)[51] This seems at first consistent with the distinction between Welsh nationalism and foreign queerness presented above, but it does not occupy the same political nationalist stance; instead, it slyly aligns foreign queer love with Welsh nationalism as acceptable subjects in Welsh education, thereby reversing the direction of Saunders Lewis, Gwenallt and Islwyn Ffowc Elis.[52] Indeed, as we will see later in further examples, John Gwilym Jones consistently troubles the heterosexual desire throughout his plays and other writings.

Recognizing such possibilities, we may look back to earlier texts, and Prosser Rhys's 'Atgof' (Reminiscence) is a good point at which to start our search for the '*cadi-ffanllyd*' in twentieth-century Welsh literature. Edward Prosser Rhys (1901–45) has gained a reputation as a gay writer based mainly on this poem that won the crown for the poet in 1924. Only a very small part of the long poem in plodding sonnets hints at homosexuality. The first part of the poem deals with the protagonist's heterosexual experiences. The word '*Rhyw*' (sex) is always capitalized, and, after his passionate lovemaking with a girl, the young man feels instant shame and regret: 'I would press down / The Sexual lust, and chase it away' ('*Gwasgwn i lawr / Flys Rhyw, a'i ymlid*').[53] He turns instead to Friendship (also capitalized). His special friend he describes as, 'a charming yellowhaired youth' ('*[l]lanc gwalltfelyn, rhadlon*').[54] They forswear any sexual activity: 'we would not yield to any fleshly enchantment' ('*Nid ildiem ni i ddim rhyw gnawdol hud*'), but what he means here is that they wouldn't have anything to do with girls.[55] Then things take an unexpected turn one night. They fall asleep together and awake:

> *A'n cael ein hunain yn cofleidio' dynn;*
> *A Rhyw yn ein gorthrymu; a'i fwynhau;*
> *A phallu'n sydyn fel ar lan y llyn ...*[56]

> And finding ourselves in a tight embrace
> With Sex overwhelming us; and enjoying it;
> And suddenly stopping as above the lake ...

He stops here as he had stopped earlier in the poem after he had made love to the girl, and this is the full extent of the same-sex scene in the poem. Hardly positive, almost as if the boys have heard a disembodied voice shouting, 'This must stop immediately!' And this is followed quickly by deep remorse:

> *Llwyr-ddeffro ... ac ystyried beth a wnaed*
> *Fe aeth f'ymennydd fel pwll tro gan boen;*
> *Roedd Cyfeillgarwch eto'n sarn dan draed,*
> *A ninnau gynnau'n siwr [sic] santeiddio'n hoen!*
> *Mi lefais: Gad fi'n llonydd bellach, Ryw,*
> *Yr wyf yn glaf, yn glaf, o eisiau Byw!*[57]

> Fully awake ... considering what had happened
> My brain became a whirlpool of pain;
> Again Friendship was a stepping-stone underfoot,
> Hadn't we just sworn to make it a sacred joy!
> I cried: Let me be now, Sex,
> I am sick, sick, for wanting to Live!

So it was all a big mistake. We should have been warned by the poet's nom de plume for the competition, Dedalus, and the quotation from Keats at the beginning of the poem, all of which prepare us to understand this time as a phase in a boy's life. Hardly the Great Gay Poem of Welsh literature: it's rather a sort of anti-sex mea culpa. Nevertheless, read alongside the passionate friendship of Amlyn and Amig or the constrained desire of Gwerful Mechain's *llatai*, one sees an enduring desire in Prosser Rhys's passing phase, which is also described in his earlier more nuanced sonnet, 'Strancio' (Fooling About):

> *Ond weithian gwybydd di*
> *Fod Fflam yn llosgi ynof, ac aml dro*
> *Yn llamu ar draws fy nghorff materol i,*
> *A'm hysu hyd fy ngyrru i maes o'm co,*
> *A strancio a wnaf eto rhag fy ffawd*
> *Nes torro'r fflam ei ffordd o'i charchar cnawd.*[58]

> But sometimes you must know
> That a Flame burned within me, and often
> Sprang from my material body
> Plaguing me until it drove me mad
> And I would taunt my fate
> Until the Flame broke free of its prison of flesh.

As in 'Atgof' the language is cryptic, the confession is guarded and then the experience is downplayed, even in the title of the poem. The poet, while acknowledging his feelings, seeks to deny and withdraw them, but it is hard to ignore the liberated language escaping in the last line, which suggests both spiritual and orgasmic release.

It has always been assumed that the blond youth mentioned in 'Atgof' and 'Strancio' by Prosser Rhys was Morris T. Williams (1900–46) and that the two men were either the Great Loves of one another's lives or just bosom buddies, depending on one's perspective. Certainly Morris Williams, who married the novelist Kate Roberts in 1928, was a deeply troubled individual who struggled with his sexuality, debts and alcoholism, each one of these problems feeding off and exacerbating the others. Morris Williams was a failed novelist. His novel 'Troi a Throsi' (Tossing and Turning), never published, was not suppressed because it was too scandalous but because the narrative was stillborn. The protagonist, Meurig Prisiart, stands for Morris Williams himself. The gay subtext is only a small fraction of the whole work. Meurig's great friend in the novel, based on Prosser Rhys, is called Arthur Morgan. This is at times an intense, emotionally deep and passionate friendship, though it never finds a physical, sexual expression. Nevertheless, I don't think the significance of the relationship should be underestimated. In his article on Morris Williams, Peredur Lynch asks,

> *O gofio am y bryddest 'Atgof', o gofio am yr ymgofleidio ar 'Ffordd Fethel' rhwng y bardd 'a'r llanc gwalltfelyn', a oes rhyw ystyr hud yn y nofel? A oes amwysedd bwriadol i'r 'cyfeillgarwch' y cyfeirir mor fynych ato? A oes yma berthynas homorywiol wedi ei sensro gan ledneisrwydd llenyddol? Y mae arnaf ofn na fydd fy ateb wrth fodd calon y wasg dabloid Gymreig.*[59]

While remembering the poem 'Reminiscence', while remembering the embraces between the poet and 'the yellowhaired youth' on the 'Bethel Road', is there some hidden meaning to the novel? Is there some intentional ambiguity in the 'friendship' so often referred to? Is there here a homosexual relationship censored by literary prudence? I am afraid my answer will not satisfy the Welsh tabloid press.

Peredur Lynch inevitably comes to the predictable conclusion that the novel's material is basically heterosexual. But in his argument, he compares the friendship between Meurig and Arthur in the novel to that of David and Jonathan in the Bible, which he understands as being 'beyond the physical, or in the words of the Second Book of Samuel, "above the love of women"' (*'y tu hwnt i'r cnawdol, neu yng ngeiriau Ail Lyfr Samuel, "y tu hwnt i gariad gwragedd"'*).[60] This is a strange analogy, as the story of David and Jonathan is usually accepted as an entirely homosexual love story and the words 'greater than the love of women' as being a clear declaration of their preference for one another rather than for women, not 'beyond the physical'. Ironically then, Peredur Lynch, in contending that the relationship between Meurig and Arthur is *not* homosexual, uses an example that for many gay readers would be the clincher in claiming 'Troi a Throsi' as a gay text. At the end of his article, Peredur Lynch points out that in 1915 Methuen had been dragged through the courts after publishing *The Rainbow* by D. H. Lawrence and that Welsh publishers probably had this in mind when considering Morris Williams's manuscript.[61] The potentially gay sexual content of the novel is dismissed somewhere in between the scandalous interests of the 'Welsh tabloid press' and the censorship of D. H. Lawrence's *Rainbow*, which perhaps says more about the mechanisms that refuse queer readings than it does about the sexual content of the novel.

The natural movement to make at this stage is to the work of Kate Roberts (1891–1985); however, as so much good work has already been carried out on this important figure in queer Welsh literature, we turn instead to one of her influences John Gwilym Jones (1904–88) who was introduced above.[62] Kate Roberts's lesbian themes were perhaps influenced by a collection of short stories offered to her by John Gwilym Jones for publication by the company she and Morris Williams ran, Gwasg Gee (Gee Press). At first, she rejected the collection but then relented and brought out *Y Goeden Eirin* (The Plum Tree) in 1946. Later in her career, she was to pay tribute to the influence these stories had on her own writing. John Gwilym Jones brought Freud and the stream of consciousness into Welsh literature with these stories. The internal monologues of many characters explore sexual conundrums and anxieties. In 'Y Cymun' (The Communion), Meurig Lewis meets a young man, Gwyn Morgan. He notices his beautiful hands: 'his hand was smooth and his long-slender fingers like a girl's' (*'yr oedd ei law yn llefn a'i fysedd yn hir-fain fel rhai merch'*).[63] He feels that the proximity of the boy has a strange effect upon him: 'Meurig felt so close to him that he needed to hurt him' (*'Teimlai Meurig mor agos ato nes yr oedd yn rhaid iddo ei frifo'*).[64] But he does no harm to him and somehow the boy's presence changes him.

This was the first of many hints at same-sex attraction that permeate the work of John Gwilym Jones. In play after play, he showed scenes of courtship between a young man and a young woman. Although these scenes often had a streak of humour running through them, they were invariably artificial and somewhat unconvincing. We sense that they were not based on much real experience, and none of these rather formal, old-fashioned courtships ever blossoms into a romance. In fact, the usual pattern is that they come to a sudden end based on weak excuses. Why John Gwilym Jones felt the need for these storylines in his plays is something of a puzzle, but many of his dramas were originally written for performance by his students and colleagues and amateur groups, so he may have felt obliged to appeal to a mixed audience with conventional tastes. On the other hand, relationships between two male friends are often much more intense. In *Hanes Rhyw Gymro* (The History of a Certain Welshman, 1964), there is a deep bond between Morgan, based on the seventeenth-century Puritan writer Morgan Llwyd (1619–59), and Siencyn, an older man and erstwhile mercenary who has seen much of life. Even though Morgan is married and has children, it is to his friend that he turns for comfort. At the end of the first scene in the play, Morgan reveals his doubts and his loneliness, whereupon Siencyn promises to join him wherever he goes. Later on, once more, Morgan is beset with uncertainty:

> Morgan: *O, Siencyn, be'sy'n digwydd imi? Be'sy'n digwydd imi? 'Rydw i ofn ... ofn ... Gafael amdana'i, Siencyn ... gafael amdana'i'n dynn ... dynn ...*
> (*Siencyn yn ei gofleidio ac yn ei siglo fel baban*).
> Siencyn: *Dyna ti, Mog bach ... dyna ti, mach i ...*
> Morgan: *Wnei di mo ngadael i, Siencyn?*[65]
>
> Morgan: Oh, Siencyn, what's happening to me? What's happening to me? I'm afraid ... afraid ... Hold me, Siencyn ... hold me tight ... tight ...
> (*Siencyn embraces him and rocks him like a baby*).
> Siencyn: There you are, Mog bach ... there you are little one ...
> Morgan: You won't leave me, Siencyn?

Of course, Siencyn is a father figure to Morgan, but there is a touching, emotional aspect to their attachment to one another. The scene in which Siencyn is dying and begs Morgan to bless him using a sacred relic, which is against Morgan's beliefs, is very moving, and this historically displaced affection between men recalls the intimacies of the earlier texts discussed above.

In later plays, John Gwilym Jones went a little further in unsettling the heterosexual codes constraining male characters who share intimate bonds. In *Ac Eto Nid Myfi* (And Yet Not Me, 1976), we still have the familiar unsuccessful boy/girl love story. In fact, the play begins with Alis ending her relationship with Huw 'Because you are you / who you are' ('*Am mai chi ydach chi*').[66] What she means by this is not clear at the start. Huw's life is examined: his father was often away from home, and his relationship with his mother is much closer, though she is preoccupied with the chapel and is rather strict. His grandmother is more indulgent of him as a child. But Alis's meaning is perhaps best answered by his relationship with his great friend Wil, which is at the heart of the play. The intimate scenes with the two in digs as students really come to life with lively banter and witty dialogue. We learn that somehow Alis has become pregnant by Huw. After a great struggle with himself, Huw offers to marry her which brings us back to the rejection scene that started the play. Alis we sense has understood Huw better than he understands himself. But the play is based on a kind of lipogram: the real reason why they can't marry is unspoken.

A more positive treatment of same-sex attraction is found in T. Rowland Hughes's novel *Yr Ogof* (The Cave, 1945), which, like John Gwilym Jones's

Hanes Rhyw Gymro, locates the desire at an enabling historical distance. This novel, set at the time of Jesus Christ with the family of Joseph of Arimathea at its centre, is highly readable, though sentimental in parts. Joseph's daughter, Ruth, is smitten with the handsome centurion Longinus but his interests lie elsewhere:

> *Ceisiai [Joseff] swnio'n garedig a thadol, a siaradai'n araf a phwyllog. Ond yr hyn a hoffai ei ddweud mewn gwirionedd oedd fod ei ferch wedi gwirioni'i phen yn lân â'r canwriad a bod gan Longinus fwy o ddiddordeb yn ei brawd Othniel nag ynddi hi. Gallai rhywun dall weld hynny, meddai wrtho'i hun.*⁶⁷

> [Joseph] tried to sound kind and fatherly, and he spoke slowly and sensibly. But what he really wanted to say was that his daughter had lost her head completely over the centurion and that Longinus had more interest in her brother Othniel than in her. A blind person could see that, he said to himself.

And Longinus's feelings for Othniel indeed seem to be reciprocated: 'When he came for a trip to Arimathea, he would spend most of the time chatting to him, Othniel, enjoying a discussion on the dialogues of the Greek philosopher Plato' (*'Pan ddeuai ar wib i Arimathea, yn ymgomio ag ef, Othniel, y treuliai'r rhan fwyaf o'i amser, gan fwynhau sgwrs am ddeialogau'r athronydd Groegaidd Plato'*⁶⁸). Much later in the novel, in turbulent surroundings, Longinus thinks of Othniel again: 'His mind drifted back again to Arimathea and Othniel and the little stream in the far part of the orchard. He would've given anything to hear the sound of that rivulet listening to the soft voice of his friend reading one of his poems to him' (*'Crwydrodd ei feddwl eto i Arimathea at Othniel a'r ffrwd fechan ym mhen pellaf y berllan. Rhoddai rywbeth am gael bod wrth su esmwyth yr afonig honno yn gwrando ar lais tawel ei gyfaill yn darllen un o'i gerddi iddo'*).⁶⁹ The friendship never breaks into anything physical: it has been made quite clear that it is 'Platonic', but nothing sexual ever happens in a novel by T. Rowland Hughes, nothing 'adult'; the desire remains undefined and Longinus is ultimately converted to Christianity through his friendship with Othniel.

The first unambiguously homosexual character in Welsh fiction appears in a story by Pennar Davies (1911–96), who was a writer of enormous intellect and learning and a Christian theologian of great sensitivity. It is no surprise, therefore, that 'Y Dyn a'r Llygoden Fawr' (The Man and the Rat, 1966) is much subtler than T. Rowland Hughes's novel, and it provides a greater *cadi*/queer indeterminacy. A synopsis of the story would perhaps remind some of 'Flowers for Algernon': a scientist writes letters to a friend about his experiments on the intelligence of rats. However, there the similarity ends, and Pennar Davies's story originally appeared in the Welsh journal *Heddiw* (Today), '*mor bell yn ôl â dyddiau cynnar yr Ail Ryfel Byd*' ('as far back as the early days of the Second World War'), many years before the science fiction tale by Donald Keyes.⁷⁰ The letters from 'The Man', never named, are interspersed with the thoughts of the most intelligent rat Repin. The scientist is pleased to see that Repin is clever enough to learn that it is only through cooperation that he and the other two rats can feed themselves from the experimental equipment. The other two stupid rats never learn this lesson. While the allegorical nature of the story is more than a little simplistic and contrived, the character of the Man is more complex. He writes imploring his friend Michail to come to stay with him: 'There is always a place for you in my bed – and there is no place for anything other than you in my heart' (*Mae lle iti bob amser yn fy ngwely – ac nid oes le i ddim amgen na thi yn fy nghalon'*).[71] At last, we have a completely unmistakable expression of homosexual love in Welsh. But the Man responds to replies from Michail, never quoted in the story, who promises to visit but never does. The love is one-sided and unrequited. When the Man receives a letter with a photograph of Michail with a woman, he responds, 'And who is the girl who is with you? A co-officer I presume. Do you like working with women? I hate to see women smiling and laughing all around the workplace. They are so uninteresting.' (*'A phwy yw'r ferch sydd gyda thi? Cydswyddog iti, mae'n debyg. Wyt ti'n hoffi cydweithio â merched? Cas gennyf weld merched yn cilwenu ac yn cilchwerthin dros y weithfa. Mae nhw [sic] mor anniddorol.'*)[72] The man may be a misogynist or this may be a pathetic attempt to distract his friend's interest in the girl from a distance. Certainly, it signifies an inability to recognize his friend's effort to show him that he is not gay, or at least his decision to try to deny a gay sexuality. Later, the Man expresses his deep disappointment and sadness on hearing that Michail has married. Still, he wishes him happiness. But he cannot comprehend Michail's choice: 'Why? That's the question that has no answer. You've left me, gone out of my abnormal, struggling, electric life to become part of that strange, meaningless, normal world that is beyond my comprehension and understanding.' (*'Paham? Dyna'r cwestiwn nad oes ateb iddo. Rwyt ti wedi fy ngadael i, wedi mynd allan o'm bywyd annormal, ymdrechgar, trydanol i ac wedi mynd yn rhan o'r byd normal, diethr, diystyr hwnnw sydd y tu hwnt i'm hamgyffred a'm deall.'*)[73] Ultimately, the conclusion of the story is disappointing, as the last letter from the Man to Michail is to inform him of his plan to throw himself off a cliff. This ending was typical of the view of gay people that prevailed when the story was written: sad, 'abnormal', unloved; inevitably they killed themselves in novels, plays and films throughout the first half of the twentieth century. However, this was a story that showed the intensity of same-sex attraction and was quite a challenging piece of fiction for the late 1930s in Welsh. The Man's self-definition as 'abnormal' is unfortunate but perhaps an accurate reflection of how some gay people felt at the time. Further, there is possibly a hidden story within this: Michail may have aligned himself with a heterosexual lifestyle because of the anti-gay pressures of the time, or perhaps the Man rejects 'normality' and embraces his sense of difference, even from within the scientific discourses that pathologize homosexuality and naturalize heterosexuality. In this way, perhaps the vague figure of 'The Man' resists essential identities that are as normal, meaningless and incomprehensible as they would be in the tale of Amlyn and Amig or the lesbian *llatai*.

From this point on, the incorporation of gay and lesbian characters in Welsh fiction begins to multiply into wilder and more unruly bodies that offer greater complexity than Islwyn Ffowc Elis's pathologized Cecil, for instance. Arguably, the starting point for this shift is Caradog Prichard (1904–80). His extraordinary, complex masterpiece *Un Nos Ola Leuad* (One Moonlit Night, 1961) explores almost every kind of sexual variation without judgement. Apart from incest, exhibitionism and child abuse, there is also cross-dressing and homosexuality. The novel could, in fact, be seen as representing the amorphous nature of gender and sexuality in general. All this is presented by the novel's (unreliable) narrator for the reader to respond to in his or her own way. *Un Nos Ola Leuad* was a very important step in the development of the Welsh novel and is mentioned here as a bridge between the 1950s and 1970s. Also, it has generated more discussion in Welsh than any other novel in the language, and in its wake our literature and our writers have followed its example, becoming more open and free in depicting the full range of sexuality.

Space in this chapter does not permit mention of every example, but a novel about university life by John Rowlands (1938–2015), *Tician Tician* (Ticking Ticking, 1978), is noteworthy. One of the lecturers, Humphrey or Wmffra James, is gay but not the usual cliché musical-hall sissy like Cecil. Instead, he is rather aggressive, a hell-raiser and a sexual predator. He likes drinking, smoking, drugs and has a reputation for holding orgies in his flat; however, just like Cecil, he is accused of forcing his unwanted attentions on a young man:

> '*Fe ddaeth e i'r gwely ata i – heb bilyn amdano fe – yn un hwlc mawr blewog.*'
> ...
> '*Ewch mlân,*' *meddai Meic,* '*mae'n rhaid ca'l y stori'n llawn. Falle fod hyn yn fater i'r polîs.*'
> '*Wel fe ...*' *Cododd y bachgen ei ben yn sydyn.* '*Fe ymosododd e arna i. Chi'n gwbod beth wi'n feddwl ...*'
> '*Yn rhywiol?*' *gofynnodd Meic.*
> '*Roedd e wedi colli arno'i hun yn lân – yn chwyrnu fel ci cynddeiriog ac yn fy mrathu fi ... Drychwch os nad ŷch chi'n coelio.*' *Agorodd ei gôt a dangos ôl dannedd yng nghnawd ei war.*[74]

> 'He came into my bed – without a stitch on – a big hairy hulk.'
> ...
> 'Go on,' said Meic, 'we have to have the whole story. This could be a matter for the police.'
> 'Well he ...' The boy lifted his head suddenly. 'He attacked me. You know what I mean ...'
> 'Sexually?' Meic asked.
> 'He had completely lost control – growling like a rabid dog and biting me ... Take a look if you don't believe me.' He opened his coat and showed teeth marks on the flesh of his neck.

Hardly an appealing picture. The gay character is threatening, unable to control his lust. He's almost a wild animal, a biting rapist. In a way, of course, this justifies the homophobia. This is not a matter of a man making a pass at another man who, being heterosexual, rejects the proposition: this is violent, and to prove it bite marks are left in the boy's flesh, 'a matter for the police'.

Siôn Eirian (1954–) explored heterosexual feelings in his 1979 crown-winning poems, though in his novel of the same year, *Bob yn y Ddinas* (Bob in the City), he has his protagonist visit a gay pub in Cardiff. He describes the experience like a visitor to a foreign country (though Bob, in this satirical novel, is something of a country bumpkin and finds many aspects of city life strange and alienating). The gay barman is an object of curiosity and amusement to him: 'This is a bar for people that are the same as Toni, you see. It wouldn't surprise me if the four that are at the bar now are the same as Toni. One of them a business man in a smart suit too' ('*Bar i bobol 'run fath â Toni ydy hwn, welwch chi. Synnwn i ddim nad ydi'r pedwar sy wrth y bar rŵan yn bobol 'run fath â Toni. Un ohonyn nhw'n ddyn busnes mewn siwt smart hefyd'*).[75] Bob is surprised when a large middle-aged woman comes into the bar and buys drinks for the boys, only to realize that it's a man in drag. And when people wander into the bar by mistake, Toni ushers them into the other lounge: 'he only wants to avoid embarrassment. Because a young lad doesn't want to bring his innocent girlfriend to a bar where she can see this big navvy here holding hands with the spindly insurance man beside him' ('*ond eisio osgoi creu embaras y mae o. Achos dydi llanc ifanc ddim am ddod â'i gariad ddiniwed i far lle y gall hi weld y nafi mawr 'ma'n gafael yn llaw y dyn siwrin eiddil yn ei ymyl'*').[76] Toni is not unlike Islwyn Ffowc Elis's Cecil, but the bar contains a wide variety of gay types – the respectable-looking businessman in the smart suit, the drag queen, the big navvy. And this is a place for gay people to hide, where straight people go by mistake and where they may be embarrassed, and embarrassment is not a bad thing when it makes a heterosexual complacency uncomfortable.

It is hardly surprising that the few twentieth-century writers who may, or possibly may not, have been gay felt too constrained to write openly about being gay, bearing in mind this atmosphere of homophobia and also the defensiveness and anger of friends and family at the suggestion, since their deaths, that they may have been gay; what possible hope could there have been to be open about being gay during their lives? Prosser Rhys, Morris Williams and John Gwilym Jones did nothing more than hint at homosexuality, and this is hardly surprising in light of the attitude towards gay people that prevailed in the first part of the twentieth century, as reflected in the work of Gwenallt, Saunders Lewis and Islwyn Ffowc Elis. Even as late as the 1970s, as seen in the novels of liberal-minded writers, such as John Rowlands and Siôn Eirian, the depiction of gay characters is at best comic and at worst ambivalent.[77] It is not until the 1980s that openly gay writers were able to produce work about their experiences in Welsh. However, this uncertainty can be productive, too, as it is in earlier texts that form the long and complicated history of expressing the *cadi*/queer experience in Welsh and, despite the negative and frustrated forms that expression has sometimes taken, it is preferable to defaulting to an English vocabulary and tradition that immediately displaces that experience outside Wales. In fact, if we make the effort, we may even enjoy the aimless wandering into the gay bar by mistake. We may revel in the embarrassment and alienation arising from cross-class gay affection or the middle-aged drag queen, for this drag queen is only Huw Arwystli's boy-in-girl's-clothes all grown up, still refusing to be straightened out, still confusing the desires of those who try to identify her in strictly heteronormative terms.

Part 2
Placing Queer Wales After 1900

5

'A queer kind of fancy': Women, Same-sex Desire and Nation in Welsh Literature[1]

KIRSTI BOHATA

Introduction

Queer women are a recurring presence in literature from Wales, and Wales itself is often portrayed as something of a queer country. As an idealized rural retreat or wild romantic terrain, the Welsh countryside has been represented as a space in which female relationships may endure, most famously in the case of the Ladies of Llangollen. The wayward difference of Wales, as constructed in dominant discourses within Britain, provides writers with some important tropes used to represent love between women and disruption of gender, particularly from the nineteenth century onwards. While Welsh writers make use of wider paradigmatic tropes to signify lesbian desires, such as jewels, 'odd' colours, sickness, obsession, and so on, they also draw on Welsh culture and history. Traditional music, nationalist rebellions, Celtic saints, witches and wise women, ghosts and the *tylwyth teg*, and more recently the politics of devolution are used to evoke, frame or encode homoeroticism and love between women. This chapter establishes a long 'tradition' of Welsh writing about female same-sex desire and observes in post-devolution Wales a flowering of literature depicting lesbian characters. These often occur in novels that are also directly concerned with nationhood and Welsh identity, providing an important opportunity to consider how sexuality and nationality intersect in literature.

Yet it has been easy to overlook the abundance of literature from Wales by or about women who love women. This chapter maps a hitherto largely neglected critical terrain: that of female same-sex desire in Welsh writing in English and Welsh-language literature in translation.[2] It outlines the primary tropes used to represent same-sex desire between women, with a particular interest in the ways in which national character is entwined with gender and sexual identity. The aim is to provide a broad chronological and thematic overview in order to bring into focus the neglected 'tradition' of homoerotic writing and lesbian history.[3] Because the aim of the chapter is to explore *representations* of same-sex desire, the literature selected for discussion includes texts by men and women, queer or otherwise. The chapter is divided into four parts. Part one is a theoretical discussion of how sexuality and national identities are linked; part two offers a broadly chronological overview from c.1650 to c.1997, noting important themes in the representation of same-sex desire and nation. Part three extends the thematic focus, moving away from chronology to examine some of the key inter-representations of sexuality and Welsh identities from 1880 to the present. Finally, the chapter turns to post-devolution fictions in which queer sexualities are bound up with queer and not-so-queer ideas of nation.

Part 1: Theorizing nation and sexuality

Sexuality is a historically contingent concept.[4] Thus while we can find love between women across history and literature, how same-sex desire has been understood, displayed and experienced has changed over time.[5] What this means is that there is no single transhistorical 'lesbian' identity that can be traced back through history. This is not the same thing as saying there was no same-sex desire or that women did not choose other women as exclusive sexual or life partners where this was economically possible, which they manifestly did.

If sexuality is historically contingent, so too are concepts of nation and gender identity. All three, moreover, are closely interrelated. The rise of the modern nation in the nineteenth century required the regulation of both gender and sexual behaviours; categories of homosexuality and heterosexuality were defined alongside, and in direct relation to, civic and ethnic national identities. Nations in the abstract are themselves gendered constructs, often represented figuratively by the mother (conveyor of culture and protector of morality) or the nubile maiden who needs to be protected by the masculine soldier or statesman. Meanwhile the state was defined by civic institutions in which only men had full representation, such as parliament and the law, the military, universities and the church.

Sexual behaviour was seen as directly related to the strength or weakness of different nations and ethnicities. As Alexander Maxwell has demonstrated, in central Europe in the nineteenth century, virile men, virtuous women and healthy mothers were the desired sexual models for a modern nation, a model that places reproduction at the centre of sexuality (thus rendering everyone implicitly heterosexual).[6] Less than virtuous women were seen as the handicap of subaltern peoples (such as the Czechs in the Habsburg context). In Wales, the Blue Books report of 1847 which accused Welsh women of sexual licentiousness confirms this pattern.[7]

If the nineteenth-century nation was a gendered concept and sexual behaviour was viewed as an essential marker of national character, sexual identities – to complete the circle of references – were also conceived in terms of gender. 'Sexual inversion' (or homosexuality), as defined in the second half of the nineteenth century, was understood in terms of 'gender inversion' and, as Marilyn R. Farwell points out, well into the twentieth century 'both positive and negative definitions of the homosexual have assumed that the lesbian or gay man crosses the gender norms of his or her culture'.[8] Thus gender, sexuality and the nation/state are intersecting, sometimes interdependent, categories.[9]

The relationship of same-sex sexualities to national identity, however, is complicated and rather different in the case of male and female homosexuality (in large part because of their different legal statuses).[10] In literature, since the *fin de siècle* at least, male homosexuality has been implicated in ideas of national identity, purity and ethnic difference. According to Eve Kosofsky Sedgwick, '[t]he decades around the turn of the century marked the precipitous popularization, not only of the new word "homosexual", but of the very concept of male-male desire based on sameness'.[11] Sedgwick illustrates how this idea of '*homo*' (same) homosexuality is represented in Oscar Wilde's *The Picture of Dorian Gray* (1890–1), in which the key erotic relationship is located in the 'domestic Same' – that is to say, between Dorian and the desired English (national) body that his own portrait represents.[12] The connection of male homosexuality with the national body, and the male-male relationship offering a bounded and pure notion of homogenous national identity, is discussed by Walter Benn Michaels with reference to modern American literature from around the start of the twentieth century. He identifies the male homosexual family as a 'solution' to a national (read racial) 'problem' of mixture where reproductive heterosexuality equates with miscegenation. '[T]he purely American family', he observes, 'must be the nonreproductive family, and if the nonreproductive family is the homosexual family, then the purest American is the [male] homosexual'.[13]

Sedgwick's reading of male homosexuality at the *fin de siècle*, and Michaels's reading of the pure modern American family as homosexual both figure dominant nations in terms of *male* homosexuality. While there is some overlap, these are not models that can be simply transferred to lesbianism and/or smaller, possibly subjugated, nations or nationalisms.[14] Certainly in the Welsh literature discussed here, when sexuality and national identity are 'interrepresented' (a term used by Sedgwick to suggest the representation of nation and homosexuality within a single figure or set of images) the tendency is to associate lesbianism – socially suspect and economically disadvantaged as it has been – with marginal or subjugated groups and beleaguered or minority nationalisms. The lesbian (alone or in a couple) tends to be on the edge, in exile, or escaping, or constructing an alternative community away from the centre.

The idea of minority (sexual) nationalism was taken up in 1970s America when Jill Johnson conceived The Lesbian Nation, a movement for a separatist lesbian feminist community. And more recently, in the 1990s, Queer Nation appropriated the concept of nationhood for a political movement of resistance. As Bonnie Zimmerman explains, 'space is a profound metaphor for lesbian writers which has a lot to do with the fact that we were scattered in such a way that we must create a concept of space because that space is not given to us'.[15] Or, as Sally Munt put it, making explicit the link with marginalized and subjugated nations: 'Like other oppressed cultures, lesbians hold fast to a dream of commonality and unification.'[16]

This desire for spatial presence and unification might perhaps make struggles for national autonomy resonate with lesbian writers. Alternatively, those fighting national oppression may see some connections with an oppressed sexual identity. But this is not an unproblematic alignment. The example of Erzsébet Galgóczi's novel, *Törvényen belül* (Within the Law, 1980), is a case in point.[17] Galgóczi's semi-autobiographical novel about a lesbian affair in Communist Hungary is a good example of the complications of an allegorical reading of sexual identity as national predicament, or vice versa. The novel is about lesbian experience in an oppressive totalitarian state. When it was adapted for screen in Hungary and premiered at Cannes in 1982 the national-sexual allegory was immediately noted by Western critics. The film, entitled *Egymásra nézve* (Another Way), begins and ends with the main character being shot dead by guards as she tries to cross the Hungarian border. The frame seemed to invite a reading in which the lesbian lovers, hounded and punished for their sexuality, apparently represent an oppressed nation. But it is an interpretation challenged by Aniko Imré who calls attention to the problems of taking lesbian characters to stand for a nation which itself offered no representational space for lesbianism. Rather than reading lesbianism as an unproblematic allegory for political dissidence, Imré argues instead that Galgóczi used a 'smokescreen of national allegory' as a way of representing her own 'unrepresentable subjectivity'.[18]

Thus, albeit sometimes problematically, we find instances of lesbian political appropriation of the concept of national space and of using an oppressed nation as an allegory for a marginalized sexual identity. Conversely, a national narrative may be articulated through the outlawed or occluded lesbian. One of the questions that underpins this chapter, then, is whether there is a discursive space in which suppressed sexualities and sexual identities (in this case those of lesbian and other forms of female same-sex desire) overlap with representations of nation and national identity in literature from a country which for much of its history has been marginal to the centre of British culture and power and, since the nineteenth century, has been struggling for greater recognition and autonomy. What begins to emerge when one looks at lesbian fiction from Wales from the late nineteenth century onwards is that writers seeking to inscribe, or encode, marginalized and 'transgressive' female relationships do draw on tropes of Welshness. It is no coincidence that one of the earliest Welsh novels about same-sex desire, Amy Dillwyn's *The Rebecca Rioter* (1880), also represents a rebellious, would-be independent Wales.[19]

Part 2: Same-sex desire in writing from Wales:
a chronological survey c.1650–c.1997

The connection between same-sex desire and Wales dates back further than the emergence of modern nationalism and sexological concepts of sexual identity. This chapter will eventually focus on that segment of literary tradition extending from the late nineteenth century to devolution, but we begin with a wider chronological survey of early representations of homoeroticism, love and desire between women from the seventeenth century.[20]

'How dear the blest retreats': nature, seclusion and love between women c.1650–c.1870[21]

In literary and historical representations from the seventeenth century, Wales is regularly represented as a rural retreat, or as a natural wilderness, and this landscape of Wales is closely bound up with representing same-sex relationships. The early poems and letters of Katherine Philips, 'The Matchless Orinda' (1632–64), are characterized by a concern with rural seclusion, love between women and political dissent. Brought to live in Pembrokeshire aged fourteen, Philips was married to a nobleman from Ceredigion and moved to the Welsh-speaking county at the age of sixteen. Despite her early marriage, her writings testify to extra-marital attachments and passions. Philips wrote a series of poems on 'Friendship', including several that she hoped would 'transmit to fame / Lucasia and Orinda's name'.[22] Lucasia was Anne Owen of Landshipping in Pembrokeshire, one of three women for whom Philips expresses love in her verse. The poems represent friendship as unification, 'Joyn'd and growing, both in one,' and merger, 'They are, and yet they are not, two.'[23] In 'To my excellent Lucasia, on our friendship. 17 July 1651', love is sublimated into spiritual enlightenment when Lucasia becomes Orinda's soul which 'guides my darken'd brest'.[24] The love of one woman for another surpasses the love of men:

> For thou art all that I can prize,
> My Joy, my Life, my rest.
> Nor Bridegroomes nor crown'd conqu'rour's mirth
> To mine compar'd can be:[25]

As Harriette Andreadis argues, '[in] Philips's poetry friendship between women is infused with the passionate intensity and rhetoric of heterosexual love as it was understood by seventeenth-century male poets'.[26] By invoking bridegrooms and kings, the speaker appropriates and usurps these male roles.

Philips also articulated same-sex love through themes of retreat and seclusion, as in 'A retir'd friendship, to Ardelia 23 Aug. 1651'.

> Come, my Ardelia, to this Bowre,
> Where kindly mingling Souls a while,
> Let's innocently spend an hour,
> And at all serious follys smile.[27]

Sarah Prescott shrewdly notes that 'retirement' is an idea which has both gendered, political and national relevance. Women were removed from the world by marriage, while 'Royalist poetics relied on the theme of retirement'.[28] Wales, moreover, was broadly sympathetic to the Royalist cause (even while Philips's Welsh husband was not). Philips, as a Royalist poet and a married woman, constructed the idea of her Cardiganshire home with its 'beloved Rocks and Rivers' as both exile and retreat in ways that chimed with her political sympathies and gender role, and, I would argue, her romantic desires.[29] Suppressed politics, gender and same-sex love thus share the same ideological retreat, one geographically located in Wales.

Philips's motif of the sequestered garden arbour, 'this Bowre', as offering an intimate space for female friendship, free from 'frowns' and 'Slavery of state',[30] was perpetuated by the Ladies of Llangollen in their retirement at Plas Newydd, which duly became renowned as a place of refuge, retirement and romantic seclusion. Lady Eleanor Butler and Sarah Ponsonby were two Anglo-Irish 'fugitives' who made their home in the Vale of Llangollen for fifty years, from 1780 to 1829/31.[31] Their androgynous riding habits, their cultivated aesthetic tastes, their romantic devotion and their shared tomb became for their admirers the iconic markers of a lifelong female partnership. And their renowned intimacy provided inspiration for other same-sex 'marriages' in the nineteenth century and beyond.[32]

The Welsh landscape became central to the projected identities of the women with reference to eighteenth-century aesthetic values, as Martha Vicinus explains:

> By means of a natural metonymy, the Welsh countryside, wild and untutored, embodied the sublime, and Plas Newydd and its garden the beautiful and the cultivated. But irrational behaviour was only partly transferred away from them and onto Wales. Their eccentric riding habits, practical for so untamed a country, invariably reminded visitors that their lives were somehow unnatural.[33]

The androgynous appearance of the ladies is in some senses excused by the ex-centricity of the country in which they live. 'A wild "male" nature might rage outside, but within the confines of their home and garden, tranquil femininity reigned.'[34] Thus femininity is dissociated from the 'wild' landscape and linked with control and cultivation, yet their mannish outfits demanded by the untamed Welsh location queer the feminine space of Plas Newydd.

Friends and visitors played a large part in constructing contemporary and subsequent representations of the household at Plas Newydd. Anna Seward (1742–1809) the 'Swan of Lichfield' (in the West Midlands) was amongst many writers who visited or corresponded with Ponsonby and Butler. She recognized theirs as a 'Davidean relationship' (the reference is to the famous biblical attachment of David to Jonathan) which reflected her own love for Honora Sneyd.[35] Seward's poem in praise of the ladies' friendship, 'Llangollen Vale', begins with a reference to Owain Glyndŵr and freedom, and constructs Wales as a stronghold that 'In vain the stern Authorities assail.'[36] The vale offers refuge for friendship and she praises the ladies' seclusion, 'Freedom' and virtue, 'in this Cambrian Valley'.[37] Seward was not the only contemporary to see their relationship as 'cemented by something more tender still than friendship', as Anne Lister (1791–1840), herself sexually active with other women, was to put it.[38] The Welsh businesswoman, editor, diarist and distant neighbour, Hester Thrale Piozzi (1740–1824), was even more direct, calling them 'damned Sapphists' in an unpublished diary, although she was friendly and generally complimentary about their household in public.[39] Virtuous recluses, androgynous oddities, suspected Sapphists: the ladies ultimately became a positive marker of same-sex love, whether that was conceived in spiritual terms or as something more corporeal. For instance, when the Welsh sculptor Mary Lloyd returned to live in Wales in the 1890s with her life partner, Frances Power Cobbe, Cobbe described herself and Lloyd as 'The Ladies of Hengwrt'.[40] And when Margiad Evans was exploring – one might say researching – her sexual identity with her one-time partner Ruth Farr, they read the *Hamwood Papers of the Ladies of Llangollen* which had been published by Macmillan in 1930.[41]

The association of same-sex desire with rural seclusion and verdant nature continues into the later nineteenth century. Gardens, arbours, unfurling flowers, as well as other natural phenomena – the moon, the stars, the sea – are staple romantic images used with passion to express female, particularly same-sex, desire. All these images appear in a love poem to an unnamed woman, 'Fy Ffrind' (My Friend, 1870), by Cranogwen (the pen-name of Sarah Jane Rees, 1839–1916, poet, lecturer and editor of the Welsh-language publication, *Y Frythones*).[42] The poem begins with a long section on friendship which makes use of garden imagery to describe her beloved, or rather their friendship, as 'a dear little tender flower' (*Blodeuyn annwyl, tyner*) with 'perfume quite enchanting / Yet his survival is strange' (*swynol ei arogledd / Ond, er mor ryfedd mae yn byw*).[43] Flowers give way to cosmic imagery, and Jane Aaron astutely observes that 'as the poem proceeds its tone becomes unambiguously lover-like':[44]

> Ah! anwyl chwaer, 'r wyt ti i mi,
> Fel lloer i'r lli, yn gyson;
> Dy ddilyn heb orphwyso ...

> Ah! dear sister you are to me,
> as the moon to the sea, constantly;
> following you restlessly ...[45]

> Mae miloedd eraill, sêr o fri,
> Yn gloewi y ffurfafen;
> Edmygaf hwy, ond caraf di,
> Fy Ngwener gu, fy 'Ogwen'.

> Thousands of other honoured stars,
> Glitt'ring on the horizon:
> I admire them all but I *love* you,
> My dearest Venus, my 'Ogwen'.[46]

'Ogwen' was 'the female love-object in a popular romantic ballad of the period', as Jane Aaron has noted, and thus Cranogwen, like Philips, 'places herself ... in the male lover's role'.[47] In another poem, 'To My Country', the poet pledges her life to the service of a country imagined as a bountiful, yet sometimes scorned, mother:

> Mi allaf ddiolch, gallaf, ar fy ngliniau,
> A chynnig iti fy ngwasanaeth goreu:

> ... *gan hynny, wele fi,*
> *Fy ngwlad, am dreulio 'mywyd i'th wasanaethu di*
>
> I can give my thanks, oh yes, down on my knees
> And offer you my heartfelt, best service;
> ... to acknowledge my due,
> My country, I shall spend my life in service unto you.[48]

This patriotic pledge of lifelong service to the nation imagined as a woman is again to usurp a masculine role, this time that of chivalric knight or soldier. It was a trope that surfaced repeatedly in feminist iconography in the second half of the nineteenth century.

National service: chivalry, the New Woman and home rule, c.1860–90

The relocation of romantic devotion and service from the garden arbour to the national stage seen in Cranogwen's poetry signalled a growing feminist consciousness which would develop into campaigns for women to be admitted as full citizens into education, politics and the professions. The androgynous figure of the woman-as-knight was a popular image in New Woman iconography and utopian fictions of female heroism. In Wales in particular, these civic aspirations were associated with the struggle for national autonomy as can be seen in literature, in Amy Dillwyn's *The Rebecca Rioter*, and in politics when Cymru Fydd enshrined women's rights in its home-rule agenda. This feminist imagery of the heroic knight and chivalric suitor had pronounced homoerotic undertones.

From at least the mid-nineteenth century, the love of one woman for another was frequently expressed through the image of chivalric devotion. The gender roles of knight, saint, maiden and suitor are deliberately blurred in the mid-nineteenth-century poem 'A Clever Woman' by London Welsh woman Sarah Williams (Sadie, 1838–63).[49] The speaker, whom we take to be a woman, imagines asking a series of questions to a hypothetical 'clever woman', which cleverly insinuate both the sacrifice and future glory clever women may expect. In the final stanza, the speaker kneels before an image of a specific woman, 'my lady', in the role of knight/lover, to declare her unquestioning devotion. As Catherine Brennan has remarked, there is a 'strong homoerotic charge' running through this poem:[50]

> Once I saw a clever woman
> In a picture frame;
> Alone I had my lady,
> But no question came.
> I just knelt and said 'I love you:'
> Echo knows her name.[51]

Although the poem clearly addresses the struggles of a feminist archetype – the 'odd' woman who seeks learning and intellectual fulfilment – it is personalized by the closing allusion to a name that Echo could repeat, suggesting the speaker has a particular woman in mind.

The figure of the female knight was, of course, modelled in part on Joan of Arc, the cross-dressing Christian soldier who in due course became adopted as an allegorical representation of France, thus linking the nation to an image of an androgynous feminist heroine.[52] John Everett Millais's painting of a kneeling and rather feminine Joan, nevertheless clad in the breastplate of a neo-medieval jousting knight, caught Amy Dillwyn's imagination when it was exhibited at the Royal Academy in May 1865 and was eventually given modified expression in her fiction. A genderqueer chivalry is not only repeatedly invoked in her novels but used as a way to express same-sex desire in her private diaries: 'I should like to have been a knight in the old days of chivalry & whether she cared for me or not I would never have deserted my ladye [sic] love while I lived.'[53] In her first novel, *The Rebecca Rioter* (1880), Dillwyn created in Evan Williams an unlikely cross-dressed knight, one of the rural protesters who from 1839 onwards had disguised themselves as women in order to destroy the hated tollgates and styled themselves 'Rebecca's Daughters'. Evan takes the oath '*Gwell angau na chywilydd*' (better death than shame) to fight for the poor and for Wales.[54] But in the end it is chivalric devotion to his beloved Miss Gwenllian, and his desire that he should not be shamed in her eyes, which causes Evan to sacrifice his liberty and ultimately his life. In the relationship between Evan and Gwenllian, we may read a representation of Dillwyn's passion for her own 'ladye love', Olive Talbot. Later, in *Jill* (1884), the novel most transparently concerned with the love of one woman for another, Dillwyn returns to the chivalric notion of service, transposing it onto a mistress/maid relationship. While in the sequel, *Jill and Jack* (1887), the eponymous characters compete in the performance of chivalric acts in the service of an imprisoned young maiden, Miss Morton.

Pathology, passion and pearls: portraying lesbianism c.1900–97

Contemporary reviewers of Miss Dillwyn's novels noted with approbation their focus on unconventional female characters, but by the end of the nineteenth century, such figures had become cause for suspicion. Androgynous or 'mannish' women were classified as gender inverts in scientific discourse; in the twentieth century, the invert or lesbian became a figure both more visible and more suspect. In literature, longstanding patterns of romantic friendship and schoolgirl-teacher crushes and jealousies become markers of a mildly ridiculed lesbian identity in such novels as Margiad Evans's *The Wooden Doctor* (1933) and Hilda Vaughan's *The Candle and the Light* (1954). Vaughan, like Evans, has a recurring interest in lesbian characters. A predatory lesbian in *The Curtain Rises* (1935) first educates the Welsh heroine before rejecting her in a fit of jealousy. But she remains a minor figure, a lonely, self-defeating 'type' reminiscent of the spinster, Miss Webster, in Vaughan's earlier novel *The Invader* (1928).[55] Lesbian characters appear centre stage in short stories and novels by Margiad Evans and Rhys Davies. Often these are associated with tropes of illness, deformity or other pathology, as in Evans's 'A Modest Adornment' (1948), which pivots on the neglectful death of one half of a lesbian couple, and 'The Haunted Window' (dated 1953, unpublished) in which two women are brought together by visions of illness and death.[56] The hunchback, Lizzie, in Rhys Davies's *The Black Venus* (1944) enjoys a special status because of her deformity and can thus indulge her penchant for odd clothes and express her odd desires with impunity. More sinister and sad is Davies's morbidly obsessive policewoman in 'The Romantic Policewoman' (1933), who prefigures the murderous couple in *Nobody Answered the Bell* (1971). In that novel, two women kill an inconvenient stepmother to set up home together, only for their lives to become dominated by the body rotting in a cupboard and for the cycle of murder and death to continue. A more intriguing cycle of murder and same-sex desire are at the centre of 'respectable' small-town Welsh life in *A Ram with Red Horns* (1996), when Rhonwen kills her adulterous husband only to begin a queer relationship with his mistress.[57] Indeed, the link between violence, criminality and queer sexual desire is apparent elsewhere in Rhys Davies's fiction, such as in 'The Chosen One'(1967) and 'Arfon' (1931).[58]

Ironically, at the time lesbianism became widely visible as a sexual identity, representing it in literature was often a matter of coded allusion. Kate Roberts's short story 'Nadolig' (1929, Christmas) uses codes familiar from other lesbian writing: friendship, pearls, the apparitional, the unspoken and oddness. The word 'strange' (*rhyfedd*) is repeatedly used in a story about the formation and betrayal of the 'strangest' (*rhyfeddaf*) friendship between two teachers.[59] In 'Y Trysor' (1972, The Treasure), Roberts again adopts several paradigmatic lesbian tropes, in addition to the 'treasure' of the title: a friendship that blossoms around an initial illness, a suggestively close mistress-maid relationship, the 'oddity' of the two women's fondness for mountain walks and the disapproval of Jane's family to the relationship (in part on economic grounds). Annoyed at her transference of loyalties, Jane's son tries to come between his mother and her friend by suggesting Martha might have a dubious sexual past:

> there was no knowing what her life had been when she was in England. After all, why had her master left her money in his will and a pension? Jane was able to make Wiliam look very foolish when she said it was a woman and not a man had been her employer.[60]

The jealous Wiliam may look foolish, yet at the same time the passage hints at a possible closeness between mistress and maid that Wiliam cannot see. The homoerotics of service and command between mistress and maid has been well used elsewhere, particularly in Victorian fiction as we see par excellence in Amy Dillwyn's *Jill*, and on into the twentieth century, including in Margiad Evans's *Turf or Stone*. Evans uses the motif again in 'A Modest Adornment' where Miss Plant comes across 'a little old woman, pumping' water wearing a

> big blue apron with pockets and a skull cap ... She kept saying 'The mistress is round the garden ...' I've often thought that she might have been me ... I'm sure there were only two of them living there and they both ate their meals in the kitchen together.[61]

And of course in the neo-Victorian novels *Affinity* and *Fingersmith* by Sarah Waters, the roles of servant and employer are exploited to the full in her lesbian narratives of power, disguise and duplicity.

The unsayable, or the desire to represent a *different* kind of bond, may be sublimated into the intensity of colour, light and gifts. In Kate Roberts's 'Nadolig', Olwen's sudden 'dawning' realization of Miss Davies's feelings for her (and perhaps Olwen's premonition of marriage as a ghosting of her own self) is foreshadowed by an odd transformative light in which faces have 'a kind of deathly pallor or a strange lavender colour' (*'rhoi iddynt ryw welwder angeuol neu ryw liw lafant dieithr'*);[62] lavender has a long association with lesbians (and gay men).[63] In 'Y Trysor', Jane also recalls her intense feelings for Martha through colours and light: 'Her memories interwove with the colours of the clothing of children who were playing on the beach and with the millions of pearls that danced on the sea and shone on the sand.' (*'Gweai ei hatgofion yn gymysg â lliwiau dillad y plant a chwaraeai ar y traeth ac â'r miliynau perlau a ddawnsiai ar y môr ac a ddisgleiriai ar y tywod.'*)[64] Jewels, and pearls in particular, are clitoral symbols and the exchange of jewellery, a proxy for the lover which nestles close to the beloved's body, was a favourite token of love in intimate female friendships. In Amy Dillwyn's *A Burglary, or Unconscious Influence* (1883), the object of Imogen's love, Ethel, has her jewels stolen from her bedroom by Imogen's döppelganger, a gentleman-thief masquerading as a local Welsh poacher.

As we begin to see in this discussion of lesbian 'codes', many tropes recur in texts from the late nineteenth century into the present. It is worth turning away from the chronological approach pursued thus far, to consider some of the ways in which lesbian motifs and national identity are intertwined in literature across time.

Part 3: National and sexual identities:
Welshness and same-sex desire c.1880–2014

Sexual identity was being categorized by sexologists in the same period that Welsh home rule was being pursued in cultural and political arenas in the late nineteenth century. Part three of this chapter considers how national and sexual identities are intertwined and inter-represented in short stories and novels from the late nineteenth century to post-devolution Wales. Negative and positive markers of Welshness are associated with same-sex desire, while the mysteriousness and 'otherness' of Wales is evoked by Welsh and non-Welsh writers to suggest the 'difference' of queer sexual identities, even as respectable and conventional Wales may appear as a stifling and inhospitable place.

'Strange haunting charm': music and same-sex desire

Music, which communicates on a level beyond language, is a sensuous, sometimes unsettling force associated with same-sex desire in stories by Margiad Evans and Rhys Davies. In Evans's short stories, music conveys a love that cannot be articulated. Miss Allensmore's oboe, with its 'hordes of sound', makes a strange music that even her partner fails to understand.[65] Josephine fascinates the young Arabella, in 'The Old and the Young', as she strides around in her 'gardening breeches' playing the violin with an abandon that is linked to female sexuality: 'she would be walking about the lawn in all the bright green plumage of the garden, laying, playing, the mouth, the eye, the fingers and the heavenly strings all singing'.[66] And Miss Potts's penetrating yet ghostly piano recital leaves a young girl transfixed and transformed:

> When she began to play I found no one to look at ... And my chest felt blank, not uncomfortable, but simply empty, as if I'd no breath and no need to breathe ... Miss Potts might have been thinking it to me as she played it.[67]

Music is stereotypically represented as a particular passion in Wales, 'land of song', but it is also linked to exoticism and thus to sexual availability in Rhys Davies's short story, 'The Doctor's Wife' (1931), in which Phoebe's female lover sings 'in a voice of strange haunting charm, the sentimental ballads of several nations'.[68] In this story, music not only represents same-sex desire but is connected specifically with Wales, both ancient and modern. Phoebe plays the harp. The instrument symbolizes her distance from her self-important husband: 'Phoebe's harp ... stood so aloofly against blue curtains' (137). The doctor, for his part, dislikes the music she plays, and her tastes in music and lovers are dismissed: the 'doctor thought [her music] trash: his attitude to the harp had never been very benevolent' (138). His philistine guests, representing modern industrial Wales, show similar intolerance: 'the guests always became a bit fidgety if the piece of music was too long'; they respond only to the suggestively gendered 'swollen floods of sound from male-voice choirs' (137–8). When Phoebe, who now lives with her 'friend', finally sends for her harp the doctor realizes their marriage is over.

If Phoebe's harp is a symbol of her sexuality, it is also Welsh. Described as 'ancient' it marks her as Celtic, feminine and representative of an older, more aristocratic pre-industrial Wales. Interestingly, this Celtic inheritance is also linked to the Decadents who so fascinated Davies:

> She loved her harp ... [and] had a sentimental and romantic regard for the ancient instrument. When she played for charity at concerts she always wore a white satin dress, and her long graceful arms, as she pecked at the strings, were like the necks of swans lifted to the music. She seemed to dream over the thing in impassioned poses and she liked best the languid reflections of Debussy's music. (137)

Debussy recalls the decadent literature and culture of the *fin de siècle*, while the term 'languid' suggests same-sex desire. Harp music also connects Phoebe to the ancient pagan deities, her swan-like arms evoke the sun-god represented by the swan.

Music, then, offers a mesmerizing, suggestive and even compulsive medium through which sexualities can be insinuated, and in Davies music is explicitly linked to both ancient, pagan, Celtic Wales and the homosexual decadence of *fin de siècle* Europe.

A 'queer-looking lot of women': genderqueering, cross-dressing and disguise[69]

Cross-dressing and masquerade have an important place in both Welsh history and literature, closely linked as they are to rebellion. In her novels, Amy Dillwyn represents an untamed Wales of genderqueer women, rebellious peasants and often criminal, violent, working-class figures who provide the backdrop for her representations of same-sex desire. On the surface, *The Rebecca Rioter* is a story of unrequited love between a working-class man turned outlaw and the squire's daughter (he is also involved in a homoerotic friendship with another young man, a sailor whom he has rescued in an act of kindness and anti-authoritarianism). Once we retune to read Evan as an instance of 'transvestite ventriloquism', the rough Welsh hero becomes a cross-dressed stand-in for a semi-autobiographical story of the desire of a masculine woman for an unobtainable lady.[70] This technique of using a (frequently thwarted) heterosexual romance as a substitute for same-sex desire is common, from Emily Faithfull's *Change upon Change* (1868) to novels and short stories by Willa Cather such as 'On the Gull's Road' (1908) and *A Lost Lady* (1923).[71]

Dillwyn's use of cross-dressing and alignment of same-sex desire with a working-class Welsh identity can be understood with reference to the Victorian conceptualization of gender inversion as sexual inversion (where mannish women take on the sexually active male role, seducing feminine women). Dillwyn certainly conceived of her own sexual/gender identity in masculine terms. In her fiction, cross-dressing and cross-class disguises are furthermore specifically connected to rebellion and Welshness. In *A Burglary*, Dillwyn's third novel, female masculinity is linked with a rebellious, rough, outdoor Welsh identity. Imogen is a 'wild Indian' and a 'savage' girl, dressed identically to her brother in 'rough and carelessly put on' costumes of 'Welsh flannel, corduroys, thick boots, etc'.[72] In *Jill*, cross-dressing is abandoned in favour of cross-class disguise, a theme already introduced in a criminal context in *A Burglary*. Although *Jill* is not so explicitly located in Wales, in this novel, Dillwyn develops many themes that are central to her depictions of Welshness, including the alignment of a genderqueer lower-class identity with same-sex desire.

Contemporary novelists, including Sarah Waters, have returned to similar themes of class, disguise and lesbianism in their historical fiction.[73] In Stevie Davies's historical novel, *Impassioned Clay* (1999), the rebellious Welsh Quaker, Hannah Emanuel, appears from over the border in 'brown breeches and a stained leather coat' and is mistaken for a 'lad' by the English labourer Isabel. The two women later become 'yoke-fellows' for life, but at first sight, Isabel recalls:

> I could hardly forbear to laugh at the tyke's singsong tongue, & said in scorn, 'Thart not neither, for thart a Welshie, get back home Welshie & let's be shot of thee, tha canna speak the king's English.'
>
> 'I am a maid,' she said then ...
>
> I stared & saw that she was what we call in our country a WILL-JILL, neither man nor woman, fish nor fowl – a hermaphrodite, you would say.[74]

Hannah is a liminal figure, neither Will nor Jill, male nor female. In this scene, she is told to get back across the border to Wales, and thus her gender and by extension sexual ambiguity is associated with border-crossing. This liminal space is also associated with crime. Isabel describes Hannah as 'the soft breeze that brings the thaw for outlaws & vagrants that bide in the open',[75] positioning her spiritual enlightenment and her Christian love outside civic and even domestic spaces. Hannah is brutally silenced for her transgression of gender boundaries – for giving public speeches in her lilting Welsh accent, most certainly not the 'king's English' – and eventually hung as a witch and outlaw.

Welshness is linked with queer sexuality through class, gender transgression and linguistic difference in the examples above. In another historical novel by Stevie Davies, *Awakening* (2013), similar markers – poverty, Welsh language and a queer gender identity – are arguably used to construct a poor Welsh minister as an adequate stand-in for the female lover Anna can't have. Anna, an English Baptist living in Wiltshire in the 1860s, has been bereaved of her female lover. She eventually takes as husband Will, or to give him his full name, Gwilym Anwyl (his surname, Anwyl, means 'dear'), whose soft femininity is associated with his poverty and his Welsh-speaking origins in Ceredigion. A liminal figure in several senses, who 'exists amongst the English in cumbrous translation', he is thus another queer Will-Jill.[76]

Welsh lesbian gothic

The gothic is a strong presence in anglophone Welsh writing. In her book on *Lesbian Gothic*, Paulina Palmer notes the commonplace 'utilization of Gothic imagery and motifs as a vehicle for discussing lesbian/homosexual issues'.[77] Arthur Machen's *fin de siècle* femme fatale, Helen Vaughan, in *The Great God Pan* (1894), is a lesbian monster whose border-Welsh identity and connection to Wales's ancient pagan past is essential to her construction as sexually different and racially threatening. Machen is clearly influenced by French literature, and in particular Theophile Gautier's *Mademoiselle de Maupin* (1835), which 'became the bible of the aesthetic-decadent literature', according to Lilian Faderman.[78] Gautier produces 'wild and exotic' lesbians, and Machen's Helen Vaughan is a literary descendant: an exotic stranger, with olive-coloured skin, 'of a very different type from the inhabitants of the village ... her features were very marked, and of a somewhat foreign character'.[79] Indefinably beautiful, she seduces a Welsh girl, with results too horrifying to be named in the text: 'At the beginning of the summer of 1882, Helen contracted a friendship of a peculiarly intimate character with Rachel M.' The two girls would spend the day until dusk in the woods, returning home 'languid and dreamy'. Eventually, Rachel, distressed and 'lying, half undressed, upon the bed', confesses 'a wild story' that we do not hear but which provokes in Clarke, who collects such diabolical stories, 'a paroxysm of horror. "My God!" he had exclaimed, "think, think what you are saying."'[80]

Helen Vaughan's unspeakable threat is not just her relations with women, but her ability to cross boundaries of class, gender and race. 'Gautier's lesbian',

Faderman writes, is 'a beautiful young woman who looks equally stunning when dressed as a man, flaunts her sexual nature and refuses classification in either of the two sexes (which the French much preferred to think of as being strictly discrete categories)'.[81] Helen – half woman, half devil – is at home amongst English aristocrats and in a brothel in Soho. She moves between Wales, London and South America with ease, changing her name as necessary, while in death she literally changes shape and sex: 'the firm structure of the human body that I had thought to be unchangeable, and permanent as adamant, began to melt and dissolve ... I saw the form waver from sex to sex'.[82] In *The Great God Pan*, unbridled sexual desire is linked with racial difference and Welshness, and is directly linked through pathology, criminology and racial discourses with lesbianism, as I have argued elsewhere.[83]

Yet if the monstrous lesbian vamp appears in some Welsh gothic fiction, there are rather more examples of texts that use gothic tropes – ghosts and witches in particular – to paint more nuanced and often positive pictures of rebellious, transformative, or simply tender, same-sex desire.

Welsh witches

Witches and lesbians have been connected through images of sexual excess and deviance since at least the sixteenth century, when a 'seminal treatise' on witchcraft, Johann Weyer's *De praestigiis daemonum* (On the Illusions of the Demons, 1583), included a chapter 'Concerning the sexual mingling of witches amongst themselves'.[84] In her book *Welsh Gothic*, Jane Aaron argues that the Celtic attitude to witches was different from that of other parts of Europe, with only a handful of executions in Wales during the early modern period in which thousands of women were executed in the rest of Britain and Europe. Amongst the common Welsh people, Aaron postulates

> a subversive identification with [an] older way of life, and with the natural forces of her long gone ancestor, the mother goddess, represented, the witch never was delivered up by Celtic communities for punishment to the same extent she was elsewhere. That sense of identification with an alternative world also permeates [literary] texts which celebrate the witch as heroine.[85]

Witches in Welsh literature, like lesbians making a space for themselves in heteropatriarchal societies, are directly associated with gender rebellion and challenging social hierarchies. Witches appear in attempts to 'liberat[e] the self from the patriarchal order, from its confining gender roles and the rigidity of the social systems of private property and inheritance on which it depends'.[86]

Jane Aaron identifies two types of Welsh witch, the wise woman or 'gwiddon ... translated in the dictionaries as "witch", but which includes within it the concept of knowing',[87] and the more rebellious and anti-patriarchal *gwrach*, although there is significant overlap between the two. The audacious lesbian witch Lizzie, in Rhys Davies's *The Black Venus*, is an example of the *gwiddon* type. A 'dwarfish hunchback' woman in 'clothes of scandalous colours', Lizzie defies conventions.[88] Her intimate knowledge of village affairs is achieved by her privileged crossing of gender, age and class boundaries: her 'reputed second sight was no more than an old knowledge, common in the people but going into wicked by-paths in her' (48). The novel is about Olwen's courting in bed of a series of men in an attempt to reform them and the resulting scandal whipped up by the church. Lizzie expresses her quasi-malevolent desire for Olwen throughout the novel.[89] Her pronouncement on the scandal is that the village women should send in a woman disguised as a man to teach Olwen a lesson. Indeed, she imagines herself in Olwen's bedroom: 'dress up as a man I wish I could – after her I would go' (106). She does finally get her wish in one sense, taking up residence in Olwen's household, wearing 'cabin boy's white trousers' (192).

Lizzie Pugh desires to serve Miss Olwen but also to consume her: 'Oh, there's love and there's hate your body I do, Miss Olwen! There's pleasure it would be for me to bathe you ... Curd and honey in your flesh! ... A darning needle I could rip in it and dip a piece of bread in the juice ...' (111–12). Margiad Evans's Miss Allensmore in 'A Modest Adornment' is another witch with cannibalistic tendencies. A fat black cauldron of a woman, she is partial to 'boys' sweets' and has a ravenous appetite that sees her frying chips shaped 'like talons' as her life-long partner Miss Plant lies dying.[90] Despite her unpalatable habits, Miss Allensmore is a sympathetically drawn figure, a witch in the construction of those who need to categorize and ostracize an odd woman, whose musicianship (discussed above) elevates her baser attributes.

Although Jane Aaron does not explicitly identify same-sex desire as an attribute of witches, characters such as Miss Allensmore and Lizzie Pugh, both explicitly marked as witches and lesbians (and figurative cannibals), along with the pagan Helen Vaughan, show a clear connection between various types of Welsh witch and lesbianism.

'A dead woman!' haunting apparitions

The apparition is a paradigmatic trope of lesbian writing. Ghosts are liminal, elusive yet insistent presences, and in *The Apparitional Lesbian*, Terry Castle sees the ghost as both literary signifier and interpretative metaphor. She describes the 'ghosting' of lesbians in culture and history, whereby lesbians are rendered invisible even when they are right in front of us. She also explores the way same-sex desire in literature is often suggested and simultaneously frustrated by the paradoxical idea of haunting – an elusive presence in absence.[91] Wales, with its ancient ruins and out-of-the-way cottages, has been a popular location for gothic romances and hauntings.

In an early twentieth-century short story, an intense, sudden affective bond between two women, triangulated via a third dead woman, springs up in a supremely gothic Welsh location on the edge of the Black Mountains. 'A House that Was' (1912) by Bertha Thomas, features a young American tourist who has become lost while trying to find a route across unreliable terrain.[92] Ivy Harvey stumbles upon an 'ancient looking and grey' house, whose door is opened '[b]y a dead woman! ... A corpse-thing.'[93] Between the fragile mistress of the house and Ivy an instant connection is made, mediated through the portrait of a beautiful, long-deceased sister which shines 'like a jewel in a vault' (136):

> The strangeness of it, that they two, only just met together, two with half a century and the ocean between their ages and their homes, who did not know so much as one another's name, should be discoursing thus, was unfelt by both, as though mutually hypnotised. (137)

'The Grey Ghost', as Ivy thinks of her host, is near death (and does die before the end of the story). Her decaying house is, we learn, 'heavily mortgaged' by previous generations, and thus is 'a mock heritage' for the feeble incumbent (140). Houses and matters of inheritance are recurring features in Welsh female gothic fiction and poetry where derelict, decaying or lost homes often function as symbols of the nation, as I have discussed elsewhere.[94] In this story, the house, 'the quaintest old tenement ... [w]ith the dearest old lady ghost hanging on to it', seems to signify an older Wales (or a tourist's idea of it), with its 'old oak flooring, settle, chest, and woodwork ... sawn before ever the *Mayflower* set sail' (135). With the passing of the failing woman, Ivy fears the spirit of old Wales will vanish and the house will 'be handed over to the speculative builder' (140), or perhaps to the old woman's immediate oppressor, the cruel housekeeper who is 'no native of here' (139). Thus the story evokes a romanticized lost Wales overcome by modernity, mourned through the fleeting, mysterious bond of female affection channelled through the haunting portrait of another, long-dead, woman.

Apparitions are a major presence in Margiad Evans's writing and similarly serve to bond women together, as in the short story 'Miss Potts and Music' – where memories of Miss Potts are triggered by an (imagined?) apparition. Or in 'A Modest Adornment' where Mrs Webb fantasies about Miss Plant in a series of ghostly visions, culminating in her dream of 'poor Miss Plant ... [who] seemed to quaver across the air, across the sunshine, weaving herself, as it were, *behind* the April light'.[95] In Evans's unpublished short story 'The Haunted Window', spectral visions of the future bring two women together in a kind of marriage.[96] Significantly, Evans also figures the borderland of Wales as a haunted landscape, where the brooding hills and clouds wait to reclaim lost territories.[97] The common imagery invites implicit connections between sexuality, desire and national identity.

Ghostly connections between female love, loss and home are made by Tristan Hughes in *Revenant* (2008). This haunting gothic novel plays with ideas of sexual awakening and adolescent friendships alongside ambivalence towards 'home' at a literal and national level. Del, who drowns in front of her friends, was the charismatic tomboy leader of a gang of four. She exerts a mesmerizing power in death as in life, particularly for Steph, the only other girl in the group. For the adults who have returned to Wales for a grim reunion ten years later, Del, the revenant, remains just out of reach, tantalizingly present yet unavailable, just as she was in life. Steph's erotically charged memory of chasing Del through a barn dissolves into an image of loss: 'At the top I try to grab her foot and she squirms away into a tunnel between the bales [of hay] ... Opening my eyes I find that Del has gone and my mouth is poised, slightly open, waiting, over vacated air.'[98] *Revenant* is set in a stagnating Anglesey seaside town – a place defined by zombie-like pensioners and abandoned buildings punctuating the countryside. Del is the absence at the centre of the novel, figured in large part through the deferred erotic attraction between her and Steph, but this void is also projected on to Anglesey and, by extension, Wales. Her absence is 'a patch of darkness that's congealed there ... Croeso, it says. Home.'[99]

Rebellious and passionate Celts: Welsh lesbians in English literature

As we have seen, Welshness itself is often aligned with queer sexuality, one linked to wildness, sensuality, a primitive landscape, passionate excesses and an ancient paganism, as well as oppositionality and 'difference'. These discursive constructions were not lost on writers outside Wales. In two of the most important British lesbian novels of the 1920s – Sylvia Townsend Warner's *Lolly Willowes* (1926) and Radclyffe Hall's *The Well of Loneliness* (1928) – English authors chose to make their central or supporting lesbian characters of Welsh origin. In Sylvia Townsend Warner's modernist fable of rural witches, the protagonist, Lolly Willowes, rejects her family duties and retreats to the countryside only to discover that she is a witch and, if we read the story waiting for us between the lines, a lesbian.[100] The pagan spirit that underpins her erotic and gender rebellion is aligned with an exotic lower-class primitivism and an ancestral Welsh identity. Lolly's grandfather had 'a roving and untraditional temperament' which led him beyond the pale to 'marry a Welsh lady'.[101] This 'Welsh-woman with a tall hat like Mother Shipton's who would carry her shoes to church, had secretly estranged him from his relations' (10), and Lolly inherits this disruptive streak, refusing to take her own place in the family as dutiful spinster aunt. She also inherits her grandmother's unusual pale grey 'Welsh eyes' (27), set wide apart in her dark skinned face to give her a 'rare' appearance 'too startling to be agreeable' (25). A celebration of a transgressive feminist and queer sexuality in an isolated rural retreat, Warner's novel anticipates the style and tone of some of Margiad Evans's best work in *The Old and the Young* (1948).

A milder, but no less impulsive, Welsh character becomes the lover of Stephen Gordon, the mannish invert in Radclyffe Hall's *The Well of Loneliness*. Stephen is seduced by Mary Llywellyn's 'Celtic pluck' and her 'ardent, courageous, impulsive nature', which Stephen sees in her wartime behaviour whilst the 'innocent' Mary is ignorant of her own strengths.[102] Mary is a lover of nature, the abused and the vulnerable. Moved by ancient Celtic urges, she falls in love with Stephen:

> For the Celtic soul is the stronghold of dreams, of longings come down the dim paths of the ages; and within it there dwells a vague discontent, so that it must for ever go quest-ing. And now as though drawn by some hidden attraction, as though stirred by some irresistible impulse, quite beyond the realms of her own understanding, Mary turned in all faith and all innocence to Stephen. (286)

Like Lolly, Mary possesses widely set, 'slightly oblique grey eyes' (287) and a widow's peak (a 'national failing' (336) she shares with her Welsh spaniel). An orphan from 'the wilds of Wales; an unwanted member of a none too prosperous household ... she had little education' (286). Stephen enters their relationship in the patronizing role of guardian, teacher and protector, extending the national symbolism (in this instance with England as Wales's overbearing protector) which weaves through this novel.

Part 4: Nation-building and sexuality: towards devolution

If reproductive heterosexuality was at the heart of the idea of the nineteenth-century European nation-state, as we saw in part one of this chapter, twentieth- and twenty-first-century literature concerned with the present and future of the Welsh nation engages with a more diverse range of erotic attachments and national futures.

Towards the end of the twentieth century, and as equal LGBTQ rights were embedded in policy-making in devolved Wales, a flowering of queer fiction took place. Inclusion of minor lesbian characters in novels such as Catherine Merriman's *State of Desire* (1996) was overtaken by texts that placed same-sex desire centre stage. Sarah Waters's choice of London settings for her lesbian historical novels has tended to reinforce the idea that Wales is too provincial and conservative to provide an imaginative space for lesbian identity. But at the same time as Sarah Waters was publishing her neo-Victorian lesbian fiction, Stevie Davies was writing about queer Welsh identities in her historical novel *Impassioned Clay*, while contemporary representations of same-sex desire became prominent in novels such as Davies's *Kith and Kin* (2004) and *Awakening*, Erica Wooff's *Mud Puppy* (2002), Tristan Hughes's *Revenant* and Rhian Elizabeth's *Six Pounds Eight Ounces* (2014).

The growth in post-devolution queer narratives has been read as part of 'a current desire to see differences in sexual as well as ethnic orientation more openly acknowledged in a more heterogeneous Welsh culture'.[103] While this is certainly true, the extent to which a celebration of queer sexual identity opens up new understandings of nation, thus queering the nation, or whether nation-building narratives tend to invoke a heteronormative model in accordance with the theory that nations are essentially heterosexist constructs will be discussed in the remainder of this chapter.

Post-devolution Wales: a queer nation?

In her essay on devolution fiction, Lynne Pearce considers some of the 'ways in which devolutionary politics relate to, and impact upon, our romantic desires and sexual relations'.[104] She discusses 'the reliance of *both* [imperialist centrism and marginal resistance] on heterosexist orthodoxies'.[105] Pearce argues that devolution may be 'our great *hope* in redrawing the sexual-political map of the British

Isles' since 'the experience and identity of *having been marginal* [may] enable us to rethink the negative and destructive forces of "othering" in favour of a more dialogic, though no less charged, dynamic of "us" and "them"'.[106] However, she is also aware of other possibilities, including 'the bleakest prospect' in which 'countries or regions retain a sense of themselves as threatened margins instead of relocated centres' with the result that a 'suspicion of outsiders' leads to 'prescribed' endogamy and 'continued reification of the heterosexual nuclear family'.[107] Given 'the history of the nation-state is inextricably linked to the heterosexual family', she writes, 'it is easy to doubt whether national and sexual desires *can* speak to one another in any more radical or subversive way'.[108] Given the marked increase in lesbian (and gay) narratives being published in post-devolution Wales, I want to conclude this chapter by considering Pearce's doubts about nation/alism and sexuality with reference to two novels in which lesbian characters play a central part, Fflur Dafydd's *Twenty-Thousand Saints* (2007) and Erica Wooff's *Mud Puppy*.

Twenty-Thousand Saints is set on Ynys Enlli, or Bardsey. The island is a retreat and refuge from the failed referendum of 1979 for a queer family of two women and their infant sons. They dream of creating their 'own little Wales out there' – a Welsh-speaking utopia, a new enchanted island of Gwales.[109] Claustrophobic isolation, however, leads to quasi-incestuous and possibly murderous behaviour. Yet in the present of the narrative, set in devolved Wales, the island is also a vibrant and seductive space of sexual fluidity and experimentation.[110] The novel opens with a beguiling scene of same-sex desire: 'The men were scarce that summer. The women of Bardsey Island had begun giving each other languorous looks ... it was only a matter of time before their glances and gestures sprouted hands and lips' (7). But despite what appears to be an affirmation of sexual fluidity and same-sex desire on the island, queer relationships seem not to survive beyond Bardsey. Returning to mainland Wales for the original exiles is an assertion of confidence in Wales, as the characters are committed to building a new nation for the future, but leaving the island also coincides with a restoration of heteronormative roles.

Island life brings same- and mixed-sex couples together and ultimately ends relationships that are less than honest. Leri, an 'out' lesbian, is making a documentary about Bardsey with the bisexual Greta. Their trip takes their friendship to a new level: 'Crossing the sea, seeing the island rising out of the depths in front of her, feeling Greta squeeze her hand, she [Leri] knew it could happen. Not straightaway, perhaps, but eventually' (40). But by the time they return to Cardiff, Leri's life is in freefall and their affair at an end: 'They embraced awkwardly, a mess of limbs, before Leri lifted Greta's face to hers. Greta pulled away, and Leri collapsed in a sea of bags in the middle of the road' (240). It is not that there are no lesbians on mainland Wales. Leri's arch-rival on the Welsh media scene has won a BAFTA Cymru award for her documentary on 'the Welsh-language gay scene', and there is 'the sorority of the Welsh-language-lesbians, whom they [Leri and Greta] avoided at all costs' (39). But these off-stage references notwithstanding, the plot closes down the main same-sex relationship, leaving the obsessive and deceptive Leri deservedly bereft.

The other central homoerotic plot revolves around Viv and Delyth. Prominent nationalist campaigners during the 1979 referendum, they rejected their no-voting husbands and went to live on the island in protest, taking their infant sons with them: 'They had left, together, a family' (131). Viv's unrequited attraction to Delyth is explored through memories sparked by watching Greta and Leri's caresses: 'Viv wanted to ask them if it was worth it, what they'd done, the one thing she and Delyth had never dared to do … It had seemed possible. She'd reached out a hand, without knowing where it was going. And Delyth had moved away before it landed' (182). When Delyth finally does kiss Viv, it is her last act before she kills herself. Viv reminisces:

> She wondered if Delyth knew. Whether she was right about that strange look Delyth gave her in the door that afternoon she disappeared, the 'Oh Viv' that had come at her like an apology before she had reached out and planted that one solitary kiss on her lips, that had ignited so much in Viv, a kiss that still tingled even in memory. Before Viv had even been able to lift her eyes to look at her properly, she was already climbing the mountain path, the peaks of her red and blue headscarf flapping behind her, waving goodbye. (183)

In a plot familiar from other lesbian literature, same-sex desire can only be acknowledged at the point of, or after, the death of one of the women.[111]

Heteronormativity is further re-established away from the island through the reinstatement of the mother and reproduction. Viv is restored as a mother (to Iestyn and an emblematic mother – a cultural conservator and conduit of national culture) at the end of the novel. It is a role in which she has failed on multiple counts – she has rejected her son believing he has murdered Delyth and, in a passage loaded with symbolism, actually drops a baby she is minding as she recalls the scene that convinced her of his guilt. The maternal role is not, of course, solely or necessarily heteronormative. The island of Bardsey is a community run by mothers, particularly the all-powerful matriarch Mwynwen, and as such could be seen as a feminist reimagination of nation with its traces of female saints and Celtic goddesses. Nor am I suggesting here that motherhood is distinct from lesbianism. Indeed, in an essay on post-devolution lesbian and gay writing from Scotland, Joanne Winning considers whether devolution may 'initiate a radical reconception of how its citizens might be "reproduced" or choose to "reproduce"', specifically invoking the possibility of queer families and gay and lesbian reproduction.[112] On the one hand, when she leaves the island Viv drives straight to the Senedd to take up a campaigning role in Wales, which is precisely what her beloved Delyth wished (and in an unlikely twist of the story, tried to engineer by her suicide). Yet Viv's return to the role of 'national mother' seems less an act of lesbian fidelity and rather a return to heteronormative roles: she relinquishes her jealous hold over Delyth's memory, acknowledges her tangled erotic history and repairs her relationship with her disowned son, Iestyn, who has been a rival for Delyth's sexual attention.

Yet the question of maternity and reproduction is complicated in this novel. Deian, who has lost his mother tongue and has been pronounced infertile by doctors in England, finds a new future with Mererid, a Welsh-language poet. Both he and his poet reject their existing English-speaking partners and this new Welsh-speaking pairing between Deian and Mererid is the only (hetero)sexual relationship to survive the return to mainland Wales. They should be the ideal (reproductive) couple, but for Deian's infertility. The novel ends on a positive note with Deian seeing a 'purpose, somehow, a direction ... hopeful ... that there were other ways of living on' (226), although the reproductive challenge which faces them raises questions about the future of the nation.

On the one hand, then, the island *is* Wales, figured here as a fluid space of sexual possibilities and linguistic survival, a liminal space of possibility. Yet the plot, which ends with a nationalist return to the 'real' nation, sees the evaporation of the same-sex relationships alongside the creation of a linguistically, if not biologically, idealized heterosexual couple. The liminal, queer, lesbian space of the island is left behind; queer families give way to conventional familial roles as women return to mothering and ensuring cultural continuity. Perhaps this is not surprising given the way nations are imagined through the metaphors of the heterosexual nuclear family, or a female body, and ultimately as a mother. As Lynne Pearce notes 'Not only might the emerging nation require its subjects to prioritize their national identification [over sexual or gender identity], but so might it also demand evidence of a more material commitment in the form of an explicitly *procreative* sexual politics.'[113] Reading the novel at the level of *plot*, rather than through the more complex detail of specific scenes and images which enrich the text, raises questions about the pressures on and influence of queer identities in a national/ist narrative.

A rather different kind of queer Wales is constructed in Erica Wooff's *Mud Puppy* in a narrative where the protagonist's sexual identity is firmly lesbian but national identity is open to constant rewriting. Symbolized by the fertile but shifting estuarine mud of Newport, national identity, like gender identity in the novel, is a drag act. In London, Daryl has traded on her difference, on her performance of Welshness:

> My name's Daryl. Funny name for a girl, I know. At least in London it is. Not so much in Wales, though. There are a lot of funny names in Wales. Being Welsh has become my special feature. My trademark. Being Welsh is very sexy at the moment. At least a certain type of Welsh is sexy. You know what I mean. Wacky, eccentric, slightly-exotic-in-an-arty-type-of-way sexy ... So I've played on the funny name and kept my accent lilting higher than the Brecon Beacons ... I am now Welsh with a capital W. Picture postcard Welsh. Dragons, daffodils and mountains.[114]

This performance of national identity is knowingly constructed for largely commercial ends (it's her trademark), and it is as false as the picture-postcard Wales. While her ambiguously gendered name Daryl, for instance, may seem less strange in Wales than it does in London, it is, we are told later, Anglo-Saxon and not Welsh in origin.

The novel cleverly revisits many of the concerns about the false promise of exported 'picture-postcard' culture that Ed Thomas explored in *House of America* (1988). Ani, Daryl's under-age girlfriend, dreams of American-style lofts she has seen in magazines and fantasizes about New York cop drag-acts and Manhattan clubs (even her step-father is an accomplished Elvis impersonator). Everyone believes Ani to be a consummate storyteller (read liar) and she meets a tragic end as an attempted suicide, but it transpires that while she visualizes them through an American lens, most of Ani's plans and stories are in fact located in the gay bars of Cardiff. In tribute, Daryl dresses up in Ani's bampy's [grandfather] teddy-boy outfit, suggestive of an indigenous queer glamour, to unveil her mud-sculpture of a dragon. This symbol of nation, formed out of local mud rather than the glass and metal her transatlantic corporate commissioners had expected, immediately begins to shift and recompose itself under persistent Welsh rain. Not an entirely successful novel, and one troubled by key elements of failure and morbidity which I have not discussed here, *Mud Puppy* nevertheless represents an example of a post-devolution imagining of nation that determinedly rejects heterosexist and endogamous narratives in favour of transformative, queer identities. In fact, once Daryl has returned to Wales, it is her sexual identity – her lesbianism – that is the only fixed, firm and immutable aspect of her life. National and gender identities are in constant flux.

Conclusion

What first strikes one from a survey of the field is the sheer abundance of what might be loosely termed lesbian literature from Wales: female same-sex desire is a recurring theme amongst canonical Welsh writers in both languages although one that has been largely ignored by critics. Furthermore, same-sex desire and Welshness are often 'inter-represented' – particularly via liminal spaces or marginal cultural positions – confirming a close relationship between sexuality and national identity.

Early writing about erotic friendship aligns Wales with retreat, the natural world or the garden: spaces of comparative freedom, romance and gender bending. The research parameters of this chapter – focusing as it does only on anglophone literature or writing in translation – may inflect the picture of Wales with reference to love between women: most of the early writers are incomers or, like Sadie Williams, writing about Wales from afar.

In the late nineteenth and early twentieth century, with Welsh writing in English on the rise, lesbian sexuality is even more closely connected to Welshness in a variety of ways: through images of class difference (as in Amy Dillwyn's novels) or represented through gothic or Celtic tropes, such as music, haunting and pagan witchcraft (as in short stories by Rhys Davies and Bertha Thomas). This alignment of an ex-centric national or ethnic identity (largely conceived of in racial terms of blood, ancestry and inheritance) with an underground sexual identity was adopted outside Wales in major lesbian novels by Radclyffe Hall and Sylvia Townsend Warner. The results of such use of national and sexual stereotypes can be both subversive and limiting, depending on the way in which writers adopt and adapt these tropes. Furthermore, major nineteenth- and twentieth-century Welsh writers in both languages, including Kate Roberts and

Margiad Evans, adopt paradigmatic tropes of same-sex desire that are familiar from other British, European and American writers. Thus Welsh literature in both languages both contributes to and extends the tropes of lesbian literature current in Western literature.

In the second half of the twentieth century, there is something of a dearth of new lesbian literature. There are important late works by Kate Roberts and Rhys Davies, and Emyr Humphreys includes a smattering of homoerotic attraction in his novels, but it is not until devolution that lesbian stories once more emerge in force. When they do, queer sexuality is again closely connected (in terms of plot and representation) to national identity. In place of the former rigid categories of an often racialized national identity and congenital sexuality (and binary sexual identities) is a more fluid sense of sexuality, gender and national identity. Thus, as well as drawing attention to the heterosexist foundations of the European nation, post-devolution anglophone literature about queer sexualities potentially begins to queer – to expand and complicate – national identities.

6
'Not friends / But fellows in a union that ends': Associations of Welshness and Non-heteronormativity in Edward Thomas

ANDREW WEBB

Queer, as a critical approach, aims to complicate and deconstruct received understandings of supposedly 'natural' identities. As Ardel Haefele-Thomas has defined it, queer 'supplies room for multiple, potentially polyvalent positions, conveying gender, sexuality, race, class and familial structures beyond heteronormative (and often bourgeois) social constructs'.[1] This is distinct from conventional, narrower definitions of 'queer' as an approach that reveals 'the gender specificity found in gay and lesbian theories and historiographies', and, in its breadth and ambition, reflects the way in which queer theory as a field has developed in recent years.[2] The ideal object of study, then, for a queer critical approach, is a text that can be situated 'astride the uneasy cultural boundary that separates the acceptable and familiar [identity] from the troubling and different'.[3] Operating in this shadowy space between the familiar and the different, between the normative mainstream and the non-normative other, such a text would express non-normative identity on its own terms, yet would also have a role within the mainstream culture; it would also serve, within the normative culture, 'to call the idea of the "norm" into question'.[4]

Cultural expressions of Welshness would in many ways seem to be an ideal object of study for a queer critical approach that is defined along these lines. Certainly, there are clear parallels between Welshness and queer. In broad terms, Wales has existed on the edges of British national space, its own national narratives marginalized by virtue of its incorporation into a British culture that is Anglocentric. There are numerous cultural expressions of this peripheral position, perhaps none more infamous than the early twentieth-century entry for Wales in the *Encyclopaedia Britannica*: 'For Wales, see England'. Of course, if all readers needed to do, in order to understand Wales, was 'see England', there would be no need for a 'Wales' entry in the first place. In this sense, the definition reveals an anxiety: Wales has a presence which cannot be elided – hence the need for definition in the first place. Its existence, however, poses a potential threat to the dominant Anglocentric narrative. To the editors of this very British publication, then, Wales is indistinguishable from England, and – in a publication which purports to speak for Britain – cannot define itself. As a marker of Anglocentrism within British culture at the turn of the twentieth century, this could hardly be clearer. When such strong Anglocentric norms prevail, any text that expresses Welshness in a British context challenges these assumptions. Such a text is particularly amenable to a queer critical approach: not only does it set out Welshness in its own terms, it also calls into question the dominant Anglocentric norms.

This chapter explores these parallels in the work of the London-based anglophone Welsh writer, Edward Thomas (1878–1917). It contends that his correspondence, prose and poetry register a queerness that – however brief its historical occurrence – suggests a conscious relation between two repressed aspects of Thomas's identity: that of his Welshness, and that of his non-heteronormativity. His texts show alertness to how the social, economic and military institutions of his historical moment constructed the subject in ways that limited the expression of both of these repressed aspects. Nonetheless, these texts also register the ways in which Thomas did find ways of leading a non-heteronormative existence, and they highlight the importance of writing, and in particular of collaborative male writing, in this case with the American poet Robert Frost, to the expression of non-heteronormative desire.

This work is situated within the broader critical field in that it heeds Judith Halberstam's call to map the ways in which non-heteronormativity does manage to find expression, even in societies where it is not allowed. Critics, Halberstam suggests, should become more adept 'at describing in rich detail the practices and structures that both oppose and sustain conventional forms of association, belonging and identification'.[5] In particular, she comes up with the notion of the 'queer place', the necessarily local geographical space in which non-heteronormativity may be expressed: a site of resistance to the centre which contains 'the concrete, the specific, the narrow, the empirical and even the bodily'.[6] Stories of non-heteronormativity, of sexual encounters and desires that occur in a society in which it is officially forbidden, form an area of subsequent concern for critics. John Howard has worked on this question in respect to the southern US states.[7] More recently still, Alison Donnell has identified some of the 'unruly, even uncategorizable, acts of living' that form what she terms 'Caribbean queer'.[8] Both of these writers identify what Donnell calls 'located and locally sensitive repertoires of non-heteronormativity' in historical spaces of 'insistent heteronormativity' where alternatives were supposedly impossible and strictly policed.[9]

It is important, then, to set out the supposed impossibility of homosexuality in Wales in the first and second decades of the twentieth century. Fifteen years before the end of the nineteenth century, in the same decade in which the term 'homosexuality' was first coined, a British Act of Parliament – the Labouchère Amendment to the 1885 Criminal Law Act – criminalized male homosexuality. In the years after 1895 when Oscar Wilde was imprisoned for 'gross indecency',

Britain was a place in which non-heteronormativity had been driven underground; self-censorship among writers had become prevalent, while expressions, particularly of male homosexual desire, had become coded in order to avoid prosecution. In Wales, non-heteronormativity was, if anything, even more suppressed. While the same laws applied, a strictly heterosexual Nonconformist culture predominated, and had undergone a recent revival in the first decade of the twentieth century. In the industrial areas, still growing until the 1920s, a macho, working-class heterosexuality was well established. Homosexuality, and broader expressions of non-heteronormativity, were arguably as much of an impossibility here as in the rest of Britain.

Thomas's poem 'The Other', written in December 1914, can be read as a coded expression of non-heteronormativity, in particular of repressed homosexuality. It presents a male protagonist in physical pursuit of another male in expected fulfilment of his 'desire of desire'.[10] The homoerotic nature of the relation is implied from the first stanza when the speaker emerges 'glad' from a 'forest' to find himself confronted by unknown interrogators:

> But 'twas here
> They asked me if I did not pass
> Yesterday this way? 'Not you? Queer.'
> 'Who then? and slept here?' I felt fear. (*ACP*, 40)

The use of 'queer' here is telling. Tomos Owen has suggested, as far as another London-based Welsh writer is concerned, that as early as 1894, 'queer' carried, among other meanings, early and derogatory connotations of homosexuality.[11] Such connotations are certainly suggested in this opening stanza: here, it can be read as an accusatory term, attracting aggressive questions from unnamed strangers concerning who slept where. Rhymed with 'fear', it is a label that the male speaker is keen to avoid. But while the poem in these ways carries a suggestion, both of homoeroticism and others' homophobia, it also masks any direct reference to either of these. Images like 'forest' function both in a literal sense and as metaphors for something that remains obscure. Similarly, it is never clear who 'the other' is, why he is being pursued, or even whether he represents a part of the speaker's self.

Through these images and masks, the poem engages in what Wayne Koestenbaum has described as 'double talk': the homoerotic is suggested, especially to a readership 'in the know', but then masked by metaphors that escape specific referents. The concept of 'double talk' appears in Koestenbaum's *Double Talk: The Erotics of Male Literary Collaboration*, a pioneering study of joint male authorship, acknowledged and covert. He principally considers collaborative work from the three decades after 1885, a date chosen because, as we have noted, in that year the British parliament explicitly criminalized sex between men.[12] Ten years later, the authorities used the 1885 Act to punish and silence Oscar Wilde. Over the following decades, it made literary collaboration between men in this period 'a complicated and anxiously homosocial act', one in which all writers 'were increasingly pressed to defend their friendships against imputations of homosexual feeling'.[13] Male writers whose literary endeavours with other men brought them into close relation with each other, thereby raising the fear of such 'imputations', were in a particularly difficult situation. Examining such authors' self-conscious attempts to understand or explain the process of collaboration, Koestenbaum discovers what he describes as a pattern of 'double talk': moments when writers 'rapidly patter to obscure their erotic burden, but the ambiguities of their discourse give the taboo subject some liberty to roam'.[14]

In Thomas's 'The Other', the narrator's pursuit of the other man is characterized, in elevated terms, as the search 'to kiss / Desire's self beyond control, / Desire of desire.' The man is described, moreover, as one who lived 'under a ban'. The pursuit ended one 'night' in which 'still / The roads lay as the ploughland rude, / Dark and naked on the hill.' This suggestively described location is the site at which the speaker, apparently alone, finds temporary satisfaction, a moment that involves:

> Happiness and powers
> Coming like exiles home again,
> And weaknesses quitting their bowers (*ACP*, 40)

If this is an allusion to a clandestine liaison between two men, the term 'exiles' here is also significant for it suggests an additional, national, dimension to the poem. The term echoes Thomas's description of himself as an exiled Welshman in a 1901 letter to his tutor O.M. Edwards, as a Welsh person forced by the need for work to live outside Wales, an experience common to hundreds of thousands of Welsh men and women of course.[15] Emigration, driven by the requirements of capitalist modernity, is complicated in this context by Wales's position within a Britain in which an ideology of Anglocentrism prevailed. British and even English identities were available to some who lived within Wales, to some of those who emigrated east to find work, and perhaps even more so to those people born in England to Welsh emigrants. Self-identifying as British or English often involved the subject's self-repression of his/her Welshness. This is a well-documented historical phenomenon among Welsh people keen to 'get on', represented most symbolically of course by those parents who did not pass the Welsh language on to the next generation. Thomas, the London-born son of Welsh emigrants, who described his own 'accidentally Cockney nativity' on more than one occasion, also recorded regret that his Welsh-speaking father had not passed the language on to him.[16]

The reference to 'exiles' also recalls the posthumous tribute poem of his friend, the Welsh bard, Gwili, who likens the London-based Thomas to a 'great exile priest', and to a Moses figure, the exiled leader of the Israelites, who would never reach the promised land.[17] In short, 'The Other' raises parallels between a state-suppressed non-heteronormativity and an unrealized Welshness. Both are registered as repressed aspects of the narrator's identity; writing, it seems, is a site at which these repressions may emerge.

Non-heteronormativity, male relations and unrealized Welsh nationhood are also evident in Thomas's short story 'The Patriot', published in the Cardiff-based journal, *Nationalist*, in 1909. Here, a Welsh soldier, on his deathbed in a 'foreign land', recalls a journey from London, where he was brought up in exile, back to Wales, 'the land of his desire'.[18] The story moves back and forth between the boy's stay in Wales, during which time he played with 'rough strange mountain boys', and his present predicament, surrounded by other British soldiers and their deathbed reassurances to him that he was about to die for his country (*P*, 38). The story's climax is the narrator's deathbed moment of self-realization that, as a Welshman, he was about to die for Britain, a country that was not his own. Visualizing Wales, he declares that 'the country he had been fighting for was not this' (*P*, 41). This story, probably set in the Boer War, is unusual in the distinction it establishes between the British and Welsh identities, and the point it makes about the impossibility of fighting or dying for Wales. This deathbed realization is also – crucially for my purposes – expressed in terms of male relations that did not come into actuality. No sooner has the narrator distinguished between fighting for Britain and failing to fight for Wales than he begins recalling his time in Wales, wondering 'where were those young men scattered?' (*P*, 41). An unrealized Welshness is expressed here then in terms of a thwarted homosociality, an alliance between the 'young men' of Wales that is prevented, in this case, by the British Army, an institution that builds a different set of male allegiances. The word 'scattered' is also interesting here: on the one hand, it is a biblical reference, this time to the diaspora of Jews after the sack of Jerusalem; on the other hand, it suggests the power of modernity and institutions like the British Army to break up Welsh communities, to encourage people away with the prospect of work. This is a circumstance experienced by the narrator, by Thomas's London Welsh family, and in the decade after Thomas wrote 'The Patriot', by hundreds of thousands of Welshmen and women who contributed to the war effort. With its connotations of 'scattered seed', it also suggests a wasted or misdirected fertility, echoing the narrator's own position as a soldier whose life has been wasted in fighting for a country not his own. There is a suggestion here, then, of the connection between a lived Welshness and thwarted male relations. Both are aspects of the narrator's identity that have not been realized in his lifetime. Indeed, similarly to the fires the boys start on the Welsh mountainside, the airing of these repressions is 'like the genii out of the imprisoning jar in the Arabian tales' (*P*, 41).

The metaphor of men as scattered seeds also occurs in a 1906 letter to his friend Gordon Bottomley. Here, he confesses the high hopes that he placed in his relations with other men, while also masking the homoerotic implications of such a confession:

> Certainly I have a devil in me as much as any man I ever read of. But if there are devils there are no exorcisers, tho a kind friend wrote to me lately to point out the security & sweetness of his refuge in the fat bosom of the Church. I feel sure that my salvation depends on a person & that person cannot be Helen [his wife] because she has come to resemble me too much or at least to play unconsciously the part of being like me with a skill that could make me weep. It is unlikely to be a woman because a woman is but a human being with the additional barricades of (1) sex and (2) antipathy to me – as

a rule. And as to men – here I am surrounded by schoolmasters, while in town I can but pretend to pick up the threads of ancient intercourse, a task as endless as the counting of poppy seeds or plovers in the air.[19]

The closing reference to 'poppy seeds' is linked to the slim chance of finding the right man and 'threads of ancient intercourse' acquired on his visits to London. This is an allusion to the poppies in Virgil's *Second Eclogue*, one of the flowers with which Corydon courts Alexis, and, according to Martin Taylor, one of the ancient, classical texts that, by the early years of the twentieth century, had become an accepted means of expressing homoeroticism.[20] The general confessional element is plain, but so too is the effort to disguise in allusion and metaphor his need for 'salvation' from a male figure. This should not be a surprise: given the taboo and criminal associations of homosexuality, any hint of it in this period is likely to be coded, if only to protect his reputation should the need arise. Here, Thomas's use of the term 'devil' to describe what ails him suggests its deviant, immoral character. The fact that there are 'no exorcisers' implies too that whatever the 'devil' is, it is too much a part of Thomas to be removed. It is also significant that 'devil' is associated with 'man', whereas the 'salvation' Thomas refuses – 'the fat bosom of the Church' – is associated with the feminine, a connection Thomas develops when he goes on to dismiss as 'unlikely' the possibility that his marriage to Helen might be a possible source of the rejuvenation he is searching for. Indeed, the misogyny of the phrases 'a fat bosom' and 'a woman is but a human being with the additional barricades of (1) sex and (2) antipathy to me' suggests a determined attempt to dismiss the possibility of finding salvation through a woman, and to concentrate instead on an exclusively male bond.

The motif of a non-heteronormative relation between men occurs in Thomas's correspondence too. It dominates the letters between Thomas and Robert Frost, seventy-seven of which survive, all written in a period from December 1913 to April 1917. As early as 19 May 1914, only six months after first corresponding, Thomas looks forward to the possibility of emigrating from Hampshire (where he lived with his wife Helen and their three children) to join Frost in New England:

> Today I was out from 12 till sunset bicycling to the pine country by Ascot and back. But it all fleets & one cannot lock up at evening the cake one ate during the day. There must be a world where that is done. I hope you & I will meet in it. I hardly expect it of New Hampshire more than of old.[21]

'New Hampshire' is a reference to their shared dream of making a living from farming, writing poetry and setting up a summer camp together. The hopes expressed here – that moments of heightened experience be recaptured in memory or art – seem bound up with Thomas's relation to Frost. 'New Hampshire' seems shorthand for a locality where non-heteronormative desire could be realized – one of Halberstam's 'queer places' where in Thomas's romantic words, 'you and I will meet'. The juxtaposing here of the 'old' and 'New' worlds again raises the relation between nation and sexuality. In this case, however, the text raises the possibility of a 'queer place' that lies, significantly, outside the bounds of the 'old' world.

In the same letter, Thomas's sense of the possibility of the 'queer place' is mirrored in the possibility of writing poetry. Indeed, it is in the same May 1914 letter that Thomas first moots the idea of turning to poetry: 'I wonder whether you can imagine me taking to verse. If you can I might get over the feeling that it is impossible – which at once obliges your good nature to say "I can".'[22] The possibility of Thomas 'taking to verse' is here dependent on Frost's say-so. The conception of poetry that is presented is not the act of the single author, but a tricky business of exchange, fraught with 'impossible' barriers which may be overcome only if the two men agree it 'can' be done. The very act of writing poetry becomes for Thomas an expression of non-heteronormative desire, the articulation of which is a surrogate action for the imagined time in the New World when 'you and I will meet'.

When, in December 1914, Thomas produced his first poem, it is therefore hardly surprising that he used a non-heteronormative sexual metaphor to connect himself, Frost and the 'impossible' event:

> I find myself engrossed and conscious of a possible perfection as I never was in prose ... Still, I won't begin thanking you just yet, tho if you like I will put it down now that you are the only begetter right enough ... My works come pouring in on you now. Tell me all you dare about them.[23]

When two men collaborate on a text, their work, suggests Koestenbaum, is 'an act of metaphorical sexual intercourse', while 'the text they balance between them' becomes 'the child of their sexual union'.[24] Thomas's phrase 'only begetter' invites us to see Frost as the father of their shared child – Thomas's poetry. It makes an allusion to the epigraph of the 1609 publication of Shakespeare's sonnets in which the author calls 'Mr W.H' their 'onlie begetter'. In the context of Thomas and Frost, the use of the phrase alludes daringly to the creative possibilities in two men conceiving a text together. This is poetry, jointly conceived, as the enactment of non-heteronormative desire.

There are many instances both from the poetry and the correspondence that support such a contention. In the same May 1914 letter to Frost in which he first raised the possibility of writing poetry, Thomas consciously alludes to two other non-heteronormative writers:

> And you really should start doing a book on speech and literature, or you will find me mistaking your ideas for mine and doing it myself. You can't prevent me from making use of them: I do so daily and want to begin over again with them and wring all the necks of my rhetoric – the geese. However, my *Pater* would show you I had got on to the scent already.[25]

Walter Pater, on whom Thomas had published in 1914, and who developed ideas in the 1870s that were to influence Wilde and the Aesthetic Movement of the *fin de siècle*, is a non-heteronormative writer. Paul Verlaine, the other non-heteronormative writer referred to here, coined a phrase that captured an influential new direction in French poetry – 'Prends l'éloquence et tords-lui son cou!' ('Wring the necks of rhetoric'). Thomas was to allude to the same phrase in the first line of his first poem, 'Up in the Wind', written in November of that year: 'I could wring the old thing's neck that put it there' (*ACP*, 31). While this implies Verlaine's influence on Thomas's poetry, any allusion to the French symbolist in correspondence between two male poets must also bring to mind his notoriety: certainly, the allusion to a homosexual poet who shocked Paris by having a very public affair with Arthur Rimbaud would have been clear to both Thomas and Frost.

Frost's collaboration on Thomas's poetry continued until Thomas's death. For example, on 16 March 1916, Thomas sent 'Home "Fair was the morning"' and 'Thaw', and voiced concerns that he had not yet received Frost's input into the previous batch of poems that he had sent.[26] Once British publication of his first collection had been arranged (Frost arranged the US publication), Thomas, in one of his last letters, written from France to Eleanor Farjeon on 31 January 1917, asked her to 'make sure that the dedication TO ROBERT FROST doesn't get left out'.[27] Frost's correspondence seems even more effusive. In August 1916, he confessed that:

> I have reached a point this evening where no letter to or from you will take the place of seeing you. I am simply down on the floor kicking and thrashing with resentment against everything as it is. I like nothing, neither being here with you there and so hard to talk to nor being so ineffectual at my years to help myself nor anyone else.[28]

And this, written to Helen on 27 April 1917, on hearing of Thomas's death:

> He was the bravest and best and dearest man you and I have ever known. I knew from the moment I first met him at his unhappiest that he would some day clear his mind and save his life. I have had four wonderful years with him. I know he has done all this for you: he's all yours. But you must let me cry my cry for him as if he were *almost* all mine too.[29]

The last two sentences, in particular 'he's all yours', conform to the propriety of the situation in that they confirm Helen as widow and keeper of her husband's memory. The insertion of 'you' into the first sentence performs the same function. Even so, the first line is a declaration of romantic love from one man to another, while the 'but' of the final line asserts Frost's right to 'cry for him' in opposition to Helen's possession of her late husband. The peculiar phrase 'let me cry my cry' makes Frost sound like the mistress talking to the widow. However, in a Whitmanesque sense, it also serves to make Frost's grief singularly different to that of Helen's. In contrast to the declaration that 'I have had four wonderful years with him' (which sounds like a nostalgic comment on a romantic relationship), the line 'let me cry my cry for him' is as close as Frost gets to an expression of non-heteronormativity, one that is safely posthumous.

While Thomas's letters contain many allusions to non-heteronormativity, his poetry, conceived with Frost, becomes an enactment of that desire. It too contains coded references to non-heteronormativity. Much anthologized, 'The sun used to shine while we two walked', written from an army camp in May 1916, is concerned with Thomas's memory of the time that he and Frost spent together in Ledington in the late summer of 1914. The homoerotic element is present in the idea of two men walking, like lovers, through the countryside. Indeed, Martin Taylor includes the poem in his anthology of 'lads' love poetry from the First

World War. The suggestion of romantic love between men is carefully framed as a male-male relation that is acceptable to society. First, the speaker is at pains to tell readers that the men 'cheerfully parted / Each night' (*ACP*, 122). At the end of stanza two:

> We turned from men or poetry
> To rumours of the war remote
> Only till both stood disinclined
> For aught but the yellow flavorous coat
> Of an apple wasps had undermined (*ACP*, 122)

In a public sense, the apple here captures the idea of a natural world that cannot remain uncontaminated by the war. But the apple is 'flavorous', a sensual description which suggests both its corruption and attractiveness. It is an odd description for a rotten apple, as is the term 'undermined', which suggests something that remains intact on the outside and yet corrupted on the inside. In this sense, it implies the sensual attractiveness of tasting corruption, indeed the men 'stood disinclined / For aught' else.

The image of the apple 'from core to rind' also occurs in Thomas's sonnet 'Some Eyes Condemn', written a week before 'The Sun Used to Shine'. It too employs metaphors for which specific referents are hard to identify. This non-specificity, along with other aspects of the poem – the thematic association of love with condemnation, the non-specified gender of the object of desire (indeed, 'he' is the poem's only indication of any gender) – are consistent with oblique references to non-heteronormativity (*ACP*, 121). 'Parting', written in February 1915 on the occasion of Frost's departure to the US, is another poem that could be read as a coded expression of non-heteronormativity. Its speaker tries to assuage his own sadness by recalling memories of the times he spent with the unnamed traveller. Here, the past is described as 'a strange land' where 'men of all kinds as equals range' in 'a kind of bliss ... / That naught can stir' (*ACP*, 60). Here, the phrase 'men of all kinds' linked to the idea of equality is particularly suggestive. The poem contrasts these treasured memories with the present's 'perished self [that] / lacks all blood and nerve and wit', a reference, oblique as ever, to Thomas's indecisiveness concerning whether or not to follow Frost to the US (*ACP*, 60).

But while non-heteronormativity appears as a coded, elusive presence in the texts, its actuality thwarted, the question of Welshness remains. Where are the parallels, evident as we have seen elsewhere in Thomas's work, between a suppressed non-heteronormative desire and Welshness?

A clue to the answer is evident in Frost's 'The Road Not Taken', written in April 1915. The poem supposedly alludes to Thomas's indecisiveness, a long-standing private joke between the two men. There is no explicit homoeroticism in the narrator's famous description of the choice between two paths, the poem instead employing metaphors that invite wider interpretations without specifying a particular referent. In this sense, it works in a similar way to Thomas's 'The Other'. But given the events at the time, one more specific referent is the agonizing decision Thomas faced over whether to enlist in the British Army or emigrate to the US to be with Frost.

This dilemma dominates Thomas's correspondence to Frost at the time. On 13 June 1915, Thomas wrote, unwittingly prophetically, 'I am thinking about America as my only chance (apart from Paradise). Tell me when would be the best time to begin.'[30] Five days later, he wavered, weighing the benefits of writing and farming with Frost against the fear of losing his editorial connections in London.[31] The dilemma is a re-framing of the tension discussed earlier: between non-heteronormative desire between men, and a Britishness whose institutions replace these potential unions with an enforced kind of all-male relation based on the army or economic need.[32] In his earlier work, this thwarted non-heteronormativity is associated with Thomas's position as an exiled Welshman. Here, the possible 'queer place' is no longer linked to Wales, but to spaces and people outside an insistently heteronormative Britain – whether to Frost and the woods of New Hampshire or Verlaine and Paris. These new spaces are ranged against the strictly heteronormative British institutions of the army, the press and family. When Thomas wrote to Frost to let him know that he had decided to enlist, he described the decision as 'punish[ing] myself with (other people's idea of) virtue & what a married man ought to do &c &c. And still when you wrote, of course, you didn't know it was all off just because I took to khaki.'[33] The mention of khaki sets up the familiar motif of the British Army juxtaposed against non-heteronormative desire. The reference to 'what a married man ought to do' presents heterosexuality as a societal obligation which is then placed in opposition to the subversive yet creative possibility of two men living, writing and teaching together. Likewise, the phrase 'it was all off' suggests abandoned marriage plans. Another letter, written in the same period, attempted to explain his decision:

> I believe you know that to find myself living near you & not working for editors would be better than anything I ever did & better than I dare expect. There is no one to keep me here except my mother. She might come too. But I couldn't in this present mess pack up again and be born again in New Hampshire.[34]

The prospect of being 'born again' in New Hampshire takes us right back to the May 1914 letter in which Thomas first mentions both the hope of emigrating to the US and the possibility of writing poetry. Once again, non-heteronormative desire is associated with America, while its suppression is linked to a range of institutions including family, work and the British Army. Queerness and Welshness, between which Thomas had earlier drawn such suggestive parallels, are no longer associated with each other. Indeed, ranged against the demands of enlistment in the British Army and the associated expectations of 'what a married man ought to do', non-heteronormativity is now postponed indefinitely, as is the Welshness with which it was briefly associated. However, there is one poem in which both Thomas's Welshness and his non-heteronormativity recur. In 'Home "Fair was the morning"', written post-enlistment from Hare Hall army camp in Essex, Thomas describes the forced fellowship of three soldiers on a morning walk out of the camp. One of the soldiers happens to mention 'home', a word that catches the soldiers unawares and, immediately, the 'union' of men and constituent nations on which the British Army is built begins to unravel:

> The word 'home' raised a smile in us all three,
> And one repeated it, smiling just so
> That all knew what he meant and none would say.
> Between three counties far apart that lay
> We were divided and looked strangely each
> At the other, and we knew we were not friends
> But fellows in a union that ends
> With the necessity for it, as it ought.
> Never a word was spoken, not a thought
> Was thought, of what the look meant with the word
> 'Home' as we walked and watched the sunset blurred.
> And then to me the word, only the word,
> 'Homesick', as it were playfully occurred.[35] (*ACP*, 114)

The speaker's yearning for more meaningful relations – not this group of 'fellows in a union that ends' – is the spectral presence of queerness, the non-heteronormativity that, in Thomas's writing, is consistently ranged against the kind of male allegiance offered by the British Army. The 'union' to which the three men belong can be read in its most immediate sense as the group of three soldiers, or in a more national sense as the British union. The 'homesickness', which is not resolved but suppressed by an act of collective soldierly will, is also uncannily familiar. While such feelings are often shared by all soldiers, regardless of where they come from, it has specific Welsh connotations in its association with *hiraeth*. Given the wider context of Thomas's work, and the concerns addressed in some of the poetry and prose, the longing for home is a longing for Wales.

To conclude, Thomas's poetry, prose and correspondence register a brief association between Welshness and non-heteronormativity. Both are detectable, often in coded forms which suggest their metaphorical affinity, and both are suppressed by the dominant social, economic and military institutions of British society at the time. These examples suggest that, even in societies like those of early twentieth-century Wales and Britain, in which it is supposedly impossible, non-heteronormativity does find localized moments of expression. These are registered, however obliquely, in the literary and cultural record, and especially in the field of collaborative writing.

7

Fairy-tale Drag and the Transgender Nation in Rhys Davies, Erica Wooff and Jan Morris

HUW OSBORNE

Transgender people are often granted the rights and privileges of citizenship based on the verifiability of their position on one or the other side of the gender line[1] where policing the borders of the body is simultaneously a policing of the borders of the state. As Aren Aizura argues, for most gender nonconforming bodies, citizenship requires that one ultimately decide to be either male or female. It requires

> fading back into the population (and exercising the rights of populist democracy) but also the imperative to be 'proper' in the eyes of the state: to reproduce; to find proper employment; to reorient one's 'different' body into the flow of nationalised aspiration for possessions, property, wealth.

In doing so, one sustains 'the public fiction that recognition of queerness or gender variance is gained under the aegis of universal entitlement, rather than because "difference" has remade itself as non-transgressive or non-threatening'.[2] These were precisely the stakes on 19 November 2014 when the Welsh Liberal Democrats led a debate on transgender rights in the Welsh government. The debate revealed a reassuring wide cross-party support for improving the safety, security and health of transgender people; however, it also raised questions regarding the terms by which trans experiences are incorporated into the state. In part, this involves making people living various forms of transgender lives productive members of the workforce so that they may, as Conservative MP for south Wales east, Mohammad Asghar, put it, make a 'full contribution to society and the economy'.[3] It also means systematizing the trans body so that it may be accommodated in a health care system accustomed to the treatment of gender conforming bodies. While Peter Black (Liberal Democrat south Wales west) prefaced the debate by subtly defining trans as all gender identity that 'changes or challenges traditional gender definitions', including the 'gender queer' who live within 'overlapping or blurred' gender categories, the subsequent amendments tended to make MTF and FTM transsexuals, or those, as one MP put it, 'clearly born into the wrong body', the default definition, implying that the language of the state is better equipped to dealing with clearly sexed bodies that will ultimately choose one or the other traditional gender category.[4] Similarly, the equality yet to be achieved for transgender people was contrasted with the success in LGB rights, signalled, the debate stressed, by the recent achievement of equal marriage, making conformity to heterosexual state institutions the benchmark for progress. One cannot doubt that the government debate is a positive step for the tens of thousands of transgender people living in Wales, but one must also be sensitive to the ways in which even (or perhaps especially) a progressive politics of recognition and inclusion is always just as much about preserving the default heterosexuality inherent in economic, medical and social institutions of the state.[5]

The question of 'home' for transgender people, therefore, is urgent and fraught, and this chapter proposes that being at home in one's body and one's body being at home in the nation are not easily achieved or even desirable. Rather, the queer translocation of the body across geography and gender requires a necessary loss of bodily and national coherence. Wales has rich literary resources that offer alternative ways of knowing a trans belonging, that are not necessarily granted on the terms of the state, that challenge the heterosexual terms of political citizenship, that are not predicated on success within the progressive politics of heteronormative place and time, and that exploit the inherent queerness of the Welsh nation. While I do not disparage important political progress in LGBTQ rights, these forward-looking efforts might be augmented by backward-looking uses of national materials, times and places that offer alternative ways of knowing and belonging to Wales. For the writers in this chapter, this queer undoing of the nation is achieved through myth, folklore, fairy tale and fantasy. These backward glances to both the imagined past of the nation and to childhood provide resources for being queer and living nationally while resisting forms of self and growth based on heteronormative definitions of maturity designed to promote a 'full contribution to society and the economy'. What happens if we turn away from such forms of fulfilment and contribution? Addressing this question, Rhys Davies, Jan Morris and Erica Wooff deploy transgender representation and themes in a fairy-tale drag that unbinds bodies from the heteronormative time and place of a nation that defines belonging in terms of maturity, 'success' and progress.

Fairy-tale drag

What I'm calling fairy-tale drag draws on queer theories of time, place and performativity.[6] It is conceived in notions of failure as defined by Judith Halberstam and Heather Love, and staged in terms of drag performance's repurposing of the past and nostalgia to fashion materials for queer communities that do not default into a straight logic of a political future and national past. Fairy tale and legend are replete with alternative embodiments and eccentric desires that defy the strictures of straight time. In the fairy tale, 'Repetition is favoured over sequence; fairy tale time (long, long ago) and mythic space (far, far away) form the fantastical backdrop for properly adolescent or childish or very often patently queer ways of life' outside the ordering bonds of heteronormative society.[7] This turn to childhood and what Judith Halberstam calls the 'silly archive' sidesteps success as defined in terms of maturation in heterosexual contexts: not getting married, not having children, not securing a career, not buying a house and not growing into a responsible adult are all forms of failure; however, for queers, being a failure in these terms has often been a necessity, and embracing these failures offers new possibilities for shaping life and forming communities. Speaking of failure, Halberstam writes,

> Under certain circumstances failing, losing, forgetting, unmaking, undoing, unbecoming, not knowing may in fact offer more creative, more cooperative, more surprising ways of being in the world. Failing is something that queers do and have always done exceptionally well; for queers, failure ... can stand in contrast to the grim scenarios of success that depend on 'trying and trying again.'[8]

The rewards of failure are in the escape from 'the punishing norms that discipline behaviour and manage human development with the goal of delivering us from unruly childhoods to orderly and predictable adulthoods'.[9]

Heather Love extends the uses of failure into the queer relationship to history. Like Halberstam, she argues that we need a 'politics forged in the image of exile, of refusal, even of failure', one that preserves a queer relationship to the past and that keeps faith with those failures. As she writes,

> For queers, having been branded as nonmodern or as a drag on the progress of civilization, the desire to be recognized as part of the modern social order is strong. Narratives of gay and lesbian progress inevitably recall the painful history of the homosexual's birth as one of modernity's backward children ... however, backwardness has the status of a lived reality in gay and lesbian life. Not only do many queers ... feel backward, but backwardness has been taken up as a key feature of queer culture. Camp, for instance, with its tender concern for outmoded elements of popular culture and its refusal to get over childhood pleasures and traumas, is a backward art.[10]

Heather Love calls for a queer approach that continues to be a drag on progress, to immaturely wear the campy and cast-off detritus of the queer past and to own the failures that this wilful immaturity implies. Love, therefore, like several theorists of queer time, looks for alternative temporalities that allow the formation of queer communities that do not default into heterosexual space and time. In this line of thinking, this chapter also draws on Elizabeth Freeman's 'temporal drag', which plays with both senses of the word drag: to be held back by things behind one and the queer repurposing of gendered cultural materials to expose the fabrication of all gender identities. Freeman finds herself 'emotionally compelled by the not-quite-queer-enough longing for form that turns us backward to prior moments, forward to embarrassing utopias, sideways to forms of being and belonging that seem, on the face of it, completely banal'.[11] She is interested 'in the tail end of things, willing to be bathed in the fading light of whatever has been declared useless'.[12] To do so, she examines camp anachronistic deployments of the past to find a 'different modality for living historically, or putting the past into meaningful and transformative relation with the present'.[13]

This longing for form, however, is a performative one. Linking drag to a queer relationship to the past opens up interesting possibilities for thinking the queer nation. In such terms, queer uses of fairy tale and myth are not retooled patriarchal materials but always-already queer. Fairy-tale drag exceeds and denaturalizes its formal patriarchal inheritance and undoes straight time's reproductive history in much the same way Judith Butler describes the effects of gender drag, where 'the replication of heterosexual constructs in non-heterosexual frames brings into relief the utterly constructed status of the so-called heterosexual original'.[14] In the stories of Angela Carter, for example, gender performativity and fairy tale come together in this way. Furthermore, the backward glance to folklore, fairy tale and myth reminds us that this is a temporal performativity as well. As Freeman puts it,

> drag can be seen as the act of plastering the body with outdated rather than just cross-gendered accessories, whose resurrection seems to exceed the axis of gender and begins to talk about, indeed talk back to, history. This drive to figure, along with our drive to love, survive, and mourn, is part of 'our history', or at least our way of becoming historical.[15]

In this same line of thinking, Freeman lingers on the word 'fabulous' printed on a patch of the AIDS Memorial Names Quilt, itself a symbol of fashioned community and unaccountable loss and trauma within the national space of Washington DC. She celebrates the word's ambivalent movement between queer camp exaggeration and an appeal to fantasy and imagination:

> Queers have, it is fair to say, fabricated, confabulated, told fables, and done so fabulously – in fat and thin art, and more – in the face of great pain. This is the legacy I wish to honor here, that of queers as close enough readers of one another and of dominant culture to gather up, literally, life's outtakes and waste products and bind them into beautiful but fictitious (w)holes.[16]

Davies, Morris and Wooff work in this spirit, confabulating and fabricating the nation to make it a less coherent place – a transgender place of belonging, loss and desire.

Customs houses, fairy palaces and painted drag kings

As a gay man in unsettled and constant movement for much of his life, Rhys Davies was sensitive to questions of queerness and national belonging and often figured this sensitivity in transgendered terms. In a scene edited out from the second draft of his autobiography, *Print of a Hare's Foot* (1967), he describes customs houses as fairy palaces of play and transgression:

> Customs sheds are fairy palaces to me. To this day they are halls of magic adventure. I would not have their guardians – apparently much-detested in Newhaven by travellers' [*sic*] coming into England – thrown into the harbour. I like their expert rummaging into my luggage and their wholesale suspicion of villainy in the human race. The charm of a

trip abroad would lose a Gilbert and Sullivan antic if these guardians were abolished. I always try to select the most blackguardly-looking officer for examination of my luggage. It is a joy to witness a foreign woman, especially if she is French, do her stuff for these cement-faced male hags. A customs shed at boat-time would make a good theme for a ballet.[17]

Davies transforms a place of regulation and power over the movement of bodies across national borders into a place of fantastic play and performance. He would have understood perfectly Aren Aizura's formulation of transgender bodies and geography:

> Borders – the state line, the airport, customs – are spaces where those who do not 'belong' are separated from those who do. Borders police a body's ability to signify as citizen/human rather than 'alien'. At the border, it is imperative to produce the right papers and look or act as if we belong – even, paradoxically, when we are sure that we do ... And if geographical borders cannot be divorced from the integrity of home, then equally, the boundaries between differently gendered bodies raise the spectre of not being 'at home' in one's body.[18]

In the scene above, Davies revels in pleasures derived from national and gendered categories that are established at borders where bodies are required to be coherent and documented. The examination of his luggage and, presumably, the clothing within provides a thrill of exposure under the authority of their inspection, but, by describing the guards as 'male-hags', he relocates a sexual threat within their own paranoid imperative to establish gender and national borders. In the processes, he renders those borders unstable.

This national and bodily delineation appears even more clearly elsewhere in the final published text of *Print of a Hare's Foot*, where the national and the sexual are implicated in a mutually unsettling mingling. While in Berlin, he witnesses the tail end of liberating Weimar decadence in the transgender nightclub, Eldorado:

> It was hard to know what to do with oneself in Berlin. The Eldorado night-club still functioned, like the antics in the thoroughfares around it. I had not visited it on my previous German trip. I danced with a slight, pretty girl who spoke excellent English. She had sat with her encouraging middle-aged escort at a table next to one where I and my two English male companions endeavoured to seem at home. 'You know she's a man?' one of my friends said when I returned to our table. I had half suspected it on the floor. Most of the other dancing 'women' did not need a second look. We invited our neighbours to a drink at our table. The girl, very pleased by my doubt, readily admitted to his sex and told me that he and his escort had been travelling by car all over Europe as a married pair – 'except', he said, a gruff note coming teasingly into his light voice, 'when we're arriving at a frontier. Then I go into the back of the car and change into men's clothes – it's less fussy than explaining to officials that my passport is really me. If we get our luggage examined they stare a bit at all my frocks and wigs, but they're used to everything.'[19]

Here we have Davies in his characteristic mode of travel and movement in a space of cosmopolitan variety and gender instability. Positions of national/gender identification ('I and my two English male companions') and the feelings of displacement implied by the attempt to 'seem at home' are followed by the unsettling of gender and knowledge in the statement of fact figured as a question: 'You know she's a man?' The pronouns change in the transitional sentence where 'the girl ... admitted his sex', and the language troubles the difference between sex and gender at the moment the 'married' couple appears in travel and movement across frontiers. Far from being a simple site of transcription and control, however, the national border is a location of teasing delight. The transgender girl's position is stressed by the distant '*men's* clothes' worn at the border and the more personally gender-identified '*my* frocks and wigs' in her travelling luggage. She therefore disguises herself as a man to appear like the picture on the passport, and only a closer examination of her luggage will reveal her femininity. The border guards' ability to police this frontier requires legally defined gender identities whose borders, they discover, are too porous to control.[20]

Davies likes the elusive and magical shape changers, whether they be Mr Simon in 'Wigs, Costumes, Masks' or Lizzie Pugh in *The Black Venus*,[21] or his own hare-like elusiveness in his autobiographical writing.[22] The hare, as Meic Stephens points out, is a 'highly secretive, shapeshifting creature in Welsh and English folklore', and one that served as 'a coded reference to [Davies's] own androgynous nature'.[23] One of Davies's principal shape-changing figures is Guy Aspen in the 1954 novel *The Painted King*. Based on the celebrity Welshman, Ivor Novello, the novel deals with themes that were central to Davies's career, especially inter-relationships between art, the market, public identity, Wales and the celebrity closet. For Davies, Novello would have been compelling due to the actor's specifically Welsh origins, not only because of Davies's public relationship to his Welsh persona, but also because the public discourse surrounding Novello refused to forget his Welshness, even as he became an international celebrity. In the first biography to appear following Novello's death, Novello's press manager, W. Macqueen-Pope, stresses the star's romantic Welsh origins. This man of 'good Welsh blood' and 'indomitable Welsh blood' had the 'essence of that land of Wales which gave him birth, that sturdy independence, that retention of national characteristic and language and that hardiness of spirit drawn from the mountains'.[24] Several years before Novello's death, Phyllis Bottome also opens her tribute to Novello by identifying him as a 'child of Welsh parents' from whom music 'poured', and she closes in reference to the 'passion of sympathy' in his 'Welsh heart'.[25] Similarly, while at the time of writing *The Painted King* Davies was actively downplaying his Welsh subjects, he cannot erase Novello's Welsh heritage from the novel. This is most evident in Guy Aspen's mother, Madame Annie (based on Clara Novello Davies). Madame Annie wants to take her choir to an annual eisteddfod and hails from 'the countryside where they sing for love ... Wild moors and valleys of rain [where] the people have this love of singing together'.[26] Guy's theatrical tribute to her life includes 'a concert in melodious Wales' (168). Furthermore, Guy's self-divided character, which gradually sacrifices 'a being of fact' for 'a mysterious changeling' (114) of the theatre, bears a striking resemblance to one of the descriptions from Macqueen-Pope's biography (though the Welshness is far less pronounced in Davies's portrait):

> There was David Ivor Davies, the dark-eyed handsome youth from Wales, and there was Ivor Novello, whom the public knew and adored and whom David Ivor Davies created ... It was Ivor Novello who trod the stage, who evoked the gasps of admiration ... It was Ivor Novello who made the world around him gay and who became so entirely a part of the fabric of the theatre ... In Ivor, Wales was deeply embedded. Not so much in Ivor Novello, who was or could be international, but in the boy from Cardiff with the Welsh name. The Welshman – with good yeoman stock from the very land of his fathers – that stock which had farmed, worked and sung as a Welshmen can – always triumphed over that somewhat exotic creation Ivor Novello.[27]

In the public imagination, Novello stood between the national Welsh belonging and international indeterminacy. His iconic face was variously described as Welsh, Celtic, classic, Latin and English, and he played in various national and ethnic roles, linking his sexual suggestiveness with wide racial exoticism.[28] For Macqueen-Pope, the 'dark-eyed handsome youth' of the publicity photographs is Welsh, but this is also the image that went into such widely signifying circulation, blurring into his many exotic roles. This shiftiness was part of 'making the world around him gay', and the meaning of the term 'gay' had been clear in the world of the theatre for at least two decades by the 1950s: 'like camp style generally, [the word "gay"] came to signify not secrecy, but acknowledgement of the demand for secrecy and ironic refusal of it'.[29] Macqueen-Pope characterizes Novello as both the rooted Welshman and as a camp international gay icon, whose public sexual and national legibility was founded in performative ambivalence. For Davies, therefore, Ivor Novello could well have been a figure of identification and transformation linked to his own transient queer Welsh belonging.

Significantly for this study, Novello was not only persistently reconnected with his Welsh national origins, but also associated with the fantasies and pleasures of childhood. For Macqueen-Pope, Novello 'had never grown up', and Phyllis Bottome claims that 'he was – and remains – a Peter Pan'.[30] This association of Novello with nostalgic childhood comes through in *The Painted King* as well: 'Fairyland, fairyland. She was no longer perplexed by the extraordinary success of Guy's musical shows. He really was a master magician. The vast audiences came to him for the ease of their holiday childhood' (182). Linking the national and temporal characteristics, Peter Noble's authorized biography describes him as the 'ever-young Welshman'.[31] These associations, further, began early in his career. In a 1927 article in *Picture Show*, Novello has 'a gay boyishness ... a love of art and a passion for music, a great touch of the Bohemian, a touch of the gipsy, possibly culled from his Welsh ancestry'.[32] Part of Novello's childishness is based on the supposedly infantile and indiscriminate pleasures of middle-brow popular audiences, which is dismissively linked to an exotic and childlike Welshness, but the silly nationalized romance surrounding Novello offers much for queer camp reclamation of his persona and work.[33] Michael Williams writes almost in terms of a 'temporal drag' when he suggests 'that the sense of obsolescence to Novello's oeuvre, or rather a wistful nostalgic longing (or be-longing) for the past, and an awareness of losing something undefined but nonetheless precious, has always been a self-conscious part of Novello's persona', one located in a camp exaggeration of identity and identity performance.[34] Novello is a camp figure of theatrical and performative transformation that corresponded with much of Davies's national and sexual identity and interests. *The Painted King*'s fictional reimagining of Novello presents the composer and actor as a figure of queer Welsh celebrity who drag-kinged romantic masculinity for a presumptively heterosexual mass audience, an audience with whom Davies had himself flirted in national and sexual terms.

The title itself, *The Painted King*, is highly suggestive of gender, state authority and performance. Not only is Guy revealed as having a predilection towards cross-dressing (129, 151), but the make-up signified by 'painted' implies a kind of drag excess that extends into forms of national performance as Guy draws on folklore, royalty and national romance. This is especially the case in his final play loosely based on the life of Ludwig II of Bavaria and which, for Guy, is a vehicle for exploring his sexually ambiguous public performance of fantasy masculinities: 'This show contains real enough stuff of autobiography – transformed ... The celibate prince, creating fairy-tale palaces and music and positively doomed by his beauty, both inner and outer' (225). The relationship between this inner and outer beauty is the thematic focus of much of the novel's treatment of Guy's unlocatable sexuality, and it is the source of Judith's frustration:

> For the last few years she had watched what she considered was the slow transformation of a human being into a protean denizen of the theatre, a changeling. The façade of the original youthful being remained, wonderfully well-preserved, but with every show he devised, in which he was always the central character, a real escape into the fantasy of other personalities was achieved. Interiorly the years, instead of solidifying the original being, chiselled away at its texture, piece by piece. It was death and also creation; it was magic – black magic, she sometimes thought. And no one really touched him. (99)

This observation comes to Judith as the two practise for Guy's ill-fated production of *Romeo and Juliet*, Guy taking the role of Juliet, claiming that he'll 'play Romeo better if [he] can be Juliet also, so to speak' (100). Speaking is precisely what the two are doing at this moment, working through the lines without the costumes or elaborate set designs that characterize Guy's shows. His being is altered as he steps linguistically into the feminine role, and Judith regards him as a changeling, perhaps not unlike the boy actors of the early modern stage. Near the end of the novel, when Guy's physical body approaches its final decline, Judith quotes Bosola in Webster's *The Duchess of Malfi* (a play that Davies presents in a homoerotic context in *Print of a Hare's Foot*) to stress the body's vanity and fragility, but it has the equal effect of alluding to a play in which bodies de-constitute themselves, not only in the context of dramatic staging but also in the wild perversity and fantastic (lycanthropic) change and transformation.

In the spirit of this performative transformation, the 'original being' that Judith laments was perhaps never there to be lost, as she fails to realize following an unsuccessful sexual encounter, which for Guy was nothing more than a need to understand the passions of Romeo. Judith looks at his naked and sleeping body, and it loses its meaning when shorn of Guy's changeling powers:

> At the sight of his slackened ordinary body, a strange pity filled her. There was nothing of the famous glamour there. A body of indoors pallor, commonplace of contour, the lightly blotched flesh anonymous. She felt no desire to know this body. It had no flavour of reality to her, meant nothing. And she knew then that she had proceeded with him so long a domain of fantasy that this effort toward reality tonight was almost bound to end in failure. He could only reach her through an impersonation. She had rejected it. (115)

The body's physical reality is stripped of the performance that repelled her, yet she does not desire the body shorn of that performance. It still lacks something that can only be a different performance, another 'flavour of reality', that more closely accords with her needs. Judith understands this as 'failure', but this is part of Guy's spectacular failure to settle into heteronormative connections of any kind, a childlike refusal of Judith's longing for marriage and a canopied bed.

Guy's death following the opening night of his last play finally thwarts the heterosexual desire that fuels his public persona. In his final role, the hero kills himself just before the arrival of the woman of his dreams, replicating the romantic failures of all Guy's plays in which he remains unattached to preserve the celebrity idol's image as an object of desire. This echoes the themes of his plays which exploit fleeting moments of pleasure rather than romantic continuity. As Penny Farfan writes of Noel Coward's plays, they offer the 'antithesis of comedy's traditional underlying emphasis on the future through its narrative drive toward heterosexual marriage, fertility, reproduction, and social continuity'.[35] Guy's plays are the same, and his beautifully romantic death off stage on the opening night of his final show prefigures his actual death in his dressing room after the performance, his final disappearance into a role.

In Novello's mercurial Welsh-international camp queer celebrity, Davies found a figure whose experience and public persona reflected much of his own work with his identity. Indeed, it reflects much of Davies's playfulness with his past, his queer undoing and redoing of the factual record of his life. As Davies wrote in a 1958 piece for the 'Our Contributors' series in *Wales* magazine,

> The blankness of the page waiting for notes about myself is more dismaying than page 1 of a projected new book. Temptations for exhibitionism! So much to conceal, evade, touch-up! Stolid facts such as 'Born 1903 in Blaenclydach, Rhondda', where I lived for eighteen years, seem to be unnecessary.[36]

Here, he sounds much like his Guy Aspen speaking of his final play in which he does not use biographical figures 'in a realistic way', preferring only 'the idea of them' (195), and one may argue that the uses to which Guy put King Ludwig II are the same as the uses to which Davies put Ivor Novello. This fellow Welshman artist found himself in a similar kind of circulation, and was often anxious about the gendered associations of his consumption in the literary market. More broadly, when seen in light of Davies's many cross-dressing and border-crossing figures, Novello/Aspen may be read as one of Wales's most famous drag kings performing camp masculinities that are both repeatedly linked to and yet operating in excess of his Welsh origins.

Welsh drag(on)s: trans space and time in Erica Wooff's Mud Puppy

Drag performance is also at the heart of Erica Wooff's *Mud Puppy* (2004), which further complicates the relationships between bodies, place and belonging through a transgender incoherence and failure that drags the nation into a queer past of myth and fairy tale. *Mud Puppy* is set in Newport and told by two queer narrators who have conflicted relationships with their Welsh homes. The novel begins with Daryl's homecoming from London following a failed art exhibit, and she returns to Newport nine years after discovering that her mother had not in fact died in a car accident, as her father had told her, but had committed suicide. Her connection to home in Wales is broken by her Welsh-speaking mother's dismissal, through suicide, of the family's future. Her alternative queer self is constructed in terms of London's metropolitan anglophone cosmopolitanism, where she capitalizes on a chic trendy Welshness that never really touches her personal Welsh past. Returning to the family home and the childhood bedroom, she is thrown back into her past, the Welsh language, the memories of her mother and her mother's fairy tales. Shortly after her arrival, she is also thrown into a present desire for the 17-year-old Ani. The younger Ani is equally unable to identify with her Welsh home, and lives in a dream world longing for a future life in New York. Her fantasy revolves around Carlos, a transgender man from New York (via Ohio) who initiates Ani into the world of drag kinging that she had previously associated with her stepfather's Elvis tribute performances. As with Daryl, her disconnection from her Welsh reality is also a temporal dislocation, as the narratives of her fantasies repeat the same scenes with increasingly surreal differences.

Carlos is at the heart of the novel's national drag. Echoing Davies's border guards, he is a policeman who first appears in uniform policing the movement of queer characters. Early in the novel, he pulls Ani over one night as she drives to Newport from a night at the clubs in Cardiff. He is not immediately identified as transgender, and this ambiguity blurs the sexual, gendered and national categories at play:

> I could hardly believe it when I heard him. This guy was straight out of some movie. He even had an American accent. America by way of Pontypridd probably, but it still sounded good on him. I mean the guy was a complete poser, right? There we were in the centre of Cardiff at two-thirty in the morning and he's acting like he's in an episode of *NYPD Blue*. You had to laugh. But at the same time you couldn't help admiring him. I mean he did it so well. He was ... he was a real dude. There's no other word for it. This guy was a real dude.[37]

Although Ani is, at this moment, unaware that the performance is as much a gendered one as it is a national one, the two are conflated: the pose of 'doing' the American cop so well has made him a 'real dude' and drawn cross-dressing into the national frame. As with Davies's drag subversion of the border guard, the site of gender incoherence has now shifted to the figure of uniformed authority, finally and unequivocally exposing the excess of the heterosexual policing of national/sexual/gendered categories.

To digress for a moment, Frank Vickery stages a similar playfulness and policing in *Drag Factor* (1994), a play about two parents, Ruby and Griff, sitting in a hospital and coming to terms with the revelation that their son, Nigel, is a gay drag queen. As the play is almost entirely a dialogue between the ostensibly straight couple, it, like the recent Welsh government debate, negotiates difference from within the borders set by institutions of medicine, marriage and family. To emphasize that this regulation is mapped onto bodies moving in and across places and communities, both parents work in occupations that involve regulating sites of movement and travel. The mother/wife, Ruby, is a lollipop lady, and the father/husband, Griff, is a British Rail Guard. Ruby's compassionate insistence on supporting her son is couched in her repeated insistence that that's 'what mothers are for'.[38] In this way, she appeals to a biological determinism that is consistent with Griff's counter position that he cannot accept queerness in his 'own flesh and blood' (135). Both speak from within the framework of heterosexual and familial control of bodies within their larger Rhondda community (represented by Ruby and Griff's social life at the club). Ultimately, however, the gender coherence of the play collapses under its own weight. Nigel never appears, but he animates the discussion between Griff and Ruby.[39] What has been absent is not simply Nigel and his sexuality, but a queerness that has always been there: in Griff's past in an impromptu drag performance of his own; and in Griff's old friend who, Griff is forced to acknowledge, harboured a secret love for him. The 'drag factor' of the play, it turns out, is not Nigel's alone; his cross-gender performance is only the most overt instance of it. Indeed, one cannot ignore the fact that both parents appear before the audience in uniform. As with Davies's border guards, the boundaries of this south Wales community are mapped onto bodies that were always operating in excess of local and national codes of gender and sexuality, an excess revealed in the transgender possibility of the drag queen child (like Novello/Aspen) who has refused to grow up in the proper way.

Carlos is also marked by productive absences that deny the supposed presence of gender categories. Not only is Carlos's ostensibly original femininity absent in his first description, he is never defined in terms of a prior or original femininity that has been left behind. Later in the novel, Ani asks for Carlos's 'real name', his 'girl's name', imagining something embarrassing and Welshy, like Angharad, but Carlos does not oblige, maintaining his gender and national incoherence.[40] When Ani sees Carlos perform, she experiences this indeterminacy first hand: 'With the lights down and the make-up you can't really tell. I mean, you can tell it's an act. But what you can't tell for sure is whether it's a "she" being a "he", or just a "he" camping it up' (84).

Carlos's drag performances may be understood in temporal terms as well. To begin with, his absent original femininity and the incoherence it sustains resists, on the one hand, a chrononormative logic that locates the essential femininity prior to the subsequent masculine 'pose', or, on the other hand, the previously unhomely body before the achievement of the more fittingly masculine home. Similarly, Carlos's drag performance, like all drag performance, draws its materials from the past. He shifts from NYPD cop, to Elvis Presley, to Tom Jones, to 'New York Dandy, in a three-piece suit and cravat' (88), playing within incongruous forms of nostalgic masculinity. In doing so, he preserves and repurposes the past to the communal needs of a queer present. As Freeman puts it, queer camp performance 'is a mode of archiving, in that it lovingly, sadistically, even masochistically brings back dominant culture's junk and displays the performer's fierce attachment to it'.[41] Drag is a kind of 'feeling backward', as Heather Love would call it: it is a 'tender concern for outmoded elements of popular culture',[42] and it is equally evident in Ani's drag, which is assembled from her grandfather's clothes, a refashioning of the clothes of her fathers in a queer context.

This temporal drag is part of the novel's general assault on time's designs on Daryl and Ani, both of whom live in their childhood rooms and indulge in escape fantasies that trouble the 'realness' of the homes to which they struggle to belong or escape. This is evident in Ani's flights of fancy that increasingly blur the setting and unravel the narrative development. While her disordered narrative represents a form of mental illness, perhaps schizophrenia, it is simultaneously a response to a life that allows few options for those living outside straight time. Her fantasy world is consistent with Daryl's celebration of fairy tale as a corrective to the limitations of history. Daryl's memories of her mother offer her access to an alternative fairy-tale Welsh past drawn from the iconography of Welsh myth and folklore but transformed into a Welsh legend that plays with gendered and national borders:

> There was a time when the women of Wales wore wings. Sounds bizarre, I know, like some fairy tale souped up to comply with a feminist agenda. But there was no political separatism involved, the skies were open to everyone. It was just that the majority of men weren't interested in flying. They were way too busy, off fighting the marauding English. (71)

Daryl draws attention to a kind of campy 'souped up'[43] deployment of fairy story, emphasizing the denaturalizing excess of this repurposed personal and national past. As the story continues, we learn that the women learned to fly from dragons and fashioned wings to fly on the thermals created by dragon breath. Eventually, the jealous and neglected men banded together and slew all of the dragons. The tale begins by resisting an antagonistic gender binary while exposing the patriarchal nation's preoccupation with the national border, a line that the transformed winged women may easily fly above and over. Not surprisingly, Daryl's desire for Ani slips into this queer Welsh flight of fantasy:

> I thought I'd closed my eyes and wished for a magic sprite, a celestial being, then opened them again and, flying out of the darkness, I'd seen bright copper hair framing a puckish face. Blue-rimmed eyes, pale cheeks. And underneath, a mouth as wide as a river. (76)

Like the women of Wales, Ani is imagined as a celestial figure of flight, flame and magical transformation. Her puckish face suggests her transgender ambiguity in the same way that Daryl's mother's fairy tale is indifferent to boundary and separation, while the river imagery (which recurs throughout the novel) paradoxically invokes division and movement. In all, Daryl's childhood stories blur the time and place of the nation that she had left for London, and they are fashioned from a fairy-tale national drag around the childish, elfin, gender-ambiguous and drag-kinging Ani who lives in a transitive dream world of Newport/Cardiff/New York.

The mythic and fairy-tale figure of the dragon is central to the novel's concern with transformative refashioning in the Welsh search for home. This is particularly evident in the titular mud puppy that has baffled biological science by turning up on the saltwater shores of Newport and, in defiance of evolutionary history, suddenly started breathing air. The children who first find the mud puppy see it as a dragon and name it Idris, and Daryl, following their childish fantasy, regards it as a 'creature of fables and legends' (63) that confirms that 'dragons can come back to Wales' (117). In this biological curiosity, the national fairy-tale transformations shift into the indeterminacy of a natural body that defies scientific classification and the supposedly irrevocable dictates of anatomy. For Daryl, the mud puppy undoes biological determinism, making sudden non-sequential change an unruly and insurgent condition of biological existence:

> Evolution. From the latin – *volvere*, to roll. *E*-volution. *Un*-roll. But who said the unrolling had to always be in the same direction or in a straight line? ...
>
> The biological environment of our planet is patchy to say the least. Different modes of life are required for different habitats and sometimes, shock horror, the habitats become so different so suddenly that a species has to transform itself pretty bloody quickly, and not over the generations as some experts would have us believe. Sometimes the change happens overnight. (116)

What's key here is the almost wilful breaking, *un*-rolling, of time's slow evolutionary progress across generations (in a 'straight line', no less) in order to make places habitable. The unrolling of generations and the passing on of traits and habits feed a heterosexual-biological reproductive time that the mythic dragon/mudpuppy has blithely defied by physically transforming itself in a single generation. In a novel so deeply implicated in queer desire and transgender indeterminacy, one cannot ignore the possibilities where anatomy is not destiny. Halberstam, referring to the work of transgender theoretical ecologist Joan Roughgarden, contends that such spontaneous transformations 'break with Darwinian readings of animal behaviour that have coded human values like competition, restraint, and physical superiority into interpretations of eclectic and diverse animal behaviours'.[44] When these animals fail to keep time with the triumphalist narratives of biological science, they upset biology and its inevitably gendered categories. *Mud Puppy*'s turn to Welsh myth and fairy tale in the mother's stories is part of a radical denial of the historical and biological mapping of heterosexual national place and time onto bodies.

The novel ends by bringing together art, myth, transformation and transgender ambiguity in one denaturalizing performance of place. Dressed in Ani's grandfather's clothes, Daryl unveils the sculpture that is meant to memorialize the joined commercial destinies of New Jersey and Newport, placing this peripheral Welsh city on the inter/national map. Instead of revealing a sculpture 'that will last forever' and make 'people remember' one, 'even after [one is] dead' (75–6) – as Ani had described Daryl's earlier work in sculpture – she unveils a 'solid, six-hundred pound, grey-green-brown dragon, shaped out of untreated river mud and supported underneath by a crude wooden frame' (276). As the rain falls, the sculpture dissolves:

> I stand perfectly still and watch the rain wash everything away. All my work, breaking down the form, the time and space. Until all you can see is mud. Mud is all there is. Mud of the highest quality. Newport comes tops in the mud department. Rivulets of mud. Nature in abundance.
>
> Running and rolling into a world of constant movement, change. A world without boundaries and borders, rules or controls. (277)

Along with rivers and bridges, the mud is a recurring and ambiguous symbol of place in the novel, one that offers a shifting belonging to the land. It is, to begin with, part of the novel's long temporal perspective in the form of evolution, naturalism and archaeology:

> Mud is a long-term preservative. Down there, down on the flatland, the marshes with their high acidity, low temperature and absence of oxygen have become repositories of past life over thousands of years. Bodies, clothing, tools, even pollen grains preserved in bogs can reveal to us now something of human life over two thousand years ago. (19)

This preservative power, however, is balanced by its intrinsic shiftiness and excessiveness. When Daryl sees 'nature in abundance', it is nature exceeding itself, nature as art, unrolling and denaturalizing a connection to home previously understood primarily in terms of her relationships to her parents. In this great moment of failure and anti-exhibit, Daryl, dressed in Ani's drag-past and watching her mother's ephemeral dragon dissolve back into the ancient earth, finds a home. This home does not appeal to a transnational metropolitan queerness of London or New York, nor does it locate a queer place within the chrononormative history of Wales. Rather, it is fashioned from anachronistic and outmoded materials of the past to evade the nation's claims upon the borders of bodies first announced by the apparition of Carlos's transgender incoherence. It makes its place in the magically denaturalized trans bodies of a nation that cannot map its borders in terms of gender.

Jan Morris and the mythic trans/nation

These questions of transgender belonging and Wales are complicated by Jan Morris, who, one may justly argue, is committed to narratives of gendered and national coherence. Her identification with Wales is romantically nationalistic and at times smacks of colonial exoticism, she is fairly content within gender binarism, and her treatment of gay men in *Conundrum* replicates the demands of straight time. On this last point, she explains that the 'truth and pathos of [the gay male] condition seemed to [her] exemplified by their childlessness'.[45] After the deaths of a devoted gay couple, she pronounces that 'A marriage as loyal as marriage could be had ended sterile and uncreative: and if the two of them had lived into old age their lives, I fear, would have proved progressively more sterile still, the emptiness creeping in, the fullness retreating.'[46] The single factor of the child is the only abiding criteria for success and maturity. Outside straight time, they fall into non-being. Despite these problems with Morris's views on gender, sexuality and nation, I am not prepared to dismiss her queer experience of Wales, and prefer to see in her somewhat kitsch turn to Welsh myth and folklore a transsexual destabilization of the place and time of the nation. Her queer embodiment in the physical landscape of Wales and her mythic sense of the Welsh past converge in a fairy-tale drag that accommodates a transgender Welshness.

Morris disrupts gendered and geographical borders as she describes her position as a small boy looking east to the Mendip Hills of her mother's English heritage and looking west to the Welsh mountains and the land of her father.[47] Katie Gramich has written on Welsh border writing by men, noting that the Welsh/English border is as much a border between gender, language, culture, time and religion as it is a border between nations, and the national divide is inseparable from these intersecting identifications.[48] The gendered nature of the border space, usually constructed in terms of a feminized Wales and masculinized England, makes the border space a site of sexual intercourse, both intimate and violent, and a potentially meaningful one for the homosexual or queer writer.[49] The seemingly whole identities in the national core are the product of the work done at the boundaries, which are 'places of continual interaction and interchange between self and Other, the native and the foreign'.[50] In Morris's gendering of her split national self, she equates her sexual journey with her national one, and *Conundrum* may be read as almost as much a narrative of choosing a Welsh home as it is of choosing a female sex. However, the gendered boundaries of this 'home' are more ambiguous than this formulation might suggest. As James Morris changes into a *woman* while finding a home in the land of her *father*, Wales itself becomes a transgendered site of crossing. In *The Matter of Wales*, Morris refers to the 'quandaries of the Anglo-Welshman' as a 'traumatic split of the emotions which can leave the sensitive man divided not only in his loyalties, but in his personality'.[51] Morris refers to the Welsh*man*, but, as Gramich and others argue, the trauma of this national split partly derives from the colonial power imbalance manifest in the misogynistic feminization of Wales. Morris's memoir complicates this gender/national binary by adopting her father's homeland and her English mother's sex, healing over (yet preserving the scars of) this national split through her transsexual and affective connection to Wales.

The bodily connection to place is explicit in several passages in *Conundrum*, where Morris sits ambiguously between mobility and belonging. She writes early on that all her life she has 'felt in places, in landscapes as in cities, an allure that seems to [her] almost sexual, purer but no less exciting than the sexuality of the body'.[52] Significantly, this feeling is associated with many places, because her transsexual experience is a borderless one predicated on mobility and change. Richard Phillips has linked Morris's transsexuality to her relationship to places and travel: always in motion, she occupies the '[i]n between places, and on the road (or aircraft, or other form of travel), Morris recovers in-between spaces of ... gendered subjectivity'.[53] At the same time, Morris displays a great deal of rootedness, and this love of mobility and change is paradoxically located in Wales, which is a place of local yet shifting possibility.

These comparisons of feelings for places to romantic and bodily excitements echo the close relationship between her body and her home. Indeed, she defines the 'matter of Wales' as a tension between a hard unyielding materiality and a responsive and bodily feeling. Writing of the Welsh landscape, she tells us that the 'substance of Welsh nature is largely rock', and while there is much on top of this substance, 'the real thing, the dominant, is hard, bare, grey and stony'.[54] But it is also a sensuous place, a place of the body and of affect: 'This means that the truest Welsh places offer experiences as much tactile as visual, for everywhere there are stones that seem to invite your stroking, your rolling, your sitting upon' (15). These stones take on the qualities of the bodies that touch them, for they are often 'warm to the touch ... unguent, yielding objects', and when a farmer picks up a stone, 'the two of them are flesh and blood' as he holds the stone 'like a baby' (15). While she defaults into a reproductive father-child relationship, this yielding bodily landscape speaks of and to a transsexual belonging. Morris's own bodily transformation is affected, we shall see, through her connection to the land; her sex was transformed to conform to her gender, making her body matter in the matter of Wales. That Morris is concerned with what she calls the 'matter of Wales' is especially telling, in that the materiality of the land, like the materiality of the body for Judith Butler, is not prior to the ways in which it comes into meaning but inseparable from them, as sex is inseparable from gender. From this assumption arises Morris's distrust of rationalist discourses, be they historical or geological, and their claims on ontology and the boundaries of the real. Morris's matter, like Butler's, is as much about the ways the land comes to matter, the way one *does* Wales in order to materialize it into a meaningful place. So while Wales is most often the home of her transsexual self, it is a place of paradoxical transbelonging somewhere between past and present, male and female, home and movement, being and doing.

As with Wooff, this transsexual destabilization of the 'matter of Wales' replaces historical and scientific ways of knowing the time and place of the nation with the ahistorical transformations of myth and fairy tale. For Morris, Wales is a magical place at odds with efforts to materialize it in fixed geographical or historical terms. It is

> at once lost and still to come – a vision of another country almost, somewhere beyond time and even geography, which has remained ever since a distillation of history and imagination, poetry and hard fact, landscape and aspiration, and which we may call, in the absence of any more exact definition, the Matter of Wales. (4)

Further, in placing Owain Glyndŵr as the mythical refrain for the book, she resists '[h]ard-headed historians' who are 'too late', for '[l]egend is far stronger than academic analysis' (5). *The Matter of Wales: Epic Views of a Small Country*, whose title encodes physical place (matter) and time (epic), is inhabited by anachronistic mythical and magical forms of knowing. Glyndŵr re-appears as the narrative moves into the future, increasingly out of joint with time. In the process, this figure of masculine and paternal national heroism becomes a queer hero who undoes history with the transformative and counter-temporal affect of legend. Indeed, for Morris, part of Glyndŵr's power is in his disappearance from history (5) and his mercurial fusing with other figures (like Arthur). Further, while he is seen as intrinsic and original, he is also a figure of heroic failure who opposes the fixed materiality of place and being: 'That he achieved nothing material in the end is only apposite, for if there is one constant to the Welsh feel of things it is a sense of might-have-been, tinged sometimes with despair' (5) – and does this not sound like an apt description of queer history? He fails in a national narrative defined in terms of *place* and *time* (nothing *material* in *the end*), but there is an ambiguity, both bodily and emotional, in the affective 'feel of things' in the imagined past-future of the 'could have been'.

Glyndŵr's mythic counter time is echoed in the many fairy tales that disrupt the historical, topographical, social and cultural surveys of *The Matter of Wales*. The tales sit within the larger historical inheritance of the book, occasionally revising hard-headed history and science with national stories that refuse easy categorization. She prefers the strange indeterminacy, 'part conundrum, part hyperbole', of ancient Welsh stories which mirror the Welsh language with their 'mutations and transpositions' (128). Before describing the Welsh fauna of horses, dogs, pigs and sheep, Morris lingers on mythic and folkloric 'creatures not visible to all eyes' in this 'land of chimerea', including the dragon, the 'ultimate chimera' and 'national creature of Wales' (28). Tales of creatures (literally created beings, like the gender re-assigned body) of multiple and unpredictable shapes that defy biological category form the backdrop to the studies that follow. When Morris begins to describe the goat, therefore, it makes perfect sense that the section begins with 'Once upon a time' (38) and continues to recount the story of a goatherd chasing a shapeshifting goat whom he refuses to wed. When the angry goat king kicks him down the mountain, he finds that fifty years have passed, and his adventure through shapeshifting desires has knocked him out of the normal course of time. This chimerical fairy-tale Wales of uncertainty, change and mutation consistently troubles the coherence of the national narrative. And these tales are part of what Morris sees as 'the slyness, the queerness tamed by convention and brought to a not-quite-absolute concord' (127) in Welsh art.[55] This sly slippage between queerness and convention describes gender drag performance as well, and the importance of this fairy-tale drag to Morris herself is evident in the book's closing pages in which she describes a Wales of inbetweenness always 'on the brink' (424). She presents herself as the embodiment of not just the present Wales but all 'the once-and-future' Wales. The words are grand, Whitmanesque, Romantic and problematically transhistorical, but at the same time, they demonstrate a chimerical and transgendered national past:

> The peasants are me, the miners, Rebecca's horsemen, are me, Pantycelyn and Anne Griffiths, the princes and their ladies, the bards, the priests – I am Owain himself, and

the divine Dafydd, and Nest, and Hywel Dda, and before them too I inhabited the ancient mysteries of stone and seer – myth-maker, shape-changer, there I go! (425)

The cross-dressing Rebecca rioters introduce two listed phrases that hold male and female figures as single units, and then the passage moves on to a diverse collection of male and female figures ending in the shape-changing potential of a Welsh embodiment on the brink of many borders.

And this brings us to the scene in *Conundrum* for which those familiar with Morris's writing have been waiting. At the height of Morris's transsexual transformation just before surgical reassignment, she returns to Wales for the summer and figures it as a landscape of mystery and magical transformation:

> Sometimes, though, on fine summer days, I made a pilgrimage to a little lake I knew high in the mountains called the Glyders, in North Wales. There I could bathe alone ... The silence was absolute. There I would take my clothes off, and all alone in that high world stand for a moment like a figure of mythology, monstrous or divine, like nobody else in those mountains had ever seen: and when, gently wading through the reeds, and feeling the icy water rise past my loins to my trembling breasts, I fell into the pool's embrace, sometimes I thought the fable might well end there, as it would in the best Welsh fairy tales. (105)

Here is the chimerical transgender creature dressed in the Welsh past of myth and legend. Morris's physical transformation across the borders of gender takes shape through repurposed Welsh fairy-tale imagery. She cites an archive of the mythic past, anachronistically placing herself in a queered national belonging. This national belonging is neither the 'ordinary English woman' nor the 'pan-sexual Middle East' exoticism identified by Marjorie Garber.[56] The particularly Welsh registers of Morris's sexual transformation are completely absent from Garber's discussion. Indeed, Garber dismisses Wales – though she does not directly mention it – within a generalized reference to Morris's 'exotic, magical ... middle stage of [her] journey'.[57] In reducing the journey to an English/Middle Eastern Orientalist othering enacted through the transsexual body, Garber ignores Wales's colonial relationship with England and the gendering of the Welsh/English national border, the Anglo-Welsh 'traumatic-split' as Morris calls it in *The Matter of Wales*. Morris's appeal here to Welsh fairy tale and myth is more than just a generalized magical exoticism. This moment of atemporal inbetweenness recalls the animal and sexual transformations of the Mabinogion and undoes the gendered national body. In this way, I resist readings of *Conundrum* that end with the homecoming to the female body; one may instead suppose that the story 'might well end here, as it would in the best Welsh fairy tales'. Indeed, when one reads the autobiography against the grain of straight time's insistence on regulated movement between states – biological or political – perhaps one *must* stop here where narrative, national and bodily coherence dissolves.

For Morris, Wales is the borderless transgendered space of queer possibility. The legally and medically credentialed Morris prior to her final surgical transition begins 'living almost entirely as a woman' but returns to 'epicene ambiguity at home in Wales'.[58] Even the fully transitioned Morris finds her Welsh community mostly indifferent to her 'moment of metamorphosis', a description that, against the narrative insistence on her final bodily destination, returns us to the mythic atemporal inbetweenness in the lake of the Glyders.[59] And it is the magic of metamorphosis at the moment of crossing that matters most, as we see in another act of crossing from *The Matter of Wales* when Morris describes riding across the Newport Transporter Bridge, one of the bridges featured (though rather less magically) in *Mud Puppy*:

> Crossing it is rather like experiencing a page of Jules Verne, or perhaps the Mabinogion. You drive your car onto its platform to be greeted by a functionary in a captain's cap, who presently disappears up a ladder into his cabin, a merry pavilion with a steeply pinnacled roof, painted blue with a bobble on top. A bell rings, the platform shudders a little, and off you glide silently high across the water. It is an eerie sensation. It is half like being in a ship, and half like being in the basket of a balloon: and since in fact not much traffic uses it nowadays, it possesses also a remote sensation of fantasy, as if you are all alone in the world with that faery captain in his gazebo, riding the wild Welsh winds above the wasteland of the docks.[60]

This outdated bridge, finally, is the pre-eminent site of a nostalgic fairy-tale drag of national belonging. Here is a moment of crossing (not at the national border, but a crossing nonetheless) that takes up Davies's characterization of customs houses as 'fairy palaces'. Morris devotes a whole section to bridges as important symbols of the Welsh past, for the 'imagery of bridges was ancient, linking Life and Death, the Known and the Unknown. Their symbolism was potent – bridges marked frontiers in Wales, bridges linked traditions, or separated dialects, and it was on bridges that agreements were made'.[61] Here is the transgender site of separation and agreement, of past and present, of stasis and motion, riding, perhaps like the fairy-tale women of Daryl's childhood, 'high on the Welsh winds'. Yes, there are risks to this turn to myth and a fairy-tale world of national belonging, but in their queer contexts, these scenes and stories of national belonging offer a performative and drag repurposing of nation. They may be dismissed as trivial and childish and perhaps, like the fabulous plays of Ivor Novello, they fail to enact any 'real-world' influence, but they are the best alternative fantasies for undoing the repressive fantasies of gendered and national belonging. As fairy-tale drag, they appeal, to repeat Freeman, to 'the not-quite-queer-enough longing for form that turns us backward to prior moments, forward to embarrassing utopias, sideways to forms of being and belonging'.[62]

Part 3
Building Queer Wales Post-Devolution

8

Lesbian Motherhood in the South Wales Valleys: A Narrative Exploration

ALYS EINION

I write this as a self-confessed lesbian and mother, brought up in the Cynon Valley in south Wales. I own this orientation and make no apology for it but, instead, use this acknowledgement of my own subjectivity to contextualize the discussion and analysis in this chapter. Lesbians were largely invisible in my childhood and adolescence, and lesbian parents unheard of. Developing my own lesbian identity in such a dramatically heteronormative space engendered a distinct sense of self as other, that is, an identity distinct from that of my peers and that of my culture and family. As such, my lesbianism set me apart from my community. At the same time, my lesbian parenthood appeared to set me apart from others in the lesbian community, such that I and my partner occupied a space outside 'community' and isolated from social support and normative social networks. We could not engage in family and community as parents without a lesbian identity, and within lesbian spaces without a parental identity. In 2001, I wrote and presented a paper entitled 'Lesbian Mothers of Sons and the Rejections of Separatism', after finding that in the newly emerging online social spaces occupied by lesbians, lesbian parents and especially mothers of sons were challenged in many ways. Separatist lesbians rejected me as the mother of a male, and in local social spaces, bringing my son into a lesbian space was seen as disruptive and unwelcome. This prompted my interest in understanding the nature of community for lesbians who are parents, a status that is both mutually exclusive and socially exclusive. Condemned as a 'breeder' by my gay peers, and as a sexual deviant by straight society, I negotiated a lonely road littered with doubts, challenges and uncertainties, with no guide and no road map other than an intellectual understanding of the social and political constructs of heteronormativity, sexism and patriarchy which defined my external landscape.

This chapter draws on narratives gained informally over a period of ten years, recounting the experience of lesbian parenting in a specific sociocultural context. I write as both insider and outsider, as an insider who was always alien in her own context, and as a woman who left that context for many years before returning to her home valley as a lesbian parent. There are advantages to this insider perspective, not the least of which is a critical understanding of the lived experience of lesbian parenting, providing a comparative mirror to the theoretical analysis of challenges facing lesbian mothers in south Wales. Acknowledging the fundamental theoretical constructs of identity formation has allowed me to explore the self-revealed narratives of the lives of a small group of lesbian mothers for whom motherhood and sexuality remain uncomfortable bedfellows.[1]

The analytical approach chosen focuses purely on the larger narratives of these women's lives, exploring not simply the statements of experience but the ways in which each narrator emplaces herself within the story-context of her life. In adopting a narrative approach, I have attempted to follow what Andreea Ritivoi describes as 'narrative as an epistemic and social transaction' which provides evidence of and is the product of 'the social nature of the "storied self"'.[2] I draw on Strawson's theories around the narrated self and identity to argue that the women whose stories inspire this chapter can be identified as diachronic, conceiving of themselves and their life experiences in narrative terms.[3] These stories were not told once, in an isolated incident within a research context, but told and re-told within the same or similar social contexts over a period of time, restated, re-evaluated and re-contextualized each time as the narrators sought to both explicate their experiences and validate them in the context of their own sense of self in time and place. Thus, they can be viewed as what Stephanie Taylor describes as situated constructions, 'the biography produced by a speaker within a particular interaction' but narratives that have been refined and given form through multiple retellings which confer identity on the speaker and create the 'lesbian mother' that they define for themselves.[4] As Kraus states, 'the author of a self-story must be seen as a person with many selves, constantly trying to reorganise ... herself into a provisional unity'.[5] I also acknowledge the fundamentals of Symbolic Interactionism, which argues that identity is formed and re-formed through interaction with others who influence and contribute to the renegotiation of identity.[6] It is not my aim to deconstruct these narratives, but instead to recount them and explore them within a theoretical and critical context as a means of elucidating the experiences of a socially and culturally unique group of women whose stories deserve to be heard and understood. Thus, this chapter first contains a summary of the stories, and then moves onto an exploration of three identified narrative motifs: identity, community and the loss script. It concludes with a discussion of lesbian motherhood as an evolutionary identity.

The stories – a summary

Andie was a single lesbian parent of her son, who returned home to the valleys to try to access social and family support when she found herself no longer able to work. Her son was four months old when she returned, and she was then joined by Jane, who moved in five months later. Andie's familial support evaporated rapidly once her lesbian identity became obvious – once she was in a relationship with another woman. Andie and Jane experienced homophobia from Andie's family – with some close relatives expressing clearly that their son would be 'damaged' by being brought up by two women – and from local communities. After five years of verbal abuse, vandalism and threats, they left the valleys to live in Cardiff.

Kim was a self-identified bisexual woman who had returned to the valleys after an abusive marriage. She identified herself as 'preferring women' but her complex gender and sexual identity meant that she also had sex with men. Kim had five children, the youngest of whom was twelve at the time of our acquaintance. Kim's identity as a bisexual parent was masked by her continuing public appearance with male partners, enabling her to integrate a little more easily into valley life but leaving her divorced from any kind of lesbian community. Kim had four sons and one daughter, and felt strongly that her intimate relationships with women had nothing to do with her family. She was not 'out' to anyone, including her own children.

Charley was a 47-year-old mother of two adult boys, who had been married for thirteen years before coming out as a lesbian. Charley's experiences were mediated by her occupying a social space within a small, tight-knit and somewhat insular village community, and her experiences as a lesbian parent were affected by the cultural dimensions of that community. 'I was married 13 years, my sons were still in school. It wasn't easy, but I didn't have no hassle.' Charley was well known within her community and had a reputation as being a 'tough' girl ('hard' in valleys parlance). She was known to be fiercely protective of her family but was deeply entrenched in valleys culture. The expectation was that she would move out of home and have a family of her own as soon as she was old enough. This was the script of life for the working-class valleys woman, a typical narrative arc relegating individuals into characteristic roles with a heavy weight of inevitability, and Charley remained fully conscious of this.

For Charley, this script was defined by the culture of her home valley, a former mining community now specified as an Objective 1 area due to the high index of deprivation and unemployment.[7] As a working-class young woman, she moved from school into employment, first in a shop and then a factory, only stopping work once she married and had children. Lesbian parenthood happened by default, through a relationship with another woman with an older teenage/young adult son whilst Charley's children were still in school, and through a second, shorter relationship with a younger woman with a child in primary school. For Charley, motherhood came first, but her exploration of her lesbian identity was not slowed or marred by 'coming out' as a parent. The key features of Charley's experience have been the continuing inclusion in her local community and social spaces, and it seems from her accounts that parenting children within those spaces granted her access to 'normative' family spaces and events in many circumstances. Simply put, she knows almost everyone in her community and is well known and respected. Despite this, she also experienced negativity from her family. One example is that of her parents: 'They hated my husband, thought he was a waste of space', she says. 'But once I was with Terry, suddenly it was oh, poor Keith, he's such a good father. Butter wouldn't melt. I think they have a better relationship with him than with me.' She refers here to the sympathy displayed for a man whose wife leaves him for another woman.

For Charley, there was never any question of her keeping her children: 'They're my kids. I brought them up. Keith, he had nothing to do with it.' Both of her previous partners, Terry and Diana, were mothers who had children in heterosexual relationships before entering into lesbian relationships. Terry's son was brought up by a relative once Terry engaged in a full-time relationship with another woman, and Terry allowed this. Subsequently, her relationship with her son was always problematic.

Dawn had two children with her husband, but fell in love with Maz quite suddenly. Maz invited her away for a weekend, and Dawn never returned home. Her husband and family fought her for custody of her children, and won, leaving Dawn estranged from her family and with a difficult relationship with her children. As a lesbian, Dawn was left at a disadvantage in terms of the battle for custody, and her lifestyle was called into account during this time: 'I lost my children because I was a lesbian. I chose happiness over my children' (Dawn). The fact that Dawn's marriage had been abusive and that there were good reasons for her wishing to leave beyond the fact that she had found a female partner did not signify. She believed that it was the culture of the valleys that resulted in her losing her children. When she spoke of them, and of their loss, the pain and anguish remained fresh and clear, even though many years had passed.

Mel was also aged forty-seven. Mel followed the same script, marrying young and having three children. When she came out as a lesbian six months after Charley, she experienced a number of challenges and also left the family to live as a lesbian, but maintained a relationship with her children. She is now a grandmother and very involved with her grandchildren. Her partner, Julie, from Cardiff, separated from the father of her two children to be with Mel. Her older child chose to live with her father, and her son agreed to live with her, but spends every weekend with his father. As a result of this, Julie's life pattern shows a marked delineation between her life as a parent (lived Monday to Friday) and her life as a lesbian (lived on weekends). Mel and Julie also exemplify the challenges of lesbian step-family construction in which the formation of a new family identity must take place, necessitating disclosure and negotiation of new family boundaries.[8]

These summaries represent narratives that have been told repeatedly, pertaining to the experiences of these lesbians as mothers. That their motherhood identity was formed and expressed long before their lesbian identity in most cases is something to be considered in the following discussion, through exploration of three emergent motifs: namely identity, community and the loss script.

Motif 1: identity

The narratives that were told and retold over the time of my acquaintance with these women represent a form of self-identity construction, in which these women revisit their experiences as mothers and as lesbians and create a meaningful narrative shape that both explicates and justifies their current position. I do not argue against the legitimacy of their stories – far from it – but instead posit that by creating these stories over time, these women have themselves engaged in an act of reflexive analysis that has defined their roles within their own (hi)stories. My aim here is to simply re-present these stories for a wider audience. Thus, we can see the characterization of lesbian parent as a negotiation of self in context, but specific to a common value system or ideology, that of the culture of the south Wales valleys.

The shape of each narrative is understandably self-referential, and the core feature of the narratives, with self as narrator, is that of emergent identity referred to through repeated tropes of the lesbian self. Identity as a lesbian is problematic, as it is a construct of both social and personal spaces and one which aligns itself with specific external identities of 'lesbian'. It can be described as something which is collectively experienced or ascribed through, for example, activist groups or association with a specific social network.[9] Gorman-Murray et al. discuss belonging as something with multiple layers, and something inevitably 'partial'.[10] For example, in my first experiences of coming out, lesbianism was firmly associated with political activism, with campaigning for LGB rights, and was associated with membership of feminist lesbian organizations. The social dimension of lesbianism was secondary to this, which is hardly surprising since the majority of lesbian socializing I experienced in my late teens was political. As such, claiming a lesbian identity was a political act and something which necessitated me leaving south Wales for a large English city. But for other lesbian mothers in south Wales, lesbian identity seems to have been primarily a sexual and personal identity, entirely dependent on emergent or manifest attraction to another woman, and the ability to act upon that attraction and engage in a lesbian relationship, having little to do with political activism. Equating this identity with that of family, with lesbian self as parent, seems particularly challenging as the sexual lesbian trope does not equate with the maternal motif.

The concept of sexual identity can appear to manifestly oppose a motherhood identity, particularly for lesbians.[11] It is not unknown for motherhood and sexuality to be perceived as mutually exclusive. Indeed, work on perceptions of motherhood identifies a split between female sexuality and the ideal of the perfect mother.[12] This is more problematic for lesbian families in which sexuality becomes the defining feature of maternal identity[13] and, I would argue, the reason for challenges to personal identity. What we can see is that there is an inherent social construction of the lesbian woman as immoral.[14] Lesbianism is viewed as 'a stigmatized characteristic'.[15] In her analysis, Jane Rule relates this to the persistence of Judaeo-Christian social constructions in which homosexuality is condemned as unnatural, resulting in a persistent sense of lesbianism as being something akin to criminal or bestial behaviour.[16] (Certainly, I have experienced this attitude in heteronormative spaces, where it has been assumed that I would engage in other immoral or questionable behaviour because I am a lesbian and therefore morally corrupt.) Whether these particular perceptions are geographically defined is a question that can be asked in relation to these women's narratives.

In this south Wales context, lesbian identity and coming out is associated with the threat of loss of community, including 'the rejection or lack of involvement from the lesbian mothers' family of origin'.[17] Research in other contexts identifies the ways in which lesbians 'create' family for themselves, affected by their social context and their wider family networks.[18] The women I have met viewed the challenges they faced as part of their process of coming out as inevitable results of their choices, including 'actual and fear of losses such as child custody, jobs, friendships and family approval; and living in a neighbourhood ... where the existence of their family form is negated'.[19] Certainly, the concept of identity for older lesbian mothers in south Wales seems strongly entrenched in lesbianism as an adjunct to motherhood, secondary to the mothering role, until such time as the children are old enough to afford their mothers the freedom to engage in a lesbian social life. Charley recalls this trend: 'I always went out, but it wasn't until I met Terry that I ever went on the gay scene. The kids were that bit older, I could leave them with their father.' Finding a lesbian identity for these women therefore meant sacrificing something of their maternal identity. As Kim put it, 'With my kids, I was a mother. I could only be a lesbian away from them.' The concept of lesbian identity as separate from maternal identity may be in part due to the way that heterosexuality can be seen as a political and social force within Welsh society, such that heterosexuality is the default position, and lesbianism, as deviance, occurs outside motherhood because motherhood is a product of heterosexuality. So for some of the women in these stories, their self-construction as lesbians involved a separation from their maternal identities. This could be related in part to internalized homophobia, a negative self-concept caused by the direction of negative social perceptions and meanings towards the self.[20] As such, self-concept as mother excluded performative lesbianism.

For some women, this involved absent motherhood. As Dawn said, 'I had to leave my kids. It was the hardest decision of my life, but I had to do it.' This concept of absent motherhood is something that seems to resonate in the older lesbians of south Wales, who, unlike those entering into parenthood since the changes in the law in 2005, faced challenges from family in relation to custody and access to their children, or who even made the decision themselves that their children would be better off in 'normative' spaces with, for example, the availability of male role models.[21] It seems that for many, the script of lesbianism excluded motherhood and this performative script was made manifest in their lives and in their choices. Certainly, this is true for Kim who never 'came out' as a bisexual to her family or to her children. However, with the evolution of social norms being more inclusive of lesbian, gay and bisexual parenting, supported by changes in the law, it might be that in future such a division in identities will become less obvious.

Motif 2: community

The largest theme for lesbians in the south Wales valleys who feature in this discussion relates to community, inclusion and exclusion. Belonging to or being part of a community is, according to Yuval-Davis, about the 'politics of belonging'.[22] This relates to social context, the personal and familial experience, and emotional connections.[23] The nature of this South Wales community is particularly important, as it occupies a space neither rural nor urban, but uniquely physically and socially located, and has a unique history. The history of the miner's strike is deeply ingrained in these communities, and social identification with the history of the valley is a key to inclusion.[24] Thus, the first challenge to inclusion is the adoption of an identity that sets the individual as 'other' or outsider.

As Andie stated, 'I knew from the moment I accepted being a lesbian that I would leave. I spent three years planning to leave. I could see no place for myself here. I still don't believe that I came back. I don't know why I expected it to be different.' Andie experienced extreme social isolation and marginalization, and after four years of what was deemed by the police as 'neighbourhood abuse' she and Jane and their 5-year-old son moved to Cardiff expressly to live in a more inclusive community. Unfortunately, their social isolation continued, such that lesbian identity and social life remained divorced from parental identity and social life, although the abuse never recurred: 'We never went out as lesbians, just as parents. And even then, at school events, there was always that feeling of being "the lesbians". If you mentioned something, like you had seen a film, or were reading a book, the other parents, especially the fathers, would assume it was something sexual' (Andie). Jones et al. discuss marginalization and belonging in rural landscapes,[25] and similarly, in this paper, inclusion and exclusion are largely dependent on social networks, although here these are more likely to be pre-existing social networks (predominantly familial). Jones et al. state that 'connectivity can be understood as the ways in which individuals identify and connect themselves with others and the ways in which this may be filtered by aspects of their age and sexuality'.[26] This is certainly the case for Andie and Jane, and for Dawn and Maz. Dawn moved away from the valleys to Cardiff to be with Maz, but it seemed that she had to make the choice between her relationship and her identity as a lesbian, and her family and local community. That she chose lesbianism over her children compounded her isolation. Charley, who lived in the same community all of her life, experienced some distancing of some family acquaintances, but retained a full sense of 'belonging'. Thus, for some, lesbianism brought an entirely different characterization of self in context, defined by inclusion versus exclusion, whilst for others identity shift did not mean a lack of access to community.

To extend this notion to that of lesbian community shows the continuing rift between lesbian motherhood and social inclusion. Andie and Jane tried to access lesbian community support when their child was small, finding social isolation an increasing strain on them personally, and as a family. However, taking their child to lesbian spaces resulted in specific challenges, where they were made to feel that their child was unwelcome:

> We were at a lesbian social event, for networking, and our son was playing with a book that made train noises. This was a monthly thing, and we were poor, you know, and the petrol to get there – it was in Swansea – was a big deal. But we felt like we needed it, we needed to be around lesbians, to make some friends. There was a playroom there, a cold and dark room with a few toys, but the socialising was all happening in the main room. Someone complained about the noise our son was making, asked us to take him in the playroom. So we were faced with the choice – one of us could stay and be with the other women, our so-called community, while the other sat and played with our son, alone, in a cold room. We felt bad, we felt rejected, unwanted, because we were parents. We got the message that the group was for lesbians, not for lesbians with children. So we stopped going. We could sit alone in a room playing with our son at home. (Andie)

In these narratives, lesbianism was placed as an adjunct to motherhood whilst the children were still of school age, with varying degrees of ownership of lesbian identity. For these mothers, some experienced what Bos et al. describe as 'minority stress' in both heteronormative and lesbian spaces.[27] Shifts in social trends, however, have increased the ability of such women to access 'lesbian' spaces within the gay scene in Cardiff, but a sense of community is derived from lesbians per se, not lesbian parents.

Yet for the most part, community for these women was experienced as a strong link to local family and friends. This might reflect the particular nature of the social context in which these women experienced motherhood and lesbianism. Charles and Davies highlight prior research which identifies particular parameters of Welsh community, referring to this as 'a set of locally meaningful social relationships and mutual responsibilities that also informed a broader Welsh cultural identity'.[28] This is an interesting dichotomy. In a research review on sexual orientation by Mitchell et al., factors that increased the likelihood of people holding discriminatory attitudes towards lesbian, gay and bisexual people included social class, preference for area in which to live and where one lives.[29] Lower educational attainment and not living in an area rich in sociocultural diversity were also cited as resulting in prejudicial attitudes.[30] All the narratives make some reference to the limited social consciousness of their context, and related this to poor education, but not all experienced homophobia: 'I never had any issues . . . that doesn't mean people haven't had any, or said anything . . . but they're ignorant, they don't know any better' (Charley). Considering this from a narrative perspective, the location of the self as protagonist in each narrative sets these women apart from their context. There is evidence in each story of self versus other, with the defining characteristic of difference being their lesbianism. However, it is not easy to pinpoint why this might be even when the women involved considered that they remained part of their community. As mothers they considered themselves included within that community for the most part (with one notable exception) but their lesbianism existed outside that community of family.

Motif 3: the loss script

The women in this chapter experienced varying degrees of separation from their family context as lesbians – either losing the extended family network of support and inclusion (to varying degrees) and/or losing or compromising their relationship with their children. As such, it is possible to argue that these narratives represent a loss script, a script that equates one choice with the loss of another choice, an either-or status which eliminates true choice. That choice in women's lives is restricted is not news. But it is interesting to note that for some of these valleys women, the choice to leave their children was apparently viewed as inevitable by many of them and, to a certain degree, based on their own belief that their children would be better off remaining within the context of the 'family' even as they, as newly fledged lesbians, stepped outside that context: 'I know that Mel, Dawn and Maz, they thought their children would be better off with their fathers, staying with their fathers' (Charley).

The internalization of heteronormative assumptions about the 'proper' sphere for bringing up children is evident here, and can also be critiqued as an extension of the critique of the limitations of social conventions of motherhood. Some illumination might be shed on this by other researchers, particularly those utilizing a feminist perspective to critique the status of motherhood within the domain of lesbian identity. For example, Julie Thompson states that the 'rhetorics of gender and sexuality function … to convince women that our "natural" duty is to reproduce … within the context of legal marriage'.[31] Much like the discourses and experiences discussed in Adrienne Rich's compulsory heterosexuality, the inevitability of women's reproductive outputs has remained, for these women, the defining script of their lives, until such time as they embrace a form of deviance inherent in choosing to live as lesbians.[32] So, for many of these women, the choice to be true to their personal identity has been at the cost of their relationship with family, friends and, most tragically, their relationship with their children. Thompson discusses the paradox of a heteronormative social context which states that lesbians cannot be mothers, but where the other choice is a lesbian social context which states that women with children are not real lesbians.[33]

Radical shifts in the UK justice system have brought about a change in the visibility and acceptability of lesbian parents, but the emphasis in current social discourse is on lesbians who choose to become parents in the context of a lesbian relationship. The women whose stories are represented here are those who seem to bear the stigmata and scars of a previous existence as 'quasi-heterosexual' women who were able to experience motherhood and family life in a normative context, but experienced loss, pain and personal damage once they chose to embrace their lesbian identity. This loss is the inevitable result of the 'ideological pressures for women to bear children [which] exist on a day to day level'.[34]

Thompson describes this as the oxymoron of the term 'lesbian mother', returning us to the concept that lesbianism with its arguably morally questionable focus on sex and sexuality is the antithesis of concepts of the selfless, nurturing mother.[35] It could therefore be argued that these women have internalized this dichotomy, and it has therefore defined the choices they have made throughout their lives. Andie, for example, reflects on her choices and still wonders whether she made the right ones for her child:

> I knew it would be difficult. But looking back over the last fifteen years, he has suffered more than I have. I've cried so many times about what he had to go through. When he was small, the other parents in his primary school wouldn't let the kids play with him outside of school. He would cry, 'Mum, why can't I go round Carl's house, why can't I play with Carl?' It broke my heart to see him so sad, and to see him blaming himself. And even though I know it's not my fault – it's the ignorance of those other parents – I still blame myself. I could have lied, I could have hidden my sexuality, raised him as a single parent and not chosen to be in a relationship, and he would never have known a lifetime of homophobia.

This concept of lesbian motherhood as something 'illegitimate' as suggested by Thompson seems manifest in the stories of these women within this context.[36] Andie experiences a 'loss script' because she mourns the 'normal' childhood her son could have had if she had not chosen to live with her partner and raise him in a lesbian family; Dawn retains a haunted look as she speaks of losing her children with continuing grief; Mel's jaw tightens when she speaks of her children and the tumult of the period in her life when she accepted her lesbian identity. This loss of the ideal is felt in a very real way by women forever divorced from the social world in which they grew and bore children, and the crushingly unavoidable fact of their continuing separation from their own perception of motherhood as defined by the valleys culture in which they themselves grew into women.

It is possible here to relate to what Rich describes as 'two strands: motherhood as experience, one possible and profound experience for women, and motherhood as enforced identity and as political institution'.[37] These women, few of whom profess to be feminists or activists in the recognized sense, are confirming this standpoint in the ways in which they relate their own mothering experiences, locating themselves in two divergent roles. That such roles can (and should) be complementary does not signify in the narrative arcs they create. The act of 'coming out' or of performative lesbianism, acting on their feelings by having lesbian relationships and owning a lesbian identity is the signifying feature of their personal narratives, the turning point, the epiphany, the causal element in the plot that they have retrospectively created to make sense of their experiences in the dichotomous, confusing space between mother and lesbian.

Lewin describes this dichotomy but from the opposite perspective, that of the lesbian who chose motherhood and rejected the limitations that lesbianism might place on her in relation to her capacity to bear children.[38] She describes a woman who used the process of becoming a mother to construct her identity as both, rather than either/or. For her, there is no loss script because she integrated lesbianism and motherhood, showing that there is not an inevitable division between the two aspects of identity. Similarly, I do not wish to paint an entirely negative picture here, because the very fact of the creation of these oral narratives, of women repeatedly utilizing the process of informal storytelling to define and generate their lesbian/maternal identity in commonly occupied, informal social spaces shows that they have renegotiated the terms of their self-identification. All of the women here retain positive relationships with their children now, especially as the children have grown up and established homes of their own. Some of them are grandmothers with a great deal of involvement with their grandchildren, and all have relationships with their families to a greater or lesser extent. 'I don't get any hassle. I still say hello, everyone says hello, no bother. I still talk to my ex-husband, his family, all my friends' (Charley).

Charley is a good example of the ability to combine her maternal and her lesbian identities. Charley remains fully integrated in her local community, with a wide and extensive network of friends and family with whom she has regular positive contact. She has not lost anything by 'coming out'. She argues that this is because she was always a rebel who 'takes no nonsense' and can 'look after herself', something respected in valleys culture. As such, hers is the paradoxical narrative in this collection, because she mostly continues to occupy the same position within her community as a lesbian parent as she did when she was within the boundaries of a heterosexual marriage. She is the exception that proves the rule. Yet even she, like her peers, experiences a sense of loss of social legitimacy. When recounting her stories, creating 'a pattern in experience', Charley, like the others, recounts a before and after, where expressing, owning or acting upon their lesbian identity changed their lives forever, featuring varying degrees of loss.[39]

Conclusion: lesbian motherhood as an evolutionary identity

This discussion contains a brief snapshot and exploration of the life narratives of a small group of women within a specific, and unique, social context, at one point in time. It illuminates these women's experiences and perspectives, and highlights challenges faced by lesbians living across the boundaries of convention and social legitimacy. It also illustrates how they have constructed narratives to assimilate their changing identities and the losses associated with the social and personal stigma of being a lesbian parent, and integrated their parenting identity as a parallel identity to their lesbian identity. They are lesbians who are also mothers, or mothers who are also lesbians. They are women who transgress the boundaries of social convention through the most conventional act of womanhood, and despite many challenges, find legitimacy, self-belief and validation as lesbians and as mothers.

Whilst Thompson proposes lesbian motherhood as a kind of hybrid identity, in this analysis, I would propose that for these women, lesbian motherhood is an evolutionary identity, in which the hybridity grows beyond the discord and dissonance of maternal/lesbian identity experienced during the childhoods of their offspring, into a more reciprocal relationship between adult children and their mothers and between self and community.[40] As such, lesbian identities as mothers must also evolve, both within the context of the heritable ideologies of social contexts such as the south Wales valleys, and the changing wider ideological and social constructs of a pluralistic society which nevertheless continues to struggle with the heteronormative imperative and the ongoing patriarchal drive to control every aspect of motherhood.

This chapter attempts to share some of the stories of lesbian parents within Wales in a critical and thoughtful manner. That such an experience is changing must be acknowledged and, indeed, these stories may be only a stage in an evolutionary journey of lesbian becoming, in which the old boundaries defining lesbian/mother become meaningless. As Sheena Wilson states, 'versions of motherhood condoned by patriarchy limit and contain women's potentialities, often denying our subjectivity as thinking, acting, becoming women who exceed our roles as mothers'.[41] In this case, it is evident that regardless of the perceived 'cost' in terms of legitimacy within the maternal role, valleys women can successfully negotiate the process of becoming that signifies their journeys as lesbians who are mothers, transgressing the boundaries of culture and creating new realities that acknowledge the strength of their history and culture whilst rejecting their limitations. The version of the motherhood narrative created by these women sees the self as mother distinct from the self as lesbian, as both the hero and the villain of the story, occupying a paradoxical narrative space in which they are both victim and perpetrator of their own particular challenges. Yet each finds their way through to a place of surety, retaining relationships with children and family to varying degrees, amid the pathos of loss and frequent isolation. These are stories of triumph. I can only hope that those beginning this journey now and in the future experience fewer or different challenges within the vibrant and unique communities of the south Wales valleys.

9
Living in Fear: Homophobic Hate Crime in Wales

MATTHEW WILLIAMS AND JASMIN TREGIDGA

This chapter takes as its focus the increasing problem of homophobic hate crime in Wales. Hate crime, defined by the Home Office as 'Any hate incident, which constitutes a criminal offence, perceived by the victim or any other person, as being motivated by prejudice or hate', has experienced an ascending position in policy agendas in England and Wales.[1] This policy focus reflects the rising tide of hate and bigotry towards lesbian, gay and bisexual people (LGB), captured in both official police statistics and victim surveys. This chapter reports on the results from the All Wales Hate Crime (AWHC) project that ran from 2010–13. As part of the project, we surveyed and interviewed 535 LGB people living in Wales on topics including community cohesion, fear of hate crime, perceptions and experiences of the police and the criminal justice system, and hate crime victimization.[2] The results reveal that the overall picture for LGB people living in Wales is a bleak one. Compared to other protected characteristics groups (ethnic and religious minorities, those with disabilities and transgender individuals), LGB respondents were second most likely to fear hate crime. Furthermore, a third of all victims of sexual-orientation-related hate crimes/incidents stated that violent crimes were the most serious they had experienced, the highest when compared to other protected characteristics groups.

Defining and counting homophobic hate crime

In England and Wales, there is no specific offence of homophobic hate crime. Instead, the Criminal Justice Act 2003 introduced enhanced sentencing provisions for crimes against LGB people that are perceived to be motivated by prejudice, and the Criminal Justice and Immigration Act 2008 introduced a new offence of inciting hatred against persons on the grounds of sexual orientation. While the Home Office's definition of hate crime is considered victim-centred given its basis upon perception, in practice, it is at odds with the evidence-driven criminal justice process where there must be proof beyond reasonable doubt that a hate crime was motivated by hostility. The available police data show that 43,927 hate crimes were recorded in England and Wales in 2012/13 (around 1 per cent of all recorded crime) with homophobic hate crimes accounting for 10 per cent of all hate crimes.[3] In 2011/12, there were 1,809 hate crimes recorded in Wales, with homophobic hate crime accounting for 13 per cent of all hate crime. An analysis of the Crime Survey for England and Wales (CSEW) 2011/12 and 2012/13 showed that around 3 per cent of crime overall was hate motivated, an estimated 278,000 incidents a year. Victims of homophobic hate crimes accounted for 39,000 of these (14 per cent).[4] While data specific to Wales can be extrapolated from the CSEW, the sampling strategy adopted by the Home Office and the Office for National Statistics means that the number of respondents reporting hate crimes/incidents is too small to conduct a robust analysis on an area by area basis, even after combining several sweeps of the survey. The Home Office and Office for National Statistics state that the CSEW is designed to provide estimates for England and Wales as one unit of analysis. The national statistician's review of crime statistics concluded 'given the sample size of the survey it cannot be used to produce robust estimates on an annual basis for those crimes that are experienced by relatively small proportions of the population or outside the current scope of coverage'.[5] The All Wales Hate Crime Survey was funded due to this restriction in existing national datasets.

Wales as a site for homophobic hate crime

Assessing the nature and impact of homophobic hate crime in Wales must take into consideration a number of geo-political issues. The Government of Wales Act 1998, 2006 created a national assembly for Wales and the Welsh government, transferring a wide range of powers to the devolved administration. However, responsibility and budget for policing and criminal justice is not devolved. In the context of hate crime, Wales is subject to the legislation outlined above, but an additional response to hate crime issues has been taken forward as part of the Community Cohesion Programme of the Welsh government which commenced in 2009. This has resulted in positive developments, including attempts to tackle negative social attitudes held towards minority communities and to increase community engagement and cohesion across Wales. Furthermore, the Welsh government, criminal justice agencies, local authorities and voluntary sector organizations have worked together to help take forward work across Wales to improve the operational and strategic response to hate crime. Much of this work, coupled with extensive Welsh-specific research into the nature and impact of hate crime victimization[6] and hate crime perpetration,[7] culminated in the Welsh government's *Tackling Hate Crimes and Incidents: A Framework for Action* in 2014.

In addition to the political context, there are a number of geo-historical characteristics that have the potential to shape the nature and impact of homophobic hate crime victimization and, in turn, challenge hate crime policy development and application in Wales. Community tensions that are particular to Wales, as compared to England, Scotland and Northern Ireland, are difficult to extrapolate from national datasets. Pinning down the provenance of such tensions in Wales that may be brought about by variances in space, place and economy and the like is a complex task, and one that is yet to be fully undertaken. However, some work has examined community cohesion in Wales specifically that assists in understanding the possible genesis of tensions that may lead to hate crime perpetration. Cooper and Innes found that nearly three-quarters of the Welsh population perceived a lack of respect and consideration as a problem in their area, with men, the young, those born in Wales and those in social housing more likely to feel this way.[8] The latter economic factor emerged as highly significant and reflects the poorer economic conditions in Wales compared to the rest of the United Kingdom. This is important in understanding homophobic hate crime in this context, especially towards LGB ethnic minorities and immigrants.[9]

There are densely populated, multicultural regions in the south-east of Wales (proximate to the cities of Swansea and Cardiff) that are at contrast with large areas to the north and west that are characterized by a highly dispersed demography, particularly in the rural and valleys locations. The All Wales Hate Crime Project highlighted how these regional factors shape hate crime experience. Within the more rural areas, minorities expressed through interviews heightened feelings of exclusion, vulnerability and fear in relation to hate victimization, citing how 'different' was often perceived as 'dangerous' in these isolated communities. Language and Welsh nationality also emerged as a particular factor, with native Welsh speakers expressing experiences that differed from non-Welsh speakers.[10] The results reported in this chapter represent a particular indigenous geo-historical context and should not be considered nomothetic. However, the factors reported above are not exclusive to Wales when compared to the other constituent regions of the United Kingdom.

This chapter corroborates much of the existing research into the nature and impact of homophobic hate crime. However, it also provides insight into the complexity of individual identity within the context of hate crime victimization and highlights prominent issues such as the role of 'misgendering' and the effect that victimization can have on personal perception of 'self' and the presentation of identity in public settings. This chapter presents findings on a range of issues within a LGB context, including community cohesion, fear of general crime and hate crime, and perceptions of hate crime impact on local communities. The chapter then moves onto hate crime experience in particular.

Community cohesion

All survey respondents were asked to provide some local community information including how long they have lived in the area and their perception of levels of interaction and integration within the local community. The responses from three survey questions were combined to generate a 'community cohesion scale'.[11] Figure 1 shows that on a scale of 3 to 12 (3 being most strongly disagree and 12 most strongly agree), heterosexual respondents most strongly feel that they live in a cohesive community with a mean score of 9.2, followed by bisexual men (mean

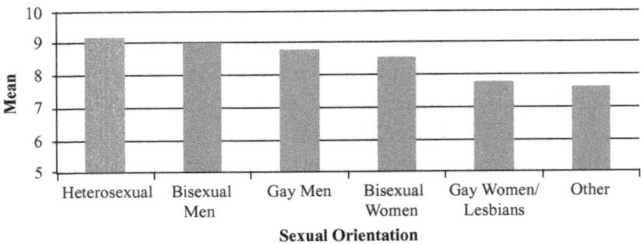

1 Sexual orientation by cohesion scale

score of 9.0). The respondents who are less likely to agree that they live in a cohesive community are gay women (mean score of 8.6) and bisexual women with a mean score of 7.8. Moreover, there are a number of significant differences in relation to community cohesion. Heterosexual respondents are significantly more likely than both gay women and bisexual women to think that they live in a cohesive community, and gay men are significantly more likely than bisexual women to agree that they live in a cohesive area.

General fear of crime and police satisfaction

Figures 2 and 3 provide information on levels of fear of crime and police satisfaction within the LGB respondent community.[12] On a general fear-of-crime scale (4 being the least fearful and 16 being the most fearful), bisexual women (9.8) were the most fearful followed by bisexual men, gay women and gay men (8.4). In fact, the data reveals that gay women and bisexual women are significantly more fearful than heterosexual respondents, and bisexual women are significantly more fearful than gay men. Moreover, there are a number of significant differences when the data is analysed in terms of the four specific crime types included in the survey. In terms of sexual violence, gay women and bisexual women are significantly more fearful than gay men and heterosexual respondents, and gay women and bisexual women are significantly more fearful of becoming a victim of threat/harassment than heterosexual respondents. This would indicate that gender has a role to play in fears around sexual violence and harassment victimization in Wales. Multiple regression that takes into account other factors, such as demographic characteristics and previous victimization, revealed that, while controlling for these other factors, respondents who said they were LGB did not emerge as statistically significantly more fearful than those that said they were not LGB.

As figure 3 shows, survey respondents within the LGB community were slightly less satisfied than heterosexual respondents (3.48 versus 3.34) with the perceived job the police were doing in their local area. This represents a significant difference between the two groups. However, there is no significant difference in satisfaction levels within the LGB community. No statistically significant findings emerged in the multiple regression analysis in relation to perceptions of general police effectiveness and LGB status.

Living in Fear

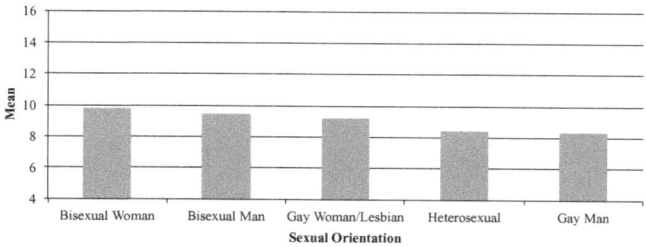

2 General fear of crime by sexual orientation

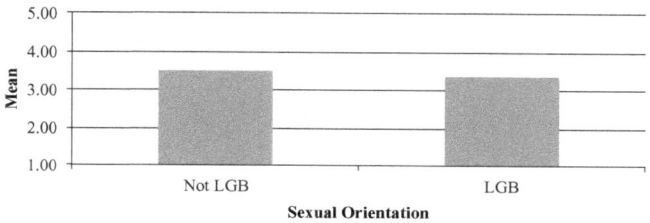

3 Sexual orientation by general satisfaction

General hate crime issues

This section shows the findings from questions regarding issues and concerns around hate crime and hate crime victimization from within a LGB context. All survey respondents could answer the questions in this section; therefore, findings include data from both victims and non-victims of hate crime. Where possible, interview data is presented in order to provide a more holistic understanding of key themes emerging from the statistical findings.

Scale and impact of hate crime on the community

Survey respondents were asked their perceptions of the scale of the hate crime problem in their local area. The data shows that on a scale of 1 to 4 (1 being not a problem at all and 4 being a very big problem), the mean value across the LGB categories was 2, indicating that the majority of respondents believe that hate crime is not a very big problem at all in their local area. However, figure 4 shows that bisexual women are more likely to believe that hate crime is a problem compared to all other LGB categories. Moreover, gay men and women and bisexual women are significantly more likely than heterosexual respondents to perceive hate crime as a problem in their local area. Multiple regression analysis did not reveal any statistically significant findings in relation to the differences in the perception of the problem and the impact it has on local communities between LGB and non-LGB respondents.

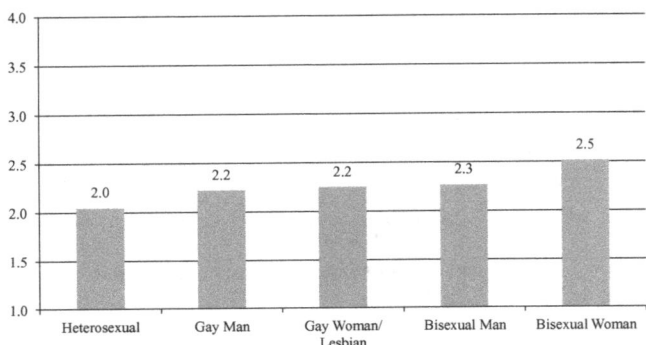

4 HC a problem in level area by SO

Perception of police performance in relation to hate crime and hate-related incidents

All respondents were asked how good a job they perceived the police to be doing to tackle hate crime and hate-related incidents in their local area. The levels of police effectiveness were measured on a scale of 1 to 5 (1 being a very poor job and 5 being an excellent job). On average, gay men view the police response most favourably (mean score of 3.4) followed by bisexual women, gay women and bisexual men (mean score of 2.8). Multiple regression analysis did not reveal any statistically significant findings in relation to the differences in the perception of police performance in relation to policing hate crimes/incidents between LGB and non-LGB respondents.

Fear of hate crime victimization and hate crime avoidance strategies

The survey was able to measure fear of hate crime on the basis of sexual orientation. Figure 5 shows bisexual women (9.8) are again the most fearful followed by bisexual men (9.4), gay women (9.3) and gay men (8.7). There are a number of statistically significant differences when these findings are broken down into specific crime types, and the sexual orientation categories are compared to each other. On a general hate crime fear scale, all LGB categories are more fearful of becoming a victim than heterosexual respondents. In terms of fear of becoming a victim of hate-related property crime, gay men and women are more fearful than heterosexual respondents. All LGB groups (except 'other') are more fearful than heterosexual respondents of becoming a victim of hate-related violent crime. In terms of fear of becoming a victim of hate-related sexual violence, gay and bisexual women are significantly more fearful than heterosexual respondents, and bisexual women are significantly more fearful than gay men. Finally, all LGB groups are significantly more fearful of hate-related harassment and threats than heterosexual respondents. Multiple regression analysis revealed statistically significant findings in relation to the differences in levels of general hate crime

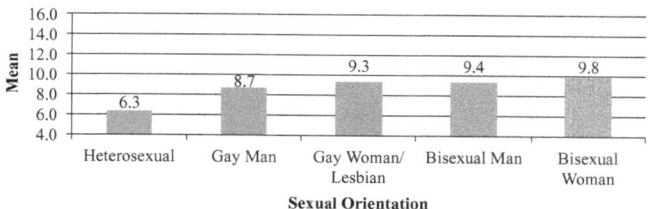

5 General fear of hate crime on the basis of sexual orientation

fear between LGB and non-LGB respondents, even when taking into account demographic and victim factors. Of all the protected characteristic groups (PCG), LGB respondents were second most likely to fear hate crime, after transgender respondents.

In association with a fear of hate crime, all respondents were asked whether they had ever attempted to conceal aspects of their identity or taken specific precautions in an attempt to reduce the risk of becoming a victim of hate crime. Forty-four per cent of survey respondents had attempted to conceal their sexual orientation in order to reduce the risk of hate crime victimization. This is the joint highest percentage across all protected characteristic groups. Additional precautions listed in the survey included improving home security, carrying personal security devices, avoiding certain areas/places, moved house/area and avoiding going out at night. We combined these measures to create a Precautions Scale (range 0–5). Those scoring higher on the scale have reported taking more precautions against hate crime. Figure 6 shows that there was a slight difference between LGB groups in relation to taking precautions but no significant findings emerged in multiple regression analysis between LGB and non-LGB respondents.

This type of avoidance behaviour or risk management was also disclosed in the research interviews.[13] Ed, a gay man living in north Wales, revealed that he keeps his sexuality a secret while at work: 'I haven't told anyone. They ask questions "have you got a girlfriend" and things, I just say no I'm single, and I just, you

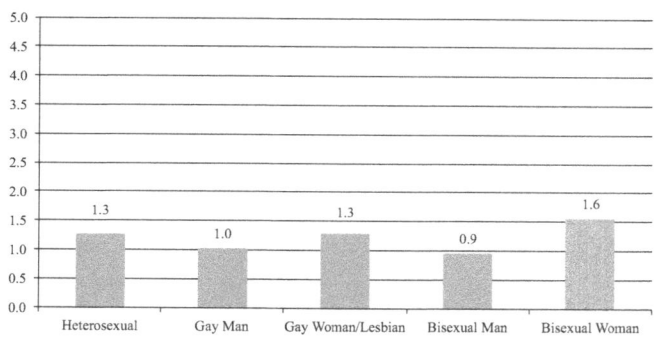

6 Precautions scale by SO

know, change the subject quick and I've not come across any prejudice yet.' And Kate, a gay woman living in south Wales comments:

> Sometimes I think I listen to my mp3 player partly to avoid making eye contact with people and partly to avoid any incidents, because I think well if you're listening to music they're less likely to try and engage with you. There was an incident where me and my partner were walking through [the park] and there was a gang of youths ahead of us who were behaving in quite an antisocial kind of way. They were shouting and being aggressive and pushing each other around and stuff, and we really backed off and stayed away from them. And then when they turned off, we went like the other direction, just that kind of risk management.

Effect of hate crime worry on quality of life

Finally, respondents were asked to measure the extent to which their quality of life was affected by the fear of hate crime victimization. The impact of hate crime worry was measured on a scale of 1 to 10 (with 1 being no effect on quality of life and 10 being total effect on quality of life). Figure 7 shows that the majority of responses were towards the lower end of the impact scale across all LGB categories indicating that worry about hate crime victimization has a relatively minimal impact on quality of life. However, the findings reveal that worry about hate crime has the biggest impact on bisexual women (mean score of 3.8), followed by bisexual men (mean score of 3.4) and gay women and gay men (mean score of 3.2). Multiple regression analysis revealed statistically significant findings in relation to the differences in levels of hate crime fear impact between LGB and non-LGB respondents, even when taking into account demographic and victim factors.

Kate's observations reflect the increased concern that some members of minority groups feel in relation to the possibility of becoming a victim of hate crime:

> I think with people often being robbed is a main fear or with women sexual assault and rape. I think when you belong to a group that's victimized by hate crime, you've got to add in the hate crime element as well, so you have the usual fears plus hate crime. It's very high in my mind definitely and I think that it's that fear that you're extra likely to be targeted because you're seen as different or you're seen as belonging to a certain group that's generally perceived with a bit of hostility. I don't know how rational that is but that's like the feeling I think.

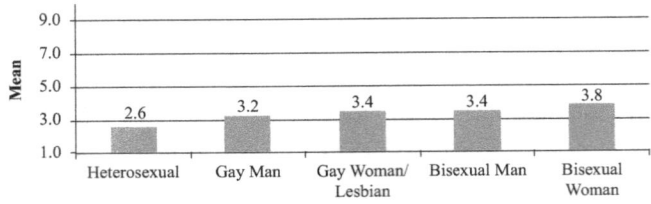

7 Impact of HC victimization worry by SO

Hate crime victim experience

This section of the chapter focuses on the findings from data provided by research participants who have been victims of hate crime in Wales. Here again, interviews voice some of the key themes emerging from the statistical findings and highlight the personal experience of hate crime victimization. The data included in the charts presented in this section highlight the nature of victimization across all protected characteristic groups. It is important to view the nature of homophobic hate crime in context and to reinforce the vital point that hate crime is not a generic phenomenon: it is a complex offence that can differ markedly between strands.

Most serious hate crime

Over a third (38.3 per cent) of all victims of sexual-orientation-related hate crimes/incidents stated that violent crimes were the most serious they had experienced, the highest amongst all strands in the AWHC survey. A similar proportion (33.7 per cent) indicated hate incidents were the most serious they had experienced, compared to just over 1 in 10 who stated threats and property crimes were the most serious (13 per cent and 9.8 per cent respectively). One in twenty (4.7 per cent) stated acquisitive crimes were the most serious experienced. Figure 8 shows that the majority of victims of homophobic hate crimes/incidents were alone at the time, while approximately one-third were with partners and 26 per cent with friends.

Figure 9 shows that 32 per cent of victims were in or just outside their own home when the hate crime incident took place; 25 per cent of victims were partaking in the night-time economy (NTE) and 26 per cent of victims were in a public street or park. Only a fraction of homophobic hate crime incidents took place on public transport.

The interviews with LGB victims highlight a broad range of types of hate crime victimization, including verbal abuse, physical and sexual assault, and criminal damage. The location of hate crime offences also varies markedly but the majority of incidents occurred in a public place. In all cases, victims were accompanied by friends or their partners which some victims believe made their sexual orientation more identifiable to others and therefore increased the chance of suffering some form of hate crime victimization.

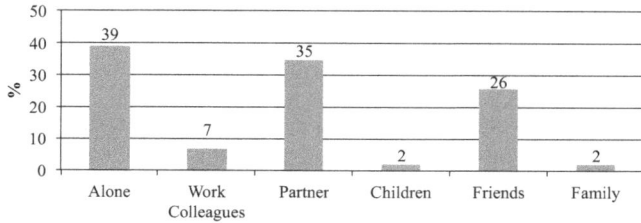

8 Who were you with at the time of the HC

Building Queer Wales Post-Devolution

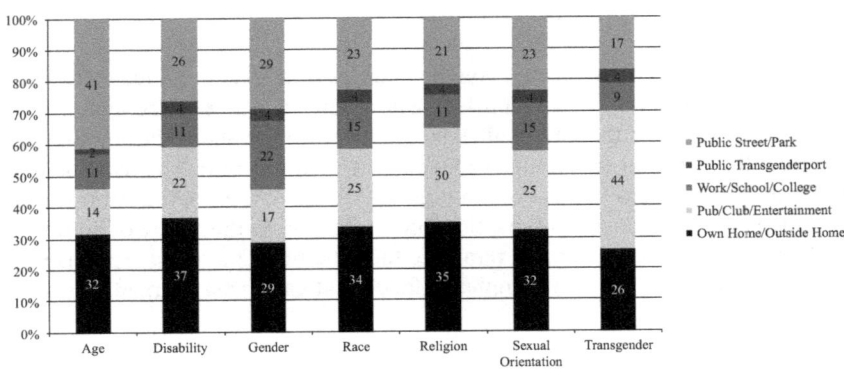

9 Where did the HC happen by PCG

The issue of 'misgendering' within the context of hate crime is highlighted as a significant issue for LGB hate crime victims. For some gay women, there is a clear relationship between gender presentation and hate crime experience. A number of women recall incidents of 'misgendering' and the unsettling effect such experiences have had on them:

> It's always men who have called me 'sir' or 'mate'. It's happened a couple of times in shops and a couple of times with club doormen. In some ways these incidents are more hostile, because that's quite deliberate and a bit more intimidating in some ways. Misgendering is hard to describe. It's quite invasive and has definitely made me quite nervous about how I'm dressing. (Kate, south Wales)

The intersectional nature of individual identity in the context of hate crime is a theme raised consistently by LGB victims. A number of LGB victims, particularly gay women, highlight the relationship between their sexuality and their gender when recalling their hate crime experiences. A number of gay women disclosed a sexual element to the abuse they experienced. As one respondent explained,

> This guy grabbed me and touched me inappropriately and said something abusive. It was definitely sexual and this incident that I had a couple of weeks ago was as well. It was me and my partner, we were walking through [the park] just arm in arm and this guy was walking towards us. He shouted at us. He was quite close, like close enough to be kind of eye to eye, and he went 'lesbianos, that's what I like to see', in a leering kind of tone of voice ... (Kate, south Wales)

Repeat victimization

Victims were asked to disclose whether they had experience of repeat hate crime victimization.[14] Figure 10 shows that 40 per cent of homophobic hate crime victims experienced cases of repeat victimization.

The majority of LGB interviews reveal that victims have experienced hate crime on a number of occasions but that each incident was an isolated event.

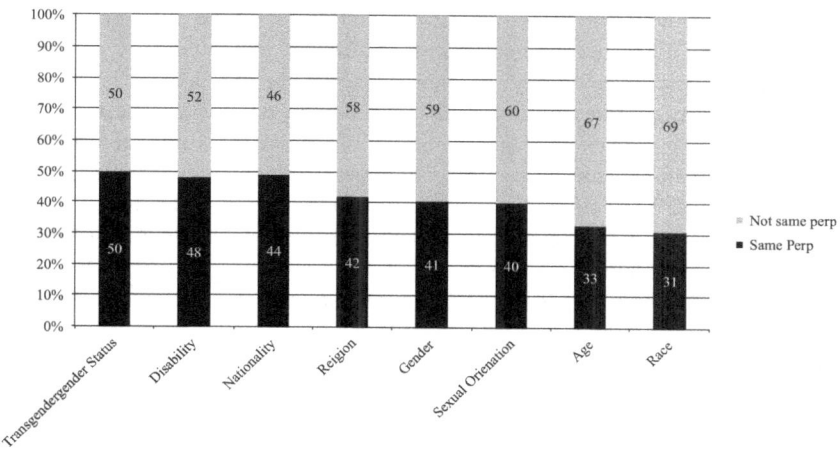

10 If you have been a victim of HC more than once, were any committed by the same perpetrator(s)?

However, one participant had experienced repeat victimization by a male neighbour, and these hate incidents culminated in physical violence.

Victim perception of offender motivation

Victims were asked what they believed motivated the offence against them. Almost 60 per cent of LGB survey respondents were left in little doubt that the offender was motivated to some degree by homophobic attitudes because of the nature of the hate speech directed towards them. Figure 11 shows that over 30 per cent of homophobic hate crime respondents felt their physical appearance/dress had contributed in some way to their victimization, and that the offender was hostile to minority groups.

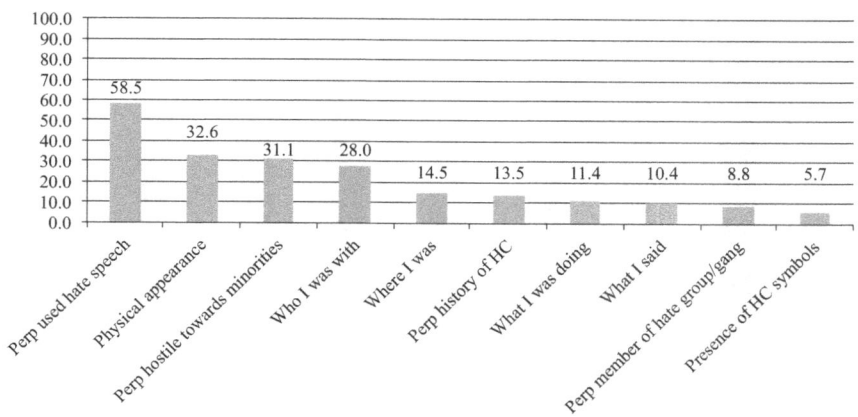

11 Perceptions of motivation for HC perpetration by SO HC victims

The interviews with LGB hate crime victims provided the opportunity to elaborate on possible explanations for offender behaviour. A number of participants, particularly gay women, once again highlighted the role of intersectionality in hate crime victimization. When articulating the relationship between gender and sexuality in the context of hate crime, some victims believe that girls who aren't seen as 'feminine' are deemed to be less worthy and there to be 'trodden on'. Others believe that if women are not seen to be sexually obtainable, or not in the dating pool, then some form of 'challenging of them' is deemed to be justified. Hannah's experience epitomizes the experiences of many victims: 'We feel that he's [offender] homophobic and, you know, he doesn't like women either, he's a misogynist. We feel we were kind of a threat to him a) because we were women and then b) because we were lesbians.' Annie in Dyfed Powys highlights the inter-relationship between age, gender and sexuality in relation to the hate crime she experienced:

> We [women] do tend to link arms as we go along, and that's quite common to see, but if you do it as you get older as well then there's something not right about it. I was actually out with my daughter. This bloke came up to me then when I was with her, and said what's an old dyke like you doing with a pretty girl like that, she should be with me, and then he started to try and chat her up.

Victim-perpetrator relationship and perpetrator characteristics

This section of the chapter details information provided by victims on key perpetrator characteristics. The data in this area is very limited across all of the protected characteristic groups. This in turn restricted the amount of statistical analysis that could be carried out and, as a result, all findings in this area should be interpreted with a large degree of caution. However, empirical research pertaining to hate crime perpetration is very limited generally in the UK, and

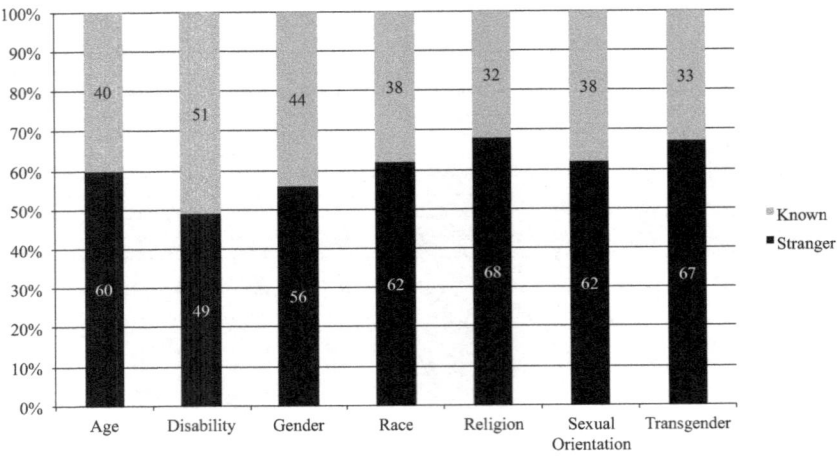

12 HC perpetrator relationship by PCG

therefore the type of data generated through the AWHC project can contribute usefully to this under-researched criminological area.

A number of LGB hate crime victims provided details of perpetrator characteristics, and the findings are presented below in figures 12–16. Figure 12 shows that in over 60 per cent of sexual orientation hate crimes, the offender(s) was not known by the victim. This is broadly comparable with the victim-perpetrator relationships detailed by victims across the other protected characteristic groups.

Figure 13 reveals that the overwhelming majority of hate crimes or hate-related incidents involving LGB victims were committed by more than one perpetrator. Eighty-six per cent of hate crimes against bisexual men were committed by more than one offender; 81 per cent of hate crimes against gay women or lesbians; 79 per cent of hate crimes against bisexual women, and 73 per cent of hate crimes

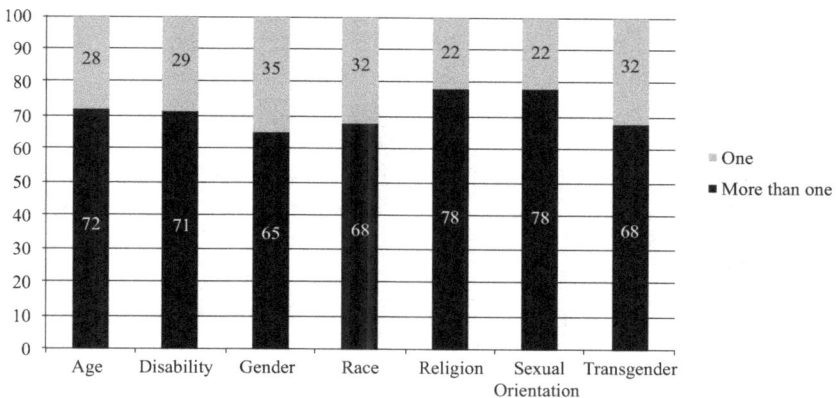

13 Number of HC perpetrators by strand

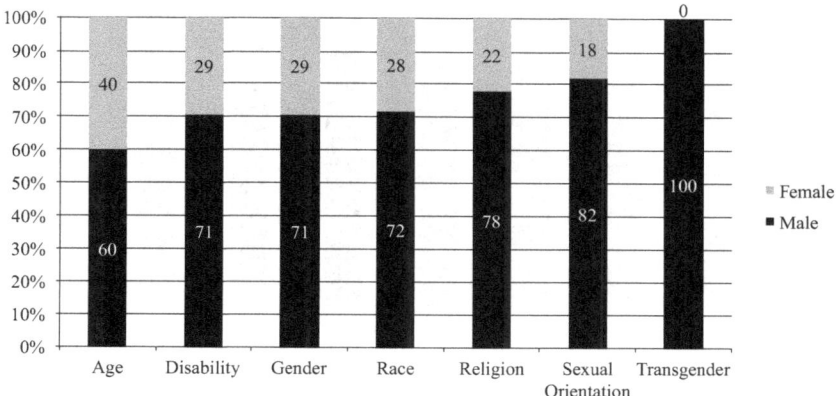

14 Gender of perpetrators by strand

against gay men. Figures 14–16 indicate that 76 per cent of perpetrators were men; 67 per cent were thirty years old or younger, and 91 per cent were white.

The interview data reflects these findings to some extent: participants report the vast majority of perpetrators were white males and ranged in age between twenties and forties. The interview data indicate that the majority of participants have been physically or verbally abused by complete strangers in a public place away from their homes. However, the data also reveals that often there is a correlation between where the hate crime took place and whether the perpetrator was known by the victim. Hannah, for example, recounts her experience of repeat victimization by a male neighbour. In this case, the hate incidents escalated in severity and culminated in attempted strangulation:

> It's a horrible thing when it's your neighbour ... coming home to that environment was awful really, because you come home to feel safe, but we were going home to almost

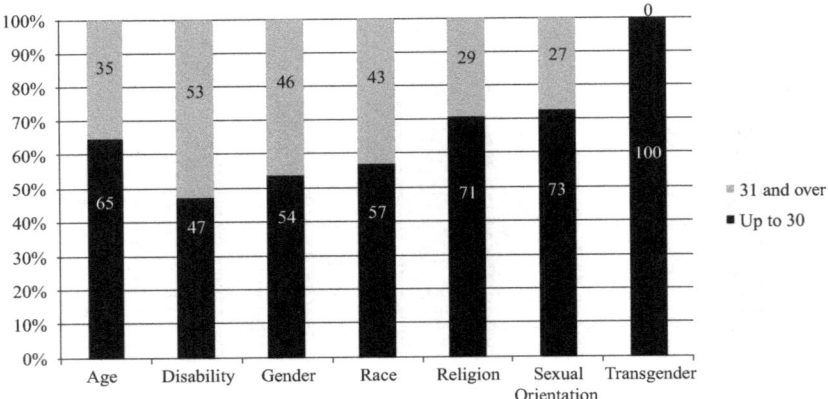

15 Age of HC perpetrators by strand

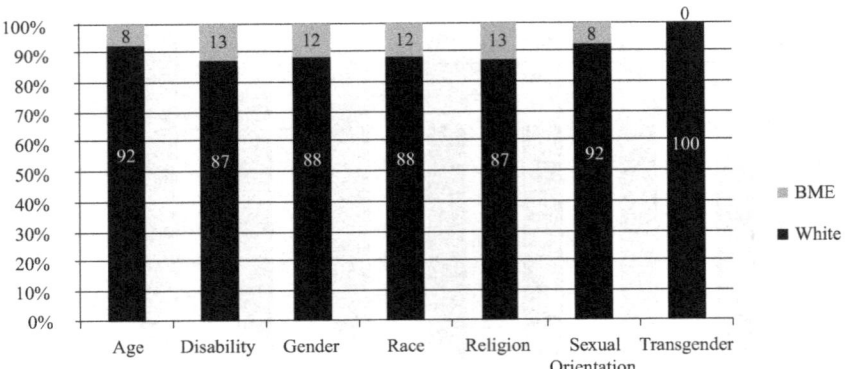

16 Race of HC perpetrators by strand

like a warzone of what would happen next. And it was tremendously stressful, you know, it was a really appalling environment to live in and we considered moving, but the market being flat none of the properties were selling in our area. So, you know, we were sort of trapped there really.

Police contact and reporting experience

This section of the chapter highlights key findings in relation to victims' experience of the hate crime reporting process in Wales. The section is framed mainly around the data generated by survey respondents. However, qualitative findings are included, where appropriate, because the interview data provide a nuanced account of victims' experiences of the police reporting process. All of the victims of sexual orientation hate crime who were interviewed had reported at least one incident to the police.

Police contact, reporting experience and levels of satisfaction

Forty-seven per cent of hate crimes perceived to have been perpetrated on the basis of sexual orientation were reported to the police. This is broadly comparable with reporting rates across the protected characteristic groups. In 71 per cent of these cases, the victims told the police explicitly that they believed the incident was motivated by homophobic attitudes or prejudice. Almost 65 per cent of the homophobic hate crime reports were subsequently recorded by the police, and 43 per cent of them initiated some form of police investigation. Sixteen per cent of homophobic hate crime reports resulted in the arrest of an offender and, in 11 per cent of cases, no further action was taken following the incident report. It is important to acknowledge that these findings are generated wholly from the victims' perspectives, and individual victims may not have been fully updated on police activity after incidents were reported.

Various reasons were given for reporting the hate crime or incident by LGB respondents. The top three reasons were that the victim wanted to prevent it from happening again, the victim hoped the offenders would be brought to justice, and the victim felt it was a serious crime/incident. The top three reasons given by victims of homophobic hate crime for not reporting were that victims believed the police could have done nothing to help, felt the incident was too trivial or it wasn't worth it, and feared retaliation by offenders. Despite these reasons for not reporting, 93 per cent of homophobic hate crime victims would encourage a victim of hate crime to report it to the police. This percentage is relatively high when comparing data across all protected characteristic groups. The interview data indicates that the perspective taken on whether to recommend reporting is often contingent on previous experience and informed by levels of satisfaction with police contact and response at the time of reporting and subsequent case investigation, and – in a minority of cases – satisfaction with the criminal justice process more generally (including case outcome). A scale of satisfaction was

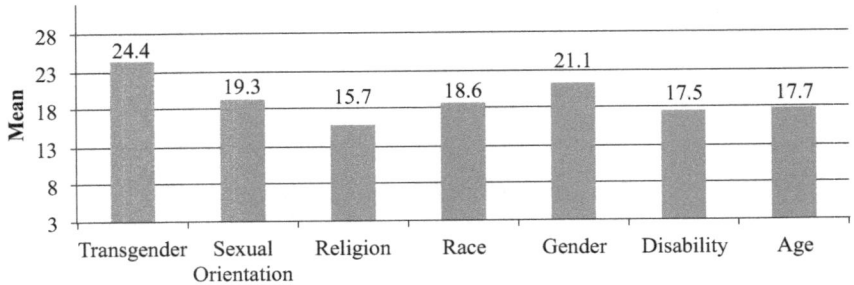

17 Satisfaction with contact with police by type of hate crime/incident reported

devised by combining the data from eight questions relating to victim satisfaction during the course of contact with the police in their local area.[15] Figure 17 shows that sexual orientation hate crime victims ranked third (mean score of 19.3) in terms of their satisfaction with the police when compared to the other protected characteristic groups. However, no statistically significant results emerged in the multiple regression analysis, indicating that the satisfaction levels of victims of sexual orientation hate crimes/incidents who reported to the police did not differ in a significant way from the satisfaction levels of other types of victims who reported.

The majority of LGB interviewees stated that they had reported incidents – either isolated events or ongoing victimization – to the police but, in some cases, they had been nervous about highlighting the hate-related aspect of the incident because they were worried about being judged or ridiculed. In some cases, fears were unfounded, as Ed in north Wales highlights:

> I was very nervous because I didn't know what sort of reaction I was going to get. A lot of people are scared if you're gay that they're [police] going to think you're some sort of weirdo/pervert. I think people need to be aware that the police are very sympathetic when you go and see them and that they [victims] will be looked after like, you know, like a burglary, a rape or anything. And I was looked after; I can't fault the police at all.

However, in a number of instances, victims were actively discouraged from highlighting the hate-related aspect of the criminal victimization. As Annie, a gay woman who lives in Dyfed Powys, recalls, 'One police officer actually turned around and said, "I don't think we want to go down that path, it'll open a whole new can of worms".' Further, a number of interviewees reveal that the hate-related element of the incident(s) was not taken seriously or that the initial report was recorded as anti-social behaviour or neighbour nuisance. Hannah's case exemplifies this:

> I think they didn't take it seriously from my point of view especially early on. We kept telling them that he doesn't like women; he doesn't like us because we're gay. They continued to call it 'neighbour nuisance' and it took the female sergeant to come up before anybody actually started saying yeah okay this may be a hate crime and, you

know, then started saying you need to keep the records and gave us some proper support. If they'd taken it seriously before it escalated to the assault and actually prosecuted him for harassment I think that would have stopped him ...

In a number of cases, LGB victims felt that there was a lack of support and information after reporting the incident to the police. Often victims felt that they had to chase for information and were obliged to repeat themselves because they found themselves talking to different police officers each time they called for information. In general, the findings highlight a lack of consistency in terms of the response and subsequent support that LGB hate crime victims receive from the police in Wales. Many victims felt that the service they received was 'hit and miss', and that their experience was positive or negative depending on the officer who dealt with them at the time.

> Most of the time I was having to repeat myself over and over again, it got very, very tedious. So if there was someone who you could specifically ring up and say, you know, this is the reference number, you know, we're at such and such a stage, rather than them saying oh we'll get back to you, because we don't know where we are with it – that doesn't help. It's me that has to do all the work. (Ed, north Wales)

In some respects, these are issues that can be addressed through a systematic assessment of police training provision. However, it is particularly worrying in cases where there is evidence of certain high risk factors, including repeat victimization and an escalation in frequency and severity of incidents. There have been a number of high-profile and ultimately tragic cases in the UK of repeated hate crime victimization that were either not taken seriously enough or recorded inaccurately as neighbour nuisance or anti-social behaviour. It is imperative that hate crime reports are taken seriously, recorded appropriately, linked together and investigated thoroughly.

Conclusions

This chapter has shown that hate crimes disproportionally impact on LGB people in Wales compared to other protected characteristics groups. In particular, LGB people were more likely to fear hate crime victimization, and victims were more likely to suffer violent crimes, to avoid certain places post victimization and to attempt to conceal some aspect of their identity to avoid future victimization. LGB victims were also most likely to be victimized by more than one perpetrator. The findings also revealed the intersectional nature of individual identity in the context of hate crime as a key issue for victims. A number of LGB victims, particularly gay women, highlight the relationship between their sexuality and their gender when recalling their hate crime experiences. The issue of 'misgendering' within the context of hate crime is highlighted as a significant issue for LGB hate crime victims. For some gay women there is a clear relationship between gender presentation and hate crime experience. Interrogating the subtle and subjective differences between multiple victim identities is complex.

'Knowing' what aspect of one's identity was 'read' and targeted is never clear, and these debates are rehearsed in court rooms by barristers defending those accused of hate crime perpetration on a weekly basis. It is therefore no surprise that this difficulty is transferred to the recording of hate crimes, both in policing and in research.

The plight of LGB hate crime victims in Wales is clearer than ever. The Welsh government's attempts to tackle negative social attitudes held towards minority communities and to increase community engagement and cohesion across Wales remain in their infancy. More expansive and deeper inter-agency working is needed between government, criminal justice, local authorities and voluntary sector organizations if an effective response to homophobic hate crime is to be achieved.

10

Heb Addysg, Heb Ddawn (Without Education, Without Gift): LGBTQ Youth in Educational Settings in Wales

JOHN SAM JONES

This chapter is a critical and personal account of education in Wales from an LGBTQ perspective.[1] Drawing on the importance of personal narrative in education, in teaching, teacher training and in student experience, it tells a story of the development of more inclusive education policies and practices that acknowledge the sexual diversity of Wales. Importantly, much of this change happened after Welsh devolution, connecting these more progressive policies to the growing independence and changing identity of the Welsh nation. Discussions of education are always national ones, in large part because they centre on the idea of the child, whose sexual life has been made into an ideological battleground for the integrity, purity and future of the nation.[2]

This chapter links a private and personal story with the public and political narrative; it joins the anecdotal experience of the author with the theoretical context of education and sexuality, and this is precisely from where a queer curriculum should emerge. Dennis Sumara and Brent Davis stress that a queer curriculum should be 'interested in understanding and interpreting differences among persons rather than categories of persons'. It should, therefore, 'wonder what circumstances lead to different identification experiences' and be 'concerned with the complex relations among past, present, and imagined experiences'.[3] This use of personal experience contributes to spaces of queer diversity in the classroom and beyond. Similarly, Guiney Yallop argues that personal narrative reimagines and challenges ways of knowing in the school experience, and James McNinch challenges teachers to teach authentically from the lived encounter and from personal experience in ways that force them to face their own assumptions about sex and sexuality rather than repress them and teach within received patterns and habits of curricula.[4] As we will see, the pedagogies and curricula that develop in a post-devolution Wales that is mindful of LGBTQ needs belongs to this context of speaking and listening to personal experience in shaping education in terms of collaboration, community and citizenship.[5]

In today's Wales, it is difficult to conjure up the values and attitudes towards homosexuality that were pervasive during the last third of the twentieth century. Contemporary society largely appreciates the contributions of the many that happen to be lesbian or gay, on the sports fields, in the theatre, in broadcasting, in literature and even in politics. The National Eisteddfod, that bastion of Welshness, has welcomed the presence of the lesbian, gay and bisexual charity, Stonewall Cymru, on to the eisteddfod field since 2002, and at the Bala Eisteddfod in 2009, after the suicide of a young gay man who had endured years of bullying and ridicule in the town, the organizers supported the distribution and use of drinks placemats in all of the refreshment outlets on the eisteddfod field with a message about homophobic hate crime. Today, when public figures in Wales who happen to be lesbian or gay celebrate their civil partnerships or the adoption of their children, the *gwerin* – even those from *cefn gwlad* – seem to celebrate with them. According to the data held by the Office for National Statistics, 1,967 civil partnerships were held in Wales from their inception in December 2005 to the end of 2011, and gay weddings in Wales can be large, family affairs.

Yes, but ...

Ben Summerskill, the chief executive of Stonewall UK (2003–14), in his introduction to *The School Report* on the experiences of gay young people in Britain's schools, published by Stonewall in 2012 (where 5 per cent of the 1,614 online respondents were from schools in Wales), writes,

> More than half of lesbian, gay and bisexual young people still report experiencing homophobic bullying and its damaging impact is just as pronounced. Over two in five gay pupils who experience homophobic bullying attempt or think about taking their own life as a direct consequence. Three in five young people say that bullying has a direct impact on their school work and straight-A students have told us it makes them want to leave education entirely.[6]

In July 2013, Plaid Cymru, through Assembly Member Lindsay Whittle, the party's equalities spokesperson, raised fears about the level of homophobic bullying in Wales's schools. Since 2008, more than seventy incidents of homophobic bullying had been recorded in schools across south-east Wales. Mr Whittle commended those schools where homophobic bullying had been acknowledged, and where action had been taken to address such bullying, but also drew attention to the fact that 'The survey carried out by Plaid Cymru indicates that many schools have no recorded incidents of homophobic bullying over the past five years', which suggests that 'not all schools identify homophobic bullying separately from bullying accusations generally'.[7] The persistence of homophobic bullying reflects a common paradox that, as sexual diversity becomes more accepted and visible in our culture as a whole, it becomes a more visible and identifiable target for discrimination in schools.[8] We must be careful, therefore, of dismissing the problems within schools based on the successes outside them; indeed, the more success one has outside schools, the more urgently reforms in schools are needed, and these reforms will happen in a complex field of competing interests in which those who have the most to lose or gain have the least amount of power. As Cris Mayo puts it in her discussion of a liberal politics of queer educational inclusion,

> children pose a particular problem for liberal theory and for queer theory. For liberals, children are nascent citizens who must be educated in a context where liberal values and practices inculcate them into eventual full participation as citizens. For queers, too, children are often future participants in queer communities, but queers may have no say in how those future community members are raised. Not only are queer children disconnected from communities in which they will eventually be members, but they are likely to be members of families, who, if disapproving of their sexuality, may well be uncertain about the future possibilities and community memberships open to those children. Furthermore, queer children are participants in school institutions that appear to be doing their level best to simultaneously socialize children into citizenship and away from queer futures. As Sedgwick argues, no other minority is so faced with medical and educational institutions intent on their eradication prior to their adulthood.[9]

How does one provide a voice to the queer citizen child? Where does one begin? Is enough being done? The observations highlighted by Stonewall and the disquiet expressed by Plaid Cymru lead those concerned about the welfare of LGBTQ students in educational settings to ask some searching questions: is latent homophobia an endemic reality within Wales's education system? Is homophobic bullying going unchallenged in some schools, and if so, in how many? Is teaching about homosexuality, in the context of valuing difference and respecting diversity, failing in its goals? Are the school managers across Wales committed to creating safe and supportive environments for LGBTQ children, young people and adults within the school system? Does public policy in Wales since devolution offer a clear steer on homosexuality as an equality issue?

What about the children?

To consider these questions in any depth, it is first necessary to reflect on the values and attitudes within British and Welsh society towards homosexuality since its decriminalization in 1967 and also to endeavour to consider how homosexuality was viewed within education in the years between decriminalization and devolution. In much of the debate over sexuality and education in this period, it is immediately apparent that the child is a particularly charged site of contestation, embodying the potential corruption of the nation and requiring the protection of the state. During February 1966, the Sexual Offences Bill, which aimed to legalize homosexual behaviour between consenting adults in public, was given its second reading in the House of Commons. All of Britain's daily newspapers carried the story of the passage of the Bill, and on 23 February 1966, a correspondent from *The Times* reported on a meeting of the Edinburgh Presbytery of the Free Church of Scotland under the strap line 'Church warning on Sex Bill'. The churchmen had drawn up a resolution which was to be sent to the prime minister, the home secretary, the secretary of state for Scotland and all Edinburgh MPs. The resolution included the following:

> While recognizing that not all sins, even heinous sins, should be made indictable offences, the presbytery deplore that the vice of homosexuality, which is abominable in the sight of God, so corrupting of public morals, so perverted and so downright destructive of the social welfare and political health of the land, should even in a limited degree be removed from the statute book.[10]

Such attitudes were not confined to the churchmen of Edinburgh. Writing in his column, 'Wales in Westminster', in the *Liverpool Daily Post* on 23 December 1966, Geraint Morgan (Conservative MP for Denbighshire from 1959 to 1983), referring to a later reading of the Sexual Offences Bill, praised the standard of debate, 'despite the disagreeable nature of the subject'.[11] These concerns with the corruption, perversion and destruction of the social welfare and public health were easily aimed at the safety of children. On 7 March 1966, Dr C. G. Learoyd wrote in the *Daily Telegraph*,

> As a doctor who has worked among homosexuals may I assure Mrs Lucille Iremonger (March 1) that 'possessive mums' and 'neglectful dads' are far more often excuses for homosexuality than causes of it. By far the commonest cause is contagion by being initiated into the habit by a practising homosexual.[12]

Similarly, Clare Shepherd, the agony aunt of the popular weekly women's magazine, *Woman's Realm*, in response to a letter from a troubled 16-year-old wrote the following in the edition published on 7 May 1966,

> At your age, many girls and boys go through what appears to be a homosexual stage. But as they grow older, they find that they are, in fact, interested in the opposite sex. For the present, go out and meet as many people of your own age, of both sexes, as possible, and keep to social relationships rather than emotional ones. This will give you a chance to develop naturally. This is a problem you may well feel you want to talk about to someone who is used to such subjects. If you confide in your family doctor, he may send you to the psychiatric department of your local hospital. All doctors who practise psychiatry are quite familiar with your kind of problem, and if you could see one you might get a great deal of comfort and help.[13]

Had this troubled 16-year-old been referred to a psychiatrist, the 'comfort and help' offered may have taken the form of aversion therapy. Throughout the late 1950s and the 1960s, the *British Journal of Psychiatry* published many articles and a lively correspondence on the aversion therapy of homosexuality – both chemical aversion and electrical aversion. John Bancroft, in his paper, 'Aversion Therapy of Homosexuality – A Pilot Study of 10 Cases', describes the electrical aversion treatment in graphic detail:

> the patient was asked to produce erotic homosexual fantasies whilst looking at photographs of males. Painful electric shocks were delivered through his arm whenever an erection developed to a certain level ... Following this initial shock, further shocks were given at 15 second intervals unless the erectile response was falling or was once again below the threshold level.[14]

Early identification of and intervention into non-heterosexual behaviour of children was common in both the United States and the UK[15] and, as illustrated above, focused the attention of politicians, legislators, educators and medical professionals, all determined to prevent the spread of homosexuality in children. Right up to the year 2000 in England, some argued for a higher age of consent for young gay men who were, echoing Dr Learoyd, in danger of falling into the hands of older gay men.[16] All of this has led to a circumstance in which schools must struggle with a long history of educating children into heterosexual family values through pathologizing and silencing sexual diversity.

There were, of course, more tolerant voices. It was Welshman, Leo Abse, MP for Pontypool in south Wales, who sponsored the Sexual Offences Bill which eventually passed into law in 1967 decriminalizing homosexual acts between men in private. But even as the Bill received its Royal Assent, Lord Arran, another of the Bill's supporters, in an attempt to minimize criticisms that the legislation would lead to further public debate and visibility of issues relating to homosexual civil rights, made the following qualification:

> This is no occasion for jubilation and certainly not for celebration. I ask those homosexuals to show their thanks by comporting themselves quietly and with dignity. Any form of ostentatious behaviour now or in the future or any form of public flaunting would be utterly distasteful and would, I believe, make the sponsors of this Bill regret that they had done what they had done.[17]

Rarely is a normalizing acceptance of difference more clear than this call for queers to be acknowledged and rendered invisible, signalling the survival pact that queer children still feel compelled to make in schools. Even as LGBTQ rights develop and make inroads in our societies, schools and classrooms remain complex spaces of knowledge and power where children's sexualities are bound up in national, religious, racial, ethnic and economic claims on their lives and bodies.

Education, sex and citizenship

As a teenager, growing up in rural mid Wales in the late 1960s and early 1970s, recognizing that I was homosexual had caused confusion and distress. Homosexuality, indeed any aspect of sexuality, was met by a wall of silence in my home (despite the public debate during the late 1960s about the decriminalization of homosexual acts) and at school (where sex and relationships education had not yet entered the curriculum). Our English teacher did encourage us to read widely, however. I describe my encounters with the press and media of the day in *Crawling through Thorns*:

> There were newspapers, magazines and what Miss Roberts called 'journals' in the school library too: *The Times*, *The Guardian*, *New Society*, *Christian* and *The British Weekly*. John didn't read them every day, but he read them often enough to know that 'homosexual' was never used much as an adjective. It was a noun, and it always appeared alongside other nouns like thief, criminal, blackmailer, alcoholic, murderer, pervert and even unstable psychotic.[18]

Throughout my university career in Aberystwyth, from 1974 to 1979, there was much to confirm that homosexuality had to remain in the shadows of the closet.

None of the members of the university gay society (that I knew well) were out, and those few lecturers who attended the clandestine meetings guarded their privacy (read secrecy), fearing for their reputation and their livelihood if their 'lifestyle' became public. The general sense of homosexuality's unacceptability was confirmed in the national psyche by the media reports of the *Gay News* blasphemy trial in 1977 and the Jeremy Thorpe 'scandal', which seemed to drag on for years in the later part of the decade.

My experiences in teacher training reinforced the silence I encountered as a student, despite many progressive developments throughout the 1970s (and perhaps because of them). The medical record of my homosexual aversion therapy during my hospitalization at the North Wales Hospital in Denbigh presented an interesting challenge during my application process for a postgraduate teacher-training course. The doctor conducting the pre-registration medical examination questioned me in detail about my sexuality and offered grave warnings about the risk I would present to the boys and young men I would come into contact with as a schoolteacher. My experience is part of a widespread and abiding sexualization of queer teachers. A similar and recent example is reported by James McNinch, whose story demonstrates how even more inclusive contemporary contexts can replicate the same kind of silence. When a young man and prospective teacher asked whether he should self-identify as gay on his application form, McNinch was confronted with the ongoing anxieties of sexuality in education. On the one hand, the form invites candidates to describe the 'circumstances related to principles of equity and inclusion which might warrant special consideration for the applicant's acceptance to the program';[19] however, this gesture towards social justice in schools may not extend into the realm of sexuality:

> Is this an invitation to disclose and be welcomed as 'special'? Would a queer narrative be read by the selection committee as a reason for accepting or rejecting a student? Sexual orientation 'doesn't matter' only when it is presumed to be heterosexual and homosexuality is masked. In applying to a teacher education program it is still probably best to leave the sexual identity baggage at home since teacher education programs have implicitly adopted the US military's [former] position: 'Don't ask; don't tell'.[20]

Only non-heterosexual teachers must contend with the question of sexual identification, inducing the feeling that any sexual identity that does not replicate heterosexual citizenship may be experienced as 'baggage'. In my experience, as I moved from my medical past to my educational future, I did not have the choice of identification but was forced to carry it with me officially, and I was aware that I had considerably less control of my personal narrative than did my heterosexual peers. Whatever the doctor wrote in his report, it did not block my acceptance to the course; this did not, however, mean that I would be taught to be a more inclusive teacher. One experience is illustrative of the barriers many faced. In early 1979, three months into my teacher-training, the pop group The Village People had a huge international hit with the song 'Y.M.C.A.' The group's fantasy personas generated much debate and discussion about homosexuality, and in one university tutorial session, gay stereotypes were discussed, and the tutor was questioned about how, as trainee teachers, we might address questions posed by our students about homosexuality. It's a discussion I remember clearly. The tutor, previously the deputy head teacher of a secondary school before taking up a university teacher-training post, was adamant that on no account should we, as trainee teachers, enter into any such debate on the subject with students at school. One of the trainee teachers then asked about the support available for gay and lesbian teachers. The tutor's response was that there was no place in the teaching profession for pederasts. This may, of course, have been a minority view, though just a few years later, 'in 1983, only 41% of the British population thought it acceptable for a homosexual person to be a teacher' in a school.[21] Something else I recall with absolute clarity from my teacher-training year is the health education module I pursued: sex education was not included in the module's curriculum, so as recently graduated biologists training to be teachers, we were given no training to deliver any aspect of sex education.

Of course, this was 1979, and much of the silence and resistance that I faced as a teacher was part of the larger context of Thatcherite Britain, where social, education and national purity became central concerns that had indelible effects on education and curricula. Prior to Margaret Thatcher's victory in the 1979 general election, schools across England and Wales were addressing sex education in terms that were eventually articulated in the curriculum documents of the 1980s, which were

> responding in a variety of ways to the need for sound sex education. Sex education is one of the most sensitive parts of broad programmes of health education, and the fullest consultation and cooperation with parents are necessary before it is embarked upon. In this area offence can be given if a school is not aware of, and sensitive to, the cultural background of every child. Sex education is not a simple matter and is linked with attitudes and behaviour. The regulations to be made under Section 8 of the Education Act 1980 will require LEAs [Local Education Authority] to inform parents of the ways and contexts in which sex education is provided.[22]

Over the decade of her tenure in Downing Street, Thatcher's twin aims for education policy in the 1980s were to convert the nation's schools system from a public service into a market, and to transfer power from local authorities to central government. The introduction of a prescriptive national curriculum became an imperative, and this included detailed national guidance on the content of sex education. The development of this new curriculum coincided with the advent of the AIDS crisis, which fuelled a toxic social climate where fear and some hysteria led to hostility towards homosexual men, who were portrayed in much of the popular press as the vectors of the new 'gay plague'. Thatcher, a trained chemist with an understanding of evidence-based practice, responded positively to the public health crisis caused by the spread of the HIV. After consultation with public health practitioners across the country, she directed funds to the NHS which enabled the mobilization of a coordinated national HIV prevention programme that was liberal and progressive, and that saw the establishment of needle and syringe exchange schemes, methadone programmes and safer-sex initiatives with groups of people perceived to be at risk, all of which generated considerable public debate about sexuality and sexual behaviour. It was a public health intervention, over many years, which proved successful in limiting the spread of HIV infection throughout the UK, despite the controversy it fuelled in the Tory heartlands and the backlash in attitude towards gay men.

Thatcher's educational policies did nothing to combat those attitudes. Indeed, she worked just as hard to eradicate the social problem of homosexuality as she did to eradicate the biological danger of HIV. Seeking to respond with sensitivity to the cultural background of individual children (as prescribed above), some schools in the large metropolitan boroughs and the Labour-controlled Inner London Education Authority introduced literature to school libraries that reflected the lives of children in lesbian or gay households. One such book was a children's picture book from Denmark called *Jenny lives with Eric and Martin*. In the book, 5-year-old Jenny lived happily with her father, Eric, and his boyfriend Martin. The three of them go to the laundrette together, and Jenny helps Martin prepare a surprise birthday party for Eric: everyday scenes of ordinary family life. The book incited wide public outrage, as many refused to accept that this children's picture book was being used in primary schools across London in the early 1980s to help children learn about different kinds of families, and help the children who came from such families to understand that there were others like them.[23] And so began the gestation of ideas which led to Section 28 of the Local Government Act 1988. In her speech to the Tory Party conference on 9 October 1987, Thatcher expressed her belief that children were being failed in their education when 'Children who need to be taught to respect traditional moral values are being taught that they have an inalienable right to be gay.'[24] The following May, the Act became law and all local authorities were prohibited from promoting homosexuality by teaching or by publishing materials. Today, the wording of Section 28 has a menacing and disturbing tone: 'A local authority shall not – (a) intentionally promote homosexuality or publish material with the intention of promoting homosexuality; (b) promote the teaching in any maintained school of the acceptability of homosexuality as a pretended family relationship.'[25]

After Section 28 was passed, there was considerable debate as to whether the legislation – which specifically cited local authorities – was actually applicable in schools. Working as a public health educator during the late 1980s, the present author visited schools regularly and witnessed the confusion amongst school governors in their discussions about the content of sex education, and experienced first-hand the anxiety amongst those teachers who were expected to deliver sex education in the classroom, fearful that they might fall foul of the new law and face prosecution. An instinct to err on the side of caution, perhaps influenced by individual personal misgivings about homosexuality by many within the world of education, led to issues related to homosexuality being erased from the curriculum in schools across the country, except in the context of disease. Schools had a legal obligation to teach about HIV and AIDS, and within this context, homosexuality (in contrast to specific risk behaviours: unprotected sexual intercourse, sharing injecting equipment) was included amongst the causal factors, thus perpetuating the myth that AIDS was a gay plague. The political, medical, familial and educational institutions were perfectly aligned to reproduce the pure heterosexual nation through protecting the heteronormative integrity of the child's body.

Devolving Wales and queering education

In the foregoing narrative and discussion, one will have noticed that the educational policies have been primarily English ones, which have necessarily and unfortunately conflated the Welsh experience of sexuality and education with the English experience, but, in truth, they cannot be so conflated. In Rhyl in 1997, the year of Welsh devolution and two years before education devolved to the Welsh assembly government, the West Rhyl Young People's Project responded to the evident needs of teenage gays and lesbians in the largely rural area of north-east Wales by setting up an LGBT support group called Deuce (later renamed VIVA). Over the winter of 1997 to 1998, with support from the local Health Promotion Department Sexuality Project, a small group of the young people attending the Deuce group shared their stories with a writer, who worked with them to produce a bilingual booklet called *Stories that Give Shape to Lives*. The first print-run of 1,000 copies was quickly depleted as *Stories* found its way into local schools and youth clubs. Within weeks, the Deuce group received requests from across Wales and the north of England for copies. A further print run of 5,000 copies was distributed in less than a year, some to a small number of schools across Wales that had decided to use it as a sex education curriculum resource with Year 9 and 10 children, despite the fact that Section 28 was still on the statute book. For the piece of work which culminated in the *Stories* booklet, the West Rhyl Young People's Project and the Deuce LGB Support Group won the Youth Work in Wales Excellence Award in 1998. This project exemplifies the priorities of an education policy that supports queer lives: these priorities put children's voices, stories, experiences, contributions and rights ahead of moralistic defences of the state.

As Sarah Oerton and Anita Naoko Pilgrim have recently pointed out, this different approach came to the fore in Welsh educational policies after devolution.[26] The fundamental difference may be found in the Government of Wales Act, which established the new Welsh Assembly Government. Part V, Section 120 of the act reads, 'The Assembly shall make appropriate arrangements with a view to securing that its functions are exercised with due regard to the principle that there should be equality of opportunity for all people.'[27] These words laid a legal precedent that all the functions of the new assembly were to be exercised in terms of social justice to protect the rights of all people. In terms of education, and sex education in particular, Oerton and Pilgrim contend that such new national policy underlined that Wales had a 'different framing of sexual morality and "family values"' than one finds in England.[28] In contrast to the English 'risk management' approach to education that is based in 'contested moral discourses around the "problem" of young people's sexualities', Wales has developed a 'social justice' model:

> In stark contrast to Westminster, Cardiff Bay enjoys cross-party consensus on the need to tackle issues of childhood and youth sexualities not just in terms of adult anxieties about over-sexualisation and/or the sexual exploitation of children, but, as importantly, as key issues of children's human rights and citizenship values. Hence, there are opportunities in Wales for an approach to SRE [Sex and Relationship Education] which is not restricted by the deployment of children's and young people's sexualities as a rallying ground for a morality politics based upon seeing sex and sexuality as 'dangerous'.[29]

Further, unlike the English model for the new millennium, which still privileged the heterosexual family, the Welsh post-devolution emphasis on the rights of the child as a citizen includes their rights to an education that fosters a healthy development in a non-discriminatory environment that does not assume the heterosexual family as the natural foundation of the nation.[30]

These changes did not happen overnight, and any account of the development of sexually inclusive educational policies and curricula in Wales must consider the role of LGB Forum Cymru, which advised ministers and ultimately the Welsh assembly on LGBTQ issues, and which evolved into Stonewall Cymru in 2003. LGB Forum Cymru, founded in the first months of 2001, was the result of several trends. The National Assembly for Wales had established an equal opportunities committee, chaired by Edwina Hart, the minister for finance, local government and communities. It had also established an equality policy unit in the Promoting Equality in Wales Project Development Fund. At the same time, Stonewall's executive director, Angela Mason, had been lobbying for the national assembly to seek out the authentic voice of LGB communities across Wales, and had talked with LGB groups across the country during the autumn of 2000 about how they might network and become a credible, representative voice that the assembly could listen to.

Meanwhile, the Public Health Department in north Wales, concerned about the lack of visibility, and therefore the lack of knowledge about the health status of lesbians and gay men across the region, was keen that the assembly should develop healthy public policy in Wales that would underpin the creation (over time) of supportive environments for the largely hidden LGBTQ community. This would (it was hoped) enable even the most isolated lesbians and gay men to have the confidence to access health care more appropriate to their needs. To this end, the director of public health in north Wales, Dr Sandra Payne, encouraged one of her education officers, an openly gay man, to be involved in any new forum that would advise the assembly on LGB issues.

At a meeting with representatives from LGB groups from across Wales on 19 December 2000, with Angela Mason from Stonewall in attendance, Edwina Hart said,

> As the chair of the Equal Opportunities Committee, I need to have a clear picture of what is going on within the LGB community in Wales, and someone I can go to for advice ... It is important to build capacity and to establish a democratic forum that could act on behalf of the LGB community in Wales. In light of the fact that Stonewall

can bring resources to the table, the Assembly will contribute financially (in some way).[31]

On 22 February 2001, at the Cathays Park offices of the assembly in Cardiff, representatives from LGB groups across Wales (including the North and South Wales Police Liaison Groups, Body Positive, FFLAG (Family and Friends of Lesbians and Gays), North Wales Lesbian Line and the National AIDS Trust), Stonewall, the Equal Opportunities Commission and North Wales Public Health Department met with civil servants from the assembly's Equality Policy Unit to formally negotiate the establishment of the LGB Forum that would represent the voice of gay and lesbian people from across Wales to the national assembly. Along with considerable practical experience, Angela Mason, on behalf of Stonewall, pledged funding of £25,000 per annum (to be reviewed annually) to the fledgling forum and, in response, the assembly's Equality Policy Unit pledged to match Stonewall's funding from the Promoting Equality in Wales Project Development Fund. A little more than a month later, on Tuesday 10 April 2001, the LGB Forum Cymru steering group met for the first time and appointed two co-chairs, Gloria Jenkins of FFLAG from Cardiff and the present author from the North Wales Public Health Department.

By June, less than two months after the forum was formally established, it was approached by the Qualifications, Curriculum and Assessment Authority for Wales (ACCAC) for advice relating to how equality of opportunity might be addressed within the school curriculum. Through Sylvia Jones (a member of the forum steering group by virtue of her membership of the North Wales LGB Police Liaison Group), who in her professional life was a senior education officer with the LEA in Denbighshire, changes were suggested to the ACCAC consultation document with regard to the inclusion of sexual orientation in the list of characteristics that any equality of opportunity strategy needed to include. In September, through Jane Davidson, the minister for education, lifelong learning and skills, the forum was asked to participate in the consultation on the Welsh assembly's own consultation paper, *Guidance on Sex and Relationships Education* (SRE). Sylvia Jones, working with the present author (whose speciality in public health was sexual health), drafted a detailed, seven-page response, which was then discussed by the entire steering group before submission. When both the ACCAC guidance on equality of opportunity and the Welsh assembly's *Guidance on Sex and Relationships Education* were finally published, most of the forum's recommendations had been accepted.

As a result, the assembly's *Guidance on Sex and Relationships Education*, which was published on 17 July 2002, constituted the most radical and inclusive statement on teaching about sexual identity and sexual orientation published by any of the administrations within the United Kingdom, and is therefore worth quoting in its entirety:

Sexual identity and sexual orientation

1.30 It is up to schools to make sure that the needs of all pupils are met in their programmes. Young people need to feel that sex and relationships programmes are relevant to them and sensitive to their needs. They might also find it difficult to talk to their parents or carers about matters of sexuality or sexual orientation. The National Assembly is clear that teachers should be able to deal with these issues honestly, sensitively and in a non-discriminatory way. They should be able to answer appropriate questions and provide factual information. It is important that young people develop an understanding and respect for others regardless of their developing sexual orientation. They should be encouraged to respect and recognise diversity and differences in human life. Section 28 of the Local Government Act 1988 does not prevent the objective discussion of homosexuality in the classroom, and schools can provide counselling, guidance and support for pupils.

1.31 The issue of sexual orientation within a school's SRE programme and what is taught in schools is an area for concern for some parents. Schools that liaise closely with parents when developing their SRE policy and programme should be able to reassure parents of the content of the programme and the context in which it will be presented.

1.32 Guidance in National Assembly for Wales Circular 3/99, 'Pupil Support and Social Inclusion' deals with the unacceptability of and emotional distress and harm caused by bullying in whatever form – be it racial, as a result of a pupil's appearance, related to sexual orientation or for any other reason. Schools should have a strong anti-bullying stance and deal with any suspicion of bullying in accordance with the schools [sic] anti-bullying policy.[32]

At the three All-Wales Personal and Social Education (PSE) advisory group meetings held in the school year immediately following the publication of the new guidance, the advisory teachers for PSE (the area within which SRE falls) in each of the Welsh local authorities reported significantly increased activity in the support offered to schools across Wales on SRE. As a member of the PSE advisory group (from 2001 to 2012, and chair for six years), the present author recalls these discussions well. Few teachers, school governors or even parents questioned the appropriateness of sensitive teaching about sexual orientation, but many teachers felt that they lacked the knowledge and experience that would enable them to cover this topic well, and most expressed their frustration at the lack of appropriate curriculum materials. It became apparent very quickly to the advisory group that the development of teachers' skills in this area and the search for appropriate curriculum support materials would be a priority. Through the middle years of the decade, considerable resources in time and finance were devoted to the development of bilingual classroom resources and the training of teachers.

Essentially, the new guidance foregrounded the responsibility to speak and know sexual diversity as an integral part of education, and the first decade of the new century saw many new initiatives across Wales. These initiatives assumed the importance of students in contributing to and leading dialogue from their own knowledge and experience. The Healthy School Scheme (Welsh Network of Health Promoting Schools) became a significant driver of (public) health issues in school settings, and the establishment of pupil/student-led school councils became mandatory in all schools. Both these initiatives have played a significant role in schools where the development of sex and relationships education is concerned. From a public health perspective, promoting health within a community (in this context, sexual health generally and the health and well-being of LGBTQ students) goes beyond healthy public policy. It requires the creation of environments where health initiatives become part of everyday life, not add-ons, and for this to happen, community action needs to be supported. Healthy School Schemes and school councils became vehicles for the creation of supportive environments and school community action.

Where school councils work well, children and young people contribute to the decision making in their school community. In curriculum areas that fall outside the prescribed national curriculum, the school council can have a say in the content of what is taught. Sex and relationships education is one such area. Despite clear and unequivocal guidance on SRE from the Welsh government, the actual content of the curriculum is the responsibility of each school's governing body. School councils, then, can directly influence the content of the sex and relationships curriculum in a school, and seek to make the content relevant to that particular group of young people's needs. Increasing numbers of secondary school councils have also been successful in ensuring that all of the sexual health services in the school's locality, including support groups for LGBTQ young people, have been advertised on school notice boards – a relatively simple action which some school councils have described as 'the school coming out as LGB friendly'.

The Healthy School Scheme is an extended programme of action on seven health topics over six phases, where each phase can be between three and six school terms (one or two academic years). Two of the health topic areas, Personal Development and Relationships and Mental and Emotional Health and Well-being, offer individual schools the opportunity to address issues relating to the support of gay, lesbian, bisexual and transgender young people. Two schools, Eveswell Primary School in Newport and Ysgol Glan Clwyd (Welsh medium) Secondary School in St Asaph (both known by the present author), have worked over a number of years to offer exemplary SRE, which is inclusive of LGBTQ issues, within the context of the Healthy School Scheme initiative. In addition, Eveswell, a large, multicultural primary school, participated in a pilot project called Tackling Homophobia over two academic years. This project involved training workshops around homophobia for the school leadership team, the staff team and parents, and it offered teacher training around a collection of teaching resources for use throughout the school, from nursery to Year 6. Eveswell was awarded the Welsh Network of Healthy Schools National Quality Award for more than a decade of work on public health issues in 2010, and the work carried out on equality issues and tackling homophobia was highly commended. In the secondary sector, Ysgol Glan Clwyd has a well-honed pastoral service which has offered support to a number of gay and lesbian students over the past decade. In a reassuring development, one of the school's ex-pupils is now the coordinator of the West Rhyl Young People's Project VIVA (LGB) Support Group and a regular visitor to the school offering workshops for both teachers and students.

Another initiative that has encouraged and facilitated the progress of anti-bullying work in schools throughout Wales is the introduction, since 2004, of

Anti-bullying Week held each November. Addressing bullying issues in schools in a systematic way is a relatively recent development. Just fifteen years ago, a school that acknowledged it had a bullying problem was considered negatively – a school with problems! Today, schools that fail to acknowledge the existence of bullying – of all kinds, including homophobic bullying – raise questions about the school's ethos and the senior management team's awareness of everyday school life. School anti-bullying policies, and strategies for dealing with bullying, now carry elements of statute, and all incidents of racial or homophobic bullying have to be reported to the local authority. School councils across Wales revisit their school's anti-bullying strategy on a regular basis, and anti-bullying work is frequently presented as part of the Healthy School Scheme. An example (known to the present author, but by no means unique) can be found at Prestatyn High School in north Wales. Over the past decade, the school community has developed an effective peer-led 'buddy' anti-bullying scheme in partnership with Childline, which has become a model of good practice for schools in the area. When homophobic bullying was announced as the major theme for the inaugural Anti-bullying Week in 2004, Jane Davidson, the minister for education, gave a ministerial lead on the need to address homophobic bullying, speaking with passion about how schools needed to be safe places for LGBTQ young people.

In all of these developments, we see the importance of voice, personal experience and dialogue that must inform a queer curriculum and community in schools. In school councils' participation in curriculum development, in workshops for school leadership, teachers and parents, and in peer-led anti-bullying programmes, the queer student is not a passive receiver of authoritative state-sanctioned pronouncements on sex and sexuality, but a speaking contributor to the changing experiences that must inform the sexual education of the diverse body of Welsh citizens. A rights-based and inclusive pedagogy that treats children and young adults with respect must attend to their voices and experiences; also, teachers seeking to connect with their students (and student teachers) must also speak from places of authentic and lived experience. Schools and classrooms are spaces where theory and practice meet, and narrative and story are often useful ways of affecting that bridge, especially in their capacity to interrupt and re-narrate the stories sustaining the traditional heteronormativity of education.[33] This is why Deuce/VIVA's *Stories that Give Shape to Lives* was such an important early contribution. Returning to Mayo's point at the beginning of the chapter, this kind of dialogue is the way to connect young people to communities based on a model of citizenship that does not exclude queer futures.

And so we return to the concerns raised by Ben Summerskill and Lindsay Whittle at the beginning of this chapter, and the questions their concerns naturally raise. Public policy in Wales since devolution is underpinned by the legal requirements of the Government of Wales Act 1998 to have due regard to the principle that there should be equality of opportunity for all people. Ministers in the Welsh Cabinet have publicly demonstrated their commitment to equality and LGBTQ issues are considered alongside other equality strands. The Welsh government works closely with Stonewall Cymru to ensure that public policy is inclusive of LGBTQ issues. Education policy is clearly inclusive, and the Welsh assembly was the first administration in the UK to offer clear, unequivocal guidance on teaching about homosexuality in schools and has highlighted the importance of developing anti-bullying and anti-homophobic bullying policy and strategy in educational settings.

To generalize on whether or not teaching about homosexuality in the context of valuing difference and respecting diversity is failing in its goals is both dangerous and difficult. There are schools that clearly rise to the challenge, with school councils offering insight into specific needs, curriculum planners responding with sensitivity, teachers delivering well-planned and well-delivered lessons and a pastoral system that offers appropriate, inclusive support. And then there are schools that struggle – because of perceived parental objections, because of 'religion' and 'belief', because the timetable is already too crammed, because children need to be protected from such issues, because homophobia is 'dressed up' in many garbs. There are schools that struggle to be inclusive where LGBTQ issues are concerned because there are still people – members of governing bodies, senior management teams and/or teaching staff – that are still tied to attitudes and beliefs about homosexuality that were common amongst Edinburgh's clergymen and magazine agony aunts in 1966. However, the present author's own experience – the story I have told – working in education in north Wales for more than a decade, suggests that homophobia is not endemic in the Welsh education system or schools across the nation. There is more truth today, which offers people who happen to be lesbian, gay, bisexual, transgender, intersexed or queer the freedom to become themselves.

Part 4
Performing Contemporary Queer Wales

11

Omnisexuality and the City: Exploring National and Sexual Identity through BBC Wales's Torchwood

REBECCA WILLIAMS AND RUTH MCELROY

Even though television continues to be a pervasive source of cultural representation and a core constituent of many people's everyday lives, queer studies has been rather slow to engage with it as a distinct medium. In the introduction to their 2009 edited collection, *Queer TV*, Glyn Davis and Gary Needham lament that there is 'nothing that could be thought equivalent to the wealth of books devoted to queer film'.[1] The disparity of critical attention paid in the field of queer studies to film and television respectively is echoed in studies of the Welsh media where individual films have, until recently (and thanks largely to the journal *Cyfrwng*), received more in-depth attention than television programmes have ever enjoyed. These tendencies say much about the relative cultural value assigned to film and its audiences, on the one hand, and television and its audiences, on the other. However, it is our conviction that an assessment of queer Wales as a mediated cultural process must attend to the relationship audiences have with the small screen and the narratives and representations of queerness that they encounter there.

One of the main reasons for doing so is that television precisely *does* offer representations of queerness. This is perhaps most obviously evidenced by the presence of queer characters in a range of fictional and popular factual genres including drama, such as *Caerdydd*, the powerful drama-documentary *Carwyn*, BBC Cymru Wales's *Belonging* and, for network, its series, *Doctor Who*, *Torchwood* and *Sherlock*; sitcom including the BBC's *Little Britain* and *Gavin and Stacey*, soap opera in the form of *Pobol y Cwm* and reality television, most recently MTV's *The Valleys*. Within the Welsh televisual landscape, the figure of Russell T. Davies looms especially large. A Welsh television writer from Swansea, he is responsible for some landmark contemporary television dramas including *Queer as Folk*, which was groundbreaking in its dramatic depictions of gay life in the 1990s on Manchester's Canal Street. As David Alderson argues, *Queer as Folk* became 'one of Channel 4's most commercially successful series internationally, in terms of both its takeup by other channels and video and DVD sales, each of which has helped to ensure its afterlife'.[2] It was also adapted in the USA for the cable channel Showtime where it gained a rather glossier hue in its new dramatic setting of Pittsburgh. Davies subsequently wrote *Casanova*, a deft adaptation of the legendary Venetian adventurer and lover's memoirs, and *Mine All Mine*, a series based on a family in Swansea who discover they own a large part of Manhattan. Much mythologized in recent television history, it was here that Davies started to work with Julie Gardner who subsequently became head of drama at BBC Wales in 2003. This relationship is commonly credited as being the basis for the successful return of *Doctor Who* in 2005 and the subsequent spin-offs *Torchwood* and *The Sarah Jane Adventures*. For many critics, BBC Wales's success in producing *Doctor Who* is almost single-handedly responsible for transforming Wales's fortunes as a centre for television drama production. Julie Gardner (with Jane Tranter) is now starting a new production company backed by the Welsh government and based in Swansea and Los Angeles. Named Bad Wolf after a motif in the *Doctor Who* universe, the new venture further links queer television to Wales's international creative industries. Queer television is therefore integral to the contemporary Welsh media story, in particular via Davies's creation of *Torchwood*, as discussed below.

In their *Look Out* report, Stonewall Cymru pay particular attention to one of Russell T. Davies's most beloved characters, Captain Jack Harkness (played by John Barrowman). Jack 'flirts with both the Doctor and his female companion in a teatime programme aimed at family audiences, yet he remains a hugely popular character whose sexuality is almost incidental to the programme'.[3] Whilst the report welcomes the visibility of gay characters in Welsh TV series (many of which are no longer on our screens), such as the soap opera *Pobol Y Cwm*, S4C's drama *Caerdydd* (Fiction Factory for S4C, 2006–9) and BBC Wales's opt-out drama series *Belonging* (1999–2009), they also note the findings of the UK-wide Stonewall report *Tuned Out*, which found that 'during 168 hours of programming' in their sample of BBC One and BBC Two transmissions, 'gay lives were represented positively for just six minutes'.[4] Not only does this reveal the complex picture of queer televisual representation, but it also exemplifies two key tendencies in the analysis of television representations of particular queer/lesbian/gay/bisexual/trans characters.

The first is a tendency to evaluate the integration of such characters into prime time, mainstream programmes as being especially positive when sexuality is integral to the character rather than a factor that is repeatedly drawn attention to or the sole reason for the character's presence on-screen. As we explore below, this may sometimes be at odds with the centrality both of characters' sexualities and a programme's overall queer sensibility and their contribution to some viewers' pleasure in watching the show. Discussing his earlier *Queer as Folk*, Davies himself spoke of the tensions in such an approach for a writer:

> I did feel this incredible pressure to be representative ... Lesbians, older gay men, monogamously gay couples, AIDS. And it's just too big, trying to represent an entire

world – that's never going to create good drama. God, it would have been bland and worthy.[5]

Davies's comment demonstrates the tension inherent in balancing drama and 'authentic' representations of the varied lived experiences of gay people.

The second tendency is a propensity for analysing television representations through an evaluative paradigm that rests on notions of positive and negative portrayal. Here the principle impetus is to assess the proximity and faithfulness of the on-screen representation to the idea of authentic 'real life' experience, what Ellis Hanson characterizes as 'the moralistic politics of representation'.[6] There are powerful political reasons for adopting such a stance, especially, one might argue, when holding public service broadcasters to account for how they may (mis)represent queer lives. This approach was certainly dominant in the responses of participants in our audience research, discussed below. However, by itself this approach can reduce what are often complex, mediated representations to fixed reflections of what are implicitly taken to be stable, even immutable, identities. This is at odds with queer theory's impulse to regard subjectivity as dynamic and in process *within* culture and, by extension, within and through a specific medium such as television. Lynne Joyrich's essay 'Epistemology of the Console' makes an important contribution to this debate when it argues against a focus on visibility (are gay lives visible on screen, for example) in favour of an approach that asks 'how TV comes to know sexuality, how it comes to construct what we even count as knowledge of sexuality'.[7]

Recognizing the distinct value and political purchase of both these approaches, we turn our focus to *Torchwood* as one of the most striking and popular examples of how television in and from Wales mediates contemporary sexualities. In doing so, we build on existing critical debates regarding *Torchwood*'s representations of sexual and national identities and insist upon 'the profound significance of the cultural politics of television, the way in which the text of a television show itself engages with the politics of its day'.[8] Indeed, what intrigues us most is *Torchwood*'s 'engagement with' Welsh sexualities – how they are made, lived and inhabited in place – rather than the direct 'representation of' Welsh sexualities. Queer theory enables us to examine representations of both national and sexual identity since it 'starts from an impulse to question, problematize, or even disclaim the very idea of a fixed abiding notion of identity'.[9] Given debates over what contemporary Welsh identity actually is, queer theory also allows us to explore the plurality of identities in process across the range of sites inhabited by *Torchwood*, from its presence on-screen to the location of its reception amongst its gay viewers. It also allows examination of the physical place where it was, for its first three series, shot and set: Cardiff Bay. As Lynda Johnston and Robin Longhurst note, space and place are often linked to sexuality: 'sexed bodies are mapped, connected, and threaded not just through bars, casinos, and sites where statues are erected but through all spaces ... Sex and space cannot be "decoupled".'[10] As the chapter goes on to discuss, the creation of a memorial for the *Torchwood* character, Ianto Jones, in Cardiff Bay offers a sense of both a queer temporality and a 'queer place', a site where fans have placed flowers, cards and posters to remember the character whose loss is felt keenly by many fans. At the same time, this memorial for a fictional construct (Ianto Jones) functions as a tangible reminder of queer identities within Cardiff: in temporal terms, the memorial simultaneously mourns and makes present queer lives thereby disrupting heteronormative temporalities that often delimit who and what may be remembered. Considering the Ianto memorial as an example of a site that functions as a fan space, a potentially queer time/space, and a sometime tourist attraction, this chapter responds to Davis and Needham's call to study the concepts of place, space and geography when considering queer television.[11]

Approaching Torchwood

Much has been written about *Torchwood*'s representations of gender and sexuality. For example, Lee Barron argues that the series has 'done much to visualise gay representation within mainstream television, to counter media heteronormativity and to blur the boundaries between straight and Queer worlds', whilst Frederick Dhaenens posits that it offers the possibility of 'queer resistance' since 'By representing the main characters as gay without fixing their sexual identity, *Torchwood* represents gay characters whose sexuality is experienced from queer subject positions.'[12] However, this is not related only to male relationships, and it has been argued that the show should be applauded for having 'female characters engage in sexual activity usually without disparaging remarks and characterizations levelled at them', and for representing the desires of female characters or audiences.[13] *Torchwood*'s representation of sexuality is often linked to its science fiction status since its 'genre trappings offer travel through time as one possibility for imagining desires across time, both affective and physical, enabled as a queer temporality'.[14] Since Rosemary Jackson's *Fantasy: The Literature of Subversion*, fantasy has come to be regarded as the pre-eminent form for dealing with alterity and transgression.[15] Many of *Torchwood*'s fans themselves attest to the importance of genre to an appreciation of the series' queer meanings. For example, in response to a critical blog titled 'Bisexual women are alien to *Torchwood*' published in 2007 on the *AfterEllen* website, one fan, Shelby, writes,

> Also Defending Torchwood!! You have these charaters [sic] in a sci-fi world where all bets are off ... No one on this show blinks whether Tosh is sleeping with an alien in a human woman's shape or if Captain Jack is kissing a man ... Sorry – I also generally agree with the thoughts on representation on television and the media on Afterellen.com but this column missed the boat by not taking into account the genre and the episode order. Torchwood isn't the L Word or Queer As Folk – who ANY of the characters sleep with is only a small part of the storytelling – not the point of it.[16]

The genre of science fiction is thus recognized by some viewers as offering the possibility of subverting and challenging straight temporalities and resisting the more reductive representations often presented in other genres. For us, it is precisely *Torchwood*'s science fiction and fantasy generic trappings that allow the series to complicate representations of Cardiff, and Welsh identities, 'because real-world spaces are transformed into fictional places via genre'.[17] So, too, does its 'combination of the "unearthly" with the everyday' allow 'the show to break new ground in terms of sexual representation'.[18]

This sexual multiplicity is also well discussed in terms of its portrayal of Wales and 'Welshness'.[19] Linnie Blake draws together the show's representation of what star John Barrowman has called 'omnisexuality' with national identity in her discussion of *Torchwood*'s wider concerns with 'questions of identity – individual, gendered, sexual, national ... human'.[20] For Blake, *Torchwood*'s narrative devices and geographical location in the city of Cardiff, situated on the 'Rift' between worlds and times, offer a space for identity play. This emphasis on the importance of place in relation to identity, particularly sexual identities, offers a response to the call by scholars of queer television such as Davis and Needham to pay more attention to the 'concept of "space" and geography for queer TV studies'.[21] With Blake, Matt Hills is one of the few scholars jointly to consider *Torchwood*'s representations of sexuality and place. Referring to a quote from creator Russell T. Davies that 'There aren't many series about bisexuals battling aliens underneath Cardiff!', Hills extrapolates that it is 'not just "fluid sexuality" that separates *Torchwood* from its cult and telefantasy competitors but also its setting in Wales', since the series 'is geographically and narratively centred on icons of the regenerated Cardiff, such as the Millennium Centre and the Bay area'.[22] Contemporary television aesthetics and economics clearly play their part here, but analysis of *Torchwood*'s national identity politics must be set against the backdrop of debates over what it means for television to be produced in specific locations and how this is understood by audiences. Whilst Welshness is contested in the contemporary era, many audience members enjoy seeing where they live portrayed on-screen and this is linked to a sense of pride and connection for these viewers.[23] Understood from within a political framework, this entails greater visibility for both sexual and national subjects in their own place. However, since cultural and social identities do not exist in a vacuum, reactions to representations of nationhood necessarily intersect with images of gender, sexual and ethnic identities. As discussed below, for viewers of *Torchwood* who identify both as Welsh and as 'queer', there are potential pleasures and problems to be found in both the text itself and in the ways in which place, sexuality and representation intersect in the real-life locations associated with the series.

Asking the audience: representing gay/Welsh characters

The data discussed in this section comes from one of the focus group interviews we conducted between 2009 and 2010 as part of a broader research project entitled *Screening the Nation* in collaboration between scholars in the Centre for Media and Culture in Small Nations at the University of South Wales (then the University of Glamorgan) and BBC Audience Council Wales. It considered how Wales and 'Welshness' were being represented on-screen, and how audiences were responding to them. Since there are 'radical differences between communities across Wales' and no 'monolithic and single "Welsh" identity', we conducted nine varied groups including English- and Welsh-speaking respondents, families, schoolchildren, the elderly, and one with members of the lesbian, gay, bisexual and transgender community within Cardiff (although there may clearly be overlaps between these demographics).[24] We were keen to meet members of this community in Cardiff precisely because *Torchwood* had already been considered progressive in its representations of 'omnisexuality' and also because we were interested in the intersections between local, national and sexual identities.

Audience responses are crucial to understanding how texts are interpreted in terms of place and from a queer perspective. Audience research helps us to avoid the assumption 'that all audiences will read representations of queer characters in similar (if not identical) ways'.[25] Our method of focus groups allows participants to discuss issues in their own words and to 'steer the direction of discussion' whilst considering 'interviewees' beliefs, interpretative frameworks, judgements and practices'.[26] Since audience research can only ever offer 'partial insights about how audiences use the media in a specific context', it is worth reiterating that the comments made by the focus group cannot be taken as representative of the views of all members of Cardiff's LGBT community.[27] The group was small, comprised of three white gay men, and does not therefore account for the views of lesbian or bisexual viewers of *Torchwood*, nor non-white gay men. Furthermore, each of the participants worked to different degrees in jobs that had strong ties to the LGBT community in Cardiff (such as working for charities) and, as such, may have had a particular awareness of issues relevant to this community. Attempts were made to conduct another, more diverse focus group in the writing of this chapter, but were unsuccessful within the timeframe and availability of interested participants. Nevertheless, these responses offer an indicative understanding of the ways in which the series represents a range of different cultural identities. Indeed, two of the key discourses discussed in the focus group were the relationship between place and sexuality (and the often inextricable representation of national and 'queer' identities) and the struggle with questions of 'authenticity', 'positive' representation and genre.

In this group, discussions of Welshness often lead into comments about sexuality and the representation of gay characters on television. Whilst this may seem like a progressive challenge to the notion of national identity as a heterosexual monolith, it is worth noting how consistently the discussion on television focused on male characters and their sexuality. Women's sexualities (lesbian, bisexual, straight) were rarely raised by participants for discussion. Still, the linkages between place and sexuality in audience discussion suggest a persistent and unresolved desire for an 'authentic' Wales that includes queer sexualities. For example, we asked a question related to the differences between *Doctor Who* (which is filmed in Cardiff but rarely set there) and *Torchwood* (which was set in Cardiff). One respondent, Matt,[28] commented,

> I quite like watching *Doctor Who* when it's in London but it's not, and I suppose because I've lived in and around London for quite a while it's quite good seeing when

they go to underground stations and you think that's not, it's Queen Street or whatever, so they do try to disguise the fact that they're really in Cardiff, they don't come out with the fact that they're filming scenes here. Sometimes with *Doctor Who* when they are in Wales, I know the Christmas special with Kylie in, they were actually on the Hayes I think and they really were on the Hayes, not a representation. I'm not sure before *Torchwood* there was much positive representation of [gay] people on TV, I think because I have a particular bugbear with the character, Daffyd from *Little Britain*, I think it's a really poor representation of Welsh and gay, as a gay man the whole overly caricatured village idiot really, who doesn't realize everybody else around him is gay, is not really the only gay in the village, so I don't know, it's not necessarily a positive role-model and it's difficult to think of other positive Welsh TV characters. You might have Welsh people who are being positive on TV, newsreaders or musicians, but actually a positive reputation.

This is worth quoting at length since Matt moves almost seamlessly from discussing filming and Cardiff locations doubling for London into his point about broader positive representations in *Torchwood*, comparing these to his issues with the character of Daffyd (played by Matt Lucas) in *Little Britain*. Although the question is not explicitly about sexuality, and the response begins by discussing representation of place (i.e. the importance of 'really being' on the Hayes), for this respondent, issues around identity and representation cannot be easily demarcated along lines of sexuality or national/local identity. This can also be seen in Will's comments in response to the kinds of programmes he would like to see BBC Wales produce:

I would like to see, not just even if a programme was literally made in Wales, but I'd like to see people on mainstream and other programmes representing Welsh people in a positive way and Welsh characters just being there with their Welsh accents, because I know lots of friends who've gone to London to live [...] being that Wales is the biggest exporter of gay people as well, I would like to see Welsh people being more ... positively, you know and I think Huw Edwards on the news that's a positive step forward.

Such responses may be symptomatic of *Torchwood*'s representational slippages between a range of different identities that take in sexuality, gender and nationality since it is 'characterised by a variety of queer representational and critical practice that undertakes a radical deconstruction of the ideologies of identity that have historically underpinned mass cultural formulations of both Welsh and British selfhood'.[29] Indeed the difference between the Welsh gay character of Daffyd from *Little Britain* and John Barrowman's representation of the omnisexual Jack Harkness in *Torchwood* is discussed at length by this group. Whilst Daffyd is perceived to be negatively stereotypical, Jack is viewed as a more positive role model and representation of queer sexuality:

Matt: I do anti-homophobia training, and when I'm talking to school pupils, let's have a positive role-model for school pupils, well let's look at the complete opposite, because [Dafydd is] such a bad role-model in that he suggests that all gay men are camp, effeminate, wear lycra, latex suits, live in their own little microcosm, I don't know, so it's a very negative gay male image, the fact that the writer of that character is a gay man himself is, you know, so it's that reinforcement that gay men are here to be laughed at

– type thing that we saw with Mr Humphries in *Are You Being Served*, you know we've not really moved on TV-wise in 30 years when we've got characters like that coming forward I think.

Our participants regard the notion that gay characters should appear on screen to be ridiculed as regressive and outdated, a hangover from attitudes dominant in the 1970s.[30] However, it is interesting to note which of Daffyd's characteristics are cited as evidence of his being a bad role model. This includes his being too camp and effeminate, his clothing, and his insularity in believing himself to be 'the only gay in the village'. This insularity may be linked to Daffyd's apparent inability to open his eyes and realize that the entire population of Llandewi Brefi is in some way 'queer' but also to the notion that, as a resident of a small Welsh village, this insularity can be linked to his being Welsh. Daffyd is inward-looking as a gay man, but also as a Welsh man.

In contrast, John Barrowman and the character of Captain Jack are valued by these respondents. Whilst their discussions of actor and character are complex, the consensus was that the portrayal of Jack, especially in his relationship with Ianto Jones (Gareth David-Lloyd), was a step forward for representations of gay characters. One respondent comments:

> Matt: I don't know if you're going to go on to talk about the current series but the one that's just been on, really really loved the Ianto and Captain Jack storyline and the death kiss, I'm sorry if you haven't watched it … You know millions of people were watching that programme and the way that was dealt with was just so good, I mean I'm sure there were the homophobes out there who were horrified that these two men kissed but what person could not believe about the love between those two men, and the feeling and emotion that was going on between those two men at that time when he was dying, you know, who would be going urgh watching it, it was just so well done. And so, I just think it's a much better way to argue our campaign to get people to accept diversity, accept lesbian and gay people.

While Welsh television production and its links to tourism was the initial focus of the group discussion here, the respondent's reply swiftly moves onto the representations of sexuality and assimilation, with the portrayal of Jack and Ianto being characterized in terms of love, emotion and feeling. Here then we can see another set of concerns emerge, alongside those of place and nationhood, namely the concern with 'positive' representation and debates over what 'authentic' textual depictions of sexuality on-screen should look like. The value of such representations lies for this speaker (at least in part) in their affective power to persuade viewers in general to become more accepting of non-heterosexual relationships, what might be termed the integrationist position characteristic of Stonewall's overall approach. The interplay between Jack Harkness and John Barrowman is also alluded to, whilst Barrowman's commitment to a civil partnership in the UK, and to marriage in the USA, becomes a key way in which Jack's queer sexuality is understood:

> Craig: I think a very good thing with *Torchwood* has been the fact that not only is John Barrowman playing a bisexual, omnisexual whatever, he's calls it pansexual

> Matt: ... he calls it pansexual
>
> Craig: I think it's been very very good that he is a gay man and he's openly gay and so yeah I think he brings something else to it, if it was either a straight actor that was doing it, the programme itself would still be fantastic I'm sure, but he brings another level to it because he then talks about it and he can relate on *Loose Women* and things like that ...
>
> Matt: So having a gay man acting a part that's not that awful camp stereotype

Here, Barrowman's own sexual identity works to valorize his portrayal of Captain Jack in a way that Matt Lucas's character of Daffyd does not allow for.

Indeed, the focus group also included a nuanced discussion about whether representation and portrayal needs to only, or always, be positive. Such issues were raised in relation to both national and sexual identity:

> Matt: There's almost a need – it's the same sort of stuff we've been talking about the gay issue – there's almost the need to counter the negative Welsh imagery that's been on TV for quite a while with some more positive until we get to that point where it doesn't really matter, you will have a Welsh porter as well as a Welsh brain surgeon so there's a whole mixture of people going on ... it's not all about London; it needs to be about outside London as well.

As Matt's comment shows, accurate representation is seen to include a range of perspectives, acknowledging the need for a move beyond the 'moralistic politics of representation'[31] which focus on more simplistic representations of 'good' Welsh, gay, female characters and so on. Furthermore, this group has complex responses to the ways in which the third series of *Torchwood* represented less positive attitudes towards Jack and Ianto as gay men:

> Researcher: ... the old guy who was a child in the 60s who says something to him, its queer or something and I wondered how you felt about that, using those sort of comments, do you think it's still quite positive acknowledging that some people can still be quite prejudiced? How do you feel about that?
>
> Matt: Well in the training, I do lots of stuff about language and the abuse of language and how it feels to be called bender and queer and stuff, but I felt at the time when I watched it, I mean I did go, 'oo', but then actually it was very appropriate; it was how Ianto's sister's husband would respond, because if he'd have said 'oh, are you gay then' that wouldn't have been right; he had to say bender, and the fact that the older guy called him queer, those are words that are used by those people. I don't know if they were challenged, maybe if they'd been challenged to it, but they were appropriate.
>
> Craig: Also I thought there wasn't a lot of malice behind it, I don't know, that was just the word that was used, it wasn't used to be confrontational.

Here, there is an acknowledgement that not all representations of queer identity on-screen need be overwhelmingly positive. In accepting that, for the characters portrayed from different class or generational backgrounds, the attitudes were appropriate, this group sees beyond the common assumption that portrayal needs to only be concerned with showing responses that are accepting, positive and non-confrontational. The value of verisimilitude to television can, in other words, override viewers' more general desire for positive representations. It is here that the value of audience research is evident, revealing as it does some fascinating insights into the process of how LGBT viewers make critical evaluations. For Matt, ideas of authenticity (expressed here as what is 'appropriate' and 'how Ianto's sister's husband would respond') can outweigh the general impulse towards potentially limiting 'positive' representation as the dominant yardstick by which to measure any individual scene. Such negotiations reveal how judgemental responses to specific gay characters may be understood along a spectrum of representation, which ranges from entirely positive through to more complex, and possibly more realistic, reflections of the continuum of gay people's experiences.

However, the general consensus of the focus group participants, that *Torchwood* has, in many ways, offered more positive portrayals of both Wales and gay people than many other dramas or comedies, is reflected in other studies. The BBC's 2012 update to the report on the *Portrayal and Inclusion of Lesbian, Gay and Bisexual Audiences* highlights that BBC shows more broadly were supported by LGBT viewers who felt that 'Gay and bisexual men seem relatively happy with the TV they consume (across all channels, not just the BBC) – lesbian and bisexual women perhaps less so' whilst the earlier report notes that 'Authenticity is crucial to improving portrayal of LGB people.'[32] Similarly, Craig Haslop's focus groups in Brighton and London found that '*Torchwood*'s portrayal of bisexuality without labelling was perceived as positive by ... respondents who were self-identified as straight and gay or queer'.[33] Furthermore, the responses here indicate the importance of genre in thinking about representations of both nationality and sexual identity since it is understood that comedy and drama, for example, have different aesthetic and narrative tropes and tackle issues of representation quite differently.

Questions of sexuality, national identity and authenticity are also key to exploring a more geographically rooted form of place, namely the presence of a memorial to the character of Ianto Jones in Mermaid Quay in Cardiff Bay. This offers a fan-created quasi-permanent space dedicated to a deceased gay fictional character that has been allowed to endure, and was even endorsed, by Mermaid Quay's management. The next section explores the memorial in terms of representations of Ianto as a 'queer' character and how this intersects with questions over space, place and tourism in contemporary Wales.

Cardiff Bay, the Ianto memorial and queer space

Cardiff Bay has seen massive investment and change over the past twenty years and is the site of 'dramatic nation-building projects' such as the National Assembly, the Senedd and the Wales Millennium Centre.[34] In addition to the impact of political devolution and the creation of the Welsh government, Cardiff Bay has benefited from an increase in media production located in the city which results largely from the 'BBC's strategic decision to move production outside London as part of its regions and nations policy'.[35] This includes the new Roath

Lock drama studios built by the BBC in the Porth Teigr development in Cardiff Bay and an associated aim to increase the economic impact of the creative and cultural industries in south Wales. New tourist opportunities have also been created in the area, primarily via the 2012 opening of the *Official Doctor Who Experience*, an interactive museum that draws heavily on the notion that Cardiff is the show's new home.

The following signage stands in a section of Cardiff Bay's Mermaid Quay, a waterfront area populated with bars, shops and restaurants and located in close proximity to the Wales Millennium Centre, the Pierhead Building and the Senedd:

Ianto Jones 1983–2009

Torchwood 3

Gave his life in defence of the children of this planet.

The management of Mermaid Quay salutes you.

NOTE: Ianto Jones was a fictional character in the BBC series Torchwood (part of the Doctor Who franchise) which is filmed in part at Mermaid Quay. Ianto died in a confrontation with an alien species known as the 456 in the Torchwood miniseries Children of Earth which was first broadcast in the UK in July 2009. This is an impromptu memorial to the much-loved character.

The sign indicates a memorial space where fans have, since 2009, placed flowers, cuddly toys, cards, signs and other memorabilia in honour of the character of Ianto Jones who was killed in *Torchwood: Children of Earth*. The memorial was originally an unofficial fan-created space, but by the middle of 2010 it was popular enough for the Mermaid Quay management officially to sanction it with the plaque above. The site is of interest to understandings of queer Wales since Ianto was in a relationship with the character Jack Harkness at the time of his death, and the decision to kill Ianto was met with disappointment and outrage by many fans.[36] This reaction, and the subsequent campaigns to have Ianto brought back from the dead, were the key instigators in the creation of the memorial site.

Audiences' links to place and space have been discussed as both pilgrimage, where they may travel to sites of relevance (for example, Graceland and Elvis fans), and a sense of 'home'.[37] Some *Torchwood* viewers do travel to visit the city of Cardiff and, in some cases, specifically to see the memorial itself, experiencing 'the rare opportunity to relocate in place a profound sense of belonging which has otherwise shifted into the textual space of media consumption'.[38] For those already resident in Cardiff, the memorial may offer a complex duality, functioning as both a site of media significance and as a more ordinary place that one passes on the way to work or when enjoying an evening out in Mermaid Quay. For non-viewers, however, the space may be viewed in a range of ways: as an interesting anomaly, as a point of bemusement or even vitriol and outrage, or overlooked entirely. As Johnston and Longhurst note in their discussion of the Stonewall Inn in Greenwich Village, New York which has a gay and lesbian monument in the park outside,

> This park is indeed a space where queer identities are accepted, yet there are also some constraints about the expression of queer identities due to factors such as time, other

park users, the placement of monuments, and even park furniture like bench seats. Homeless park users share this space with Western tourists like us.[39]

Queer space can also be created and subverted in other ways. For example, Mark Vicars discusses the way in which the street sign for Canal Street in Manchester, at the heart of the city's gay scene, has been queered by covering the first letter of the street name. He argues that this 're/texualization' of the

> obliterated 'C' remakes Canal Street into Anal Street. The signage becomes a provocative making visible of dissident sexuality and as a narrativizing sexual/textual practice, it is a challenge to tacit hetero-norming social and cultural practices of place making.[40]

Such everyday activism, he argues, 'makes visible the lines of appearance and disappearance of sexual subjectivities, practices and cultures in public domains' and 'queers the disciplined spaces of everyday life'.[41] On the other hand, Alderson notes how urban regeneration in areas such as Canal Street and, by extension, Cardiff Bay have intensified 'an already commodified and individualistic gay sexuality' which tends publically to valorize specifically gay but not lesbian citizenship as expressed through the market. For some critics, then, new urban queer spaces have 'functioned increasingly as one of the ethnic spaces in consumer culture, serving as a marker of cosmopolitanism, tolerance and diversity for the urban tourist'.[42] Queer spaces are often provocative and contested. What we seek to understand here is why the Ianto memorial space has endured and become such an integral part of Mermaid Quay's space. This section explores how the site functions as a touristic space and point of interest to locals and visitors to Cardiff, with particular emphasis upon how it operates in relation to national and sexual identities. As in the focus groups discussion, national identity and sexuality, along with other axes of identity, cannot be easily disentangled. Thus, we consider both the Ianto memorial's links to 'Welshness' and how it functions as a significant visual reminder of a gay fictional character, exploring whether this space operates as a queer site within the contemporary cityscape of Cardiff.

Doctor Who and *Torchwood* have clearly impacted on tourism in Cardiff, but this is related to a specific 'new' Cardiff, one that is largely rooted in the Bay and is heavily reliant on the gentrification of this area. The Bay has been constructed as modern and cosmopolitan and its associations with the creative and cultural industries and a young, affluent crowd of residents and visitors mean that it is promoted as one of the most attractive destinations in Cardiff. Mermaid Quay's official website states 'Overlooking the Bay and with a chic, cosmopolitan atmosphere, Mermaid Quay is where Cardiff comes to relax.'[43] Given this emphasis on cosmopolitanism, it is possible that the Ianto memorial has been allowed to endure partly as a visible signifier of the inclusivity and tolerance of such a space. As a memorial to a queer character, the site stands as a testament to the fact that the Bay is welcoming to a range of contemporary identities and lifestyles. Interestingly, despite being home to several restaurants and bars, there is no identifiable gay social scene in the Bay area with the majority of Cardiff's gay bars and clubs being found on Charles Street or Churchill Way in the city centre. The Bay is thus unable to make such claims to inclusivity directly but can, we argue, do so via the continuing presence of the memorial, allowing the area to claim some status as a queer space. It has been noted that queer spaces more broadly are often seen as evidence of being inclusive and are often 'tentatively promoted by cities both as equivalent to other ethnic neighbourhoods and as an independent indicator of cosmopolitanism'.[44] It is therefore plausible that it is the Bay's very modern positioning that allows the memorial to remain, and to work as a liminal space for a range of identities to be explored.

In addition to functioning as a queer site, the memorial embodies and visualizes *Torchwood*'s status as a specifically Cardiff-based series. Located on a site that was diegetically used for filming (as the doorway to the fictional Cardiff Bay visitor centre that was the entrance to *Torchwood* base, The Hub), the memorial works as an on-going visual and spatial reminder of the series' links to the city. Even after the fourth series, *Miracle Day*, adopted a more global focus, the memorial remains as a site of focus for viewers unhappy with this shift. For a period of time, a large banner adorned the memorial stating 'We Want *Torchwood* Cardiff', testament perhaps to precisely the kind of homogenizing cosmopolitanism that Alderson critiques in his reading of Davies's *Queer as Folk*. *Torchwood*'s association with the Bay is officially sanctioned by Cardiff Council and the Wales Tourist Board,[45] but it is the space of the memorial that is perhaps most intriguing in terms of this representation. It has been allowed to stand, according to Quay staff because

> We support anything to do with local talent and production and we will do our best to keep the shrine undisturbed. We pride ourselves on keeping Mermaid Quay neat and tidy and enjoyable for everybody. We get international visitors, there are mementos and things left there from all around the world and it is good for Mermaid Quay, Cardiff Bay and Cardiff.[46]

Visibility is deemed positive and framed as an attraction, one that is distinctly Welsh in origin but international in its possibility for consumption. As Melissa Beattie argues,

> one reason the site was allowed to stand was because of the fact that the character to which the memorial is predominantly dedicated is Welsh, as well as the connection of the series to Wales ... conversations with wardens at the site support the view that local residents did appreciate these connections and were proud of the fact that Wales was being presented on Anglophone television in a non-stereotypical way.[47]

According to this discourse, it is the impact on tourism as well as the association with local production that allows the memorial to be maintained. In such public statements about the site, however, the queering of the space that the memorial offers is discursively exnominated. Welsh identity and associations are to be privileged, respected and maintained, but the potential for queering of city space is rendered silent in such comments. This is perhaps unsurprising given that such spatial queering is not always unanimously accepted. Johnston and Longhurst note the presence in Hamilton, New Zealand of a statue of the character Riff Raff from the stage and film musical *The Rocky Horror Show*. They argue that the presence of such a statue, of a character from a musical that celebrates difference and fluid gender and sexual identities, has 'queered' the city and upset 'the idea that city statues have to be heteronormative, commemorate, and celebrate conservative family values'.[48] Although the presence of this statue was questioned, its enduring presence in the city of Hamilton offers, according to Johnston and Longhurst, a space for queer identity to become visible and has, for both *Rocky Horror* fans and LGBT activists, become a site of pilgrimage and importance. There is no evidence that the Ianto memorial has become such a beacon for members of the LGBT community in Cardiff; indeed, in our focus group research, the site was not discussed at all by our participants. Despite this, however, our research suggests clear overlaps in relation to issues around space, contemporary queer urban identities and representations, and issues of visibility: both the textual visibility of Captain Jack Harkness and the literal visibility of the artefacts at the Ianto memorial site. Research into their views of the site would be useful in uncovering greater information about who exactly is maintaining the memorial that has been largely supported by female fans of the character of Ianto or the Ianto/Jack relationship. Either way, the fact that images, cards and writings about a homosexual relationship can still be seen at the site and have been able to endure for, at the time of writing, almost five years has something to tell us about the relationship between cities, places and queer representation.

In conclusion, as a television series that functions as a nexus for debates over both sexual and national Welsh – or, more specifically, a Cardiff – identity, *Torchwood*, its audiences and the existence of the Ianto memorial offer an instructive case study for examination of queer Wales in relation to contemporary television drama. Moreover, as we have argued in the first part of this chapter, such detailed textual and audience research, when combined, can reveal the complex and often paradoxical ways in which questions of authenticity, representation and genre work in productive tension for viewers whose desires for 'good portrayal' may be contested (or simply not delivered) by a queer text that has its own modality and way of mediating alterity. Given that *Torchwood* 'set out to explore exactly what it is to be enculturated (as British and as Welsh) to call oneself a man or woman, straight or gay',[49] this chapter has argued that identity politics can be usefully understood through examination of media texts from a queer perspective. As Samuel A. Chambers argues, queer theory is neither 'a narrow field concerned only with lesbian and gay sexuality nor [a] mere theoretical technique (a type of reading one would "apply" to texts)'.[50] Accordingly, since television drama continues to 'afford sites of identification and resistance, sites of negotiation of our place in a fast-changing world',[51] analysis of how television fictions such as *Torchwood* offer the space, both narratively and beyond, for such negotiations remains key to our understanding of how national and sexual identities are understood, defined and challenged in contemporary Wales.

12

Queer/Welsh and Welsh/Queer: Performing Hybrid Wales

STEPHEN GREER

In a country with two national theatre companies – the Welsh-language Theatr Genedlaethol Cymru and the English-language National Theatre Wales (NTW) – negotiations between language, national identity and cultural production through performance are an issue of live debate in which claims on belonging blur with claims on place. In reading two recent performance works by Dafydd James and Ben Lewis – James and Lewis's *The Village Social* (2012) and James's *Llwyth* (2010) – this chapter examines the status of queerness in that ongoing dialogue, and suggests how hybrid formulations of queer/Welsh and Welsh/queer identity can inform our understanding of cultural attachments to the local and the status of the local in our broader conception of Wales. Understanding contemporary performance in Wales to be engaged in the staging of Welsh identity both to itself and the wider world, the following discussion is also an attempt to locate a discourse of queerness in Welsh theatre in relation to what Helen Gilbert describes as 'formative moments in the ongoing narrative of nationhood, a means by which communities register, reiterate and/or contest modes and models of national belonging'.[1] This impulse is informed, in turn, by a desire to respond to the provocation offered by Steve Blandford: that 'in cases where nationhood does not bring with it the full power of the state, cultural practice becomes a crucial site where such contested definitions are played out'.[2] As a discourse that challenges assumed definitions of identity and subjectivity, how might queerness inform our understanding of that dispute?

While following Jen Harvie's assertion that 'national identities are neither biologically nor territorially given: rather they are creatively produced or staged', I am keen to explore the ways in which conceptions of the local and locatedness nonetheless inflect the claim on belonging and shared culture – particularly when, as Harvie notes, a nation's cultural space is not coterminous with a formal state's borders.[3] In this, I am conscious the porousness of given borders – and the perceived threat posed by subjects whose affiliations are plural rather than singular – may give rise to specific kinds of antagonistic nationalism (an issue to which I will return in discussion of *Llwyth*'s overseas staging). This much is a recurring preoccupation of James's recent work for the theatre: a concern for the conditions and consequences of claims on nation and belonging, and the tensions between the celebration of a Welsh-language culture and the policing of its borders; an interest in the slipping points, if you will, between an egalitarian or pluralist nationalism and a potentially authoritarian one. Welsh cultural identity is not evenly distributed, either within or without Wales; as I will explore below, the status of both of the works discussed in this chapter as touring productions is not incidental to their meaning, but describes their role in a broader cultural project intended to simultaneously affirm and challenge a stable sense of Welsh identity.

My broader contention here is that desire to belong may be held in complex tension with the desire to view national identity/identities as open to change, not only dynamic and 'inherently troubled' but elaborating a form of performative critique – that is, the (re)writing of culture within a scene of national constraint.[4] This perspective offers a consciously queer reading of Harvie's argument that

> UK identities are multiple, mutually contingent, and mutually embedded – simultaneously holding in tension multiple determinants from affinities with locale, region, and nation to affinities with Europe, global subjectivity and diasporic communities.[5]

Though Harvie resists an account which might segregate identities into 'us' and 'them' or resolve multiple identifications into a single coherent claim, the performance works discussed in this chapter suggest the persistent allure of such projects, even when they are known to be injurious or self-destructive. There are, if you will, bad habits of belonging which are not easily refused, practices of desire with which we engage despite ourselves because – perhaps – they are not entirely unwilled. Such a queer politics of belonging might well resemble the terms of Lauren Berlant's notion of cruel optimism, describing our attachment to something which actively impedes the aim that brought us to it initially.[6] While *Llwyth*'s encounter with belonging and place is ultimately more affirmative – and certainly less psychotropically murderous – than *The Village Social*, the following reading of those plays does not assert the simple efficacy of a pluralizing, hybrid model for understanding identity. The account that I want to offer here is more discomforting without necessarily being pessimistic, closely attuned to Berlant's apprehension that 'recognition is the misrecognition you can bear, a transaction that affirms you without ... necessarily feeling good or being accurate'.[7] Such thinking may cohere with Jose Esteban Muñoz's sense of hybridity as a modality 'where meaning or identifications do not properly line up'.[8] Might queer belonging be understood as that which persists in and through attachments that do not 'properly' line up? As attachments described by persistently 'disorient' orientations? As Dee Heddon's exploration of autotopography – a blending of the terms of mapping and narration to imagine 'autobiography as cartography of self' – suggests, a desire for 'original place' as an origin of self might involve the longing for something that was always 'fractured, layered, multiple and contested'.[9]

As such, my intention here is less to affirm a fluid, intersectional model for queerness than to examine the labour of a located hybridity by reading this chapter's case studies in the context of their material production and reception. In doing so, I hope to better acknowledge how the multiple 'contingencies, determinants and affinities' of identity are not given but worked at in relation to space and place, through affirmations and exclusions that spill into and sustain each other. To that end, I am drawn to the claim in Lucy Lippard's *The Lure of the Local* that 'All places exist somewhere between the inside and the outside views of them, the ways in which they compare to, and contrast with, other places.'[10] Such a split orientation may, in turn, pose hybridity in the terms of Sara Ahmed's discussion of (dis)orientation: that the phenomenality of space is caught between familiarity and strangeness, where the familiar is shaped by actions that 'reach out towards objects that are already within reach' and where 'the work of inhabiting space involves a dynamic negotiation between what is familiar and unfamiliar, such that it is possible for the world to create new impressions, depending on which way we turn'.[11] Perhaps perversely, the absence of 'fit' may also register as a form of attachment, a way of belonging. In this, the figure of the hybrid is never resolved as a new, coherent subject but marks an ongoing, reflexive project of hybridization – hybridity, if you will, as performativity. Set against the possibility of 'newness', then, is an apprehension of how bodies and their relations to space are materialized and 'made historical' through repetition, through gestures that makes certain kinds of labour disappear as they become 'effortless'.[12] On those terms, might we begin to understand belonging as a kind of methodology of place, a way of 'doing the local' to which we might become habituated? Which we pursue in the *hope* of habit, that it might become effortless rather than demanding our conscious labour? Or which we take up, queerly, in the hope of rewriting its terms to better include us?

Touring the local

National Theatre Wales's first year – framed as a 'Theatre Map of Wales' – premiered twelve pieces of work in twelve locations across Wales. Though encompassing conventional theatre venues, NTW's desire to look beyond theatre's 'traditional' boundaries was perhaps most clearly articulated through works commissioned in response to specific sites and communities. This strand of work included Volcano Theatre and Welsh National Opera's *Shelf Life* (2010), staged in Swansea's old public library; Marc Rees's excursionary exploration of the Welsh seaside at Barmouth, *For Mountain, Sand & Sea* (2010); Pearson and Brooke's staging of *The Persians* (2010) in Cilieni, a mock village built as a military training site in the Brecon Beacons; Rimini Protokoll's *Outdoors* (2011–12), an audio-promenade work for the streets of Aberystwyth performed every Tuesday for a year; and *The Passion* (2011), a weekend-long re-telling of the passion story in and around Port Talbot that involved some 1,000 community volunteers. This decentred approach, Steve Blandford suggests, may be understood as part of the company's attempt to reinvent and repossess the idea of a national theatre, and 'to some extent, the very idea of the nation'.[13] Amongst the opening twelve productions, *The Dark Philosophers* (2010) and the season's opening production Alan Harris's *A Good Night Out in the Valleys* (2010) toured between venues, the latter beginning in Blackwood Miners' Institute before moving to Blaengarw Workmen's Hall, Pontardawe Arts centre, Bedwas Workman's Hall and the Coliseum in Aberdare. For *A Good Night Out in the Valleys*' production designer, Angela Davies, 'the heart of the story [was] the building itself, the Miners' Institute', representing 'the man and the living breathing community in which it stands'.[14]

Against the first year's programme of broadly site-specific and site-responsive practice, *The Village Social*'s tour of the local to the local in NTW's second year may be understood as site-generic rather than site-specific – that is, as a performance generated for a series of like sites.[15] Even as the tour's chosen venues affirmed the communities of small town and village life, their specificity was characterized by a certain inter-changeability. While praising NTW's extension of the precedent set by *A Good Night Out in the Valleys* by touring to 'a diverse range of communities right across Wales', Dylan Moore's review for *The Arts Desk* suggested that Cae Bach's localism ultimately bore 'more resemblance to Royston Vasey, the north English village in BBC comedy *The League of Gentleman* than Llangwm, Llandinam, Llansilin or any of the other actual places the piece will visit'.[16] A mixed review from *Buzz Mag* which opened in seeming condemnation of the work's appropriation of the local – 'once more, out-of-city audiences have been targeted by a work which patronizingly uses their familiar social club as a starting point' – reached the similar conclusion that the 'fictional setting of Cae Bach could represent any small settlement in Wales or, indeed, any place that needs a lesson in letting it all hang out'.[17] The depiction of the local, then, was perceived as the cipher for a wider commentary about belonging and place.

In my own experience of the production at Aberaeron Memorial Hall, the production's detailed rendition of a 'local' space – balloons, streamers, light refreshments – seemed to simultaneously confirm and challenge the authenticity of the event. Though the distinction between dramatic and architectural space was blurred – not least through the mingling of NTW staff and cast members in character as front-of-house crew – the machinery of the touring production remained present to me, even as the production's carefully dressed space invoked familiar childhood memories of church hall social events in similar venues. The resulting affect, I think, expressed that *The Village Social*'s relationship to its 'local' venues involved an appropriation seeking to both celebrate and challenge the logic of communal belonging. In turn, Lewis and James's programme note declared an interest in the shared social space of the village hall as an archetypal expression of a particular kind of located togetherness:

> The village hall. What is it for? A place for the people of the community to gather together in shared activity: to celebrate, commemorate, debate, learn about local history, to sing, dance, exercise, to be entertained, to entertain? But what if it became a place where all the darkest secrets, the unconscious desires of that community of ordinary people were unleashed? What would that be like?[18]

If *A Good Night Out in The Valleys* sought to establish a located association with place in the name of authenticity – engaging with the working-class history of miners' institutes and foregrounding, for example, that the cast were 'all originally from the Valleys' – *The Village Social*'s tour implied the vertical logic of metonymic association, an exploration of rhetorical contiguity between spaces of overlapping use.

The Village Social

Framed in pre-publicity as loosely inspired by Euripides' *The Bacchae* and by its creators as '*The Vicar of Dibley* meets *The Wicker Man*', the narrative of *The Village Social* was structured as an evening of light entertainment and fundraising: a night of 'much-needed fun and jollity' following undisclosed 'recent unfortunate events' which had involved the death of twenty-seven cats and the burning of the community's much-loved ancient yew tree. A clairvoyant – Madame Isis – has been invited to provide the evening's entertainment but is running late, so the residents fill in by sharing tales of the village's history, stories relating to the Celtic otherworld of Annwn. As a group, the locals form a kind of fractured family: middle-aged Lawrence, the clipboard-wielding chairman of the village hall committee; folklorist, yoga instructor and 'community liaison officer' Lisa-Jen; germ-phobic pensioner and health and safety officer Jean; local beauty Yvonne and her security-obsessed husband Dave; and, finally, Lawrence's teenage son, Dion.

Though the stories that structure the play's first act are initially comic, it becomes clear that Cae Bach has been founded – and repeatedly renewed – through violent acts of foreclosure, and that the first human settlers of the land were themselves invaders. The celebratory anthem which opens the evening poses the condition of community as the quotidian elimination of outside threats:

> We'll shield and not neglect to
> Repel that which infects you
> This little field of ours.[19]

The commitment to land and place is figured as a commitment to work that can never be completed, only endless labour for an 'original' settlement that does not exist. As self-appointed local historian, Lisa-Jen's narration of the settlement's mythic history is laced with disapproval, envy and prurient curiosity. The original inhabitants 'whom the ancient Celts called gods and faeries' had 'no moral code in the modern sense, feasting on food and drink whenever they felt like it and enjoying long, uninterrupted session of coitus with whomsoever they chose with no disapproval or judgment'. The queerly hybrid bodies of these otherworld creatures are repellent – resembling 'subjects of a genetic experiment gone wrong, half animal, half human' – and alluring, 'And the biggest party animal of all was the great god, Cernunnos. A strapping great hunk with the head of a stag and thighs like tree trunks.' Coveting the fertile land of the clearing and unwilling to share it with the 'strange creatures' of Annwn, 'who actually make them feel slightly uncomfortable', the humans drive the original inhabitants away with sharp spears and burning torches.

The second legend's account of repelled Roman invaders repositions the invading humans as the 'local tribe' to restate a bloody claim on the land. Though a lone surviving Roman soldier is framed as an uncivilized animal, 'hunting down foxes and rats and boars and what have you in the woods at night with his bare hands and then eating their raw flesh like a bloody wolf or something', it is Dave's own account of the tribe's violent revenge that approaches pornographic detail:

> Then they cut him down, pin him to the tree trunk, cut off his feet, gouge out his knee-caps, pull all of his fingers one by one and stamp them into the ground, then they slice him open from his neck to his stomach and yank out all his guts. And he's like, 'No, no, please don't hurt me! I can't take it anymore! I'm Italian so I'm a big poof!'

Echoing Lisa-Jen's erotic fixation with the hybrid bodies of the creatures of Annwn, Dave's avidity betrays his own anxieties and, given his later transformation as 'Little Missy' in pink skirt and ringlets, enacts a kind of overcompensation for masculinity under threat. In turn, the third story – the legend of a filthy, stinking monk, Papa Begw – centres on a disgusted fascination with the body. Yvonne's delight in the detail of the story ('he looks an absolute state, he really did, he's just this sort of brown, smelly beast with eyes lookin' out') repeats the pattern of a violent policing of norms: Begw is burnt as a witch. As a darkly comic sequence, these stories seem to play out the scene of a primal repression of that which 'disturbs identity, system, order. What does not respect borders, positions, rules. The in-between, the ambiguous, the composite.'[20] As the evening continues, Madame Isis (later revealed as a disguised Dion) exposes through song the suppressed desires of the villagers and the tone shifts from observational comedy to absurdist horror: to quote from the script's description of the play's first song which foreshadows events ahead, 'like a scene from *The Wicker Man* performed by the cast of *Glee*', equally disturbing and energetic.

Dion, we later learn, has spiked the *cawl* with hallucinogens in an act of revenge for the death of his mother some ten years earlier on the night of the autumn village social: distracted by the promise of a soda stream in the raffle, no one had noticed her descent through mental illness to suicide. If Dion's mother's death was due in part to a kind of disinterested neglect by a community that – oriented on external threats – did not notice that one of its own was already absent from herself, Lewis and James's script makes plain that Cae Bach's community is capable of fiercely policing its borders, turning vigilante to chase a group of travellers from the village. Madam Isis's mocking of the community's sense of propriety presents as the moment where *The Village Social*'s satire finds its sharpest edge. Addressing Lawrence as Cae Bach's patriarch, Madam Isis sings:

> Oh brutal man
> Leading your clan
> Clutching your pitchfork and your petrol can
> Staking your claim

> This is your shame
> You downed a bottle of Chianti
> Then became a vigilante
> Shouting out 'you fucking gyppos!'
> With one flick, you lit your zippos!

The villagers' justifications for vigilantism are depressingly familiar, if not the formula of tabloid columnists: the travellers are criminals, tax-dodgers and human eye-sores and – anyway – all official channels of complaint had been exhausted.

> Lisa-Jen: They're just bunch of horrible, pikey chavs and I'm glad they're gone!
>
> Madame Isis: They were descendants of the Kale. A tribe who have lived in this part of Wales since the 16th century. How long have you been here?
>
> Lisa-Jen: Since 1998.

Rather than confirming a history of place, Cae Bach's legends – or the re-telling of them – come to represent the attempt to compensate for a desperate *lack* of belonging.

Might we understand *The Village Social*'s events as the consequences of disastrous over-compensation for that lack? As a kind of autotopography that fails in the communal attempt to (re)write place, an attempt that in denying the possibility of disorient orientations and discordant desires begins to consume itself? In the second half of the play, denial of desire and violence becomes the narrative's driving force as the inhabitants of Cae Bach become psychotropically transformed as embodiments of that which they would suppress. Denial, it seems, is only ever recuperative: it returns to the position of strength the very thing that it would exclude. Jean's concealed appetite for lurid crime dramas erupts into the murder of her neighbour's pit-bull dog, which continually fouls her garden: she returns to the hall on her mobility scooter, bloodied and wearing its head on her own. Yvonne, in turn, becomes Papa Begw: huge, hairy, encrusted with filth, belching and farting. While there is a certain horror and madness in these transformations, there is also delight in the release of libidinal energies. Yvonne sings, 'I've waited for thirty-six years to let go / To not use deod'rant and let my pits grow.'

If *The Village Social* can be read as any kind of morality tale – cautioning against the suppression of desire, or the violence of parochialism – the play's suddenly downbeat ending would refuse any reassuring sense of closure and return to normality. At the least, the exit of Lawrence to die as a sacrifice at the hands of cultists (seemingly a group of the village's young people) would stall any claim on the figure of the child as the symbol of optimist renewal. Dion's onstage overdose – a desirable and queerly morphous young man who has appeared in disguise as Madame Isis and, at the play's climax, as the god Cernunnos, with blood running from his mouth – might even figure the denial of 'reproductive futurism' and embrace of the death drive called for in Lee Edelman's queer polemic, *No Future* (2004).[21] Accordingly, Lewis and James's appropriation of *The Bacchae* – of Bacchanalian sacrifice and madness through music – might also be read through the lens of Joe Orton's re-writing of the same myth in *The Erpingham Camp* (1966), the story of respectable English holidaymakers whose 'innocent' pleasures turn to riot under the prudishly authoritarian control of Erpingham. In Orton's work, the holiday camp functions as a microcosm that demonstrates 'not only the repressive nature of society but also the farcical willingness with which its members accept and perpetuate that system', a farce that exceeds the terms of palatable social critique by refusing to 'return the audience to the safety and stability of the status quo'.[22] The status quo to which *The Village Social* returns, such as it is, are the circumstances that have led to the evening's disastrous events – offering not the closure of catharsis but rather anticipation of inevitable repetition: we have been here before, and we will be here again.

Llwyth

If Lewis and James' joint encounter with belonging and the local suggests the catastrophic consequences of a suppressed queerness, then James's drama *Llwyth* may offer an alternative and less destructive heuristic for belonging. Originally commissioned by Sgript Cymru and developed at Sherman Cymru, *Llwyth* opened at the Chapter Arts Centre, Cardiff, before touring venues throughout Wales and appearing at the Oval House Theatre in London. Restaged by Sherman Cymru and Theatr Genedlaethol Cymru for the 2011 British Council Edinburgh festival showcase, *Llwyth* toured Wales for the second time that autumn. In 2012, the work was revived for a third time for the Taipei Arts Festival, Taiwan. Though centred on the story of Aneurin – the prodigal son returning to Wales to face his extended kin – *Llwyth*'s tribe of friendships articulates a complex and sometimes contradictory web of queer and Welsh identifications across a night out in Cardiff on the day of the rugby international.[23]

Aneurin is writing a novel – a 'queer transhistorical love story' – that imagines the *Goddodin* as an ancient troop composed of gay lovers, echoing the Sacred Band of Thebes. Aneurin re-reads the *Goddodin*'s praise for martial prowess ('Swift long-maned steeds / Under the thigh of a handsome youth') as homoerotic, a re-writing presented as not only possible but obvious. At its most bullish, Aneurin's desire to queer Welshness presents as a kind of revenge for his exclusion – the re-coding of iconic Welsh cultural tropes to not only include queer subjects, but to refute their straightness. His relationship with the Welsh language and culture – with *Cymraeg* and *Cymreig* – is antagonistic and dedicated. Of *Llwyth*'s characters, only Aneurin speaks in poetic verse and in forms that echo the metre of cynghanedd; Aneurin professes to loathe the eisteddfod – 'it's a freaky cult ... it's just like a fascist rally' – but plans to compete in it, writing a poem to win the crown. Aneurin's appropriation of Welsh culture, as in the queer account of performativity, takes place through an occupation of its practices. This restive affiliation to Welshness finds its counter in Aneurin's relationship with the gay community – or, less fraternally, to the gay community's splintering image cults posed against the 'straights' and then against each other. Aneurin stands as part of that tribe of tribes – 'The jocks and the geeks, The Bears, the Cubs and the Chasers, The Bel Ami Twinks and the Triga Chavs' – and apart from it, knowing the precariousness of any queer claim on shared belonging on the grounds of sexuality alone.

Aneurin's friends also experience belonging as a form of potential alienation. For Rhys and Gareth, Welsh speech reveals an emotional fault-line, exposing different orders of emotional and cultural fidelity. Gareth has only begun to speak Welsh since dating Rhys; though marking access to a community of Welsh/gay culture, it also registers an estrangement from his Welsh but not Welsh-speaking (and, not incidentally, straight) friends. In turn, Rhys's possessiveness – or, more kindly, his fear of losing Gareth – blurs communities of speech and sexuality.

> Rhys: I'm just saying that you always say how much your life has changed. How you've grown as a person since meeting my friends, learning my language.
>
> Gareth: *Your* friends. *Your* language, Oh for Christ's sake!

Gareth's increasing fluency in Welsh marks both an affirmation of his bond to a queer/Welsh tribe and, for Rhys, the threat of independence – that fluency in the terms of both queerness and Welshness might lead him away. In turn, Dada's exchanges with Gavin – in part, an older gay man introducing a teenager to the dignified sensibility of camp – suggest how particular kinds of dedication to a language culture might enable – or at least make space for and support – divisions *within* that same culture. Gavin's protest at the formal gendering of grammar is countered, gently, by Dada:

> Gavin: But it pisses me off, like. Like why does every word have to be masculine or feminine? It's sexist.
>
> Dada: Some can be masculine and feminine, Gavin.

If Aneurin's queering is forceful – the determined and confrontational self-authoring of a Welsh queerness in the present through the re-writing of its cultural tropes – then Dada's counselling of Gavin renders queerness as an ideality, a doing towards the future whose terms are not yet known.[24] To be queer and Welsh might demand an ongoing act of translation, and the acceptance that any such translation will be partial and oriented on what *might be*, rather than what simply *is*. Though *hoyw* might 'sound gay' to Gavin, it might offer a form of recognition that – recalling Berlant – is a misrecognition that one can bear because it orients the self as to bring others within reach, others with whom one might form a tribe.

As I have argued elsewhere, *Llwyth*'s attentiveness to the possibilities for queer recognition within Welsh is marked by the play's use of different registers of speech, and the communities of practice and place that they might represent.[25] Here, the shifting register of Welsh-English or 'Wenglish' appears not just as a blending of 'the intonation and accent of the Welsh language with the speech rhythms of spoken English' but with the sense of a quotidian negotiation through speech.[26] In interview, James has described the play's multiple registers of speech as part of his own habitual hybridization of English and Welsh. In turn, the casting of *Llwyth* – a process that saw the refinement of Gareth as a character in the process of learning Welsh – was an attempt to reflect a broad range of linguistic perspectives and tones. Given the working history of Wenglish, it is not incidental that Gavin's negotiation of Welsh and queerness is marked by the register of class, protesting that 'Cynghanedd just doesn't sound nice with a Barry accent apparently.'

While Gavin imagines leaving for London as a way of re-inventing himself, Aneurin's return to Cardiff suggests that the attachments of place are not so easily discarded. There may be hard limits to a queer project of fluid affiliation and self-invention. At the play's climax, Dada challenges Aneurin's unwillingness – or inability – to prove his professed loves through actions.

> Dada: ... Love's a verb, you see. Something you do. Something you show. Not something you say. It means a commitment Aneurin. When the shit hits the fan, you don't run, you don't choose something or someone else. Love means you've already made your choice.
>
> Aneurin: That isn't love, that's loyalty.
>
> Dada: For Christ's sake Aneurin, that's what love is.

Nation and family are not a matter of simple choice but attachments that carry a kind of ethical imperative as forms of belonging that demand our participation. In this, love is both chosen as a commitment and lived as something over which one has no control: the choice has already been made, extending backwards and forwards in time. In Ahmed's terms, 'to say "we are committed" is not simply a pledge or promise that points to the future. Such a statement might suggest that it is too late to turn back, and that what will happen "will happen" as we are already "behind" it.'[27] Love, it seems, is a choice which is not a choice at all. Wales, the Welsh language and Welshness, then, are bound to sexuality and queerness in *Llwyth* in ways that are in turn optimistic and regressive, oriented on the future and demanding recognition of the past. The refrain, though, may be that queerness articulates the ongoing work in the present that is both required of and demanded by belonging. That is to say, membership of a tribe cannot be assumed but must be renewed and continually (re)negotiated.

Llwyth *in the UK*

Critical reception of *Llwyth* has sought to position the play in relation to constituencies of sexuality, language and national identity. Nathan Williams's praise for *Llwyth*'s original staging at the Chapter Arts Centre in 2010 framed the work as 'a raucous homage to Cardiff's gay scene' in which 'specificity to Cardiff residents is both its biggest strength and weakness'. For Williams, *Llwyth* spoke to and from a tightly located community: 'The details are as exciting for those who get them as they are alienating for those who don't. But then, that defiant, uncompromised presentation of subculture is kind of the point of Llwyth...'[28] Jamie Rees's review for south Wales culture magazine *Buzz* addressed *Llwyth*'s negotiation of overlapping communities of language, sexuality and recognition:

> It's a play about communities and communication and the lack of understanding that exists between different tribes in our culture, even in this age where we all know so much about each other ... It's patriotic and parochial but unlike most Welsh based theatre it will travel ... This play is Welsh yet universal.[29]

In structure, Rees's claim of 'Welsh yet universal' would seem to echo Williams's critique of a work that, through the force of its locatedness and specificity of idiom and phrase, spoke beyond the immediate tribe represented within it. In turn, Catrin Rogers's review for *Tu Chwith* praised the work for capturing a sense of queer Welsh schizophrenia: of being Welsh with 'one foot in London', of being gay amidst a (presumptively heterosexual) rugby culture, attached to family and yet desperate to escape.[30] Rogers, too, saw the play as a landmark work for Welsh theatre, not least in addressing the inadequacy of existing representations of gay life in Welsh culture. Gareth Evans's review for *Barn* similarly noted the rarity of *Llwyth*'s unapologetically frank handling of sex on the Welsh-language stage. Though acknowledging that the unabashed depiction of the sex lives of four gay men and a teenager might alone mark the work as pioneering, Evans asserted that *Llwyth* 'is not a gay play; homosexuality is not a subject, and the sexuality of the characters provide the basis for little drama'.[31] Averring the centrality of sexuality, Evans nonetheless identified *Llwyth* as the first Welsh play that was 'intentionally queer', mobilizing the self-aware aesthetic of camp with an audacity and certainty that did not seek to resolve its queerness.

If reviews in Wales located *Llwyth*'s queerness in relation to registers of Welsh-language culture and its attendant poetic and musical traditions, those elements have been conspicuously absent in responses produced elsewhere. Edd McCracken's review of the play for *fest* during the 2011 Edinburgh Festival noted the potentially clichéd registers of gay culture – 'Liza Minelli, show tunes, Kylie' – but in common with many other reviewers omitted any reference to the presence of Welsh music beyond a passing reference to a Welsh voice choir.[32] Steve Cramer's largely dismissive review for *The List* made no mention of the work's musical register, or even that the work presented made use of Welsh. Though David Kettle's review for *WhatsOnStage* noted the presence of Welsh, the 'decision to present [the play] in Welsh and English, often mixed up within the same sentence' was framed as a challenge to audience comprehension (requiring careful reading of surtitles) rather than articulating a distinct language culture.[33] In turn, writing for *A Younger Theatre*, Jake Orr praised the play's switches 'between Welsh and English' as part of director Arwel Gruffydd's success in creating a fluid sense of time and space, arguing that '*Llwyth* is camp but grounded, it's distinctly Welsh, but also universal'.[34] Though structured by Welsh and gay identities, the work was not defined by them; rather, the specifics of nation and desire allowed the play to speak more broadly to an audience who might share neither quality.

Amongst all of *Llwyth*'s reviews published during the Edinburgh festival, only Joyce McMillan's notice for *The Scotsman* made extended reference to the play's 'fabulous mixture of English, Welsh, and the kind of 21st century "Wenglish" – Welsh structure, English vocabulary', reading its presence as part of a reclaiming of 'huge tracts of traditional Welsh male culture' that might otherwise have seemed incompatible with gay identity.[35] Writing after the festival, Andrew Dickson picked up the thread of Welsh-language politics in a longer piece on the *Guardian*'s theatre blog on the emerging 'voice' of Welsh theatre through the work of *Llwyth*'s director Gruffydd as artistic director of Theatr Genedlaethol Cymru, acknowledging

> a play that took on far-reaching questions of language and sexuality without a hint of preachiness, performed in an uninhibited torrent of Welsh, English and a gloriously rich Wenglish that often bested both ... The question of who speaks Welsh, and how well, is a major concern of the play – as is the contested question of what exactly Welshness means.[36]

Llwyth's enquiry into the nature of Welshness, as such, was seen as successful in that it was able to simultaneously celebrate and challenge the known limits of a Welsh cultural identity.

Reviewing *Llwyth* at Theatr Mwldan in late 2011 during its second Welsh tour, Adam Somerset similarly praised the irreverent treatment of 'cultural shibboleths' and asserted the universality of fears faced by the characters. For Somerset, *Llwyth*'s critical saturation with consciously and identifiably Welsh tropes – suggesting that 'much in Dafydd James' writing escaped audiences in Scotland' – was indicative of the work's strength and of a broader cultural shift: 'A culture capable of self-irony, that can laugh at itself is one that has come of age.'[37] The cultural politics performed by *Llwyth*, then, was not merely paranoid but reparative, addressing and overcoming a misplaced sense of cultural inferiority. Roger Owen's commentary for *Barn* following his second viewing of the play asserted a similar sense of the work's burgeoning significance, borne not least of the play's success outside Wales. While the production appeared generally the same, Owen suggested that the play was more 'boldly explicit' in its return to Wales, significant for its restaging (a sign of uncommon success for works of Welsh language and culture) and crossing a boundary between being an interpretation of a drama and becoming a 'theatrical phenomenon' that had established its own brand, with a reputation beyond its dramatic content. The fact that *Llwyth* was now 'out there' had made the experience of viewing the work 'richer and more complicated as a result'.[38]

Llwyth *in Taiwan*

The metaphorical terms of Owen's 'out there'-ness might be readily informed by the particular cultural politics of the British Council's biennial Edinburgh showcase, in which *Llwyth* had been selected to appear earlier that year. Curated since

1997 by the council's drama and dance department with the advice of a panel of external advisors, the showcase has been framed by the council as a project intended to 'help grow and support collaborative working links between artists and organisations in the UK and their international counterparts', and 'to develop new markets and broker new collaborations between the British Council's global network and UK practitioners'.[39] Though open to the public, the showcase's works – drawn from 'outstanding' established and emerging companies working on the small- to middle-scale touring circuit – are presented to an invited audience of promoters and delegates from the international performing arts sector, a group including key programmers, producers and agents. The showcase's productions are viewed as both a product of British culture and the means for cultural dialogue, centred on a claim for theatre's particular ability to 'give an extraordinarily vivid insight into a country's values, challenges, and preoccupations: its sense of itself'.[40] Theatre's capacity to stage Britain to other parts of the world, in other words, is predicated on theatre's capacity to stage Britain to itself. In 2011, the showcase's emphasis on creativity, 'best practice' and excellence was refined to prioritize companies and practitioners seen as groundbreaking, pioneering and innovative, 'whose work exemplifies intelligent risk-taking' while simultaneously offering a form of 'quality assurance' to overseas delegates looking to promote UK work.[41] Accordingly, to read *Llwyth* as 'out there' in respect of the British Council's agenda may be to acknowledge several overlapping narratives: recognition of James's ability as a playwright and the quality of Sherman Cymru's production of *Llwyth*; an acknowledgement of the increasing profile of Welsh-language performance within Britain's network of professional practice; and, perhaps most provocatively, the affirmation of a hybrid Welsh queerness as an 'innovative' or 'groundbreaking' lens through which Britain and other nations might come to examine their own cultural identities.

This latter claim – of Welsh queerness as a paradigm for understanding the intersection of different kinds of belonging – would appear present in the discourse surrounding *Llwyth*'s staging at the Taipei Arts Festival in Taiwan in summer 2012. Interviewed for Fiction Factory's documentary for S4C, filmed during the festival, James offered a distinction between the politics of belonging and the politics of identity, averring that *Llwyth* 'isn't a play about being gay or being Welsh. It's story which explores the concept of belonging to a tribe.'[42] In Taiwan as in Wales, that exploration of belonging was inflected by a history in which the possibility of national identity – and an independent one, at that – has been fought through the terms of language culture and education. Following the end of Japanese rule at the end of the Second World War, the ascension of Mandarin under the ruling Chinese Nationality Party (Kuomintang, or KMT) in the late 1940s saw the formal downgrading of other languages – including Taiwanese Hokkien, Hakka and aboriginal languages – to the status of 'local dialects'.[43] The nationalist government's aggressive promotion of Mandarin – known in Taiwan as *Guoyu*, or 'national language' – also banned the use of Japanese and local languages in schools, government and local media. In this, Mandarin emerged as both a subject and the medium of instruction and developed as the dominant mode of cultural production and reproduction to the detriment of other language cultures.[44]

Echoing the punitive 'Welsh not' of late nineteenth- and early twentieth-century Wales, language use in Taiwanese schools was policed through physical punishment, fines and dunce boards – a practice which only came to an end in the mid-1990s following a process of political liberalization that saw the legalization of the opposition party, the Democratic Progressive Party (DPP), and the lifting of martial law in 1987. In the period that followed, the use of *muyu* or 'local mother tongues' emerged as a complex, multiple signifier of political and cultural identity: 'as a symbol of defiance against the establishment, as an expression of democratisation, as a sign of localism, and as an assertion of ethnolinguistic identity'.[45] Following the election of DPP officials in the 1990s, educators began to be directed to develop curricula at the elementary level in each region's local language, a practice that spread throughout Taiwan following 2001.[46] In contemporary Taiwan, public language history and culture remains politically charged, though the correlation between language use and support for either unification or independence movements is not straightforward: identifications through language are further inflected by conceptions of a distinct Taiwanese identity as opposed to Taiwanese identity as a *subset* of Chinese identity. Such hybrid identifications, then, might be considered both queer in their refusal – or, at least, frustration – of fixed, uniform or categorical terms for national identity.

Performed in its original Welsh/English/Wenglish, *Llwyth*'s performances in Taipei were subtitled in English and Mandarin. Speaking to the play's reception by Taiwanese audiences, James suggested that

> They see in the play similarities between the situation in Wales and their experiences in Taiwan. Some of the Taiwanese people seek independence from China. They're very passionate about the Taiwanese national identity as opposed to the Chinese identity.[47]

At the same time, and though acknowledging the antagonism between competing national identities, the logic offered by James for his own nationalism resisted the heuristic of distinction through opposition alone:

> I don't measure my national identity against that of England ... The major conflict in the play is the conflict I felt between my identity as a gay man and my identity as a Welsh man. I don't know whether the conflict is an external or an internal one. Did I create that conflict inside myself?

In other words, *Llwyth*'s tribal politics might not offer a straightforward mapping of Welsh-English to Taiwanese-Chinese tensions, but instead the possibility of a coming to terms with seemingly contradictory claims on belonging and self-identity – to return to the frame offered at the beginning of this chapter, in orientations which might not 'line up'. That said, Taipei Arts Festival's artistic director Yi-Wei Keng's location of the work within the cultural space of Taiwan was perhaps more pointed in its reading of Anglo-Welsh politics as a cypher for China-Tawainese relations:

> An English man may not realize his existence is a threat to a Welshman ... Wales has its own unique language. When we understand this, we see its experience reflects our

experience. And when we see how others face questions about their identity we learn to face our own questions.[48]

Here, the possibility of hybrid relations between cultures and cultural identifications gives way to a more directly oppositional logic, where minority culture – given to belong to a stable and discrete population – is threatened by a majority one. In this, Keng's commentary may bring into sharp relief how the potential of Welsh queerness as a cipher for understanding difference may carry within it a history of conflict. That is to say, the potential of plural and hybrid identification does not merely replace but works alongside and within rather older, dominant logics of nation and belonging. Such tension – between universalizing and minoritarian accounts of difference – marks the territory of Welsh/queer and queer/Welsh performance as one of ongoing negotiation between orientations and attachments which may persist in their discordance. While claims made for the distinctive representation of Welsh and/or queer culture and identity discussed above have oftentimes been accompanied by the assertion of their universality, the broader project of Welsh queer performance may be one which challenges and broadens the scope of the cultural recognition: a rendering of Welsh identity that attempts to continually revisit its borders.

Notes

Notes to the Introduction

1. Santiago Fouz-Hernández, 'School Is Out: The British "Coming Out" Films of the 1990s', in Robin Griffiths (ed.), *Queer Cinema in Europe* (Bristol and Chicago: Intellect, 2008), pp. 145–164, 145.
2. Judith Halberstam, *In a Queer Time and Place: Transgender Bodies, Subcultural Lives* (New York and London: New York University Press, 2005), pp. 36–7.
3. Richard Phillips and Diane Watt, 'Introduction', in Richard Phillips, Diane Watt and David Shuttleton (eds), *Decentering Sexualities: Politics and Representations Beyond the Metropolis* (London and New York: Routledge, 2000), p. 1.
4. Phillips and Watt, 'Introduction', p. 1.
5. Lee Edelman, *No Future: Queer Theory and the Death Drive* (Durham, NC and London: Duke University Press, 2004), p. 17.
6. Homonormativity refers to the normalization of queer lives through domesticity and consumption. The progress of LGBTQ rights and the increased representation of LGBTQ people (and really only the select, generally white middle-class few) in media is a form of acceptance through rendering queers institutionally invisible. See, for instance, Jasbir K. Puar, *Terrorist Assemblages: Homonationalism in Queer Times* (Durham, NC and London: Duke University Press, 2007), pp. 38–9; Heather Love, *Feeling Backward: Loss and the Politics of Queer History* (Cambridge: Harvard University Press, 2007), p. 10.
7. Love, *Feeling Backward*, p. 32.
8. Love, *Feeling Backward*, p. 17.
9. Stevie Davies, *Impassioned Clay* (London: The Women's Press, 1999), p. 32.
10. A similar relation to the past may be found in Margiad Evans, as discussed in Katie Gramich's 'Gothic Borderlands: The Hauntology of Place in the Fiction of Margiad Evans' and Kirsti Bohata's 'The Apparitional Lover: Homoerotic Lesbian Imagery in the Writing of Margiad Evans', both of which appear in Kirsti Bohata and Katie Gramich (eds), *Rediscovering Margiad Evans: Marginality, Gender and Illness* (Cardiff: University of Wales Press, 2013), pp. 513–68 and pp. 107–28, respectively. See also Carla Freccero, *Queer/Early Modern* (Durham, NC and London: Duke University Press, 2006), p. 71.
11. In their oft-cited introduction, Andrew Parker et al. tell us that nations 'are forever haunted by their various definitional others. Hence, on the one hand, the nation's insatiable need to administer difference through violent acts of segregation, censorship, economic coercion, physical torture, police brutality. And hence, on the other hand, the nation's insatiable need for representational labour to supplement its founding ambivalence, the lack of self-presence at its origin or in its essence.' See Andrew Parker, Mary Russo, Doris Sommer and Patricia Yaeger (eds), *Nationalisms and Sexualities* (New York and London: Routledge, 1992), p. 5.

[12] Roni Crwydren, 'Welsh Lesbian Feminist: A Contradiction in Terms?', in Jane Aaron, Teresa Rees, Sandra Betts and Moira Vincentelli (eds), *Our Sister's Land: The Changing Identities of Women in Wales* (Cardiff: University of Wales Press, 1994), pp. 294–300. While Crwydren problematically refers to 'choosing to become a lesbian' (p. 20), the essay as a whole is sensitive to the incommensurable hybridities across gendered, national, linguistic and sexual affiliations that de-constitute the national body.
[13] Crwydren, 'Welsh Lesbian Feminist', p. 294.
[14] Crwydren, 'Welsh Lesbian Feminist', p. 295.
[15] See, for instance, Katie Gramich, '"Those Blue Remembered Hills": Gender in Twentieth-century Welsh Border Writing by Men', in Jane Aaron, Henrice Altink and Chris Weedon (eds), *Gendering Border Studies* (Cardiff: University of Wales Press, 2010), pp. 142–62.
[16] Crwydren, 'Welsh Lesbian Feminist', p. 297.
[17] Elizabeth Freeman, *Time Binds: Queer Temporalities, Queer Histories* (Durham, NC and London: Duke University Press, 2010), p. 16.
[18] José Estaban Muñoz, *Cruising Utopia: The Then and There of Queer Futurity* (New York: New York University Press, 2009), p. 11.
[19] Muñoz, *Cruising Utopia*, p. 1.
[20] Carolyn Dinshaw, *Getting Medieval: Sexualities and Communities, Pre- and Postmodern* (Durham, NC and London: Duke University Press, 1999), p. 3.
[21] See Matt Cook, *A Gay History of Britain: Love and Sex between Men since the Middle Ages* (Oxford and Westport, CT: Greenwood World Publishing, 2007), p. 3. Rebecca Jennings calls for a practice that instead analyses 'systems of knowledge about sexuality, exploring different ways in which sexuality has been thought and described', *A Lesbian History of Britain* (Oxford and Westport, CT: Greenwood World Publishing, 2007), p. xvi. Brian Lewis challenges chronological approaches to queer histories: 'Deep burrowing in archives and a theoretical mindset conducive to a bonfire of taxonomies have expanded our localised knowledge of the multiplicity of sexual practices and beliefs but rendered "our queer ancestors" less knowable.' Brian Lewis, *British Queer History: New Approaches and Perspectives* (Manchester: Manchester University Press, 2013), p. 4.
[22] For a similar example, see the construction of a queer heritage and tourism associated with the Ladies of Llangollen and located at Plas Newydd. Rebecca Dierschow, 'Faro and the LGBT Heritage Community', in John Schofield (ed.), *Who Needs Experts: Counter-mapping Cultural Heritage* (Farnham: Ashgate, 2014), pp. 93–100.
[23] Halberstam, *In a Queer Time and Place*, p. 5.
[24] Freeman, *Time Binds*, p. 10. See also Love, *Feeling Backward*; Freccero, *Queer/Early Modern*; Edelman, *No Future: Queer Theory and the Death Drive*; Dinshaw, *Getting Medieval: Sexualities and Communities, Pre- and Postmodern*.
[25] Halberstam, *In a Queer Time and Place*, p. 5.
[26] Jonathan Goldberg and Madhave Menon, 'Queer History', *PMLA*, 120/5 (2013), 1608–17, 1609.
[27] Scott Herring, *Another Country: Queer Anti-urbanism* (New York and London: New York University Press, 2010), p. 29.

Notes to chapter 1

1. Peter W. Trinder, *Mrs Hemans* (Cardiff: University of Wales Press, 1984), p. 3.
2. Jennifer Breen (ed.), *Woman Romantic Poets, 1785–1832* (London: Dent, 1992), p. 160.
3. Susan Wolfson, 'Introduction', in Felicia Hemans, *Felicia Hemans: Selected Poems, Letters, Reception Materials*, ed. Susan Wolfson (Princeton: Princeton University Press, 2010), p. xvii.
4. National Library of Wales, MS.10959E. Reproduced in *The Literary Manuscripts of Felicia Hemans (1793–1835)* (Adam Matthews Publications), Reel 2; emphasis in the original.
5. Henry Fothergill Chorley, *Memorials of Mrs. Hemans, with Illustrations of Her Literary Character from her Private Correspondence*, 2 vols (New York: Saunders and Otley, 1836), vol. I, p. 70.
6. Chorley, *Memorials of Mrs. Hemans*, pp. 165–6; emphasis in the original.
7. Chorley, *Memorials of Mrs. Hemans*, p. 167.
8. Jane Aaron, '"Saxon, Think not all is Won": Felicia Hemans and the Making of Britons', *Cardiff Corvey: Reading the Romantic Text*, 4 (May 2000), 1–3. Available online, *http://www.cardiff.ac.uk/encap/journals/corvey/articles/cc04_n01.pdf* (accessed 11 October 2012).
9. William D. Brewer, 'Felicia Hemans, Byronic Cosmopolitanism, and the Ancient Welsh Bards', in Gerard Caruthers and Alan Rawes (eds), *English Romanticism and the Celtic World* (Cambridge: Cambridge University Press, 2003), p. 169.
10. For an account of gender and desire as 'becoming undone' see Judith Butler, *Undoing Gender* (New York and London: Routledge, 2004), pp. 1–16.
11. Elizabeth Freeman, *Time Binds: Queer Temporalities, Queer Histories* (Durham, NC and London: Duke University Press, 2010), p. 45.
12. Jerome McGann, *The Poetics of Sensibility: A Revolution in Literary Style* (Oxford and New York: Clarendon Press, 1996), pp. 184, 186, 190. I describe McGann's argument as 'veiled' because the essay takes the form of a fictional debate between three academic (and anagrammatic) avatars: G. Mannejc, J. J. Rome and A. Mack.
13. McGann, *The Poetics of Sensibility*, p. 189.
14. McGann, *The Poetics of Sensibility*, p. 193.
15. Felicia Hemans, 'The Homes of England', in Felicia Hemans, *The Poetical Works of Mrs. Hemans*, ed. W. M. Rosetti (London: E. Moxon, 1873), pp. 413–14. All further references to Hemans's poems are to this edition.
16. Heather Love, *Feeling Backward: Loss and the Politics of Queer History* (Cambridge and London: Harvard University Press, 2007), p. 24.
17. Love, *Feeling Backward*, p. 23.
18. Leo Bersani, *Homos* (Cambridge: Harvard University Press, 1995), p. 108.
19. Lee Edelman, *No Future: Queer Theory and the Death Drive* (Durham, NC and London: Duke University Press, 2004), p. 3.
20. For an extended reading of the queer and transnational dimensions of this poem, see my 'Felicia Hemans, Herman Melville and the Queer Atlantic', in Julia M. Wright and Kevin Hutchings (eds), *Transatlantic Literary Exchanges, 1783–1863* (Burlington: Ashgate, 2011), pp. 61–74.
21. Tim Fulford, *Romantic Indians: Native Americans, British Literatures, and Transatlantic Culture, 1756–1830* (Oxford: Oxford University Press, 2006), p. 202.

22 Miriam Elizabeth Burstein, *Narrating Women's History in Britain, 1770–1902* (Aldershot: Ashgate, 2004), p. 76.
23 Brewer, 'Felicia Hemans', pp. 168, 170.
24 Brewer, 'Felicia Hemans', pp. 179–80.
25 Chorley, *Memorials*, p. 127.
26 Clare Simmons, *Popular Medievalism in Romantic-Era Britain* (New York: Palgrave, 2011), pp. 76–9.
27 Gary Kelly, 'Introduction', in Gary Kelly (ed.), *Felicia Hemans: Selected Poems, Prose and Letters* (Peterborough: Broadview, 2002), p. 33.
28 Reprinted in Kelly (ed.), *Felicia Hemans*, p. 421.
29 James Mulholland, *Sounding Imperial: Poetic Voice and the Politics of Empire, 1730–1820* (Baltimore: Johns Hopkins University Press, 2013), p. 84.
30 Lynda Pratt, 'Introduction', in Robert Southey, *Poetical Works, 1793–1810: Madoc*, ed. Lynda Pratt (London: Pickering & Chatto, 2004), vol. II, p. xxix.
31 Shawna Lichtenwalner, *Claiming Cambria: Invoking the Welsh in the Romantic Era* (Newark: University of Delaware Press, 2008), p. 149.
32 For a sense of the original layout of the notes in relation to the poems, one should consult Felicia Hemans, *A Selection of Welsh Melodies with Symphonies and Accompaniments by John Parry and Characteristic Words by Mrs. Hemans* (London: Power, 1822), reprinted in Felicia Hemans, *Tales and Historic Scenes; Stanzas to the Memory of the Late King; Dartmoor; Welsh Melodies*, ed. Donald H. Reiman (New York and London: Garland, 1978). It is worth noting that this original scored publication of the melodies printed the poems in a different order from all later nineteenth-century printings of the collection in anthologies and also provided alternative titles and fewer poems than these later editions.
33 Chorley, *Memorials*, I, pp. 70–1.
34 Chorley, *Memorials*, I, p. 39.
35 Simmons, *Popular Medievalism*, p. 58.
36 Tricia Lootens, 'Hemans and Home: Victorianism, Feminine "Internal Enemies", and the Domestication of National Identity', *PMLA*, 109/2 (1994), 247–8.
37 Brewer, 'Felicia Hemans', p. 176.
38 Edward Davies, *Celtic Researches, on the Origins, Tradition, and Language of the Ancient Britons* (London: Booth, 1804), p. 173.
39 Davies, *Celtic Researches*, pp. vi–vii.
40 While Davies does distinguish between priestly druids and poetical bards, the two terms also often circulate as interchangeable in his work, as they do for Hemans whose 'Druid Chorus on the Landing of the Romans' resembles closely the incantatory form of the 'Chant of the Bards Before Their Massacre by Edward I'. Davies notes how 'the language of' the Celtic 'race' afford '*a pertinent similitude of terms*': 'From *Bard*, the character in which *Druidism* originated, the system was called *Barddas*, and the most familiar term for *Druid* in their *Triads*, was *Mab Bardd, a son of the Bard*', p. 551.
41 Davies, *Celtic Researches*, p. 172.

Notes to chapter 2

1 [Cranogwen], 'Cwestiynau ac Atebion' (Questions and Answers), *Y Frythones*, ix (1887), 69. Throughout this chapter, the translations are mine unless otherwise cited.

2. [Cranogwen], 'Cwestiynau ac Atebion', *Y Frythones*, iii (1881), 290.
3. D. G. Jones, *Cofiant Cranogwen* (Caernarfon: Argraffdy'r Methodistiaid Calfinaidd, n.d. [1932]), p. 164.
4. [Cranogwen], 'Cwestiynau ac Atebion', *Y Frythones*, iii (1881), 355. Throughout this chapter, the emphasis is Cranogwen's.
5. [Cranogwen], 'Cwestiynau ac Atebion', *Y Frythones*, v (1883), 131.
6. [Cranogwen], 'Cwestiynau ac Atebion', *Y Frythones*, x (1888), 34.
7. Jones, *Cofiant Cranogwen*, p. 73.
8. [Catherine Jane Prichard], 'Cranogwen', *Caniadau Buddug: wedi eu casglu a'u dethol gan ei phriod* (Caernarfon: Swyddfa'r 'Cymru', 1911), p. 24; see also Katie Gramich and Catherine Brennan (eds), *Welsh Women's Poetry 1460–2001* (Dinas Powys: Honno Press, 2003), pp. 142–3, for a reproduction and translation of this poem.
9. See, for example, Jones, *Cofiant Cranogwen*, pp. 147–8; and Gerallt Jones, *Cranogwen: Portread Newydd* (Llandysul: Gwasg Gomer, 1981), pp. 35 and 49.
10. Nantlais [William Nantlais Williams], 'Cranogwen', quoted in Jones, *Cofiant Cranogwen*, pp. 161–2.
11. [Cranogwen], 'Cranogwen', *Y Frythones*, v (1883), 5–6.
12. [Cranogwen], 'Cranogwen', 6.
13. Jones, *Cofiant Cranogwen*, p. 131.
14. Cranogwen, 'Y Cyflwyniad' (The Dedication), *Caniadau Cranogwen* (Dolgellau: R[obert] O[liver] Rees, n.d. [1870]), p. 3; see also Gramich and Brennan (eds), *Welsh Women's Poetry*, pp. 122–3, for a reproduction and translation of this poem.
15. [Cranogwen], 'Cranogwen', *Y Frythones*, v (1883), 7.
16. [Cranogwen], 'Hunan-goffa' (Autobiography), 39.
17. [Cranogwen], 'Hunan-goffa', 79.
18. [Cranogwen], 'Esther Judith', *Y Frythones*, ii (1880), 332; see also Jane Aaron and Ursula Masson (eds), *The Very Salt of Life: Welsh Women's Political Writings from Chartism to Suffrage* (Dinas Powys: Honno Press, 2007), pp. 91–108, for a reproduction and translation of 'Esther Judith'.
19. [Cranogwen], 'Esther Judith', *Y Frythones*, iii (1881), 81.
20. [Cranogwen], 'Dyfodol Merched Cymru' (The Future of Welsh Women), *Y Frythones*, ix (1887), 200.
21. [Cranogwen], 'Hunan-goffa', *Y Frythones*, v (1883), 374.
22. Jones, *Cofiant Cranogwen*, p. 60.
23. Cranogwen, 'Y Fodrwy Briodasol' ('The Wedding Ring'), *Caniadau Cranogwen*, pp. 7–18, 12–13.
24. *Report of the Commission of Inquiry into the State of Education in Wales ... In Three Parts. Part I, Carmarthen, Glamorgan and Pembroke. Part II, Brecknock, Cardigan, Radnor and Monmouth. Part III, North Wales* (London, 1847), ii, p. 56.
25. *Report*, ii, p. 60.
26. See John May, *Reference Wales* (Cardiff: University of Wales Press, 1994), p. 96.
27. *Report*, ii, p. 61.
28. Quoted in W. Gareth Evans, 'Y ferch, addysg a moesoldeb: portread y Llyfrau Gleision 1847', in Prys Morgan (ed.), *Brad y Llyfrau Gleision: Ysgrifau ar Hanes Cymru* (Llandysul: Gwasg Gomer, 1991), p. 95.
29. *Yr Haul* (The Sun), August 1847, 261–5.
30. *Report*, ii, p. 57.
31. See Martine Segalen, *Love and Power in the Peasant Family*, trans. Sarah Matthews (Oxford: Blackwell, 1983), p. 20.

32 [Cranogwen], 'Cwestiynau ac Atebion', *Y Frythones*, vii (1885), 98.
33 Catrin Stevens, *Arferion Caru* (Llandysul: Gwasg Gomer, 1977), p. 67.
34 [Cranogwen], 'Cwestiynau ac Atebion', *Y Frythones*, ii (1880), 130.
35 [Cranogwen], 'Cwestiynau ac Atebion', *Y Frythones*, ii (1880), 226.
36 [Cranogwen], 'Cwestiynau ac Atebion', *Y Frythones*, iv (1882), 130.
37 See Henry Havelock Ellis, *Studies in the Psychology of Sex: Vol. I. Sexual Inversion* (London: Wilson and Macmillan, 1897); Richard von Krafft-Ebing, *Psychopathia Sexualis* [1882], trans. C. G. Chaddock (Philadelphia and London: F. A. Davies and Co., 1892).
38 See Lillian Faderman, *Surpassing the love of men: Romantic friendship and love between women from the Renaissance to the present* (1981; London: The Women's Press, 1985), pp. 147–230, on the popularity of 'romantic friendships' between women during the nineteenth century.
39 Cranogwen, 'Fy Ffrynd' (My Friend), *Caniadau Cranogwen* (Dolgellau: R. O. Rees, n.d. [1870]), pp. 74–6; see also Gramich and Brennan (eds), *Welsh Women's Poetry*, pp. 128–33, for a reproduction and translation of this poem.
40 [Cranogwen], 'Phania', *Y Frythones*, viii (1886), 165–8, 165–6.
41 [Cranogwen], 'Phania', 167.
42 Cranogwen, 'Fy Ffrynd', p. 75.
43 [Cranogwen], 'Phania', 207.
44 [Cranogwen], 'Y Traethodau', *Y Frythones*, i (1879), 67.
45 Cranogwen, 'Miss Ellen Hughes, Llanengan', *Y Gymraes*, iv (1900), 5–8, 7.
46 [Cranogwen], 'Dyrchafiad Merched' (The Elevation of Women), *Y Frythones*, 8 (1886), 235–7, 236.
47 Judith Butler, *Gender Trouble: Feminism and the Subversion of Identity* (London: Routledge, 1990), p. 141.

Notes to chapter 3

1 For more on the legends and the history of the house, see Juliette Wood, 'Nibbling Pilgrims and the Nanteos Cup: A Cardiganshire Legend', in Gerald Morgan (ed.), *Nanteos: A Welsh House and Its Family* (Llandysul: Gomer, 2001), pp. 219–53. For a fictional, dark romantic take on the haunted estate in the mid-eighteenth century, see Jane Blank, *The Shadow of Nanteos* (Talybont: Y Lolfa, 2015).
2 George Powell, letter to Theodore Watts, 29 August 1878; in *The Swinburne Letters*, ed. Cecil Y. Lang (New Haven: Yale University Press, 1959–62), vol. 4, pp. 57–8.
3 Morgan, *Nanteos*, p. 93; Glyn Jones, *The Dragon Has Two Tongues: Essays on Anglo-Welsh Writers and Writing*, ed. Tony Brown (Cardiff: University of Wales Press, 2001), p. 8; Anthony Powell, review of *The Swinburne Letters*, ed. Cecil Y. Lang, *Daily Telegraph* (1961); in *Some Poets, Artists and 'A Reference for Mellors'* (London: Timewell, 2005), p. 98; Philip Henderson, *Swinburne: The Portrait of a Poet* (London: Routledge and Kegan Paul, 1974), p. 149.
4 According to Census reports, Powell was born in Cheltenham.
5 Cecil Y. Lang, foreword, *The Swinburne Letters*, vol. 1, p. xl.
6 Anne Dzamba Sessa, *Richard Wagner and the English* (Cranbury, NJ: Associated University Presses, 1979), p. 92.
7 Richard Brinkley, 'George Powell of Nanteos: A Further Appreciation', *Anglo-Welsh Review*, 21/48 (1972), 130–4, 130.

8 Elizabeth Berridge, 'A Real Sea Adventure', *Cornhill Magazine*, 1064 (1970), 99–112, 102.
9 William Michael Rossetti, diary entry 4 January 1872; in *The Diaries of W. M. Rossetti, 1870–1873*, ed. Odette Bonard (Oxford: Clarendon Press, 1977), p. 144.
10 Herbert M. Vaughan, *The South Wales Squires* (1926; Carmarthen: Golden Grove, 1988), p. 102; Berridge, 'A Real Sea Adventure', 100.
11 Lang, foreword, *The Swinburne Letters*, vol. 1, p. xl.
12 Thomas Owen Morgan, *New Guide to Aberystwith and Its Environs*, 5th edn (London: Whittaker, 1869), p. 134.
13 Powell, letter to Swinburne, 3 February 1881; in Terry L. Meyers, *Uncollected Letters of Algernon Charles Swinburne*, ed. Terry L. Meyers (London: Pickering and Chatto, 2005), vol. 2, pp. 246–7.
14 Edmund Gosse, *The Life of Algernon Charles Swinburne* (London: Macmillan, 1917), p. 178.
15 Algernon Charles Swinburne, letter to Edmund Yates, 29 November 1882; in Meyers, *Uncollected Letters of Algernon Charles Swinburne*, vol. 2, p. 312.
16 Meyers, introduction, *Uncollected Letters of Algernon Charles Swinburne*, vol. 1, p. xix.
17 For speculations on Powell and Swinburne's experience of 'male-male fun', see Deborah Lutz, *Pleasure Bound: Victorian Sex Rebels and the New Eroticism* (New York: Norton, 2011), pp. 140–3.
18 Swinburne, letter to Powell, 13 August 1867; in Lang, *The Swinburne Letters*, vol. 1, pp. 259–60; emphasis in the original.
19 Swinburne, letter to Dante Gabriel Rossetti, 10 November 1871; in Lang, *The Swinburne Letters*, vol. 2, p. 167.
20 Lang, foreword, *The Swinburne Letters*, vol. 1, p. xl.
21 Ludwig Richter, *Swinburne's Verhältnis zu Frankreich und Italien* (Naumburg a. S: Lippert, 1910), p. 18.
22 Powell, review of *The Swinburne Letters*, 98. An attempt to write a life of Powell was apparently made around 1905 by Revd George Eyre Evans; see George R. Thomas, 'George E. J. Powell, Eiríkr Magnússon and Jón Sigurðsson: A Chapter in Icelandic Literary History', *Saga-Book of the Viking Society*, 14 (1953–7), 113–30, 126.
23 Aside from Maupassant's 'L'Anglais d'Étretat', fictionalizations include Anthea Ingham's *Dreams of Impossible Pangs* (Gamlingay: Bright Pen, 2014) and Judith Grossman's 'De Maupassant's Lunch at Étretat', *North American Review*, 275/2 (1990), 28–32). See also, Julian Barnes, 'An Unlikely Lunch: When Maupassant Met Swinburne', *Public Domain Review*, 24 January 2012, http://publicdomainreview.org/2012/01/24/an-unlikely-lunch-when-maupassant-met-swinburne/ (accessed 4 November 2015). The article is accompanied by a new translation of Maupassant's 'L'Anglais d'Étretat' by Elliot Lewis. For an artist's interpretation of 'L'Anglais d'Étretat', see Walton Ford's *Chaumière de Dolmancé, 1868* (2009).
24 Brinkley, 'George Powell of Nanteos', 130. For a discussion of Powell's bequest to Aberystwyth University see Harry Heuser, 'Bigotry and Virtue: George Powell and the Question of Legacy', *New Welsh Reader* 110 (winter 2015), 18–29.
25 David Lewis Jones, 'George Powell: Swinburne's "Friend of Many a Season"', *Anglo-Welsh Review*, 19/44 (1971), 75–85, 80.
26 Jones, 'George Powell', 75.

Notes

27 Rikky Rooksby, 'Swinburne in Miniature: "A Century of Roundels"', *Victorian Poetry*, 23/3 (1985), 261.
28 Raymond Garlick, *An Introduction to Anglo-Welsh Literature* (Cardiff: University of Wales Press, 1972), p. 93.
29 Jones, 'George Powell', 75–85, 84.
30 Russell Davies, *Hope and Heartbreak: A Social History of Wales and the Welsh, 1776–1871* (Cardiff: University of Wales Press, 2005), p. 102.
31 Unidentified newspaper clipping; in Powell, 'Gleanings', unpublished scrapbook, 40 (Aberystwyth: School of Art archives, Aberystwyth University, n.d.).
32 Unidentified newspaper clippings; in Powell, 'Gleanings', 50.
33 David R. Evans, 'Blow's Court Odes: A New Discovery', *Musical Times*, October 1984, 567–9, 67.
34 George Powell, letter to Swinburne [July 1880]; Meyers, *Uncollected Letters of Algernon Charles Swinburne*, vol. 2, pp. 226–7.
35 Powell, letter to Swinburne, 26 May 1880; Meyers, *Uncollected Letters of Algernon Charles Swinburne*, vol. 2, pp. 225–6.
36 Miölnir, Nant-Eos [George Powell], *Poems: Second Series* (Aberystwith [*sic*], 1861), p. 115.
37 Miölnir, Nant-Eos [George Powell], 'True Friends', *Poems* (Aberystwith [*sic*], 1860), p. 51.
38 Berridge, 'A Real Sea Adventure', 103.
39 Miölnir, Nant-Eos [George Powell], 'The Wreaths', *Poems: Second Series*, p. 57.
40 Jones, 'George Powell', 84.
41 National Library of Wales, Minor Deposit 1408A, 32; quoted in Morgan, *Nanteos*, p. 100.
42 Powell, letter to Swinburne, 12 December 1868; in Meyers, *Uncollected Letters of Algernon Charles Swinburne*, vol. 1, p. 139.
43 Herbert M. Vaughan, *The South Wales Squires* (1926; Carmarthen: Golden Grove, 1988), p. 103; this story is retold by Henderson, *Swinburne: The Portrait of a Poet*, p. 110.
44 William G. Cherry, 'Statement of Facts', prepared for Weston Cracroft Amcotts, n.d. (Ceredigion Archives, file ADX 86/4/10).
45 W. T. R. Powell, letter to William G. Cherry, 31 December 1853 (Ceredigion Archives, file ADX 86/5/2).
46 Cherry, 'Statement of Facts'.
47 Rosa Powell, letter to George P. Wilton, 4 June 1854 (Ceredigion Archives, ADX 86/5/21); emphasis in the original.
48 Cherry, undated notes in defence of Rosa Powell (Ceredigion Archives, file ADX 86/1/2).
49 Rosa Powell, letter to George P. Wilton, 7 June 1854 (Ceredigion Archives, file ADX 86/5/24).
50 W. T. R. Powell, letter to William G. Cherry, 25 December 1853 (Ceredigion Archives, ADX 86/1/1); emphasis in the original.
51 Weston Cracroft Amcotts from Pickering, Smith and Company, lawyers to Colonel Powell, 13 February 1854 (Ceredigion Archives, file ADX 86/2/5).
52 Rosa Powell to George P. Wilton, 24 February 1854 (Ceredigion Archives, file ADX 86/2/11).
53 Hughes and Roberts, letter to George P. Wilton, 30 May 1856 (Ceredigion Archives, file ADX 86/11/38); Hughes and Roberts, letter to George P. Wilton, 10 July 1856 (Ceredigion Archives, file ADX 86/8/23).

54 Rosa Powell, letter to George P. Wilton, 14 July 1856 (Ceredigion Archives, file ADX 86/8/24).
55 Cherry, 'Statement of Facts'.
56 Rosa Powell, undated memorandum (Ceredigion Archives, file ADX 86/4/9).
57 Cherry, undated note (Ceredigion Archives, file ADX 86/1/2).
58 Rosa Powell, undated memorandum (Ceredigion Archives, file ADX 86/4/9); emphasis in the original.
59 Rosa Powell, letter to G. P. Wilton, 7 June 1854 (Ceredigion Archives ADX 86/5/24); Weston Cracroft Amcotts, letter to George P. Wilton, 11 May 1860 (Ceredigion Archives, ADX 86/1/11).
60 Miölnir [Powell], 'Autumn Wind', *Poems*, pp. 53–4.
61 Vaughan, *South Wales Squires*, p. 104.
62 George E. Haggerty, *Queer Gothic* (Urbana, IL: University of Illinois Press, 2006), p. 2.
63 Ellis Hanson, 'Queer Gothic', in Catherine Spooner and Emma McEvoy (eds), *Routledge Companion to Gothic* (London: Routledge, 2007), pp. 174–82, 176.
64 Miölnir, Nant-Eos [George Powell], 'Vale', *Poems: Second Series*, pp. 145, 146.
65 Miölnir, Nant-Eos [George Powell], 'What Spirit', *Poems: Second Series*, p. 106.
66 Miölnir, Nant-Eos [George Powell], 'A Fever Vision', *Poems*, pp. 10–12.
67 George Powell, 'An Eye-witness at a Bazaar', *'Quod-Libet'* (Aberystwith [sic]: 1860), pp. 35–42, 35, 39.
68 Powell, 'Eye-witness', pp. 40–2.
69 George Powell, letter to Principal T. C. Edwards, 4 April 1879; in Moira Vincentelli, 'The U. C. W. Museum and Art Collections 1872–1918', *Ceredigion: Journal of the Cardiganshire Antiquarian Society*, 8/4 (1979), 389–403, 402.
70 *University College of Wales Calendar Advertiser*, 2nd edn (Manchester: Cornish, 1883), p. 70. For a contemporary inventory, see J. Mortimer Angus, 'Mr. Powell's Bequest', *University College of Wales Magazine* (March 1883), 161–5.
71 Objects from the Powell bequest were on display at Aberystwyth University's School of Art in the exhibition *Queer Tastes* (18 May to 11 September 2015).
72 Neal Holland, 'George Powell of Nanteos', in Robert Meyrick and Neil Holland (eds), *To Instruct and Inspire: 125 Years of the Art and Crafts Collection* (Aberystwyth: School of Art Press, 1997), pp. 3–6, 6.
73 George Powell, letter to Swinburne, 11 September 1876, in Brinkley, 'George Powell of Nanteos', 131.
74 Holland, 'George Powell of Nanteos', p. 5.
75 Powell, *'Quod-Libet'*, preface; emphasis in the original.
76 Powell, *'Quod-Libet'*, p. 52.
77 Powell, 'Gleanings', 61.
78 Richard Dellamora, *Masculine Desire: The Sexual Politics of Victorian Aestheticism* (London: University of North Carolina Press, 1990), p. 22.
79 Dellamora, *Masculine Desire*, p. 17.
80 Thaïs Morgan, 'Perverse Male Bodies: Simeon Solomon and Algernon Charles Swinburne', in Peter Home and Reina Lewis (eds), *Outlooks: Lesbian and Gay Sexualities and Visual Cultures* (London: Routledge, 1996), pp. 61–85, 77–8.
81 G. Mackenzie Bacon, *On the Writing of the Insane* (London: John Churchill, 1870), pp. 7, 18–19.
82 Anonymous, *My Experiences in a Lunatic Asylum by a Sane Patient* (London: Chatto and Windus, 1879), pp. 1–2.

83 Anonymous, *My Experiences*, p. 1.
84 Algernon Charles Swinburne, letter to Theodore Watts, 1 December 1873; in *The Swinburne Letters*, vol. 2, p. 261.
85 Algernon Charles Swinburne, letter to Theodore Watts, 1 December 1873; in *The Swinburne Letters*, vol. 2, p. 261.
86 Anonymous, 'Emerson: A Literary Interview', *Frank Leslie's Illustrated Newspaper*, 3 January 1874, 245; in Clyde K. Hyder, 'Emerson on Swinburne: A Sensational Interview', *Modern Language Notes*, March 1933, 180–2.
87 Henry Wilson and James Caulfield, *The Book of Wonderful Characters* (London: Chatto and Windus, 1869), pp. 1, 402.
88 George Powell, 'The Femme de Chambre', *'Quod-Libet'*, pp. 11–19, 11–12.
89 H. G. Cocks, 'Secrets, Crimes and Diseases, 1800–1914', in Matt Cook (ed.), *A Gay History of Britain: Love and Sex between Men since the Middle Ages* (Oxford: Greenwood, 2007), pp. 107–44, 124.
90 Unidentified newspaper clipping; in Powell, 'Gleanings', 66.
91 Unidentified newspaper clipping; in Powell, 'Gleanings', 93.
92 John Thomas Evans, *The Church Plate of Cardiganshire* (Stow on the Wold: Alden, 1914), p. 94, n. 5.
93 Algernon Charles Swinburne, letter to Theodore Watts, 8 November 1882; in Lang, *Swinburne Letters*, vol. 4, p. 311.
94 Algernon Charles Swinburne, 'A Dead Friend', *A Century of Roundels* (London: Chatto and Windus, 1883), pp. 14, 17.
95 Simeon Solomon, letter to Swinburne, *c*.7 November 1872; in Meyers, *Uncollected Letters of Algernon Charles Swinburne*, vol. 1, p. 248.
96 *The Morning Post* (London), 3 April 1871, 7.
97 *London Daily News*, 7 April 1871, 6.
98 Eiríkr Magnússon, letter to George Eyre Evans, 23 March 1905; in Thomas, 'George E. J. Powell, Eiríkr Magnússon and Jón Sigurðsson', 126.
99 Judith Halberstam, *The Queer Art of Failure* (London: Duke University Press, 2011), p. 2.
100 Miölnir, Nant-Eos [George Powell], 'A Psalm of the New Year', *Poems: Second Series*, p. 19.

Notes to chapter 4

1 Angharad Elen, 'Golygyddol', *Taliesin*, 151 (2014), 11. I would like to thank Dr Huw Osborne for inviting me to write this chapter, and I am indebted to him for his painstaking and constructive help. Thanks to Prof. Jane Aaron for encouraging me to write this, my first paper in English. I am very grateful to my colleagues Dr Cathryn Charnell-White and Dr Huw Meirion Edwards of the Welsh Department, Aberystwyth University, for their help on many occasions. I am also very grateful to Dr Paul Bryant-Quinn for drawing my attention to a number of texts and studies that became large portions of this research. In particular, I would like to thank Dr T. Robin Chapman for his support and patience and for reading the chapter carefully and for his invaluable comments and help with my English.
2 All translations in this article are my own, unless otherwise cited.

3   This is a brilliant piece of wordplay on the traditional chant 'Y Gwir yn Erbyn y Byd', 'The Truth against the World' made by the audience in the National Eisteddfod during the crowning, chairing and medal presentation ceremonies.
4   Dafydd James, 'Y Queer yn Erbyn y Byd', *Taliesin*, 151 (2014), 75. For more discussion of Dafydd James's plays, see Stephen Greer's chapter, 'Queer/Welsh and Welsh/Queer: Performing Hybrid Wales', in the current volume.
5   Dafydd Johnston (ed.), *Canu Maswedd yr Oesoedd Canol/Medieval Welsh Erotic Poetry* (Caerdydd: Tafol, 1991), pp. 120–1.
6   For similar discussions of queerness and language see Sharyn Graham Davies, *Gender Diversity in Indonesia: Sexuality, Islam and Queer Selves* (London and New York: Routledge, 2010); Tze-lan D. Sang, 'From Flowers to Boys: Queer Adaptation in Wu Jiwen's *The Fin-de-siècle Boy Love Reader*', in Howard Chiang and Ari Larissa Heinrich (eds), *Queer Sinophone Cultures* (London and New York: Routledge, 2014), pp. 67–83; Roni Crwydren, 'Welsh Lesbian Feminist: A Contradiction in Terms?', in Jane Aaron, Teresa Rees, Sandra Betts and Moira Vincentelli (eds), *Our Sister's Land: The Changing Identities of Women in Wales* (Cardiff: University of Wales Press, 1994), pp. 294–300; Elaine Pigeon, '*Hosanna!* Michel Tremblay's Queering of National Identity', in Terry Goldie (ed.), *In a Queer Country: Gay and Lesbian Studies in the Canadian Context* (Vancouver: Arsenal Pulp Press, 2001), pp. 27–49.
7   James, 'Y Queer yn Erbyn y Byd', 82.
8   Richard Crowe, 'Creu Traddodiad Llenyddol Hoyw Cymraeg', *Tu Chwith* (1998), 133.
9   Here, Crowe plays on the word camp in Welsh: the literal meaning, 'an achievement', is nuanced by the anglicized meaning of camp.
10 Here again there is a play on the meanings of the word camp in Welsh and in English.
11 The poet Twm Morys has used the idea of the playfulness and magical nature of the hare throughout his poetry, making it a constantly changing image. Here, perhaps, Richard Crowe is alluding to the belief that hares are hermaphrodite, as well as inviting us to use Twm Morys's word *sgwarnogrwydd* as something very similar in spirit to *camp*.
12 Carolyn Dinshaw, *Getting Medieval: Sexualities and Communities, Pre- and Postmodern* (Durham, NC and London: Duke University Press, 1999), pp. 3, 11.
13 Dinshaw, *Getting Medieval*, p. 142.
14 There is much between these periods but the discussion of these two extremes will suffice with the space of this chapter.
15 Dinshaw, *Getting Medieval*, pp. 205, 196.
16 Dinshaw, *Getting Medieval*, p. 39.
17 The earliest version of this tale is a poem in Latin by a monk from Fleury, Radulphus Tortarius, although most hagiographic tellings of the tale come from a prose text, again in Latin, dating from the twelfth century, *Vita Sanctorum Amici et Amelii*. From this, a Welsh version was derived which is to be found in *Llyfr Coch Hergest* (The Red Book of Hergest, c.1382–1410).
18 Patricia Williams (ed.), *Kedymdeithyas Amlyn ac Amic* (Caerdydd: Gwasg Prifysgol Cymru, 1982), p. 7.
19 Williams (ed.), *Kedymdeithyas Amlyn ac Amic*, p. 2.
20 Williams (ed.), *Kedymdeithyas Amlyn ac Amic*, p. 2.
21 A recent twentieth-century analogue is the recently 'rediscovered' *pryddest* by Elwyn Evans, which came close to winning the crown in 1948. The *pryddest* 'O'r Dwyrain' (From the East) deals with the poet's experiences in the army in the Middle East. The speaker remembers one of his fellow soldiers: 'A young Englishman I loved lies /

Under a sea of sand in a plain dwelling' ('*Mae ifanc Sais a gerais yn gorwedd / Dan fôr o dywod mewn dinod annedd*'). In another part of the poem, he talks frankly about what happened between soldiers at night: 'But I know that desire surfaces and blooms / In scores of beds at night – / The beds of men in a country beyond the love of women –' (*Ond gwn fod chwant yn brigo a blodeuo / Mewn ugeiniau o welyau gyda'r nos – Gwelyau gŵr mewn gwlad tu hwnt i gariad gwragedd* –). And he recalls, 'his smooth face beneath the hard moonlight' ('*ei wyneb llyfn dan galed olau'r lloer*') and a little later the love of David and Jonathan is specifically evoked and echoed in the words 'Very dear was he ...' ('*Cu iawn fu ef ...*'). It might be tempting to dismiss these lines as nothing more than chaste comradeship, but a beautiful *englyn*, '*Milwr*' (Soldier) and a separate poem of the same title echoes the *pryddest*. The second is even more uncompromisingly homoerotic: 'In the daytime I often saw him / Lying on his dusty cot / And all the damp golden curls / Clustered on his brow. / So brilliant in the dark, hot tent / Was his naked beauty' (*Liw ddydd fe'i gwelais lawer gwaith / Yn gorwedd ar ei lychlyd wâl / A'r holl gudynnau aur yn llaith / A ymglystyrai hyd ei dâl / Mor ddisglair yn y babell dywyll, boeth / Ydoedd ei harddwch noeth*). See Elwyn Evans, *Amser a Lle* (Llandysul: Gomer, 1975).

22 Saunders Lewis might have used his *Amlyn ac Amig* (1940) to expand the homoerotic possibilities of the fable, but that would not have been within his make-up. He does allow the two to swear their oath of love to one another, speaking together: 'I will not fail in love nor advice / Nor in anything that is worthy in a friend for a friend' ('*Na phallaf fyth o gariad nac o gyngor / Na dim fo'n iawn i gyfaill dros ei gyfaill*'). For Saunders Lewis, this is nothing more than nationalistic brotherly love. See Saunders Lewis, *Amlyn ac Amig* (Llandysul: Gomer, 1976), p. 21.

23 One may think of this in terms of Eve Kosofsky Sedgwick's discussion of homosociality in *Between Men: English Literature and Male Homosocial Desire* (New York: Columbia University Press, 1985), where the male-bonding between men in patriarchal culture operates on the threshold of greater intimacy and desire. See also Carla Freccero's discussion of a 'masculine sodomitic relation that bears fruit' in sixteenth-century French law, in *Queer/Early/Modern* (Durham, NC and London: Duke University Press, 2006), p. 57. Freccero, citing Sedgwick, finds a similar queer destabilization through a homosocial figuration of the nation in the exchange of blood, body and semen between men.

24 Peter Busse, 'The Poet as Spouse of his Patron. Homoerotic Love in Medieval Welsh and Irish Poetry?', *Studi Celtici*, 2 (2003), 177.

25 Comprised of rhyming couplets, each line being of seven syllables, developed in the fourteenth century.

26 Thomas Parry (ed.), *Gwaith Dafydd ap Gwilym* (Caerdydd: Gwasg Prifysgol Cymru, 1972), p. 21.

27 In this line, the poet references The Song of Solomon.

28 Rachel Bromwich (trans., ed.), *Selected Poems of Dafydd ap Gwilym* (Harmondsworth: Penguin, 1985), p. 168.

29 Busse, 'The Poet as Spouse of his Patron', 179.

30 *Guto'r Glyn.net*, poem edited and translated by Eurig Salisbury (accessed 14 May 2014).

31 *Guto'r Glyn.net*.

32 Freccero, *Queer/Early/Modern*, pp. 20–30. One may also read the hymns of William Williams, Pantycelyn (1717–91) in this context. Arguably the hymns insert a queer longing into the space of spiritual devotion.

33 *Guto'r Glyn.net*.
34 *Guto'r Glyn.net*.
35 Amazingly, we have Siân Griffiths's reply to Marged Harri: she sends her love via a lark as *llatai*. And there are a number of other *llatai* poems between women (and I know of no such *llatai* between men). The nature of the relationships in these poems is 'officially' viewed as 'Platonic', 'passionate friendship'. But the lexicon of sisterhood/ brotherhood was the usual way of describing and rationalizing and, in fact, legitimizing same-sex relationships in the past. One thinks of the *enfrerements* in France, which were in all but name civil partnerships if not marriages and of the sisterhood in Boston marriages in nineteenth-century America, or the 'passionate female friendship' of the Ladies of Llangollen.
36 Cathryn A. Charnell-White (ed.), *Beirdd Ceridwen: Blodeugerdd Barddas o Ganu Menywod hyd tua 1800* (Abertawe: Cyhoeddiadau Barddas, 2005), p. 101. I would like to thank my colleague Dr Cathryn Charnell-White for drawing my attention to these poems. I have attempted the translations here.
37 Charnell-White (ed.), *Beirdd Ceridwen*, pp. 120–1.
38 Charnell-White (ed.), *Beirdd Ceridwen*, pp. 120–1.
39 Charnell-White (ed.), *Beirdd Ceridwen*, pp. 120–1.
40 Charnell-White (ed.), *Beirdd Ceridwen*, pp. 122–3.
41 Charnell-White (ed.), *Beirdd Ceridwen*, p. 121; Dinshaw provides a relevant discussion of medieval transvestism in *Getting Medieval*, pp. 100–42, which offers more possibilities for the transgender lives in the period.
42 Saunders Lewis, *Cymru Fydd* (Llandysul: Gomer, 1967), p. 15.
43 For a discussion of George Powell of Nant-Eos, see Heuser, '"Please don't whip me this time": The Passions of George Powell of Nant-Eos' in this volume.
44 Gwenallt, *Eples* (Llandysul: Gomer, 1957), p. 35.
45 Gwenallt, *Eples*, p. 35.
46 Gwenallt, *Eples*, p. 5.
47 Islwyn Ffowc Elis, *Ffenestri Tua'r Gwyll* (Llandysul: Gomer, 1980), p. 12.
48 Elis, *Ffenestri Tua'r Gwyll*, p. 14.
49 Elis, *Ffenestri Tua'r Gwyll*, p. 227.
50 The reference is to Romans 1:27. As is often the case, the Welsh translation of the Bible does not correspond exactly to the English. The Welsh of Romans 1:27 could be translated as 'men with men doing filth'.
51 John Gwilym Jones, *Yr Adduned* (Llandysul: Gomer, 1979), pp. 48–9.
52 This coded literary shorthand is consistent with what we know (or don't know) about John Gwilym Jones's life. He was a very well-known and popular figure in Wales throughout his long life. He never married, and he never made a clear public declaration that he was gay. Since his death, relatives and friends have built up a barrier around his memory making it difficult even to question his sexuality. In his autobiography, his final important piece of work which was published when he was in his eighties, he did not say anything about any sexual feelings or romantic experiences. But very near the end of the memoir, he does leave a final little hint: 'at the moment I'm reading Truman Capote and having enormous pleasure' ('*Rwyf wrthi'n darllen Truman Capote ar hyn o bryd ac yn cael pleser dychrynllyd*'). See John Gwilym Jones, *Ar Draws ac ar Hyd* (Caernarfon: Gwasg Gwynedd, 1986), p. 117.
53 E. Prosser Rhys, 'Atgof', in E. Vincent Evans (ed.), *Cofnodion a Chyfansoddiadau Eisteddfod Genedlaethol 1924* (Caerdydd: Cymdeithas yr Eisteddfod Genedlaethol, 1924), p. 54.

54 Rhys, 'Atgof', p. 55.
55 Rhys, 'Atgof', p. 55.
56 Rhys, 'Atgof', p. 55.
57 Rhys, 'Atgof', p. 56.
58 E. Prosser Rhys, *Gwaed Ifanc* (Wrecsam: Hughes a'i Fab, 1923), p. 70.
59 Peredur Lynch, 'Morris T. Williams y Nofelydd', *Taliesin* (spring 1994), 19–20.
60 Lynch, 'Morris T. Williams y Nofelydd', 20.
61 Mention of Lawrence brings to mind something A. L. Rowse said about the critic John Middleton Murry: 'Murry told me that when Lawrence imparted to him that he was Gerald Crich [the character in *Women in Love* who wrestles naked with Birkin, the character that Lawrence used to represent himself], "you could have knocked me down with a feather." If sincere – he was not a wholly sincere man – this was extraordinarily imperceptive of him; but, then, there is no one so imperceptive as a 100 per cent hetero.' See A. L. Rowse, *Homosexuals in History* (London: Carroll & Graf, 1977), pp. 286–7.
62 Katie Gramich draws attention to several scenes between women that are very sensual if not verging on the erotic in her Writers of Wales series book *Kate Roberts* (Cardiff: University of Wales Press, 2011). Even earlier, in her MPhil thesis, Kate Crockett analysed two of Kate Roberts's stories 'Nadolig' ('Christmas', 1929) and 'Y Trysor' ('The Treasure', 1972), finding evidence of same-sex attraction between women and described her as 'an embryonic lesbian writer' (*'llenor lesbiaidd embryonig'*). See her 'Rhai Agweddau ar Rywioldeb yn Llenyddiaeth Gymraeg yr Ugeinfed Ganrif' [Some aspects on sexuality in twentieth-century Welsh literature'] (unpublished MPhil thesis, University of Wales, Aberystwyth, 2000), 44. Certainly, examples of close, intense emotional bonds between women can be found in her work from every period. Her long novel, *Y Byw sy'n Cysgu* (The Living Sleep, 1956), starts with a woman, Lora Ffennig, having been left by her husband. The story then goes on to detail her struggle to come to terms with her sense of rejection and feeling that now that she is outside the approved structure of marriage and family she is a failure. But the convoluted route of her thoughts in her narrative ends with her setting up a strikingly alternative family for the time. She goes to live in her bachelor uncle's house with her children and her friend Loti. On a very positive note, she concludes that there are ways of living other than the conventional ones.
63 John Gwilym Jones, *Y Goeden Eirin* ([Dinbych]: Gwasg Gee, 1946), p. 38.
64 Jones, *Y Goeden Eirin*, pp. 38–9.
65 John Gwilym Jones, *Hanes Rhyw Gymro* (Liverpool: Brython, 1964), p. 36.
66 John Gwilym Jones, *Ac Eto Nid Myfi* (Dinbych: Gwasg Gee, 1976), p. 7.
67 T. Rowland Hughes, *Yr Ogof* (1945; Llandysul: Gomer, 1975), p. 30.
68 Hughes, *Yr Ogof*, p. 39.
69 Hughes, *Yr Ogof*, p. 206.
70 W. Pennar Davies, *Caregl Nwyf* (Llandysul: Gomer, [1966]), p. 9.
71 Davies, *Caregl Nwyf*, p. 36.
72 Davies, *Caregl Nwyf*, p. 40.
73 Davies, *Caregl Nwyf*, p. 42.
74 John Rowlands, *Tician Tician* (Llandysul: Gomer, 1978), p. 42.
75 Siôn Eirian, *Bob yn y Ddinas* (Llandysul: Gomer, 1979), p. 29.
76 Eirian, *Bob yn y Ddinas*, pp. 29–30.
77 To be fair to Siôn Eirian, he did go on to write possibly the first truly gay play in Welsh, *Wastad ar y tu Fas* (Always on the Outside, 1986) and to include a very positive gay character in his film *Gadael Lenin* (Leaving Lenin, 1993, made with Endaf Emlyn).

But these works belong to the period of opening up of gay and lesbian depictions in Welsh that we see from the mid-1980s onwards.

Notes to chapter 5

1. Amy Dillwyn, *The Rebecca Rioter: A Story of Killay Life* (1880; Dinas Powys: Honno, 2001), p. 44.
2. Some notable discussions include Linden Peach's chapter on 'Unspoken Desires: Writing Same-sex Relationships', *Contemporary Irish and Welsh Women's Fiction: Gender, Desire and Power* (Cardiff: University of Wales Press, 2007), pp. 44–71 and Jane Aaron's discussion of Cranogwen in *Nineteenth-Century Women's Writing in Wales: Nation, Gender and Identity* (Cardiff: University of Wales Press, 2007), pp. 133–43. Representations of lesbians in work by men are discussed in Huw Osborne, *Rhys Davies* (Writers of Wales) (Cardiff: University of Wales Press, 2009) and Linden Peach, *The Fiction of Emyr Humphreys: Writing Wales in English* (Cardiff: University of Wales Press, 2011), pp. 78–81. See also Alan Llwyd, *Kate: Cofiant Kate Roberts 1891–1985* (Talybont: Y Lolfa, 2011) for a discussion of possible autobiographical contexts for Roberts's representations of same-sex relationships.
3. Whilst recognizing the anachronism of applying the term 'lesbian' to female same-sex relations of past centuries, I adopt it here to apply to contemporary historical research done in that field.
4. Until the late nineteenth century, sexual *acts* were not synonymous with personal *identity*. With the rise of sexology from the 1860s, sexual orientation became a matter of *who* or *what* one was. Thus sexuality became an innate identity – linked to gender – which did not necessarily require the performance of any sexual acts at all.
5. See, for instance, Sharon Marcus, *Between Women: Friendship, Desire and Marriage in Victorian England* (Princeton: Princeton University Press, 2007); Valerie Traub, *The Renaissance of Lesbianism in Early Modern England* (Cambridge: Cambridge University Press, 2002); Noreen Giffney, Michelle M. Sauer and Diane Watt (eds), *The Lesbian Premodern* (New York: Palgrave Macmillan, 2011).
6. Alexander Maxwell, 'Nationalizing Sexuality: Sexual Stereotypes in the Habsburg Empire', *Journal of the History of Sexuality*, 14/3 (2005), 266–290. See also V. Spike Peterson, 'Sexing Political Identities/nationalism as Heterosexism', *International Feminist Journal of Politics*, 1/1 (1999), 34–65.
7. On the treatment of Welsh women's (hetero)sexuality in the Blue Books and its cultural contexts, see Jane Aaron, 'The Hoydens of Wild Wales: Representations of Welsh Women in Victorian and Edwardian Fiction', in Tony Brown (ed.), *Welsh Writing in English: A Yearbook of Critical Essays*, 1 (Cardiff: New Welsh Review, 1995), pp. 23–39.
8. Marilyn R. Farwell, 'Androgyny', in Bonnie Zimmerman (ed.), *Lesbian Histories and Cultures: An Encyclopedia* (New York and London: Garland Publishing, Inc., 2000), pp. 35–6, 35.
9. See, for example, Nira Yuval-Davis, *Gender and Nation* (London: Sage Publications, 1997); Andrew Parker, Mary Russo, Doris Sommer and Patricia Yeager (eds), *Nationalisms and Sexualities* (New York and London: Routledge, 1992); Tamar Meyer (ed.), *Gender Ironies of Nationalism: Sexing the Nation* (London: Routledge, 2000).
10. Jeffrey Weeks, *Sex, Politics and Society: The Regulation of Sexuality since 1800* (2nd edn; Harlow: Longman Group, 1989), pp. 96–121. See also Alison Oram and Annmarie

Turnbull (eds), *The Lesbian History Sourcebook: Love and Sex between Women in Britain from 1780–1970* (London and New York: Routledge, 2001), pp. 155–8.

[11] Eve Kosofsky Sedgwick, 'Nationalisms and Sexualities in the Age of Wilde', in Parker et al. (eds), *Nationalisms and Sexualities*, pp. 235–45, 242.

[12] Sedgwick, 'The Age of Wilde', p. 242. Sedgwick complicates this idea of national homogeneity by reference to the disruptive presence of Wilde's own corporeal performance and presence and his position as an Irishman with nationalist connections.

[13] Walter Benn Michaels, *Our America: Nativism, Modernism, and Pluralism* (Durham, NC: Duke University Press, 1995), p. 49.

[14] Male homosexuality and its relation to the (generally American) state is a well-discussed topic; there is less material on lesbianism and the nation/state. Important discussions include Sally Munt's chapter 'The Lesbian Nation' in her book *Heroic Desire: Lesbian Identity and Cultural Space* (London and Washington: Cassell, 1998). See also Éibhear Walshe (ed.), *Sex, Nation and Dissent in Irish Writing* (Cork: Cork University Press, 1997); Joanne Winning, 'Crossing the Borderline: Post-devolution Scottish Lesbian and Gay Writing', in Berthold Schoene (ed.), *The Edinburgh Companion to Contemporary Scottish Literature* (Edinburgh: Edinburgh University Press, 2007), pp. 283–91; Jodie Medd, *Lesbian Scandal and the Culture of Modernism* (Cambridge: Cambridge University Press, 2012). On identity politics and space, see also Affrica Taylor, 'Lesbian Space: More than One Imagined Territory', in Rosa Ainley (ed.), *New Frontiers of Body, Space, and Gender* (London: Routledge, 1998); David Bell and Gill Valentine (eds), *Mapping Desire: Geographies of Sexualities* (London: Routledge, 1995) and Richard Phillips, David Shuttleton and Diane Watt (eds), *Decentring Sexualities: Politics and Representations Beyond the Metropolis* (London: Routledge, 2000).

[15] Bonnie Zimmerman, 'From Lesbian Nation to Queer Nation', interview with Susan Sayer, *Hectate*, 21/2 (1995), 29–43, cited in Zimmerman (ed.), *Lesbian Histories and Cultures*, p. 462.

[16] Munt, *Heroic Desire*, p. 143.

[17] Erzsébet Galgóczi, *Törvényen belül* (Within the Law, 1980), published in English as *Another Love*, trans. Ines Reider and Delice Newman (San Francisco: Midnight Editions, 2007).

[18] Aniko Imré, 'Lesbian Representation and Postcolonial Allegory', in Elzbieta H. Oleksy (ed.), *Intimate Citizenships: Gender, Sexualities, Politics* (Abingdon: Routledge, 2009), pp. 157–73.

[19] On rebellion see Tomos Owen, '"Never again stop the way of a Welshman": Rioting and Rebellion in Amy Dillwyn's *The Rebecca Rioter*', in David Bell and Gerald Porter (eds), *Riots in Literature* (Newcastle: Cambridge Scholars Publishing, 2008), pp. 51–74.

[20] One might make a case that the celebration of female sexuality in Gwerful Mechain's (1462?–1500) erotic poetry, such as 'I'r Cedor' (to the female genitals) is open to homoerotic readings, alongside heterosexual or auto-erotic contexts, but this is not pursued here. For a discussion of this poem's potential representation of same-sex desire, see Mihangel Morgan's chapter in the present volume. For a contemporary translation, see Katie Gramich and Catherine Brennan (eds), *Welsh Women's Poetry 1460–2001* (Dinas Powys: Honno, 2003).

[21] Illuminated legend to Eleanor Butler's journal, 1788, quoted in Elizabeth Mavor, *The Ladies of Llangollen: A Study in Romantic Friendship* (Harmondsworth: Penguin, 1974), p. 63.

22. Katherine Philips, 'Friendship in Emblem, or the Seale, to my dearest Lucasia', in *The Collected Works of Katherine Philips, The Matchless Orinda, Volume 1: The Poems*, ed. with notes and textual commentary Patrick Thomas (Stump Cross: Stump Cross Books, 1990), pp. 106–8.
23. Philips, 'Friendship in Emblem', pp. 106, 107. On union in Philips's poetry see Harriette Andreadis, 'Re-Configuring Early Modern Friendship: Katherine Philips and Homoerotic Desire', *Studies in English Literature, 1500–1900*, 46/3 (summer 2006), 523–42, www.jstor.org/stable/3844519 (accessed 10 August 2015).
24. Philips, 'To my excellent Lucasia', *The Collected Poems*, pp. 121–2, 121.
25. Philips, 'To my excellent Lucasia', pp. 121–2.
26. Harriett Andreadis, 'The Sapphic-Platonics of Katherine Philips, 1632–1664', *Signs*, 15/1 (autumn 1989), 39, www.jstor.org/stable/3174705 (accessed 2 January 2015).
27. Philips, 'A retir'd friendship, to Ardelia, 23 Aug. 1651', *The Collected Works*, pp. 97–8, 97.
28. Sarah Prescott, '"That Private Shade, Wherein My Muse Was Bred": Katherine Philips and the Poetic Spaces of Welsh Retirement', *Philological Quarterly*, 88/4 (fall 2009), 345–64.
29. Katherine Philips, letter, 5 April 1662, cited in Prescott, 'That Private Shade', 353. For a reading of 'A retir'd friendship' as a poem about political instability in west Wales, see Prescott, 'That Private Shade', 355–6.
30. Philips, 'A retir'd friendship', p. 97.
31. Sarah Ponsonby, cited in Mavor, *The Ladies of Llangollen*, p. 41.
32. Martha Vicinus, *Intimate Friends: Women Who Loved Women, 1778–1928* (Chicago: University of Chicago Press, 2004), p. 14. See also Mavor, *The Ladies of Llangollen* and Lillian Faderman, *Surpassing the Love of Men: Romantic Friendship and Love between Women from the Renaissance to the Present* (1981; London: The Women's Press, 1985).
33. Vicinus, *Intimate Friends*, p. 13.
34. Vicinus, *Intimate Friends*, p .13.
35. Seward, cited in Emma Donoghue, 'Ladies of Llangollen', in Zimmerman (ed.), *Lesbian Histories and Cultures*, p. 433.
36. Anna Seward, *Llangollen Vale with other poems 1796* (Oxford: Woodstock Books, 1994), pp. 1, 6.
37. Seward, *Llangollen Vale*, p. 9.
38. Lister, cited in Donoghue, 'Ladies of Llangollen', p. 433.
39. Hester Thrale Piozzi, unpublished diary, cited in Liz Stanley, 'Romantic Friendship? Some Issues in Researching Lesbian History and Biography', *Women's History Review*, 1/2 (1992), 196.
40. Frances Power Cobbe, letter of 1896. Cited in Vicinus, *Intimate Friends*, p. 14.
41. On Evans and Farr, see Kirsti Bohata, 'The Apparitional Lover: Homoerotic and Lesbian Imagery in the Writing of Margiad Evans', in Kirsti Bohata and Katie Gramich (eds), *Rediscovering Margiad Evans: Marginality, Gender and Illness* (Cardiff: University of Wales Press, 2013), pp. 107–28.
42. On the identity of the woman who inspired this poem, see Jane Aaron's chapter in this book.
43. Sarah Jane Rees [Cranogwen], 'Fy Ffrind'/'My Friend', in Gramich and Brennan (eds), *Welsh Women's Poetry*, pp. 128, 129.
44. Aaron, *Nineteenth-Century Women's Writing in Wales*, p. 139.
45. Sarah Jane Rees [Cranogwen], 'Fy Ffrind', in Aaron, *Nineteenth-Century Women's Writing*, translated by Aaron, p. 139.

46 Rees [Cranogwen], 'Fy Ffrind'/'My Friend', pp. 132, 133.
47 Aaron, *Nineteenth-Century Women's Writing*, p. 140.
48 Sarah Jane Rees [Cranogwen], 'Fy Ngwlad'/'My Country', in Gramich and Brennan (eds), *Welsh Women's Poetry*, pp. 140, 141.
49 Sarah Williams was born and raised in London, but she attributed her gift for poetry to her Welsh father and wrote several poems about Wales and what it represented for her. See Aaron, *Nineteenth-Century Women's Writing*, pp. 119–22; and Catherine Brennan, *Angers, Fantasies and Ghostly Fears: Nineteenth-century Women from Wales and English-language Poetry* (Cardiff: University of Wales Press, 2003). 'A Clever Woman', reproduced in Brennan, was published posthumously in the 1872 edition of *Twilight Hours*.
50 Brennan, *Angers, Fantasies and Ghostly Fears*, p. 133.
51 Sarah Williams [Sadie], 'A Clever Woman', in Brennan, *Angers, Fantasies and Ghostly Fears*, p. 131. In Greek mythology, Echo is cursed by Hera so that the nymph could only repeat recently spoken words.
52 Marina Warner, *Joan of Arc: The Image of Female Heroism* (Oxford: Oxford University Press, 2013).
53 Swansea University, Richard Burton Archives, Dillwyn Papers, 2012/11/7 Notebook '1867–68', entry for 17 January 1868. I am indebted to Dr David Painting for permission to quote from Amy Dillwyn's diaries.
54 Dillwyn, *The Rebecca Rioter*, p. 65.
55 My thanks to Lucy Thomas for drawing my attention to the lesbian character in *The Curtain Rises*.
56 On fictional and biographical representations of lesbian pathology in Margiad Evans's writing, see Bohata, 'The Apparitional Lover'.
57 There is a long history of associating 'deviant' sexuality with criminality. See, for instance, Daniel Pick, *Faces of Degeneration: A European Disorder c. 1848–1918* (1989; Cambridge: Cambridge University Press, 1993); Lynda Hart, *Fatal Women: Lesbian Sexuality and the Mark of Aggression* (London: Routledge, 1994); Lisa Duggan, *Sapphic Slashers: Sex, Violence and American Modernity* (Durham, NC and London: Duke University Press, 2000).
58 On Davies and homosexuality, see M. Wynn Thomas, '"Never seek to tell thy love": Rhys Davies's Fiction', in Meic Stephens (ed.), *Rhys Davies: Decoding the Hare* (Cardiff: University of Wales Press, 2001), pp. 260–82. For the fullest account of Davies's treatment of homosexuality, male and female, see Osborne, *Rhys Davies*.
59 Kate Roberts, 'Nadolig', *Rhigolau Bywyd a Storiau Eraill* (Aberystwyth: Gwasg Aberystwyth, 1929), pp. 29–36. See, for instance, '*Ac o bo cyfeillgawch a fu ar wyneb daear erioed, dyma'r rhyfeddaf ym meddwl Olwen*' (And of all the friendships that there had ever been on the face of the earth, this was the strangest in Olwen's view, p. 30); '*Ac ar ddiwedd yr awr, gwnaeth beth rhyfedd iawn – rhoes gusian i Olwen ar ei boch.*' (And at the end of the free hour, she did a very strange thing – she gave Olwen a kiss on the cheek, p. 32). Translations by kind permission of Katie Gramich. I am indebted to Professor Gramich for her translation of this story. For a discussion of female friendships in 'Nadolig' and 'Y Trysor', see Katie Gramich, *Kate Roberts* (Writers of Wales) (Cardiff: University of Wales Press, 2011), pp. 40, 103. Gramich notes that *Tywyll Heno* (Dark Tonight) is another story which concerns female affect and friendship (p. 40).
60 Kate Roberts, 'The Treasure', in *The World of Kate Roberts: Selected Stories 1925–1981*, trans. Joseph P. Clancy (Philadelphia: Temple University Press, 1991), pp. 326–31, 329.

61 Margiad Evans, *The Old and the Young*, ed. Ceridwen Lloyd-Morgan (1948; Bridgend: Seren, 1998), p. 131.
62 Roberts, 'Nadolig', p. 30.
63 Christy Stephens, 'Symbols', in Zimmerman (ed.), *Lesbian Histories and Cultures*, pp. 747–8, 747.
64 Kate Roberts 'Y Trysor', *Gobaith a Storiau Eraill* (2nd edn; Denbigh: Gwasg Gee, 1982), pp. 26–7. Translated as 'The Treasure' by Clancy, *The World of Kate Roberts*, p. 331.
65 Margiad Evans, 'A Modest Adornment', *The Old and the Young*, p. 135. On this and other lesbian and homoerotic imagery in Margiad Evans, see Kirsti Bohata, 'The Apparitional Lover'.
66 Evans, *The Old and the Young*, p. 157.
67 Margiad Evans, 'Miss Potts and Music', *The Old and the Young*, pp. 112–13. Both Josephine and Miss Potts play Beethoven, a composer often associated with sexual desire in Evans's writing. Proust compares the non-verbal communication of gestures and looks between homosexuals to 'those questioning phrases of Beethoven's, indefinitely repeated at regular intervals'. Proust cited in Robb, *Strangers: Homosexual Love in the Nineteenth Century* (2003; London: Picador, 2004), p. 145.
68 Rhys Davies, 'The Doctor's Wife', in Meic Stephens (ed.), *Rhys Davies: Collected Stories, Volume 3* (Llandysul: Gomer Press, 1998), pp. 137–49, 139. Hereafter page references are cited in parentheses.
69 Dillwyn, *The Rebecca Rioter*, p. 81.
70 On 'transvestite ventriloquism' (and intersecting class and gender identities), see Diana Wallace, 'Ventriloquizing the Male: Two Portraits of the Artist as a Young Man by May Sinclair and Edith Wharton', *Men and Masculinities*, 4/4 (April 2002), 322–33.
71 Emily Faithfull's novel about the love of a relatively poor man for his flighty cousin, Tiny Harewood, is a disguised version of the tragic love affair between Faithfull and Helen Codrington. On Willa Cather, see Sharon O'Brien, '"The Thing Not Named": Willa Cather as a Lesbian Writer', *Signs*, 9/4 (summer 1984), 592–8.
72 Amy Dillwyn, *A Burglary, or Unconscious Influence* (1883; Dinas Powys: Honno, 2009), pp. 1, 26, 2 respectively.
73 For a discussion of Amy Dillwyn's *Jill* (1884) in comparison with Sarah Waters's *Affinity* (1999), see Kirsti Bohata, 'Rough Tumbles and Cracked Crowns', *New Welsh Review*, 101 (2013), 60–8.
74 Stevie Davies, *Impassioned Clay* (London: The Women's Press, 1999), p. 99.
75 Davies, *Impassioned Clay*, p. 100.
76 Stevie Davies, *Awakening* (Cardigan: Parthian, 2013), p. 94; a further contemporary example is found in Erica Woof's *Mud Puppy* (London: The Women's Press, 2002), which is discussed in part 4 below.
77 Paulina Palmer, *Lesbian Gothic: Transgressive Fictions* (London and New York: Cassell, 1999), p. 13.
78 Faderman, *Surpassing the Love of Men*, p. 264. See also the chapter on 'Monsters' in Emma Donoghue's *Inseparable: Desire between Women in Literature* (Berkeley: Cleis Press, 2010), pp. 106–39; Jennifer Waelti-Walters, *Damned Women: Lesbians in French Novels, 1796–1996* (Montreal: Mc-Gill-Queens University Press, 2000).
79 Faderman, *Surpassing the Love of Men*, p. 265; Arthur Machen, *The Great God Pan* (1894; Cardigan: Parthian, 2010), p. 17.
80 Machen, *The Great God Pan*, pp. 21–2.
81 Faderman, *Surpassing the Love of Men*, p. 265.

82 Machen, *The Great God Pan*, p. 69.
83 Bohata, *Postcolonialism Revisited* (Cardiff: University of Wales Press, 2004), pp. 29–34. See also Darryl Jones, 'Borderlands: Spiritualism and the Occult in Fin de Siècle and Edwardian Welsh and Irish Horror', *Irish Studies Review*, 17/1 (2009), 31–44 and Jane Aaron, *Welsh Gothic* (Cardiff: University of Wales Press, 2013), pp. 75–7.
84 Sherry Velasco, *Lesbians in Early Modern Spain* (Nashville, TN: Vanderbilt University Press, 2011), pp. 64–5; Jacqueline Murray, 'Twice Marginal and Twice Invisible: Lesbians in the Middle Ages', in Vern L. Bullough and James A. Brundage (eds), *Handbook of Medieval Sexuality* (New York: Garland, 1996), pp. 191–222; Patricia Simons, 'Lesbian (In)Visibility in Italian Renaissance Culture: Diana and Other Cases of *donna con donna*', *Journal of Homosexuality*, 27 (1994), 81–122.
85 Aaron, *Welsh Gothic*, pp. 154–5.
86 Aaron, *Welsh Gothic*, p. 145.
87 Aaron, *Welsh Gothic*, p. 148.
88 Rhys Davies, *The Black Venus* (London: William Heinemann, 1944), pp. 45, 47. Hereafter page references are cited in parentheses.
89 For a fuller discussion of sexuality (and race) in this novel, see Kirsti Bohata, '*The Black Venus*: Atavistic Sexualities', in Stephens (ed.) *Rhys Davies: Decoding the Hare*, pp. 231–43.
90 Evans, 'A Modest Adornment', pp. 116, 118.
91 Terry Castle, *The Apparitional Lesbian: Female Homosexuality and Modern Culture* (New York: Columbia University Press, 1993).
92 Bertha Thomas, 'A House That Was', originally published in Bertha Thomas, *Picture Tales from Welsh Hills* (1912), is reprinted in Bertha Thomas, *Stranger within the Gates: Short Stories* (Dinas Powys: Honno, 2008), pp. 131–44. There is a discernible interest in 'odd' women in Bertha Thomas's writing, most notably in the androgynous, cross-dressing servant turned actress in *Elizabeth's Fortune* (1887). In life, Thomas's close personal connections to Amy Levy, Vernon Lee and particularly Helen Zimmern with whom she shared a house in Canterbury, give a broader context to a possible interest in representing same-sex relationships. See Linda Hunt Beckman, *Amy Levy: Her Life and Letters* (Ohio: University of Ohio Press, 2000).
93 Thomas, 'A House That Was', pp. 131–44, 133, 134. Hereafter page references are cited in parentheses.
94 See Kirsti Bohata, '"Unhomely Moments": Reading and Writing Nation in Welsh Female Gothic', in Diana Wallace and Andrew Smith (eds), *The Female Gothic: New Directions* (Basingstoke: Palgrave Macmillan, 2009) pp. 180–195.
95 Evans, 'A Modest Adornment', pp. 127–8; emphasis in the original.
96 Margiad Evans, 'The Haunted Window', National Library of Wales MS 23365 D, ff. 57–71 (May 1953). I discuss this in detail in Bohata, 'The Apparitional Lover'.
97 See Katie Gramich, 'Gothic Borderlands: The Hauntology of Place in the Fiction of Margiad Evans', in Bohata and Gramich (eds), *Rediscovering Margiad Evans*, pp. 53–68.
98 Tristan Hughes, *Revenant* (London: Picador, 2008), pp. 135–6.
99 Hughes, *Revenant*, p. 13.
100 Jane Garrity provides a highly persuasive lesbian reading of *Lolly Willowes* in 'Encoding Bi-Location: Sylvia Townsend Warner and the Erotics of Dissimulation', in Karla Jay (ed.), *Lesbian Erotics* (New York: New York University Press, 1995), pp. 241–68.

101 Sylvia Townsend Warner, *Lolly Willowes* (1926; London: Virago Press, 2000), pp. 9, 10. Subsequent references given parenthetically.
102 Radclyffe Hall, *The Well of Loneliness* (1928; London: Virago Press, 1982), pp. 292, 287. Subsequent references given parenthetically.
103 Jane Aaron and M. Wynn Thomas, '"Pulling You through Changes": Welsh Writing in English Before, Between and After Two Referenda', in M. Wynn Thomas (ed.), *A Guide to Welsh Literature, Volume 7: Welsh Writing in English* (Cardiff: University of Wales Press, 2003), pp. 278–309, 305.
104 Lynne Pearce, 'Devolutionary Desires', in Phillips, Shuttleton and Watt (eds), *Decentring Sexualities*, pp. 241–57, 241.
105 Pearce, 'Devolutionary Desires', p. 241; emphasis in the original.
106 Pearce, 'Devolutionary Desires', p. 245; emphasis in the original.
107 Pearce, 'Devolutionary Desires', p. 248.
108 Pearce, 'Devolutionary Desires', p. 245.
109 Fflur Dafydd, *Twenty Thousand Saints* (Talybont: Alcemi, 2008), p. 113. Subsequent references are given parenthetically.
110 Ynys Enlli/Bardsey Island is an important location in gay men's fiction. In 'Gethin Llyr – The Wonder at Seal Cave' published in John Sam Jones's first collection *Welsh Boys Too* (Cardigan: Parthian, 2000), the Seal Cave provides the liminal retreat and expansive quasi-spiritual space for a first sexual encounter between two boys.
111 See Castle, *The Apparitional Lesbian*, on the recurring presence of death and ghosts in representations of lesbian desire in literature and cultural history.
112 Winning, 'Crossing the Borderline', p. 285.
113 Pearce, 'Devolutionary Desires', p. 245.
114 Wooff, *Mud Puppy*, p. 1.

Notes to chapter 6

1 Ardel Haefele-Thomas, *Queer Others in Victorian Gothic: Transgressing Monstrosity* (Cardiff: University of Wales Press, 2012), p. 4.
2 Haefele-Thomas, *Queer Others in Victorian Gothic*, p. 3.
3 William Hughes and Andrew Smith, 'Introduction', in *Queering the Gothic* (Manchester: Manchester University Press, 2009), pp. 1–10 (p. 1).
4 Haefele-Thomas, *Queer Others in Victorian Gothic*, p. 3.
5 Judith Halberstam, *In a Queer Time and Place: Transgender Bodies, Subcultural Lives* (New York: New York University Press, 2005), p. 4.
6 Halberstam, *In a Queer Time and Place*, p. 11.
7 John Howard, *Men Like That: A Southern Queer History* (London: University of Chicago Press, 1999).
8 Alison Donnell, 'Caribbean Queer: New Meetings of Place and the Possible in Shani Mootoo's *Valmiki's Daughter*', in *Contemporary Women's Writing*, 6.3 (November 2012), 213–32, 218.
9 Donnell, 'Caribbean Queer', 218.
10 Edward Thomas, *Edward Thomas: The Annotated Collected Poems*, ed. Edna Longley (Newcastle: Bloodaxe, 2008), p. 41. Hereafter cited as *ACP* with page references in parentheses.
11 Tomos Owen, 'Notes', in Arthur Machen, *The Great God Pan* (Cardiff: Library of Wales, 2010), pp. 177–93, 180.

[12] Wayne Koestenbaum, *Double Talk: The Erotics of Male Literary Collaboration* (New York: Routledge, 1989), p. 3.
[13] Koestenbaum, *Double Talk*, p. 2.
[14] Koestenbaum, *Double Talk*, p. 3.
[15] Hazel Davies, 'Twelve unpublished letters to O. M. Edwards', *National Library of Wales Journal*, 28/3 (1994), 335–45, 343. For a more thorough exploration of Thomas's Welshness, and how this informs his writing, see Andrew Webb, *Edward Thomas and World Literary Studies: Wales, Anglocentrism and English Literature* (Cardiff: University of Wales Press, 2013).
[16] Cited in Thomas Seccombe, foreword, in Edward Thomas, *The Last Sheaf* (London: Jonathan Cape, 1928), p. 7.
[17] Gwili, *Poems* (London: n.p., 1917), p. 93.
[18] Edward Thomas, 'The Patriot', *Nationalist*, 3/29 (1909), 39. Hereafter cited as *P* with page numbers in parentheses.
[19] Edward Thomas, *Edward Thomas: Letters to Gordon Bottomley*, ed. R. George Thomas (London: Oxford University Press, 1968), p. 129.
[20] Martin Taylor (ed.), *Lads: Love Poetry of the Trenches* (London: Constable, 1989), p. 31.
[21] Robert Frost and Edward Thomas, in Matthew Spencer (ed.), *Elected Friends: Robert Frost and Edward Thomas to One Another* (New York: Handsel Books, 2003), p. 9.
[22] Frost and Thomas, *Elected Friends*, p. 10.
[23] Frost and Thomas, *Elected Friends*, p. 38.
[24] Koestenbaum, *Double Talk*, p. 3.
[25] Frost and Thomas, *Elected Friends*, p. 9.
[26] Frost and Thomas, *Elected Friends*, p. 126.
[27] Eleanor Farjeon, *Edward Thomas: The Last Four Years* (Oxford: Oxford University Press, 1958), p. 247.
[28] Farjeon, *Edward Thomas*, p. 108.
[29] Farjeon, *Edward Thomas*, p. 189; emphasis in the original.
[30] Frost and Thomas, *Elected Friends*, p. 62.
[31] Frost and Thomas, *Elected Friends*, p. 69.
[32] One frank example of this occurs in a confessional letter to Bottomley, dated 18 June 1915, in which Thomas writes:

> What a thing it is to be nearing 40 & to know what one likes & know one makes mistakes & yet is right for oneself. How many things I have thought I ought to like & found reasons for liking. But now it is almost like eating apples. I don't pretend to know about pineapples & persimmons, but I know an apple when I smell it, when it makes me swallow my saliva before biting it. Then there are pears, too, & people who prefer pears. It is a fine world & I wish I knew how to make £200 a year in it without sucking James Milne's —.

It is tempting to read the images discussion of apples and 'people who prefer pears' in the context of 'what one likes' and 'what one ought to like' as a coded discussion of sexuality. The final sentence – referring to the editor of *The Daily Chronicle*, a daily paper in which Thomas published – makes a connection between economics, sexuality and the pear/apple symbolism of previous sentences. The physical act of 'sucking James Milne's —' echoes the physicality of 'swallow[ing] my saliva before biting [the apple]'. The pleasure of biting the apple – the forbidden fruit – an act synonymous with the Fall of Man in *Genesis*, is therefore implicitly linked to the act of performing fellatio. Thomas's critical writing has become a humiliating act of prostitution, one upon which his family life economically depends, but one which is held in opposition to his experience of the 'fine world', shared in the correspondence to Bottomley.

33 Frost and Thomas, *Elected Friends*, p. 84.
34 Frost and Thomas, *Elected Friends*, p. 82.
35 The Faber edition of Thomas's *Collected Poems*, edited by R. George Thomas, has the word 'countries' instead of 'counties', a significant change in the text which supports the more nationally conscious reading that I am proposing here. Edna Longley's edition of Thomas's poetry makes the change to 'counties' without referring to the Faber edition.

Notes to chapter 7

1 Aren Aizura, 'Of Borders and Homes: The Imaginary Community of (Trans)sexual Citizenship', *Inter-Asia Cultural Studies*, 7/2 (2006), 289–309, 293.
2 Aizura, 'Of Borders and Homes', 295–6. Aizura responds to dominant narratives of transgender experience that maps the journey to be at home in one's own body, to cross the borders of gender to find one's true and authentic self. Jay Prosser's *Second Skins: The Body Narratives of Transsexuality* (New York: Columbia University Press, 1998) is the oft-cited defender of this definition of transsexual experience as a homeliness denied by theories of gender ambiguity, and Jan Morris's *Conundrum* arguably follows this trajectory as well. Opposing perspectives are found in Judith Halberstam, *Female Masculinity* (Durham, NC: Duke University Press, 1998), pp. 141–73; Aizura, 'Of Borders and Homes'; Nael Bhanji, 'Trans/scriptions: Homing Desires, (Trans)sexual Citizenship and Racialized Bodies', in Susan Stryker and Aren Aizura (eds), *The Transgender Studies Reader 2* (New York: Routledge, 2013), pp. 512–26.
3 'Welsh Liberal Democrats Debate: The Transgender Community', *Your Senedd*, 19 November 2014, *www.yoursenedd.com/debates/2014–11–19-welsh-liberal-democrats-debate-the-transgender-community* (accessed 4 November 2015).
4 'Welsh Liberal Democrats Debate: The Transgender Community'.
5 'Welsh Liberal Democrats Debate: The Transgender Community'.
6 See, for example, Elizabeth Freeman, *Time Binds: Queer Temporalities, Queer Histories* (Durham, NC and London: Duke University Press, 2010); Heather Love, *Feeling Backward: Loss and the Politics of Queer History* (Cambridge, MA: Harvard University Press, 2007); Carla Freccero, *Queer/Early Modern* (Durham, NC and London: Duke University Press, 2006); Judith Halberstam, *In a Queer Time and Place: Transgender Bodies, Subcultural Lives* (New York and London: New York University Press, 2005); Lee Edelman, *No Future: Queer Theory and the Death Drive* (Durham, NC and London: Duke University Press, 2004); Carolyn Dinshaw, *Getting Medieval: Sexualities and Communities, Pre- and Postmodern* (Durham, NC and London: Duke University Press, 1999).
7 Judith Halberstam, *The Queer Art of Failure* (Durham, NC and London: Duke University Press, 2011), p. 119.
8 Halberstam, *The Queer Art of Failure*, pp. 2–3.
9 Halberstam, *The Queer Art of Failure*, p. 3.
10 Love, *Feeling Backward*, pp. 71, 7.
11 Freeman, *Time Binds*, p. xiii.

12 Freeman, *Time Binds*, p. xiii.
13 Freeman, *Time Binds*, p. 16.
14 Judith Butler, *Gender Trouble: Feminism and the Subversion of Identity* (London and New York: Routledge, 2006), p. 41.
15 Freeman, *Time Binds*, p. xxi.
16 Freeman, *Time Binds*, p. xxi–xxii.
17 Rhys Davies papers, National Library of Wales, 21533 C 148.
18 Aizura, 'Of Borders and Homes', 289.
19 Rhys Davies, *Print of a Hare's Foot: An Autobiographical Beginning* (1968; Bridgend: Seren, 1998), p. 162.
20 Despite Davies's playfulness with authority and gender, in the background of this scene is the near future of the Holocaust in which the violent policing of queer bodies took a horrible and traumatic turn in the forging of the fixed territory of the German nation and the German body. In this late 1960s recounting of Weimar freedom, the deadly serious sexual stakes of national identity are an ever-present political reality. Davies's 'Cherry-Blossoms on the Rhine' develops this theme further in his depiction of a nascent Hitler Youth and its claims on 'natural' bodies.
21 See Kirsti Bohata, *Postcolonialism Revisited* (Cardiff: University of Wales Press, 2004), pp. 40–5.
22 See Barbara Prys-Williams, 'Rhys Davies as Autobiographer: Hare or Houdini?', in Meic Stephens (ed.), *Rhys Davies: Decoding the Hare* (Cardiff: University of Wales Press, 2001), pp. 104–37; Huw Osborne, *Rhys Davies* (Writers of Wales) (Cardiff: University of Wales Press, 2009), pp. 104–46.
23 Meic Stephens, 'Introduction', in Stephens (ed.), *Rhys Davies: Decoding the Hare*, pp. 1–28, 3. For further discussions of Davies, cross-dressing and performativity, see Katie Gramich 'The Masquerade of Gender in the Stories of Rhys Davies', in Stephens (ed.), *Rhys Davies: Decoding the Hare*, pp. 205–15; Osborne, *Rhys Davies*, pp. 55, 94–5, 116–21. For more on hare-likeness and Welsh queer representation see Mihangel Morgan's chapter in the current volume.
24 Macqueen-Pope, *Ivor: The Story of an Achievement* (London: W. H. Allen, 1951), pp. 22, 52, 519.
25 Phyllis Bottome, *From the Life* (London: Faber and Faber, 1944), pp. 47, 60.
26 Rhys Davies, *The Painted King* (London: Heinemann, 1954), pp. 94, 51. Subsequent page references are cited in parentheses.
27 Macqueen-Pope, *Ivor*, pp. 20–1.
28 Michael Williams, *Ivor Novello: Screen Idol* (London: British Film Institute, 2003), p. 7, 12–13.
29 Alan Sinfield, *Out on Stage; Lesbian and Gay Theatre in the Twentieth Century* (New Haven and London: Yale University Press, 1999), p. 113.
30 Macqueen-Pope, *Ivor*, p. 19; Bottome, *From the Life*, p. 52.
31 Peter Noble, *Ivor Novello: Man of the Theatre* (London: The Falcon Press, 1951), p. 16. The modifiers in this quotation are confusing, and one assumes that the association is between Welshness and music rather than Welshness and gypsy exoticism, but, given Novello's mobile racial persona, it is hard to say.
32 Quoted in Williams, *Ivor Novello: Screen Idol*, p. 6.
33 Novello's national and racial associations are varied, complex and shifting, but the Welsh or Celtic mystique was always underwriting his popular identity.
34 Williams, *Ivor Novello: Screen Idol*, pp. 9, 34–5. Williams also makes much of the camp nostalgic use of Ivor Novello in the cross-dressing comedy acts of Hinge and Bracket, p. 25.

35 Penny Farfan, 'Noel Coward and Sexual Modernism: *Private Lives* as Queer Comedy', *Modern Drama*, 48/8 (winter 2005), 677–88, 684.
36 Rhys Davies, 'Our Contributors, No 1 Rhys Davies', *My Wales* (September 1958), 7.
37 Erica Wooff, *Mud Puppy* (London: The Women's Press, 2002), p. 15.
38 Frank Vickery, 'The Drag Factor', in Phil Clark (ed.), *Act One Wales* (Bridgend: Seren, 1997), p. 134. Subsequent page references are cited in parentheses.
39 In this way, he is very much like the changeling boy of *A Midsummer Night's Dream* as discussed by Marjorie Garber in *Vested Interests: Cross-dressing and Cultural Anxiety* (New York: Routledge, 1997), pp. 90–2. 'The phrase "changeling boy" reminds us that boys, and boy actors, *are* changelings, are not only in the process of change but are significations of change, and *e*xchange, in and of themselves ... But the changeling boy whom Titania and Oberon both desire ... is most notable by his absence ... [T]he whole point of the changeling boy is that he is *not* there, that he is an idea that can never be realized or possessed. Like the transvestite marking the space of representation itself, the changeling boy is that which, by definition, can never be present. For the minute he comes to be embodied, it is clear that he cannot be that which is so desperately sought' (92). Nigel is the changeling boy whom both Ruby and Griff desire as a form of self-definition but whose excess and absence unsettles and exposes their efforts at categorization as such. There are also useful comparisons to be made to Davies's *The Painted King*.
40 Wooff, *Mud Puppy*, p. 87. Subsequent page references are cited in parentheses.
41 Freeman, *Time Binds*, p. 68.
42 Love, *Feeling Backward*, p. 7.
43 The passage perhaps alludes to Helene Cicoux's 'Laugh of the Medusa' in which '[f]lying is a woman's gesture – flying in language and making it fly'. *Signs*, 1/4 (summer 1976), pp. 875–93, 887.
44 Halberstam, *The Queer Art of Failure*, p. 81.
45 Jan Morris, *Conundrum* (London: Penguin, 1988), p. 63.
46 Morris, *Conundrum*, p. 63.
47 Morris, *Conundrum*, pp. 12–13.
48 Katie Gramich, '"Those Blue Remembered Hills": Gender in Twentieth-century Welsh Border Writing by Men', in Jane Aaron, Henrice Altink and Chris Weedon (eds), *Gendering Border Studies* (Cardiff: University of Wales Press, 2010), pp. 142–62, 142.
49 Gramich, 'Those Blue Remembered Hills', p. 144.
50 Gramich, 'Those Blue Remembered Hills', p. 159.
51 Jan Morris, *The Matter of Wales: Epic Views of a Small Country* (London: Penguin, 1984), pp. 201–2.
52 Morris, *Conundrum*, p. 21.
53 Richard Phillips, 'Decolonising Geographies of Travel: Reading James/Jan Morris', *Social and Cultural Geography*, 2/1 (2001), 5–24, 16–17.
54 Morris, *Matter of Wales*, p. 15. Subsequent page references are cited parenthetically.
55 There are many other tales that lend themselves to queering time and place. One example comes from the section titled 'The Order of Things', which is concerned with family, education and religion. In this section, Morris slips into a description of 'other kinds of kinship' that are 'above the family' (220), such as the homosocial comradeship of men who once lived in the ruined castle of Ewloe 'sunk in a thickly wooded dell' in a 'more or less perpetual half-light, dappled by the trees: a neat and elegant little stronghold, all alone, deep in its secret hollow'. She exclaims 'How tight a comradeship sustained the prince and his soldiers down there!' (220) and the magical world of male-bonding seems completely divorced from the heterosexual kinships of family beneath

it. Similarly, Morris's retelling of the story of Bran the Blessed (128–9) is, among other things, a tale of homosocial bonding centred around a figure of male devotion that is both dead and articulate (melancholically lost and unmourned). The male bonds are threatened by both a repression of, and an exposure to, an unacknowledged history of loss.

[56] Garber, *Vested Interests*, pp. 140, 337.
[57] Garber, *Vested Interests*, p. 337. Indeed, one must read this passage of mythic possibility against the one that immediately follows dealing with Kennedy Airport customs (Morris, *Conundrum*, pp. 105–6), one that Garber privileges (*Vested Interests*, p. 107) but does not have in its proper focus without the direct contrast to the Welsh scene. The Kennedy Airport scene offers another site of policing at the borders of gender and nation, a scene very much like those that Rhys Davies provides in *Print of a Hare's Foot*. It is less a moment in Morris's 'halcyon if confusing days of biological multivalence' (Garber, *Vested Interests*, p. 107) than one of complete subservience to the mechanisms of gender prescription within the dominant optic.
[58] Morris, *Conundrum*, p. 116.
[59] Morris, *Conundrum*, p. 139.
[60] Morris, *Matter of Wales*, p. 306.
[61] Morris, *Matter of Wales*, p. 302.
[62] Freeman, *Time Binds*, p. xiii.

Notes to chapter 8

[1] These stories were gathered informally over a period of ten years. All women were allocated a pseudonym and I did not include any details that could identify them to the reader.
[2] A. C. Ritivoi, 'Explaining People: Narrative and the Study of Identity', *Storyworlds: A Journal of Narrative Studies*, 1 (2009), 25–41.
[3] G. Strawson, 'Against Narrativity', *Ratio*, 27 (2004), 428–52.
[4] S. Taylor, 'Narrative as construction and discursive resource', in M. Bamberg (ed.), *Narrative – State of the Art. Benjamins Current Topics 6* (Amsterdam: John Benjamins Publishing Company, 2007), pp. 113–22.
[5] W. Kraus, 'The Narrative Negotiation of Identity and Belonging', *Narrative Inquiry*, 16/1 (2006), 103–11.
[6] K. M. Bergen, E. A. Suter and K. L. Daas, '"About as Solid as a Fish Net": Symbolic Construction of a Legitimate Parental Identity for Nonbiological Lesbian Mothers', *Journal of Family Communication*, 6/3 (2009), 201–20.
[7] R. Payne, K. Wakely and K. Maddy, 'Where do they go? A Study of Progression in the South Wales Valleys', *Journal of Adult and Continuing Education*, 11/2 (2005), 170–87.
[8] M. A. Van Dam, 'Mothers in Two Types of Lesbian Families: Stigma Experiences, Supports and Burdens', *Journal of Family Nursing*, 10/4 (2004), 450–84.
[9] S. Gilmore and E. Kaminski, 'A Part and Apart: Lesbian and Straight Feminist Activists Negotiate Identity in a Second-Wave Organisation', *Journal of the History of Sexuality*, 16/1 (2007), 95–113.
[10] A. Gorman-Murray, G. Waitt and C. Gibson, 'A Queer Country? A Case Study of the Politics of Gay/Lesbian Belonging in an Australian Country Town', *Australian Geographer*, 39/2 (2008), 171–91, 173.

[11] M. Waites, 'The Fixity of Sexual Identities in the Public Sphere: Biomedical Knowledge, Liberalism and the Heterosexual/Homosexual Binary in Later Modernity', *Sexualities*, 8/5 (2005), 539–69.
[12] A. Friedman, H. Weinberg and A. M. Pines, 'Sexuality and Motherhood: Mutually Exclusive in Perception of Women', *Sex Roles*, 38/9–10 (1998), 781–800.
[13] J. Gabb, 'Desirous Subjects and Parental Identities: Constructing a Radical Discourse on (Lesbian) Family Sexuality', *Sexualities*, 4/3 (2001), 333–52.
[14] J. Rule, *Lesbian Images* (London: Pluto Press, 1989), pp. 12–30.
[15] Van Dam, 'Mothers in Two Types of Lesbian Families', 451.
[16] Rule, *Lesbian Images*, pp. 12–30.
[17] Van Dam, 'Mothers in Two Types of Lesbian Families', 452.
[18] A. Perlesz, R. Brown, J. Lindsay, R. McNair, D. deVaus and M. Pitts, 'Family in Transition: Parents, Children and Grandparents in Lesbian Families Give Meaning to "Doing Family"', *Journal of Family Therapy*, 28 (2006), 175–99.
[19] Van Dam, 'Mothers in Two Types of Lesbian Families', 452.
[20] J. H. Meyer, 'Prejudice, Social Stress and Mental Health in Lesbian, Gay and Bisexual Populations: Conceptual Issues and Research Evidence', *Psychological Bulletin*, 129 (2003), 674–97.
[21] V. Clarke and C. Kitzinger, '"We're not Living on Planet Lesbian": Constructions of Male Role Models in Debates about Lesbian Families', *Sexualities*, 8/2 (2005), 137–52.
[22] N. Yuval-Davis, 'Belonging and the Politics of Belonging', *Patterns of Prejudice*, 40 (2006), 197–214, 203.
[23] K. Jones, L.-A. Fenge, R. Read and M. Cash, 'Collecting Older Lesbians' and Gay Men's Stories of Rural Life in South West England and Wales: "We were Obviously Gay Girls ... (So) He Removed his Cow from our Field"', *Qualitative Social Research*, 14/2 (May 2012), 1–21.
[24] D. Beale, 'Shoulder to Shoulder: An Analysis of a Miners' Support Group During the 1984–5 Strike and the Significance of Social Identity, Geography and Political Leadership', *Capital and Class*, 29 (2005), 125–50.
[25] Jones, Fenge, Read and Cash, 'Collecting Older Lesbians' and Gay Men's Stories'.
[26] Jones, Fenge, Read and Cash, 'Collecting Older Lesbians' and Gay Men's Stories', 2.
[27] H. M. W. Bos, F. van Balen, D. C. van den Boom and Th. G. M. Sandfort, 'Minority Stress, Experience of Parenthood and Child Adjustment in Lesbian Families', *Journal of Reproductive and Infant Psychology*, 22/4 (2004), 1–14.
[28] N. Charles and C. A. Davies, 'Studying the Particular, Illuminating the General: Community Studies and Community in Wales', *The Sociological Review* (Oxford: Blackwell Publishing, 2005), pp. 672–90, 673.
[29] M. Mitchell, C. Howarth, M. Kotecha and C. Creegan, *Sexual Orientation Research Review 2008. Equality and Human Rights Commission Research Report 34* (Manchester: Equality and Human Rights Commission, 2008).
[30] Mitchell et al., *Sexual Orientation Research Review 2008*.
[31] J. M. Thompson, *Mommy Queerest* (Massachusetts: University of Massachusetts Press, 2002), p. 2.
[32] A. Rich, 'Compulsory Heterosexuality and Lesbian Existence', in S. Jackson and S. Scott, *Feminism and Sexuality* (New York: Columbia University Press, 1996), pp. 130–41.
[33] Thompson, *Mommy Queerest*, pp. 2–5.
[34] Thompson, *Mommy Queerest*, p. 3.
[35] Thompson, *Mommy Queerest*, p. 3.

36 Thompson, *Mommy Queerest*, p. 3.
37 A. Rich, 'Motherhood in Bondage. 1976', *On Lies, Secrets and Silence: Selected Prose* (New York: W. W. Norton, 1995), pp. 196–7.
38 E. Lewin, *Lesbian Mothers: Accounts of Gender in American Culture* (London: Cornell University Press, 1993), p. 376.
39 R. V. Bullough and S. Pinnegar, 'Guidelines for Quality in Autobiographical Forms of Self-study Research', *Educational Researcher*, 20/3 (2001), 13–21.
40 Thompson, *Mommy Queerest*, pp. 2–5.
41 S. Wilson, 'Networks of Relations: Introduction to Writing Motherhood', in S. Wilson and D. Davidson (eds), *Telling Truths: Storying Motherhood* (Bradford, Ontario: Demeter Press), pp. 1–15, 3.

Notes to chapter 9

1 Home Office, *Hate Crime Action Plan: Challenge it, Report it, Stop it* (London: Home Office, 2013).
2 Of the 535 respondents who stated that they were LGB, 228 (43 per cent) identified as gay men; 179 (33 per cent) identified as gay women or lesbians; 72 (14 per cent) identified as bisexual women, and 37 (7 per cent) identified as bisexual men. Only a minority identified as other (nine or 2 per cent), where 'other' includes self-referenced pansexual, polysexual, asexual/celibate.
3 Home Office, *Statistical News Release: Hate Crimes, England and Wales 2011/12* (London: Home Office, 2012).
4 Home Office, *Statistical News Release*.
5 Office for National Statistics, *National Statistician's Review of Crime Statistics: England and Wales* (London: Office for National Statistics, 2011), 11.
6 See M. L. Williams and J. Tregidga, *Time for Justice: All Wales Hate Crime Research Project* (Cardiff: Race Equality First and Cardiff University, 2013); M. L. Williams and J. Tregidga, 'Hate Crime Victimisation in Wales: Psychological and Physical Impacts across Seven Hate Crime Victim Types', *British Journal of Criminology*, 54 (2014), 946–67.
7 C. Roberts, M. Innes, M. Williams, J. Tregidga and D. Gadd, *Understanding Who Commits Hate Crime and Why They Do It* (Cardiff: Welsh government, 2013).
8 H. Cooper and M. Innes, *The Causes and Consequences of Community Cohesion in Wales: A Secondary Analysis* (Cardiff: Universities' Police Science Institute, 2009).
9 D. Gadd, 'Aggravating Racism and Elusive Motivation', *British Journal of Criminology*, 49 (2009), 755–71.
10 Williams and Tregidga, *Time for Justice*.
11 The questions were: to what extent do you agree or disagree that your local area is a place where people from different backgrounds got on well together; to what extent do you agree or disagree that residents in their local area respect differences between people, and, how strongly do you feel you belong to your local area? The strength of agreement and sense of belonging were interpreted as proxy values for community cohesion. Each question operated on a scale of 1 to 4 (1 being definitely disagree or not at all strongly belong, and 4 being definitely agree or very strongly belong). When the three questions were combined, the cohesion scale included mean values that ranged from 3 to 12 (3 being least cohesive and 12 being most cohesive).

12 The general fear of crime scale was constructed by combining the data from a survey question that asked respondents to state how worried they were about being a victim of 1) property crime; 2) violent crime; 3) sexual violence and 4) harassment, verbal abuse or threats. Each question operated on a scale of 1 to 4 (1 being not at all worried and 4 being very worried). When the four crime types were combined the general fear of crime scale included mean values that ranged from 4 to 16 (4 being the least worried and 16 being the most worried). The findings can be used as an effective proxy for 'vulnerability'.

13 However, it must be acknowledged that interviews took place with hate crime victims, and therefore it is possible that their previous experience of victimization may have prompted them to adapt their behaviour.

14 It is important to note that the term 'repeat victimization' refers to more than one incident perpetrated by the same offender or group of offenders. It is distinct from multiple, unconnected experiences of hate crime victimization by different perpetrators at various points in people's lives.

15 The eight questions captured satisfaction levels according to the following criteria: ease of police contact; treatment by police officers/staff; how well police listened to the victim; how seriously victim information was taken; how quickly the police responded to initial contact; the way in which subsequent information was provided by the police; the extent to which police took account of personal circumstances/minority identity, and the outcome of police investigation. Each question operated on a scale of 1 to 4 (1 being very dissatisfied and 4 being very satisfied). When the eight questions were combined, the police satisfaction scale included mean values that ranged from 8 to 32 (8 being the least satisfied and 32 being the most satisfied).

Notes to chapter 10

1 The chapter approaches the subject in the widest possible terms, but understands that queer experiences of youth in schools cannot be generalized and must attend to the difference between gay, lesbian, bisexual and transgendered experience. These differences constitute one of the challenges of the area, as Caitlyn Ryan and Ian Rivers point out in 'Lesbian, Gay, Bisexual and Transgender Youth: Victimization and Its Correlates in the USA and UK', *Culture, Health, and Sexuality*, 5/2 (2003), 103–19. Cris Mayo also stresses the importance of intersectionality in student experiences, which 'reminds us that all identities work in strategies and counterstrategies, that categories are insufficient, crucial, and unstable, and that no category of identity works alone. Assumptions about the Whiteness of the category "gay," may, for instance, work against recognizing gay relationships in non-White contexts', see Cris Mayo, 'Intersectionality and Queer Youth', *Journal of Curriculum and Pedagogy*, 4/2 (2007), 69–71.

2 See, for instance, Cris Mayo, 'Unsettled Relations: Schools, Gay Marriage, and Educating for Sexuality', *Educational Theory*, 63/5 (2013), 543–58; and Cris Mayo, 'Pushing the Limits of Liberalism: Queerness, Children, and the Future', *Educational Theory*, 56/4 (2006), 469–87.

3 Dennis Sumara and Brent Davis, 'Interrupting Heteronormativity: Toward a Queer Curriculum Theory', *Curriculum Inquiry*, 29/2 (1999), 204–5;

4 John Guiney Yallop, 'Gay and Out in Secondary School: One Youth's Story', in James McNinch and Mary Cronin (eds), *I Could Not Speak My Heart: Education and Social*

Justice for Gay and Lesbian Youth (Regina, SK: University of Regina Press, 2004), pp. 29–30; and James McNinch, 'Playing by the Rules: Building a Rationale to Offer a Course on Schooling and Sexual Identities in a Faculty of Education', in McNinch and Cronin (eds), *I Could Not Speak My Heart*, pp. 228–9.

5   Sarah Oerton and Anita Naoko Pilgrim, 'Devolution and Difference: The Politics of Sex and Relationships Education in Wales', *Critical Social Policy*, 34/1 (2014), 6–7.
6   April Guasp, *The School Report: The Experience of Gay Young People in Britain's Schools in 2012* (Stonewall: University of Cambridge Centre for Family Research, 2012), p. 1.
7   Gareth Evans, 'Plaid Cymru Raises Fears About the Level of Homophobic Bullying in Wales' Schools', *Wales Online*, *www.walesonline.co.uk/news/wales-news/plaid-cymru-raises-fears-level-4879801* (accessed May 2013).
8   Ryan and Rivers, 'Lesbian, Gay, Bisexual and Transgender Youth', 107.
9   Cris Mayo, 'Pushing the Limits of Liberalism',469–87.
10 'Church Warning on Sex Bill', *The Times*, 22 February 1966.
11 G. Morgan, 'Wales in Westminster', *Liverpool Daily Post*, 23 December 1966.
12 C. G. Learoyd, 'Letters, Sex Bill', *Daily Telegraph*, 7 March 1966.
13 C. Shepherd, 'May I Help You?', *Woman's Realm*, 7 May 1966.
14 J. Bancroft, 'Aversion Therapy of Homosexuality – A Pilot Study of 10 Cases', *British Journal of Psychiatry*, 115, (1969), 1417–31. A more personal, first-hand account of the electrical aversion described by Bancroft can be found in *Crawling Through Thorns* (Cardigan: Parthian Books, 2008), the present author's autobiographical novel, relating to his own experiences at the North Wales Hospital in Denbigh as late as 1975.
15 Ryan and Rivers, 'Lesbian, Gay, Bisexual and Transgender Youth', 107–9.
16 Ryan and Rivers, 'Lesbian, Gay, Bisexual and Transgender Youth', 108.
17 Lord Arran, *The Times*, 26 July 1967.
18 Jones, *Crawling Through Thorns*, p. 19.
19 James McNinch, 'Playing by the Rules: Building a Rationale to Offer a Course on Schooling and Sexual Identities in a Faculty of Education', in McNinch and Cronin (eds), *I Could not Speak my Heart*, p. 236.
20 McNinch, 'Playing by the Rules', p. 236.
21 R. Ramesh, 'Britons More Liberal, Cynical and Individual than 30 Years Ago, Says Survey', *The Guardian*, 10 September 2013.
22 The School Curriculum, Department of Education and Science/Welsh Office (London: Her Majesty's Stationery Office, 1981), para. 26.
23 'Jenny Is Still an Outcast After 20 Years', *Times Educational Supplement*, 4703 (15 September 2006), 3.
24 Margaret Thatcher, 'Speech to Conservative Party Conference', *Margaret Thatcher Foundation*, *www.margaretthatcher.org/document/106941* (accessed May 2013).
25 Local Government Act 1988, Part IV, Section 28, *www.legislation.gov.uk/ukpga/1988/9/section/28* (accessed May 2013).
26 Oerton and Pilgrim, 'Devolution and Difference', 3–22.
27 The Government of Wales Act, Part V, Section 120, *www.legislation.gov.uk/ukpga/1998/38/section/120* (accessed May 2013).
28 Oerton and Pilgrim, 'Devolution and Difference', 4.
29 Oerton and Pilgrim, 'Devolution and Difference', 16, 18.
30 Oerton and Pilgrim, 'Devolution and Difference', 12–13, 16.
31 Letter to Welsh LGB groups from Edwina Hart dated February 2001. Private collection of the author.

32 National Assembly for Wales, *Guidance on Sex and Relationships Education*, Circular 11/02, 17 July 2002, p. 11.
33 See Thomas Conway and Ruthann Crawford-Fisher's discussion of the value of gay-straight alliances in promoting queer community and curriculum in schools in their discussion piece, 'The Need for Continued Research on Gay-Straight Alliances', *Journal of Curriculum & Pedagogy*, 4/2 (2007), 125–9. See also Sumara and Davis's discussion of experience and narrative in 'Interrupting Heteronormativity', 204–25.

Notes to chapter 11

1 G. Davis and G. Needham, 'Introduction: The Pleasures of the Tube', in G. Davis and G. Needham (eds), *Queer TV: Theories, Histories, Politics* (London and New York: Routledge, 2009), p. 1.
2 D. Alderson, 'Queer Cosmopolitanism: Place, Politics, Citizenship and *Queer as Folk*', *New Formations*, 55 (2005), 73–88, 7.
3 Stonewall Cymru, 'Look Out: Fair Coverage of Lesbian, Gay and Bisexual People in Wales', *www.stonewallcymru.org.uk/cymru/english/what_we_do/look_out__portrayals_of_lgb_people_in_the_media_in_wales/default.asp* (accessed August 2013).
4 K. Cowan and G. Valentine, 'Tuned Out: The BBC's Portrayal of Lesbian and Gay People', Stonewall (n.d.), p. 6, *www.stonewall.org.uk/documents/tuned_out_pdf_1.pdf* (accessed August 2013).
5 Russell T. Davies cited in Alderson, 'Queer Cosmopolitanism', 83.
6 E. Hanson, 'Introduction: Out Takes', in E. Hanson (ed.), *Out Takes: Essays on Queer Theory and Film* (Durham, NC: Duke University Press, 1999), pp. 1–19.
7 L. Joyrich, 'Epistemology of the Console', in Davis and Needham (eds), *Queer TV*, pp. 15–47, 17.
8 Samuel A. Chambers, *The Queer Politics of Television* (London: I.B. Tauris, 2009), p. 3.
9 Chambers, *The Queer Politics of Television*, p. 13.
10 L. Johnston and R. Longhurst, *Space, Place and Sex: Geographies of Sexualities* (New York: Rowman and Littlefield, 2010), p. 3.
11 Davis and Needham, 'Introduction', p. 10.
12 L. Barron, 'Out in Space: Masculinity, Sexuality, and the Science Fiction Heroics of Captain Jack', in A. Ireland (ed.), *Illuminating Torchwood: Essays on Narrative, Character and Sexuality in the BBC Series* (Jefferson, NC: McFarland, 2010), pp. 213–25, 224; F. Dhaenens, 'The Fantastic Queer: Reading Gay Representations in *Torchwood* and *True Blood* as Articulations of Queer Resistance', *Critical Studies in Media Communication*, 30/2 (2013), 1–15, 5.
13 S. Ginn, 'Sexual Relations and Sexual Identity Issues: Brave New Worlds or More of the Old One?', in Ireland (ed.), *Illuminating Torchwood*, pp. 165–80, 167; C. Pullen, '"Love the coat": Bisexuality, the Female Gaze and the Romance of Sexual Politics', in Ireland (ed.), *Illuminating Torchwood*, pp. 135–52, 137.
14 G. Needham, 'Scheduling Normativity: Television, the Family, and Queer Temporality', in Davis and Needham (eds), *Queer TV*, pp. 143–158, p. 154.
15 R. Jackson, *Fantasy: The Literature of Subversion* (London: Routledge, 1981).
16 K. Kregloe, 'Bisexual Women are Alien to *Torchwood*', *After Ellen*, 6 March 2007, *www.afterellen.com/bisexual-women-are-alien-to-torchwood/03/2007/* (accessed August 2013).

17. S. Lacey, '"When you see Cardiff on film, it looks like LA" (John Barrowman): Space, Genre and Realism in Torchwood', in R. Williams (ed.), *Torchwood Declassified: Investigating Mainstream Cult Television* (London: I.B. Tauris, 2013), pp. 137–53, 141.
18. C. Haslop, 'The Shape-shifter: Fluid Sexuality as Part of *Torchwood*'s Changing Generic Matrix and "Cult" Status', in Williams (ed.), *Torchwood Declassified*, pp. 209–26, 209.
19. See M. Beattie, 'A Most Peculiar Memorial: Cultural Heritage and Fiction', in J. Schofield (ed.), *Who Needs Experts? Counter-Mapping Cultural Heritage* (Aldershot: Ashgate, 2014), pp. 215–24; S. Blandford, S. Lacey, R. McElroy and R. Williams, *Screening the Nation: Wales and Landmark Television* (2010), http://culture.research. glam.ac.uk/news/en/2010/jul/19/screening-nation-update/ (accessed August 2013); L. Porter, '*Torchwood*'s Spooky Do's', in A. Becker (ed.), *Welsh Mythology and Folklore in Popular Culture: Essays on Adaptations in Literature, Film, Television and Digital Media* (Jefferson, NC: McFarland, 2012), pp. 140–59; R. Williams, 'Cannibals in the Brecon Beacons: *Torchwood*, Place and Television Horror', *Critical Studies in Television*, 6/2 (2011), 61–73.
20. F. Topel, '*Torchwood*'s "Omnisexual" John Barrowman', *Edge Boston*, Wednesday 20 February 2008, http://www.edgeboston.com/index.php?ch=entertainment&sc=televisi on&sc3=&id=56376 (accessed August 2013); L. Blake, '"You guys and your cute little categories": *Torchwood*, The Space-Time Rift and Cardiff's Postmodern, Postcolonial and (avowedly) Pansexual Gothic', *The Irish Journal of Gothic and Horror Studies*, 9 (2009), http://irishgothichorrorjournal.homestead.com/Torchwood. html (accessed August 2013).
21. Davis and Needham, 'Introduction', p. 10.
22. Russell T. Davies, quoted in B. Cook, 'Underground Adventures', *Doctor Who Magazine*, 391 (2008), 54–8, 55; M. Hills, '*Torchwood*', in D. Lavery (ed.), *The Essential Cult TV Reader* (Lexington, Kentucky: The University Press of Kentucky, 2010), pp. 279–80.
23. See Blandford et al., *Screening the Nation*.
24. Blandford et al., *Screening the Nation*, p. 5.
25. Davis and Needham, 'Introduction', p. 2.
26. R. McElroy and R. Williams, 'The Appeal of the Past in Historical Reality Television: *Coal House at War* and Its Audiences', *Media History*, 17/1 (2011), 79–86, 85.
27. K. Schroder, K. Drotner, S. Kline and C. Murray, *Researching Audiences* (London: Arnold, 2003), p. 17.
28. To ensure the anonymity of our respondents each has been assigned a pseudonym which is used throughout.
29. Blake, 'You guys and your cute little categories'.
30. See also P. Tatchell, cited in S. Lockyer, 'Introduction: Britain, Britain, *Little Britain...*', in S. Lockyer (ed.), *Reading Little Britain: Comedy Matters on Contemporary Television* (London: I.B. Tauris, 2010), pp. 1–18.
31. Hanson, 'Introduction', p. 5.
32. BBC, 'Portrayal of Lesbian, Gay and Bisexual People on the BBC: Research Update', November 2012, p. 4, http://downloads.bbc.co.uk/diversity/pdf/lgb_portrayal_ update_2012_withquotes.pdf (accessed August 2013); BBC, 'Portrayal of Lesbian, Gay and Bisexual People on the BBC: Executive Summaries and Recommendations', p. 7.
33. Haslop, 'The Shape-shifter', pp. 210–11.

34 R. McElroy, 'The Local, the Global and the Bi-Cultural: Welsh-Language Television Drama', *Critical Studies in Television*, 2/2 (2007), 77–95, 83.
35 R. McElroy, '"Putting the Landmark Back into Television": Producing Place and Cultural Value in Cardiff', *Place-Branding and Public Diplomacy*, 7/3 (2011), 175–84, 177.
36 See L. Cubbison, 'Russell T. Davies, "Nine hysterical women", and the Death of Ianto Jones', in B. Williams and A. A. Zenger (eds), *New Media Literacies and Participatory Popular Culture Across Borders* (London: Routledge, 2012), pp. 135–50.
37 Hills, M., '*Doctor Who* Discovers ... Cardiff: Investigating Trans-generational Audiences and Trans-national Fans of the BBC Wales Production', *Cyfrwng: Wales Media Journal*, 3 (2005), 56–74.
38 C. Sandvoss, *Fans* (Cambridge: Polity, 2005), p. 64.
39 Johnston and Longhurst, *Space, Place and Sex: Geographies of Sexualities*, pp. 84–5.
40 M. Vicars, 'Queering the Text: Online Literary Practices, Identities, and Popular Culture', in Williams and Zenger (eds), *New Media Literacies and Participatory Popular Culture Across Borders*, pp. 167–80, 173.
41 Vicars, 'Queering the Text', p. 173.
42 D. Rushbrook, 'Cities, Queer Space and the Cosmopolitan Tourist', *GLQ: A Journal of Lesbian and Gay Studies*, 8/1–2 (2002), 183–206, 188.
43 Mermaid Quay Cardiff Waterfront, official webpage (n.d.) *www.mermaidquay.co.uk/* (accessed August 2013).
44 Rushbrook, 'Cities, Queer Space and the Cosmopolitan Tourist', 183.
45 See Visit Cardiff (n.d.), 'On Location', *www.visitcardiff.com/things-to-do/on-location* (accessed August 2013).
46 L. Simmonds, Mermaid Quay centre manager, quoted in S. Gaskell, 'Plaques Presented at *Torchwood*'s Ianto Jones "Shrine"', *Wales Online*, 17 February 2010, *www.walesonline.co.uk/news/wales-news/plaques-presented-torchwoods-iantojones-1935595* (accessed August 2013).
47 Beattie, 'A Most Peculiar Memorial', p. 221.
48 Johnston and Longhurst, *Space, Place and Sex*, p. 3.
49 Blake, 'You guys and your cute little categories'.
50 Chambers, *The Queer Politics of Television*, p. 10.
51 R. Nelson, 'TV Fiction Exchange: Local/Regional/National/Global', *Critical Studies in Television*, 2/2 (2007), 4–17, 5.

Notes to chapter 12

1 Helen Gilbert, 'Foreword', to J. Lo (ed.), *Staging Nation: English Language Theatre in Malaysia and Singapore* (Hong Kong: Hong Kong University Press, 2004), p. vii.
2 Steve Blandford, *Theatre & Performance in Small Nations* (Bristol: Intellect, 2013), p. 4.
3 Jen Harvie, *Staging the UK* (Manchester: Manchester University Press, 2005), p. 2.
4 Harvie, *Staging the UK*, p. 3.
5 Harvie, *Staging the UK*, p. 7.
6 Lauren Berlant, *Cruel Optimism* (Durham, NC and London: Duke University Press, 2011).
7 Berlant, *Cruel Optimism*, p. 26.

[8] Jose Esteban Muñoz, *Disidentifications: Queers of Color and the Performance of Politics* (Minneapolis: University of Minnesota Press, 1999), p. 133.
[9] Deirdre Heddon, *Autobiography and Performance* (Basingstoke: Palgrave Macmillan, 2008), pp. 88, 100.
[10] Lucy Lippard, *The Lure of the Local: Senses of Place in a Multicentered Society* (New York: The New Press, 1997), p. 33.
[11] Sara Ahmed, *Queer Phenomenology: Orientations, Objects, Others* (Durham, NC and London: Duke University Press, 2006), pp. 7–8.
[12] Ahmed, *Queer Phenomenology*, p. 56.
[13] Blandford, *Theatre & Performance in Small Nations*, p. 61.
[14] National Theatre Wales, *A Good Night Out in the Valleys Programme* (Cardiff: National Theatre Wales, 2010).
[15] Fiona Wilkie, 'Mapping the Terrain: a Survey of Site Specific Performance in Britain', *New Theatre Quarterly*, 18/2 (2002), 140–60, 149–50.
[16] Dylan Moore, 'The Village Social', *TheArtsDesk.com*, 24 October 2011, www.theartsdesk.com/theatre/village-social-national-theatre-wales (accessed July 2013).
[17] Amelia Forsbrook, 'The Village Social – Stage Review', *Buzz*, 9 November 2011, www.buzzmag.co.uk/reviews/the-village-social-stage-review/ (accessed July 2013).
[18] National Theatre Wales, *The Village Social Programme* (Cardiff: National Theatre Wales, 2011).
[19] Ben Lewis and Dafydd James, 'The Village Social' (unpublished script, 2011). The following excerpts are taken from this text; I would like to extend my thanks to the authors for granting me permission to quote from it.
[20] Julia Kristeva, *Powers of Horror* (New York: Columbia University Press, 1982), p. 4.
[21] Lee Edelman, *No Future: Queer Theory and the Death Drive* (Durham, NC and London: Duke University Press, 2004).
[22] Joan Dean, 'Joe Orton and the Redefinition of Farce', *Theatre Journal*, 34/ 4 (1982), 480, 481–92, 491.
[23] The following excerpts are taken from the unpublished English surtitle script. I would like to extend my thanks to Dafydd James for granting me permission to quote from it.
[24] See Jose Esteban Muñoz, *Cruising Utopia: The Then and There of Queer Futurity* (New York and London: New York University Press, 2009), pp. 22–3.
[25] Stephen Greer, *Contemporary British Queer Performance* (Basingstoke: Palgrave Macmillan, 2012), pp. 93–6.
[26] Robert Lewis, *Wenglish: The Dialect of the South Wales Valleys* (Tal-y-bont: Y Lolfa, 2008), p. 9.
[27] Ahmed, *Queer Phenomenology*, p. 19.
[28] Nathan Williams, 'Sherman Cymru: Llwyth (Tribe)', *Guardian*, 21 April 2010, www.guardian.co.uk/cardiff/2010/apr/21/sherman-cymru-chapter-arts-centre-llwyth-review (accessed July 2013).
[29] Jamie Rees, 'Llwyth – Theatre Review', *Buzz*, 21 April 2010, www.buzzmag.co.uk/uncategorized/llwyth-theatre-review/ (accessed July 2013).
[30] Catrin Rogers, 'Llwyth: adolygiad gan Catrin Rogers', *Tu Chwith*, 26 April 2010, http://tuchwith.com/2010/04/llwyth-adolygiad-gan-catrin-rogers/ (accessed July 2013).
[31] Gareth Evans, 'A Love Letter', trans. G. Evans, *Barn*, 568, May 2010, 50.
[32] Edd McCracken, 'Llwyth – Tribe', *fest*, 21 August 2011, www.festmag.co.uk/archive/2011/100727-llwyth_tribe (accessed July 2013).

33 David Kettle, 'Llwyth (Tribe)', *WhatsOnStage.com*, 22 August 2011, *www.whatsonstage. com/edinburgh-theatre/reviews/08–2011/llwyth-tribe_7392.html* (accessed July 2013).
34 Jake Orr, 'Review Edinburgh Fringe: Llwyth (Tribe)', *A Younger Theatre*, 23 August 2011, *www.ayoungertheatre.com/review-edinburgh-fringe-llwyth-tribe-st-georges-west-sherman-cymru-theatr-genedlaethol-cymru/* (accessed July 2013).
35 Joyce McMillan, 'Theatre Review: Llwyth (Tribe)', *The Scotsman*, 25 August 2011.
36 Andrew Dickson, 'Has Welsh Theatre Found Its Voice?', *Guardian*, 1 September 2011, *www.guardian.co.uk/stage/theatreblog/2011/sep/01/welsh-theatre-theatr-genedlaethol-cymru* (accessed July 2013).
37 Adam Somerset, 'Llwyth – Landmark Piece of Theatre Deserving Its Second Tour', *Theatre in Wales*, 27 September 2011, *www.theatre-wales.co.uk/reviews/reviews_details.asp?reviewID=2658* (accessed July 2013).
38 Roger Owen, 'Llwyth – Event', trans. G. Evans, *Barn*, 585, October 2011, 36–7.
39 British Council, 'British Council Showcase Returns to Edinburgh Fringe' (British Council, 2009), *www.britishcouncil.org/scotland-arts-enews-edinburgh-showcase-2009.htm* (accessed July 2013); British Council, 'Edinburgh Showcase 2011' (British Council 2011), *http://dramaanddance.britishcouncil.org/projects/2012/edinburgh-showcase-2011/* (accessed July 2013).
40 British Council, *Edinburgh Showcase 1997–2007: Celebrating 10 Years of New UK Theatre on the World Stage* (London: British Council, 2007).
41 British Council, 'Edinburgh Showcase 2011 Artist's Information' (London: British Council, 2011).
42 Fiction Factory, Llwyth: *Y Daith i Taiwan* (Llwyth: *The Journey to Taiwan*) (Cardiff: Fiction Factory, 2013).
43 Todd Sandel, 'Linguistic Capital in Taiwan: The KMT's Mandarin Language Policy and Its Perceived Impact on Language Practices of Bilingual Mandarin and Tai-gi Speakers', *Language in Society*, 32 (2003), 523–51, 529.
44 See John Kwock-Ping Tse, 'Language and a Rising New Identity in Taiwan', *International Journal of the Sociology of Language*, 143 (2000), 156; and A-Chin Hsiau, 'Language Ideology in Taiwan: The KMT's Language Policy, the Tai-yu Language Movement, and Ethnic Politics', *Journal of Multilingual and Multicultural Development*, 18/4 (1997), 308.
45 Tse, 'Language and a Rising New Identity in Taiwan', 161.
46 Sandel, 'Linguistic Capital in Taiwan', 530.
47 Fiction Factory, Llwyth: *Y Daith i Taiwan*.
48 Fiction Factory, Llwyth: *Y Daith i Taiwan*.

Select Bibliography

Aaron, Jane, 'The Hoydens of Wild Wales: Representations of Welsh Women in Victorian and Edwardian Fiction', in Tony Brown (ed.), *Welsh Writing in English: A Yearbook of Critical Essays*, 1 (Cardiff: New Welsh Review, 1995), pp. 23–39.

——, '"Saxon, Think not all is Won": Felicia Hemans and the Making of Britons', *Cardiff Corvey: Reading the Romantic Text*, 4 (May 2000), 1–3.

——, *Nineteenth-Century Women's Writing in Wales: Nation, Gender and Identity* (Cardiff: University of Wales Press, 2007).

——, *Welsh Gothic* (Cardiff: University of Wales Press, 2013).

Aizura, Aren, 'Of Borders and Homes: The Imaginary Community of (Trans)sexual Citizenship', *Inter-Asia Cultural Studies*, 7/2 (2006), 289–309.

Andreadis, H., 'The Sapphic-Platonics of Katherine Philips, 1632–1664', *Signs*, 15/1 (autumn 1989), 34–60, *www.jstor.org/stable/3174705* (accessed 2 January 2015).

——, 'Re-Configuring Early Modern Friendship: Katherine Philips and Homoerotic Desire', *Studies in English Literature, 1500–1900*, 46/3 (summer 2006), 523–42, *www.jstor.org/stable/3844519* (accessed 10 August 2015).

Bell, David and Gill Valentine (eds), *Mapping Desire: Geographies of Sexualities* (London: Routledge, 1995).

Bergen, K. M., E. A. Suter and K. L. Daas, '"About as Solid as a Fish Net": Symbolic Construction of a Legitimate Parental Identity for Nonbiological Lesbian Mothers', *Journal of Family Communication*, 6/3 (2009), 201–20.

Blake, L., '"You guys and your cute little categories": *Torchwood*, The Space-Time Rift and Cardiff's Postmodern, Postcolonial and (avowedly) Pansexual Gothic', *The Irish Journal of Gothic and Horror Studies*, 9 (2009), *http://irishgothichorrorjournal.homestead.com/Torchwood.html*.

Blandford, S., S. Lacey, R. McElroy and R. Williams, *Screening the Nation: Wales and Landmark Television* (2010), *http://culture.research.glam.ac.uk/news/en/2010/jul/19/screening-nation-update/* (accessed August 2013).

—— and S. Lacey, 'Screening Wales: Portrayal, Representation and Identity – a Case Study', *Critical Studies in Television*, 6 /2 (2011), 1–12.

——, *Theatre & Performance in Small Nations* (Bristol: Intellect, 2013).

Bohata, Kirsti, *Postcolonialism Revisited* (Cardiff: University of Wales Press, 2004).

—— and Katie Gramich (eds), *Rediscovering Margiad Evans: Marginality, Gender and Illness* (Cardiff: University of Wales Press, 2013), pp. 107–28.

Brennan, Catherine, *Angers, Fantasies and Ghostly Fears: Nineteenth-century Women from Wales and English-language Poetry* (Cardiff: University of Wales Press, 2003).

Brewer, W. D., 'Felicia Hemans, Byronic Cosmopolitanism, and the Ancient Welsh Bards', in Gerard Caruthers and Alan Rawes (eds), *English Romanticism and the Celtic World* (Cambridge: Cambridge University Press, 2003).

Brideoake, Fiona, '"Extraordinary Female Affection": The Ladies of Llangollen and the Endurance of Queer Community', *Romanticism on the Net*, 36–7 (November 2004).

Brinkley, Richard, 'George Powell of Nanteos: A Further Appreciation', *Anglo-Welsh Review*, 21/48 (1972), 130–4.
Buddug [Catherine Jane Prichard], 'Cranogwen', *Caniadau Buddug: wedi eu casglu a'u dethol gan ei phriod* (Caernarfon: Swyddfa'r 'Cymru', 1911), p. 24.
Castle, Terry, *The Apparitional Lesbian: Female Homosexuality and Modern Culture* (New York: Columbia University Press, 1993).
Chambers, S. A., *The Queer Politics of Television* (London: I.B. Tauris, 2009).
Clarke, V. and C. Kitzinger, '"We're not Living on Planet Lesbian": Constructions of Male Role Models in Debates about Lesbian Families', *Sexualities*, 8/2 (2005), 137–52.
Cook, Matt, *A Gay History of Britain: Love and Sex between Men since the Middle Ages* (Oxford and Westport, CT: Greenwood World Publishing, 2007).
Cowan, K. and G. Valentine, 'Tuned Out: The BBC's Portrayal of Lesbian and Gay People', *Stonewall* (n.d.), www.stonewall.org.uk/documents/tuned_out_pdf_1.pdf (accessed August 2013).
Crockett, Kate, 'Rhai Agweddau ar Rywioldeb yn Llenyddiaeth Gymraeg yr Ugeinfed Ganrif' [Some Aspects on Sexuality in Twentieth-century Welsh Literature'], (unpublished MPhil thesis, University of Wales Aberystwyth, 2000).
Crowe, R., 'Creu Traddodiad Llenyddol Hoyw Cymraeg', *Tu Chwith*, 9 (1998).
Crwydren, R., 'Welsh Lesbian Feminist: A Contradiction in Terms?', in Jane Aaron, Teresa Rees, Sandra Betts and Moira Vincentelli (eds), *Our Sister's Land: The Changing Identities of Women in Wales* (Cardiff: University of Wales Press, 1994), pp. 294–300.
Cubbison, L., 'Russell T. Davies, "Nine hysterical women", and the Death of Ianto Jones', in B. Williams and A. A. Zenger (eds), *New Media Literacies and Participatory Popular Culture Across Borders* (London: Routledge, 2012), pp. 135–50.
Davis, Glyn and Gary Needham (eds), *Queer TV: Theories, Histories, Politics* (London and New York: Routledge, 2009).
Dellamora, Richard, *Masculine Desire: The Sexual Politics of Victorian Aestheticism* (London: University of North Carolina Press, 1990).
Dhaenens, F., 'The Fantastic Queer: Reading Gay Representations in *Torchwood* and *True Blood* as Articulations of Queer Resistance', *Critical Studies in Media Communication*, 30/ 2 (2013), 1–15.
Dinshaw, Carolyn, *Getting Medieval: Sexualities and Communities, Pre- and Postmodern* (Durham, NC and London: Duke University Press, 1999).
Donoghue, E., 'Ladies of Llangollen', in Bonnie Zimmerman (ed.), *Lesbian Histories and Cultures: An Encyclopedia* (New York: Garland Publishing, 2000), pp. 432–3.
——, *Inseparable: Desire between Women in Literature* (Berkley: Cleis Press, 2010).
Edelman, Lee, *No Future: Queer Theory and the Death Drive* (Durham, NC and London: Duke University Press, 2004).
Elen, A., 'Golygyddol', *Taliesin*, 151 (2014), 10–14.
Faderman, Lillian, *Surpassing the Love of Men: Romantic Friendship and Love between Women from the Renaissance to the Present* (1981; London: The Women's Press, 1985).
Freccero, Carla, *Queer/Early Modern* (Durham, NC and London: Duke University Press, 2006).
Freeman, Elizabeth, *Time Binds: Queer Temporalities, Queer Histories* (Durham, NC and London: Duke University Press, 2010).
Friedman, A., H. Weinberg and A. M. Pines, 'Sexuality and Motherhood: Mutually Exclusive in Perception of Women', *Sex Roles*, 38/9–10 (1998), 781–800.
Gabb, J., 'Desirous Subjects and Parental Identities: Constructing a Radical Discourse on (Lesbian) Family Sexuality', *Sexualities*, 4/3 (2001), 333–52.

Garber, Marjorie, *Vested Interests: Cross-dressing and Cultural Anxiety* (New York: Routledge, 1997).
Giffney, Noreen, Michelle M. Sauer and Diane Watt (eds), *The Lesbian Premodern* (New York: Palgrave Macmillan, 2011).
Goldberg, J. and M. Menon, 'Queer History', *PMLA*, 120/5 (2013), 1609.
Goldie, Terry (ed.), *In a Queer Country: Gay and Lesbian Studies in the Canadian Context* (Vancouver, B.C.: Arsenal Pulp Press, 2001).
Gramich, K., '"Those Blue Remembered Hills": Gender in Twentieth-century Welsh Border Writing by Men', in Jane Aaron, Henrice Altink and Chris Weedon (eds), *Gendering Border Studies* (Cardiff: University of Wales Press, 2010).
——, *Kate Roberts* (Writers of Wales) (Cardiff: University of Wales Press, 2011).
Greer, Stephen, *Contemporary British Queer Performance* (Basingstoke: Palgrave Macmillan, 2012).
Griffiths, Robin (ed.), *British Queer Cinema* (New York: Routledge, 2006).
Guasp, April, *The School Report: The Experience of Gay Young People in Britain's Schools in 2012* (Stonewall: University of Cambridge Centre for Family Research, 2012).
Haefele-Thomas, Ardel, *Queer Others in Victorian Gothic: Transgressing Monstrosity* (Cardiff: University of Wales Press, 2012).
Haggerty, George E., *Queer Gothic* (Urbana, IL: University of Illinois Press, 2006).
Halberstam, Judith, *In a Queer Time and Place: Transgender Bodies, Subcultural Lives* (New York and London: New York University Press, 2005).
——, *The Queer Art of Failure* (Durham, NC and London: Duke University Press, 2011).
Hanson, Ellis (ed.), *Out Takes: Essays on Queer Theory and Film* (Durham, NC: Duke University Press, 1999).
Herring, Scott, *Another Country: Queer Anti-Urbanism* (New York and London: New York University Press, 2010).
Heuser, Harry, 'Bigotry and Virtue: George Powell and the Question of Legacy', *New Welsh Reader*, 110 (winter 2015), 18–29.
Holland, N., 'George Powell of Nanteos', in Robert Meyrick and Neil Holland (eds), *To Instruct and Inspire: 125 Years of the Art and Crafts Collection* (Aberystwyth: School of Art Press, 1997), pp. 3–6.
Howard, John, *Men Like That: A Southern Queer History* (London: University of Chicago Press, 1999).
Hughes, William and Andrew Smith, *Queering the Gothic* (Manchester: Manchester University Press, 2009).
Ireland, Andrew (ed.), *Illuminating Torchwood: Essays on Narrative, Character and Sexuality in the BBC Series* (Jefferson, NC: McFarland, 2010).
James, D., 'Y Queer yn Erbyn y Byd', *Taliesin*, 151 (2014), 66–85.
Jennings, Rebecca, *A Lesbian History of Britain: Love and Sex between Women since 1500* (Oxford and Westport, CT: Greenwood, 2007).
Johnston, Lynda and Robin Longhurst, *Space, Place and Sex: Geographies of Sexualities* (New York: Rowman and Littlefield, 2010).
Jones, D. G., *Cofiant Cranogwen* (Caernarfon: Argraffdy'r Methodistiaid Calfinaidd, n.d. [1932]).
Jones, D. L., 'George Powell: Swinburne's "Friend of Many a Season"', *Anglo-Welsh Review*, 19/44 (1971), 75–85.
Jones, Gerallt, *Cranogwen: Portread Newydd* (Llandysul: Gwasg Gomer, 1981).
Jones, K., L-A. Fenge, R. Read and M. Cash, 'Collecting Older Lesbians' and Gay Men's Stories of Rural Life in South West England and Wales: "We were Obviously Gay Girls ... (So) He Removed his Cow from our Field"', *Qualitative Social Research*, 14/2.

Joyrich, L., 'Epistemology of the Console', in G. Davis and G. Needham (eds), *Queer TV: Theories, Histories, Politics* (London and New York: Routledge, 2009), pp. 15–47.

Koestenbaum, Wayne, *Double Talk: The Erotics of Male Literary Collaboration* (New York: Routledge, 1989).

Lewin, Ellin, *Lesbian Mothers: Accounts of Gender in American Culture* (London: Cornell University Press, 1993).

Lewis, Brian, *British Queer History: New Approaches and Perspectives* (Manchester: Manchester University Press, 2013).

Llwyd, Alan, *Kate: Cofiant Kate Roberts 1891–1985* (Talybont: Y Lolfa, 2011).

Lockyer, Sharon (ed.), *Reading Little Britain: Comedy Matters on Contemporary Television* (London: I.B. Tauris, 2010).

Lootens, T., 'Hemans and Home: Victorianism, Feminine "Internal Enemies", and the Domestication of National Identity', *PMLA*, 109/2 (1994), 238–53.

Love, Heather, *Feeling Backward: Loss and the Politics of Queer History* (Cambridge, MA: Harvard University Press, 2007).

Lutz, Deborah, *Pleasure Bound: Victorian Sex Rebels and the New Eroticism* (New York: Norton, 2011).

Lynch, P., 'Morris T.Williams y Nofelydd', *Taliesin* (spring 1994), 7–25.

McElroy, R., 'The Local, the Global and the Bi-Cultural: Welsh-Language Television Drama', *Critical Studies in Television*, 2/2 (2007), 77–95.

—— and R. Williams, 'The Appeal of the Past in Historical Reality Television: *Coal House at War* and Its Audiences', *Media History*, 17/1 (2011), 79–86.

——, '"Putting the Landmark Back into Television": Producing Place and Cultural Value in Cardiff', *Place-Branding and Public Diplomacy*, 7/3 (2011), 175–84.

Marcus, Sharon, *Between Women: Friendship, Desire and Marriage in Victorian England* (Princeton: Princeton University Press, 2007).

Mavor, Elizabeth, *The Ladies of Llangollen: A Study in Romantic Friendship* (Harmondsworth: Penguin, 1974).

Maxwell, A., 'Nationalizing Sexuality: Sexual Stereotypes in the Habsburg Empire', *Journal of the History of Sexuality*, 14/3 (2005), 266–90.

Mayo, C., 'Pushing the Limits of Liberalism: Queerness, Children, and the Future', *Educational Theory*, 56/4 (2006), 469–87.

——, 'Intersectionality and Queer Youth', *Journal of Curriculum and Pedagogy*, 4/2 (2007), 69–71.

——, 'Unsettled Relations: Schools, Gay Marriage, and Educating for Sexuality', *Educational Theory*, 63/5 (2013), 543–58.

Meyer, J. H., 'Prejudice, Social Stress and Mental Health in Lesbian, Gay and Bisexual Populations: Conceptual Issues and Research Evidence', *Psychological Bulletin*, 129 (2003), 674–97.

Muñoz, Jose Esteban, *Disidentifications: Queers of Color and the Performance of Politics* (Minneapolis: University of Minnesota Press, 1999).

——, *Cruising Utopia: The Then and There of Queer Futurity* (New York and London: New York University Press, 2009).

Munt, Sally, *Heroic Desire: Lesbian Identity and Cultural Space* (London and Washington: Cassell, 1998).

Oerton, S. and A. N. Pilgrim, 'Devolution and Difference: The Politics of Sex and Relationships Education in Wales', *Critical Social Policy*, 34/1 (2014), 3–22.

Oram, Alison and Annmarie Turnbull, *The Lesbian History Sourcebook: Love and Sex between Women in Britain from 1780–1970* (London and New York: Routledge, 2001).

Osborne, Huw, *Rhys Davies* (Writers of Wales) (Cardiff: University of Wales Press, 2009).

Owen, T., '"Never again stop the way of a Welshman": Rioting and Rebellion in Amy Dillwyn's *The Rebecca Rioter*', in David Bell and Gerald Porter (eds), *Riots in Literature* (Newcastle: Cambridge Scholars Publishing, 2008), pp. 51–74.

Palmer, Paulina, *Lesbian Gothic: Transgressive Fictions* (London and New York: Cassell, 1999).

Parker, Andrew, Mary Russo, Doris Sommer and Patricia Yaeger (eds), *Nationalisms and Sexualities* (New York and London: Routledge, 1992).

Peach, Linden, *Contemporary Irish and Welsh Women's Fiction: Gender, Desire and Power* (Cardiff: University of Wales Press, 2007).

Perlesz, A., R. Brown, J. Lindsay, R. McNair, D. deVaus and M. Pitts, 'Family in Transition: Parents, Children and Grandparents in Lesbian Families Give Meaning to "Doing Family"', *Journal of Family Therapy*, 28 (2006), 175–99.

Phillips, R., 'Decolonising Geographies of Travel: Reading James/Jan Morris', *Social and Cultural Geography*, 2/1 (2001), 5–24.

Phillips, Richard, David Shuttleton and Diane Watt (eds), *Decentring Sexualities: Politics and Representations Beyond the Metropolis* (London and New York: Routledge, 2000).

Prescott, S., '"That Private Shade, Wherein My Muse Was Bred": Katherine Philips and the Poetic Spaces of Welsh Retirement', *Philological Quarterly*, 88/4 (fall 2009), 345–64.

Roberts, C., M. Innes, M. Williams, J. Tregidga and D. Gadd, *Understanding Who Commits Hate Crime and Why They Do It* (Cardiff: Welsh Government, 2013).

Rushbrook, D., 'Cities, Queer Space and the Cosmopolitan Tourist', *GLQ: A Journal of Lesbian and Gay Studies*, 8/1–2 (2002), 183–206.

Ryan, C. and I. Rivers, 'Lesbian, Gay, Bisexual and Transgender Youth: Victimization and Its Correlates in the USA and UK', *Culture, Health, and Sexuality*, 5/2 (2003), 103–19.

Stephens, Meic (ed.), *Rhys Davies: Decoding the Hare* (Cardiff: University of Wales Press, 2001).

Sumara, D. and B. Davis, 'Interrupting Heteronormativity: Toward a Queer Curriculum Theory', *Curriculum Inquiry*, 29/2 (1999), 204–5.

Taylor, A., 'Lesbian Space: More than One Imagined Territory', in Rosa Ainley (ed.), *New Frontiers of Body, Space, and Gender* (London: Routledge, 1998).

Thompson, J. M., *Mommy Queerest* (Massachusetts: University of Massachusetts Press, 2002).

Van Dam, M. A., 'Mothers in Two Types of Lesbian Families: Stigma Experiences, Supports and Burdens', *Journal of Family Nursing*, 10/4 (2004), 450–84.

Vicinus, Martha, *Intimate Friends: Women Who Loved Women, 1778–1928* (Chicago: University of Chicago Press, 2004).

Wallace, Diane and Andrew Smith (eds), *The Female Gothic: New Directions* (Basingstoke: Palgrave Macmillan, 2009).

Walshe, Éibhear (ed.), *Sex, Nation and Dissent in Irish Writing* (Cork: Cork University Press, 1997).

Weeks, Jeffrey, *Sex, Politics and Society: The Regulation of Sexuality Since 1800* (2nd edn; Harlow: Longman Group, 1989).

Williams, M. L. and J. Tregidga, *Time for Justice: All Wales Hate Crime Research Project* (Cardiff: Race Equality First and Cardiff University, 2013).

—— and ——, 'Hate Crime Victimisation in Wales: Psychological and Physical Impacts across Seven Hate Crime Victim Types', *British Journal of Criminology*, 54 (2014), 946–67.

Williams, Michael, *Ivor Novello: Screen Idol* (London: British Film Institute, 2003).

Williams, Rebecca (ed.), *Torchwood Declassified: Investigating Mainstream Cult Television* (London: I.B. Tauris, 2013).

Winning, J., 'Crossing the Borderline: Post-devolution Scottish Lesbian and Gay Writing', in Berthold Schoene (ed.), *The Edinburgh Companion to Contemporary Scottish Literature* (Edinburgh: Edinburgh University Press, 2007), pp. 283–91.

Zimmerman, Bonnie (ed.), *Lesbian Histories and Cultures: An Encyclopedia* (New York and London: Garland Publishing, Inc., 2000).

Index

Aaron, Jane 16, 97, 105, 106
Aberystwyth 45, 47, 49–50, 55, 181
Aberystwyth University 6, 45, 48–9, 50, 56, 57, 58, 60, 62, 181–2
abjection 214
Ac Eto Nid Myfi (And Yet Not Me), John Gwilym Jones 84
Adduned, Yr (The Promise), John Gwilym Jones 80
Ahmed, Sara 211, 218
AIDS epidemic *see* HIV/AIDS
AIDS Memorial Names Quilt 129
Aizura, Aren 126, 130
Alderson, David 195, 206, 207
All Wales Hate Crime Project and Survey 159–76
Amlyn and Amig *see Kedymdeithyas Amlyn ac Amic*
Andreadis, Harriette 95
Anglocentrism 8, 115–16, 118
Arwystli, Huw 75–6
'Atgof' (Reminiscence), Edward Prosser Rhys 81–2
audiences 40, 84, 133, 195, 198, 199–204, 208
  see also Torchwood
'Autumn Wind' (George Powell) 54
aversion therapy 180, 182
Awakening (Stevie Davies) 104

backwardness and queerness 17, 68, 128–9, 137, 144
Bala Eisteddfod 178
bardic tradition 5, 15, 16, 20–8
Barron, Lee 198
Barrowman, John 196, 199, 201–3
Beattie, Melissa 207
Beautiful Thing (film) 1
belonging 1, 4–5, 7, 9–11, 16–21, 127–9, 132, 135, 139–41, 143–4, 151, 153, 205, 209–11, 215
  see also local, the; loss of community; queer places(s), space(s)

Berlant, Lauren 210
Berridge, Elizabeth 47, 51
Bersani, Leo 17–18
bisexuality 67, 110, 149, 152, 154, 161–6, 170, 178, 198, 199, 202–3, 204
Black Venus, The (Rhys Davies) 100, 105–6, 131
Blake, Linnie 199
Blandford, Steve 209, 211
Blue Books *see Report of the Commission of Inquiry into the State of Education in Wales*
Bob yn y Ddinas (Bob in the City), Siôn Eirian 87–8
Book of Wonderful Characters, The (Henry Wilson and James Caulfield) 61
borders 130–1, 134–7, 139, 140, 143–4, 209–10, 214, 223
Bottome, Phyllis 131, 132
Brewer, William D. 16, 20, 25
bridges 144
Brinkley, Richard 49
Buddug *see* Prichard, Catherine Jane
bullying, homophobic 178–9, 188–91
bundling *see* courting on beds
Burglary, A (Amy Dillwyn) 101, 103
Burne-Jones, Edward 56
Burns, Robert 20
Busse, Peter 71–2
Butler, Judith 44, 129, 141
Bydd yn Wrol (Be Brave; film) 2
Byron, Lord 20

Cader Idris 25–6
cadi tradition 6–7, 67–77, 80–1, 85, 88
camp 6, 68–9, 128–9, 132–4, 136–7, 201–3, 217, 219, 234n11, 247n34
Caniadau Cranogwen 34, 41
Cardiff 11, 88, 110, 113, 135, 149, 153, 154, 161, 198, 199, 200, 206
Cardiff Bay 11, 186, 197–8, 204–8
Carter, Angela 129
'Casabianca' (Felicia Hemans) 18–20

Index

Castle, Terry 106
Cather, Willa 103
Chambers, Samuel A. 208
Chawner, Claude Fox 51, 56, 62
child safety, and the decriminalization of homosexuality 179–81
Chorley, Henry 23
citizenship 3, 9–11, 126–7, 177, 179, 181–2, 186, 190, 206
civil partnerships 178, 202, 236n35
'Clever Woman', A (Sarah Williams) 98
Cocks, H. G. 61–2
colonialism 5, 7, 8, 15, 17, 22, 23, 28, 139, 140, 143
collaboration, male literary 117–18, 121–5
  see also Robert Frost, Edward Thomas
community 4, 7, 9, 69, 93, 129, 143–4, 147–50, 152–4, 157
  see also loss of community
community cohesion 161–2
Community Cohesion Programme 160
Conundrum (Jan Morris) 8, 139–41, 143
cosmopolitanism 6, 11, 16, 21, 130, 135, 206–7
courting on beds 39
Coyne, Joseph Stirling 62
Cranogwen 5–6, 29–44, 97–8
Crawling Through Thorns (John Sam Jones) 181
creative industries 10, 11, 196, 205–6
crime, associated with same-sex desire 103–5, 151
crime, fear of 162–3
  see also hate crime
cross-dressing 61–2, 87, 99, 103–4, 133–5, 143, 243n92, 247n34, 248n39
  see also drag; fairy-tale drag
cross-dressing, Victorian 61–3
Crowe, Richard 6, 68, 69
Crwydren, Roni 4
Cymru Fydd (Wales to Come) Saunders Lewis 77–8
Cynon Valley (south Wales) 147–58

Dafydd, Fflur 110–12
Dance, Charles 62
Davies, Edward 25, 26
Davies, Pennar 85–6
Davies, Rhys 8, 99–102, 105–6, 129–34
Davies, Russell T. 195–7
  see also Torchwood
Davies, Stevie 3, 103–4, 109
Davis, Brent 177
Davis, Glyn 195, 199

Dellamora, Richard 59–60
Deuce *see* VIVA
devolution 8–10, 91–2, 94, 101, 109–14, 177, 179, 185–6, 190, 204
  see also Wales, post-devolution
Dhaenens, Frederick 198
Dickson, Andrew 220
Dillwyn, Amy 8, 94, 98, 99, 103
Dinshaw, Carolyn 69
disguise 99, 103–4, 106, 131, 199, 214, 215
'Doctor's Wife, The' (Rhys Davies) 102
Doctor Who 195–6, 200–1, 205, 206
domesticity 5, 7, 9, 15, 17–21, 27, 224n6
  see also home
Donnell, Alison 116
'Draenog, Y' (The Hedgehog) Gwenallt 79–80
drag 8, 73, 88, 112–13, 128–9, 133–8
  see also cross-dressing
Drag Factor (Frank Vickery) 136
druids 26
'Dyn a'r Llygoden Fawr, Y' (The Man and the Rat) Pennar Davies 85–6

Edelman, Lee 2, 17–18, 215
educational settings 177–91
Eirian, Siôn 87–8
Elen, Angharad 65
Elis, Islwyn Ffowc 79–80
Elizabeth, Rhian 109
Ellis, Havelock 40, 61
enfranchisement of women 44
English literature, Welsh lesbians in 108–9, 113–14
'Esther Judith' (Cranogwen) 35
Eton 48, 53, 61
Étretat 47, 52, 59
Euripides 213, 216
Evans, Elwyn 234–235n21
Evans, Margiad 8, 97, 99–102, 106, 107, 108
evolution 138–9
exile 18, 20, 22, 93, 95, 110, 118–19, 124, 128

Faderman, Lilian 104, 105
failure and queerness 1, 3, 4, 6, 17, 64, 113, 127–8, 134–5, 139
fairy-tale drag 8, 127–44
Faithfull, Emily 103
family 7, 9, 34, 69–71, 77–8, 93, 108, 110–12, 124, 136, 147, 151, 152, 155, 186, 213, 218, 219

see also lesbian motherhood; lesbian mothers; queer parenthood
Farwell, Marilyn R. 92–3
female friendship 2, 96, 101, 236n35, 241n59
feminism and lesbianism 4, 8, 93, 98–9, 151
feminist iconography 98
'Fever Vision, A' (George Powell) 54–5
Ffenestri Tua'r Gwyll (Windows Towards Twilight) Islwyn Ffowc Elis 79–80
fires 18, 19, 23–4, 119
flogging 48, 59
Forest Sanctuary, The (Felicia Hemans) 18
France 46, 47, 99, 236n35
Freccero, Carla 73
Freeman, Elizabeth 4, 8, 16, 128, 129, 137, 144
Freud, Sigmund 83
Frost, Robert 8, 116, 120–5
Frythones, Y (The Female Briton) 29, 33, 35, 39, 41, 42, 43
Fulford, Tim 19
'Fy Ffrynd' (My Friend) Cranogwen 41–2, 97, 229n39

Galgóczi, Erzsébet 94
Garber, Marjorie 248n39
Garlick, Raymond 49
Garnier, Étienne-Barthélémy 57
Gauthier, Theophile 104–5
gay adoption 3, 178
gay marriage 3, 140
gender inversion 92–3, 103
  see also sexual inversion
genderqueer revolution 8
genderqueering 103–4
geography and gender 2, 127, 130–1, 198–9
  see also queer place(s)
ghosts, and same-sex desire 106–7
Gilbert, Helen 209
Glyn, Guto'r 72–3
Glyndŵr, Owain 96, 141–2
Goeden Eirin, Y (The Plum Tree) John Gwilym Jones 83
Good Night Out in the Valleys, A (Alan Harris) 212–13
Gosse, Edmund 47
gothic literature 54, 106
  see also lesbian gothic
Gramich, Katie 140, 237n62, 241n59
graves 18, 22, 23, 27, 42, 71
Gray, Thomas 24

Great God Pan, The (Arthur Machen) 104–5
Guidance on Sex and Relationships Education 187–8
Gwenallt 78–80, 88
Gwili 118
Gwilym, Dafydd ap 71–2
Gymraes 43

Haefele-Thomas, Ardel 115
Haggerty, George E. 54
Halberstam, Judith 64, 116, 127–8, 138
Hall, Radclyffe 108–9
Hamilton, New Zealand 207–8
Hanes Rhyw Gymro (The History of a Certain Welshman) John Gwilym Jones 84–5
Hanson, Ellis 54, 197
hares 69, 70, 80, 131, 234n11
harps 102
Harris, Alan 212
Harvey, Jonathan 1
Harvie, Jen 209–10
hate crimes 9–10, 159–76
hate crimes, fear of and avoidance strategies 164–6
hate crimes, perpetrator characteristics 170–3
hate crimes, police responses to 162–4, 173–5
hate crimes, scale and impact 163–4, 166
hate crimes, victim experiences 167–73
Haul, Yr (The Sun) 38
Healthy School Scheme 189–90
Heddon, Dee 210
Hemans, Felicia 5, 15–28
  see also bardic tradition
heteronormative citizenship 3
Hills, Matt 199
HIV/AIDS 3, 129, 183–5, 196
Holland, Neil 56
home 9, 10, 17–19, 27, 95, 96, 107–8, 124–5, 127, 130–1, 135–6, 138–41, 143, 205, 246n2
  see also belonging; domesticity
'Home "Fair Was the Morning"' (Edward Thomas) 122, 124–5
'Homes of England, The' (Felicia Hemans) 15, 17, 27
homonormativity 3, 9, 224n6
houses, as symbols of old Wales 107
'House that Was, A' (Bertha Thomas) 106–7
Howard, John 116

hoyw 65–8
Hughes, Ellen 43
Hughes, Tristan 107–9
Hughes, T. Rowland 84–5
Humphreys, Emyr 114
hybridity 10–11, 209–23

Impassioned Clay (Stevie Davies) 3, 103–4
Imré, Aniko 94

Jackson, Rosemary 198
James, Dafydd 4, 11–12, 65–8, 209, 216–23
Jenny Lives with Eric and Martin 184
jewels, as symbols of lesbian desire 91, 101
Jill (Amy Dillwyn) 99, 103
Jill and Jack (Amy Dillwyn) 99
Joan of Arc 99
Johnson, Jill 93
Jones, Alice Gray *see* Peris, Ceridwen
Jones, David Lewis 49
Jones, D. James *see* Gwenallt
Jones, Ianto (TV character) 11, 197–8, 202–6, 208
Jones, John Gwilym 80, 83–4, 88, 236n52
Jones, Mary Oliver 43
Jones, Reverend D. G. 32, 36, 42
Jones, Sylvia 187
Jones, Terry Dyddgen 2
Jones, Tom 136
Joyrich, Lynne 197

Kedymdeithyas Amlyn ac Amic (The Friendship of Amlyn and Amig) 70–1, 73, 77, 81, 86, 235n22
Kelly, Gary 20
Koestenbaum, Wayne 117–18, 121
Kraus, W. 148
Kümpel, Wilhelm 56

Labouchère Amendment to the 1885 Criminal Law Act 116, 117
Ladies of Llangollen 8, 40, 91, 96–7
Lang, Cecil Y. 46, 48
L'Anglais d'Étretat 47, 48
Lawrence, D. H. 83
Legends of Iceland (George Powell) 49
Lesbia Brandon (Algernon Swinburne) 48
lesbian gothic 104–7
lesbian identity 4, 8, 92, 99, 109, 147–58
lesbian motherhood 9, 147–58
Lesbian Nation, The 93

lesbianism in Welsh literature 7–8, 91–114
Lewis, Ben 209
Lewis, Saunders 77–8, 80
LGB Forum Cymru 186–7
Lippard, Lucie 211
Lister, Anne 96
Little Britain (TV series) 195, 201–2
Llangrannog 33, 34–5
llatai 75, 77, 81, 86, 263n35
Lloyd, Mary 97
Llwyth (Dafydd James) 11, 12, 65–7, 209, 216–23
local, the 2, 4, 6, 9, 10, 11, 15–16, 69, 113, 116, 141, 147, 149, 153, 154, 157, 161–4, 174, 176, 200–1, 207, 209–23, 225n21, 251n11
Lolly Willowes (Sylvia Townsend Warner) 108
London 1, 2, 109, 112, 135, 138, 184, 200, 201, 203–4, 218, 219
Longfellow, Henry Wadsworth 48, 51, 56
Lootens, Tricia 25
loss 1, 3–5, 16–28, 107–8, 127, 129, 150, 152, 158, 249n55
loss of community 147, 152–4
   see also belonging; lesbian motherhood
loss script 155–7
Love, Heather 3, 17, 127–8, 137
love between women in Welsh literature 73–5, 91–114
   see also individual authors
Lynch, Peredur 82–3

Mabinogi/Mabinogion 68–70, 77, 80, 143, 144
MacDonald, Hettie 1
Machen, Arthur 104
Macqueen-Pope, W. 131–2
Madoc (Robert Southey) 22
Magnússon, Eiríkr 49, 51, 64
Marmion (Walter Scott) 17
marriage 3, 5, 7, 19–20, 36, 39, 40, 60, 70, 71, 75–8, 95, 96, 107, 124, 127, 134, 136, 140, 155, 157, 202, 236n35, 237n62
Masoch, Sacher 59
Mason, Angela 186–7
Math fab Mathonwy (The Fourth Branch) 68–9, 75
Matter of Wales, The (Jan Morris) 8, 140–4
Maupassant, Guy de 47
Maxwell, Alexander 92
Mayo, Chris 179, 190
McGann, Jerome 17

McNinch, James 177, 182
Mechain, Gweful 73–5
medieval Welsh literature 6–7, 69–77
Memoirs of a Woman of Pleasure (John Cleland) 53
memorialization, memorialism 5, 11, 19, 21, 22, 27, 51, 138
Mendelssohn, Felix 48, 56
Mermaid Quay 204–7
Merriman, Catherine 109
Metronormativity 2, 9, 10
Meyers, Terry L. 47–8
Michaels, Walter Benn 93
Middle Ages, sexuality in 70–7
Millais, John Everett 99
miscegenation 93
misgendering 161, 168, 175
'Miss Potts and Music' (Margiad Evans) 107
Mitford, Mary Russell 20
'Modest Adornment, A' (Margiad Evans) 100, 106
Moore, Thomas 20
Morris, Islwyn 2, 129
Morris, Jan 8, 139–44
Morris, Twm 234n11
motherhood 111–12, 148–58, 156, 158
  see also lesbian motherhood
Mud Puppy (Erica Wooff) 8–9, 109, 110, 112–13, 135–9, 144
Mulholland, James 21
Muñoz, José Estaban 5, 210
Munt, Sally 93
music, and same-sex desire 101–2
My Experiences in a Lunatic Asylum 60
myth 8, 21–2, 26–7, 127, 129, 135, 137–44, 213, 216, 241n51, 249n57
mythography of loss 21–2

Nant-Eos 45–7, 51, 53, 55, 78
Nantlais 33
narrative, national 2, 6, 7, 8, 68, 94, 115, 142
narrative, personal 10, 147–58, 177, 181–7, 191
national belonging 4, 5, 11, 16–21, 129, 143–4, 209
  see also Welsh nationalism, identity
national drag 135, 138
National Eisteddfod 32, 36, 131, 178, 216, 234n3
national identities and sexuality 9, 92–4, 114, 195–208
National Melody 24

National Theatre Wales 209–23
nationhood and theatre 209–23
Needham, Gary 195, 199
Nighy, Bill 1–2
Noncomformism 38, 39, 117
non-heteronormativity and Welshness 115–25
Novello, Ivor 131–4, 136, 144, 247n31, 247n33, 247n34

Oerten, Sarah 185–6
Ogof, Yr (The Cave; T. Rowland Hughes) 84–5
'Old and the Young, The' (Margiad Evans) 101
omnisexuality 199–201
Orton, Joe 216
'Other, The' (Edward Thomas) 117–18
Owen, Tomos 117
Oxford University 51, 52, 61

Painted King, The (Rhys Davies) 8, 131–4
Palmer, Paulina 104
Parry, John 20
'Parting' (Edward Thomas) 123
Pater, Walter 59, 121
'Patriot, The' (Edward Thomas) 118–19
Pearce, Lynn 109–10
performativity 8, 11, 29, 127, 129, 211, 216, 247n23
Peris, Ceridwen 43
personal experience, use in educational settings 177–91
Philips, Katherine 8, 95–6
Phillips, Richard 2
Picture of Dorian Gray, The (Oscar Wilde) 93
Pilgrim, Anita Naoko 185–6
Piozzi, Hester Thrale 96–7
Plaid Cymru 178
police, handling of hate crimes 162–4, 173–5
police, satisfaction with 162–4
policing of gender 10, 87, 126, 130–1, 135–6, 247n20, 249n57
Portrayal and Inclusion of Lesbian, Gay and Bisexual Audiences (BBC report) 204
Powell, Frederick York 48
Powell, George 6, 7, 45–64
preachers, female 31–2
Prescott, Sarah 95
Presley, Elvis 113, 135, 136, 205
Prichard, Caradog 86–7

Prichard, Catherine Jane 32
Pride (film) 1–3, 4, 7
Print of a Hare's Foot (Rhys Davies) 129–31, 133
Prosser Rhys, Edward 81–2

queer anti-urbanism 9
Queer as Folk (television series) 195–6, 198, 207
queer children 178–81, 185, 189–90
  see also bullying, homophobic
queer curriculum 177, 190
  see also educational
queer educational inclusion 179
queer future(s), 2, 5, 11, 179, 190, 217
queer history(ies), 1–7, 17–18, 69, 128–9, 138, 139, 141–2, 153, 212–13, 215, 225n21
queer history of Wales 5, 7
queer memorialization 11, 19
Queer Nation 2, 67, 93
queer nation(s), 1, 2, 4, 109–13, 129
queer parenthood 9
  see also lesbian motherhood
queer pedagogy 10
  see also educational settings
queer place(s) and space(s), 116, 120–1, 124, 153, 197–9, 206–8
  see also Cardiff Bay
queer teachers 182–3
  see also educational settings
queer television 195
  see also Doctor Who; Queer as Folk; Torchwood
queer theory 44, 67–8, 115, 127, 197, 208
queer time/temporalities 11, 127–9, 198
  see also temporal drag
queering education 185–91
'*Quod-Libet*' (George Powell) 55, 58–9, 61

Rebecca Rioter, The (Amy Dillwyn) 94, 98, 99, 103
Records of Woman (Felicia Hemans) 19–20
Rees, Fanny 42–3
Rees, Jamie 219
Rees, Sarah Jane *see* Cranogwen
Report of the Commission of Inquiry into the State of Education in Wales 6, 37–40, 92, 238n7
Revenant (Tristan Hughes) 107–8
Rhys, Matthew 2
Ritivoi, Andreea 148

'Road Not Taken, The' (Robert Frost) 123–4
Roberts, Kate 8, 82, 83, 100, 101, 113, 114
'Rock of Cader Idris, The' (Felicia Hemans) 24–8
Rocky Horror Show, The 207–8
Rogers, Catrin 219
Rossetti, Dante Gabriel 47, 48
Rossetti, William Michael 47
Rowlands, John 87
Rule, Jane 151
rural life and spaces, rurality 1–2, 8, 39, 91, 95, 97, 108, 153, 161, 181, 185

Sade, Marquis de 47
Salesbury, William 66
Sand, George 60
Schnetzer, Ben 3
Schumann, Robert 56
science fiction 198–9
  see also Torchwood
Scott, Walter 17
Section 28 of the Local Government Act 1988, 184, 185
Sedgwick, Eve Kosofsky 93, 179
Selection of Welsh Melodies, A (Felicia Hemans) 20–1, 23–7
self-identity construction and perception 10, 150–2, 157
Seward, Anna 96
sex and relationships education 181, 183–5, 187–9
sexology 238n4
sexual inversion 40, 103
  see also gender inversion
Shakespeare, William 121
Solomon, Rebecca 48
Solomon, Simeon 48, 50, 56, 60, 61, 63
Somerset, Adam 220
Southey, Robert 22
South Wales Women's Temperance Union 41
Spedding, James 59
Stevens, Catrin 39
Stonewall Cymru 178, 186–7, 190, 196
Stonewall Inn (New York City) 205–6
Stonewall UK 178
Stories that Give Shape to Lives 185, 190
straight time 3, 4, 127, 129, 137, 139, 140, 143, 198
'Strancio' (Edward Prosser Rhys) 82
Strawson, Peter F. 148
Sumara, Dennis 177
Summerskill, Ben 190

'Sun Used to Shine While We Two Walked, The' (Edward Thomas) 122–3
Swinburne, Algernon Charles 46–8, 51, 56, 59, 60, 61, 63
Symbolic Interactionism 148
Symonds, John Addington 59

Tackling Hate Crimes and Incidents: A Framework for Action 160
Taiwan 220–3
Taylor, Stephanie 148
television and nationhood 195–208
temporal drag 8, 128, 132, 137–9
Tennyson, Alfred 59
Thatcher, Margaret 183–4
theatre and nationhood 209–23
Thomas, Bertha 106–7
Thomas, Edward 8, 112, 115–25
Thomas, Jane 30, 42, 43
Thompson, Julie 155, 156, 157
Thorpe, Jeremy 182
Tician Tician (Ticking Ticking) John Rowlands 87
time, queer theories of 8
  see also queer time/temporalities; temporal drag
'To My Country' (Cranogwen) 97–8
Torchwood (TV series), 2, 11, 195–208
Törvényen belül (Within the Law) Erzsébet Galgóczi 94
tourism 11, 202, 204, 206–7
transgender rights in Wales 126–7
transgenderism 68–9, 75–7, 126–44, 159, 165, 168–72, 174
transgressive female relationships 8, 94, 108
(trans)nationalism 5, 18–20, 27–8
transsexuality 8, 126, 139–44, 246n2
transsexuality and place 140–1
trauma 1, 3–4, 37, 128, 129, 140, 143
tropes of Welshness 8, 94, 216, 220
'Trysor, Y' (The Treasure) Kate Roberts 100, 101
Twenty Thousand Saints (Fflur Dafydd) 110–12
Tyrwhitt, St John 59

Un Nos Ola Leuad (One Moonlit Night) Caradog Prichard 88

'Vale' (George Powell), 54
van der Burch, Jacques-Hippolyte 57
Vaughan, Hilda 99

'ventriloquism,' 23–5, 27–8, 103
Verlaine, Paul 121–2
Vicars, Mark 206
Vicinus, Martha 96
Vickery, Frank 136
Village People, The 182–3
Village Social, The (Ben Lewis) 11, 209, 212–16
Virgil 120
VIVA 185, 189, 190

Wagner, Cosima 48
Wagner, Richard 56
Wales, post-devolution 8, 9, 10, 91, 109–14, 160, 177, 185–91
  see also educational settings; hate crimes; lesbian motherhood
Wales as a borderland 8
Warner, Sylvia Townsend 108
Waters, Sarah 100, 103, 109
Watt, Diane 2
'Wedding Ring, The' (Cranogwen) 36–7, 39
Well of Loneliness (Radclyffe Hall) 108–9
Welsh Airs (Felicia Hemans) 22
Welsh emigration 118, 201
Welsh identity 8, 91, 92, 103, 104, 108, 109, 119, 197, 199, 200, 207, 209, 210, 223
Welsh-language queerness 6–7, 12, 65–70, 210, 216–22
  see also cadi tradition
Welsh media 11, 110, 195–6, 199, 201, 204
  see also Torchwood
Welsh myths and legends 5, 8, 21, 26–7, 45, 127–44, 213–15
  see also hares
Welsh nationalism 5, 9, 10, 11, 16, 21, 80, 94
Welsh nationality and female same-sex desire 91, 101–14
Welshness 8, 12, 20, 23, 47, 49, 77, 94, 101–5, 108, 112, 113, 115–25, 131, 132, 135, 140, 178, 199–204, 206, 216, 218, 220, 245n15, 247n31
Welsh revivalism 21, 22
Welsh television 195–208
Welsh theatre 209–23
Westall, Richard 57, 58
West Rhyl Young People's Project 185, 189
'What Spirit?' (George Powell) 54
Whittle, Lindsay 190
Wilde, Oscar 6, 47, 64, 93, 116, 117

Williams, Michael 132–3
Williams, Morris T. 82–3
Williams, Nathan 218–19
Williams, Patricia 71
Williams, Sarah 98
Williams, Waldo 80
Wilson, Sheena 158
Winning, Joanne 111
witches, and lesbian desire 8, 91, 105–6, 108, 113
Wolfson, Susan 15

Wooff, Erica 2, 8–9, 109, 112–13, 129, 135–9
working class 1, 2, 3, 36, 103–4, 117, 149, 213

Yallop, Guiney 177
youth, LGBTQ 177–91

Zimmerman, Bonnie 93
Zwecker, Johann Baptist 57